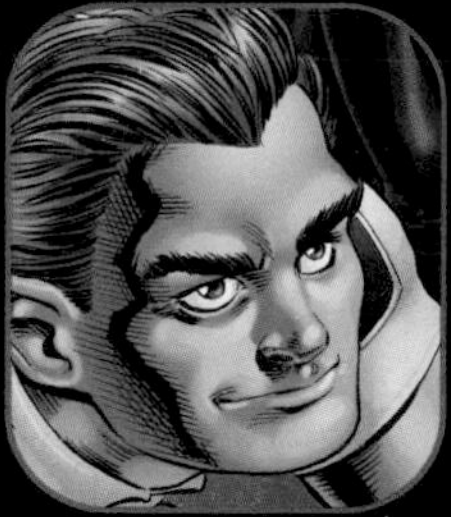

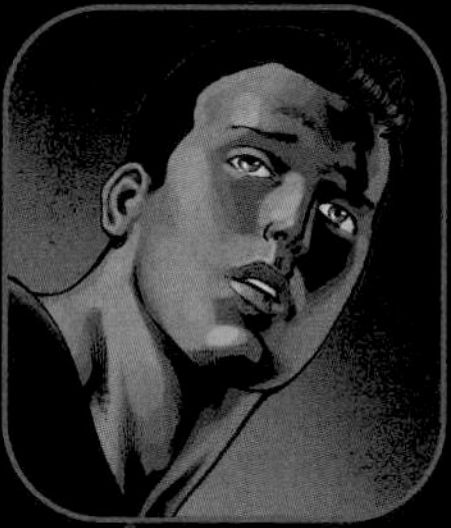

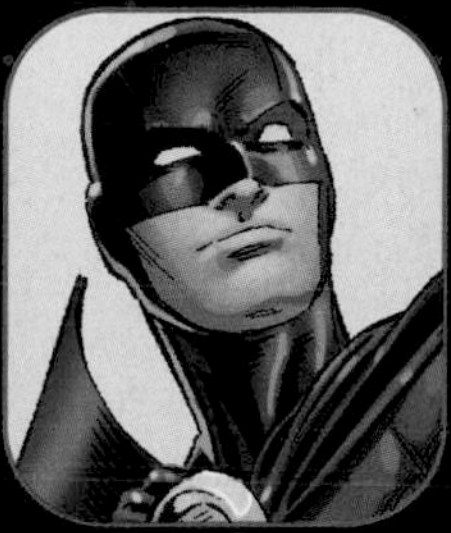

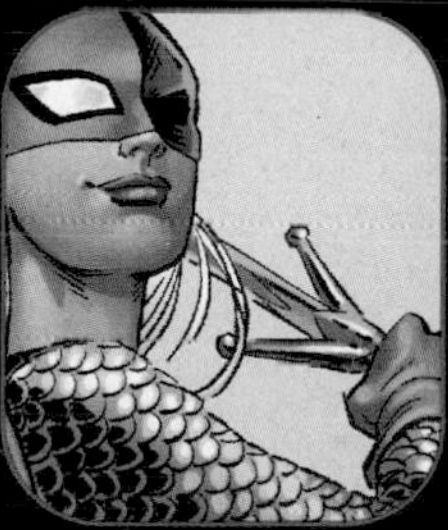

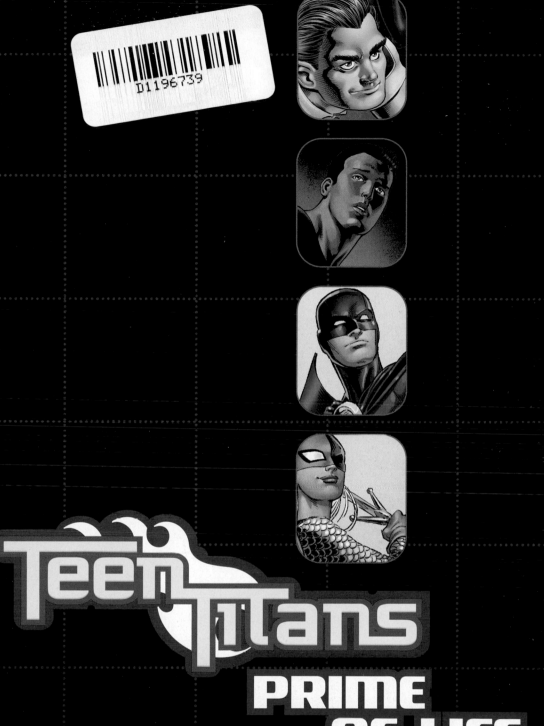

Teen Titans

PRIME OF LIFE

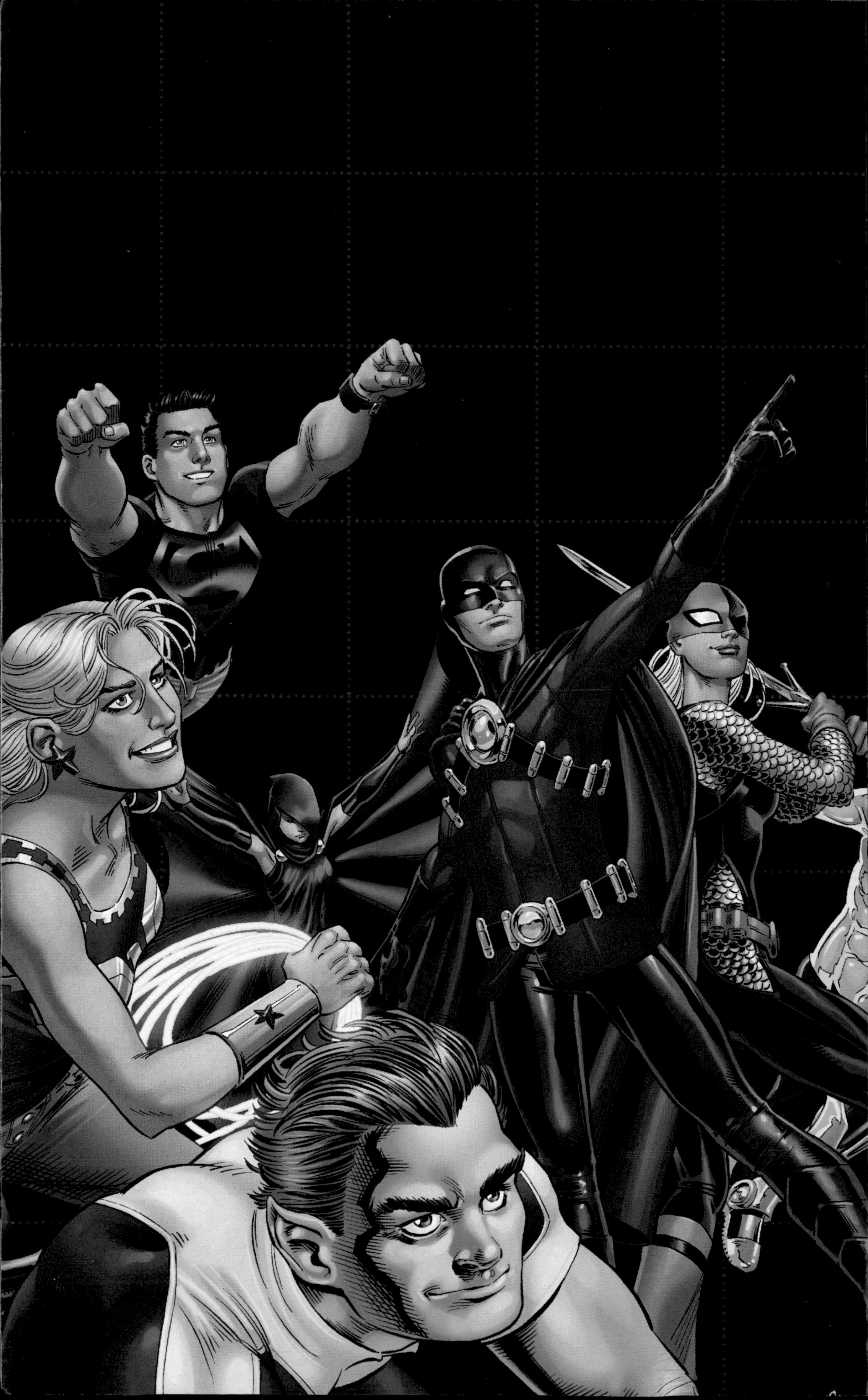

J.T. Krul
Writer

Nicola Scott
José Luís
Eduardo Pansica
Pencillers

Doug Hazlewood
Sandro Ribeiro
Jonas Trindade
Eber Ferreira
Greg Adams
J.P. Mayer
Jack Purcell
Inkers

Jason Wright
Colorist

Sal Cipriano
Carlos M. Mangual
Travis Lanham
Letterers

Nicola Scott &
Doug Hazlewood
with Jason Wright
Cover Artists

Teen Titans
PRIME OF LIFE

Rachel Gluckstern
Editor – Original Series

Rickey Purdin
Assistant Editor – Original Series

Robin Wildman
Editor

Robbin Brosterman
Design Director – Books

Eddie Berganza
Executive Editor

Bob Harras
VP – **Editor-in-Chief**

Diane Nelson
President

Dan DiDio and **Jim Lee**
Co-Publishers

Geoff Johns
Chief Creative Officer

John Rood
Executive VP – Sales, Marketing and Business Development

Amy Genkins
Senior VP – Business and Legal Affairs

Nairi Gardiner
Senior VP – Finance

Jeff Boison
VP – Publishing Operations

Mark Chiarello
VP – Art Direction and Design

John Cunningham
VP – Marketing

Terri Cunningham
VP – Talent Relations and Services

Alison Gill
Senior VP – Manufacturing and Operations

David Hyde
VP – Publicity

Hank Kanalz
Senior VP – Digital

Jay Kogan
VP – Business and Legal Affairs, Publishing

Jack Mahan
VP – Business Affairs, Talent

Nick Napolitano
VP – Manufacturing Administration

Sue Pohja
VP – Book Sales

Courtney Simmons
Senior VP – Publicity

Bob Wayne
Senior VP – Sales

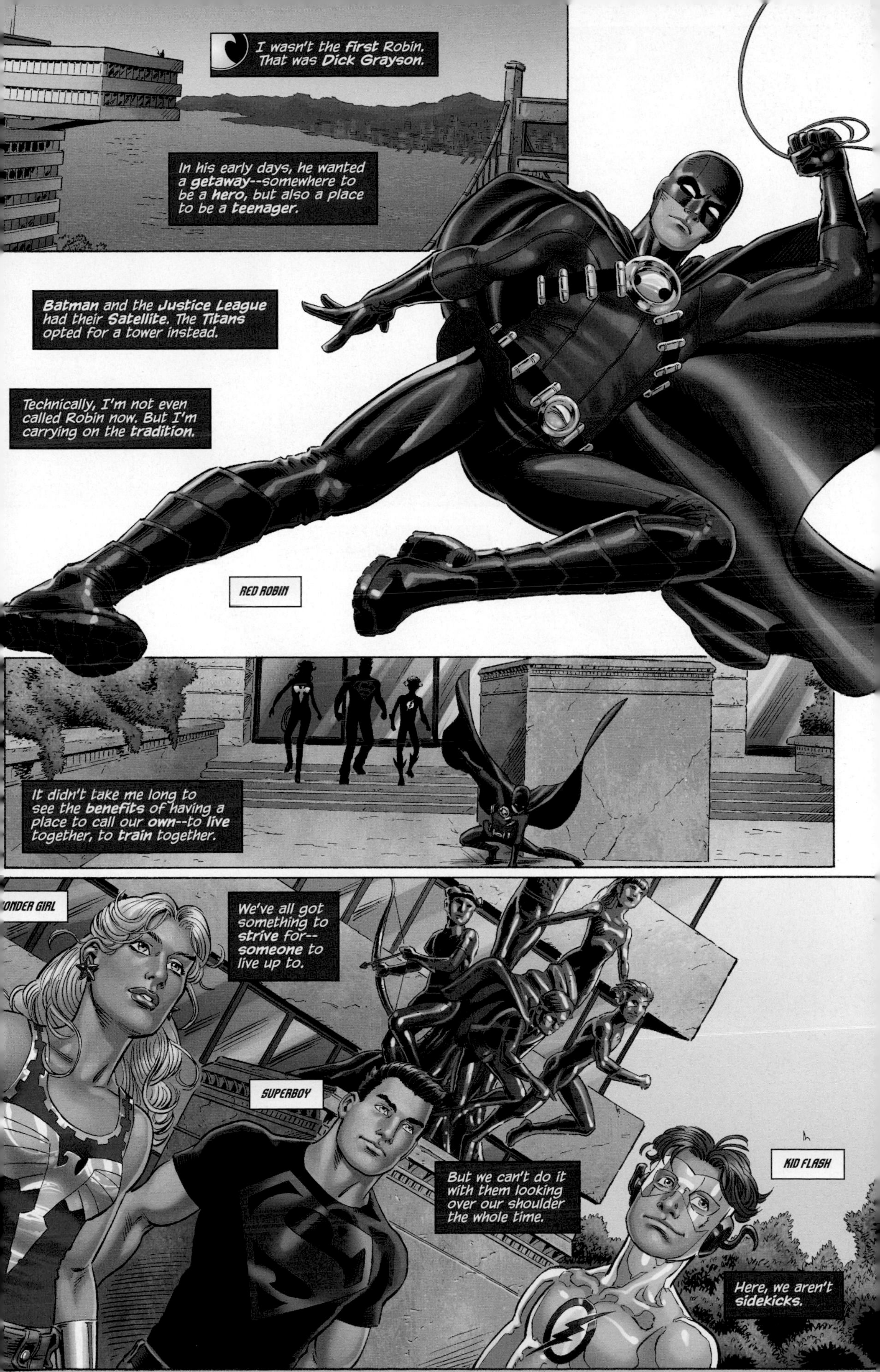
I wasn't the first Robin. That was Dick Grayson.
In his early days, he wanted a getaway--somewhere to be a hero, but also a place to be a teenager.
Batman and the Justice League had their Satellite. The Titans opted for a tower instead.
Technically, I'm not even called Robin now. But I'm carrying on the tradition.
RED ROBIN
It didn't take me long to see the benefits of having a place to call our own--to live together, to train together.
ONDER GIRL
We've all got something to strive for--someone to live up to.
SUPERBOY
But we can't do it with them looking over our shoulder the whole time.
KID FLASH
Here, we aren't sidekicks.

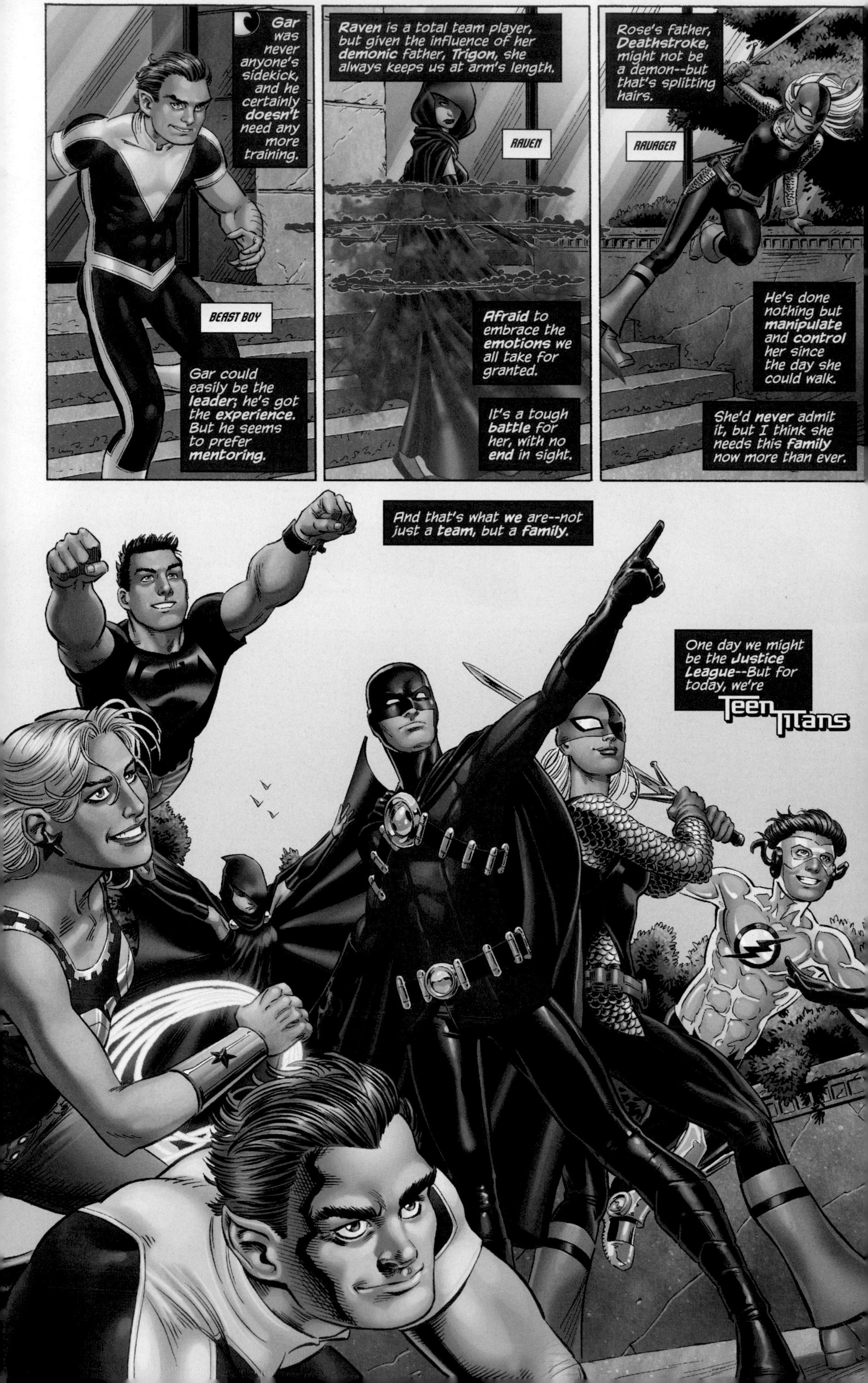

Gar was never anyone's sidekick, and he certainly doesn't need any more training.
BEAST BOY
Gar could easily be the leader; he's got the experience. But he seems to prefer mentoring.
Raven is a total team player, but given the influence of her demonic father, Trigon, she always keeps us at arm's length.
RAVEN
Afraid to embrace the emotions we all take for granted.
It's a tough battle for her, with no end in sight.
Rose's father, Deathstroke, might not be a demon--but that's splitting hairs.
RAVAGER
He's done nothing but manipulate and control her since the day she could walk.
She'd never admit it, but I think she needs this family now more than ever.
And that's what we are--not just a team, but a family.
One day we might be the Justice League--But for today, we're
Teen Titans

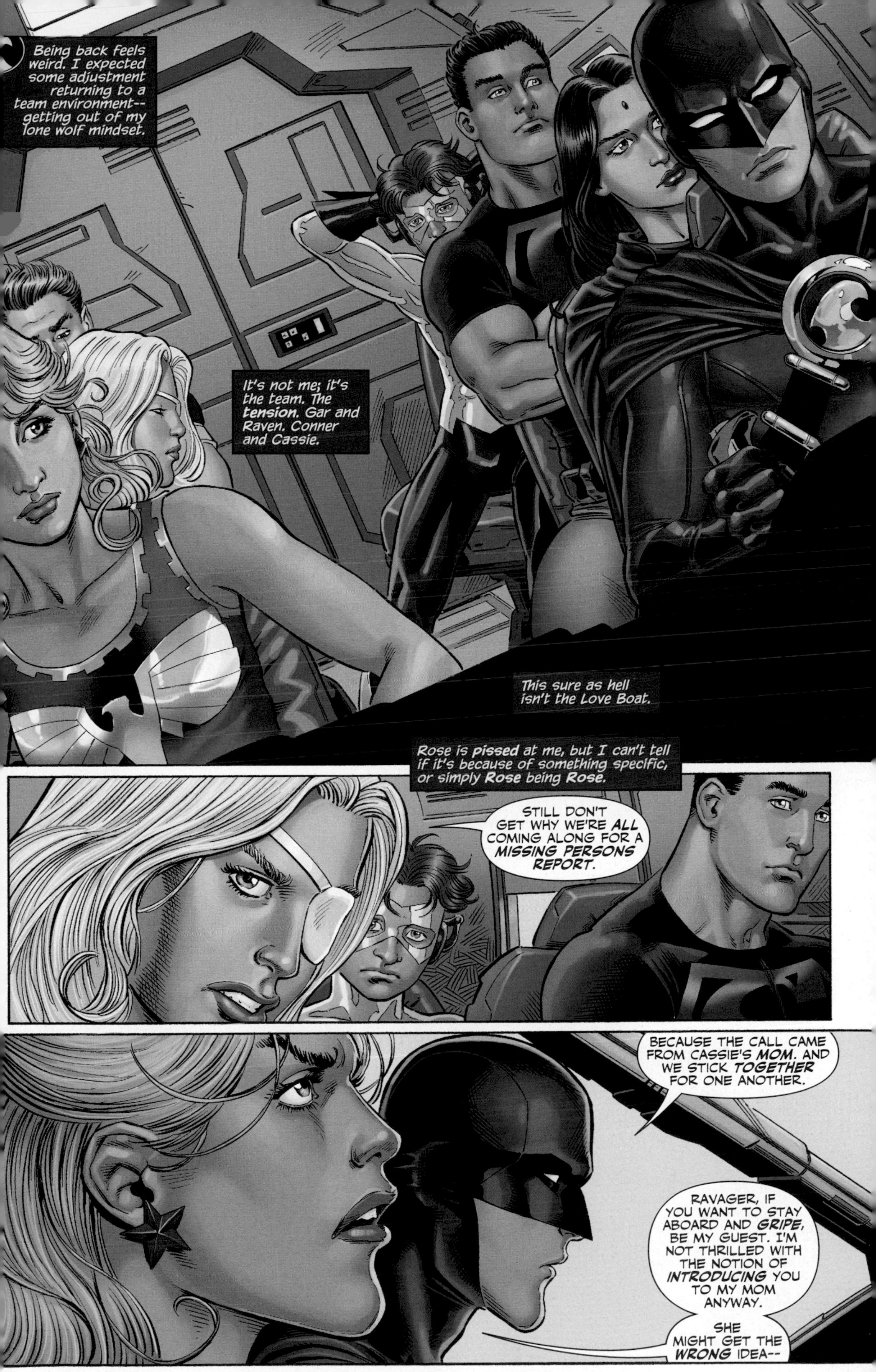
Being back feels weird. I expected some adjustment returning to a team environment-- getting out of my lone wolf mindset.
It's not me; it's the team. The tension. Gar and Raven. Conner and Cassie.
This sure as hell isn't the Love Boat.
Rose is pissed at me, but I can't tell if it's because of something specific, or simply Rose being Rose.
STILL DON'T GET WHY WE'RE ALL COMING ALONG FOR A MISSING PERSONS REPORT.
BECAUSE THE CALL CAME FROM CASSIE'S MOM. AND WE STICK TOGETHER FOR ONE ANOTHER.
RAVAGER, IF YOU WANT TO STAY ABOARD AND GRIPE, BE MY GUEST. I'M NOT THRILLED WITH THE NOTION OF INTRODUCING YOU TO MY MOM ANYWAY.
SHE MIGHT GET THE WRONG IDEA--

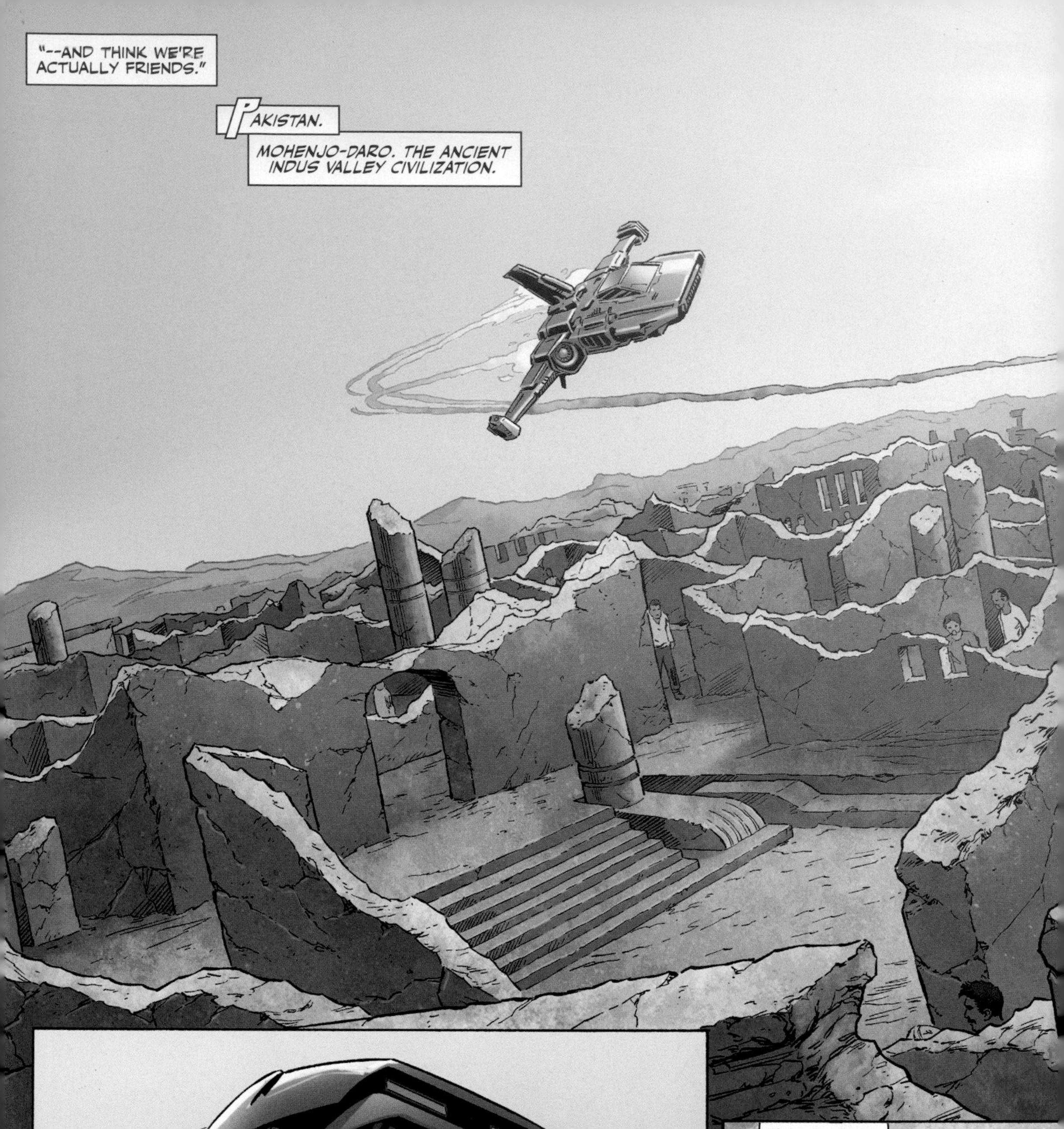
"--AND THINK WE'RE ACTUALLY FRIENDS."
PAKISTAN.
MOHENJO-DARO. THE ANCIENT INDUS VALLEY CIVILIZATION.
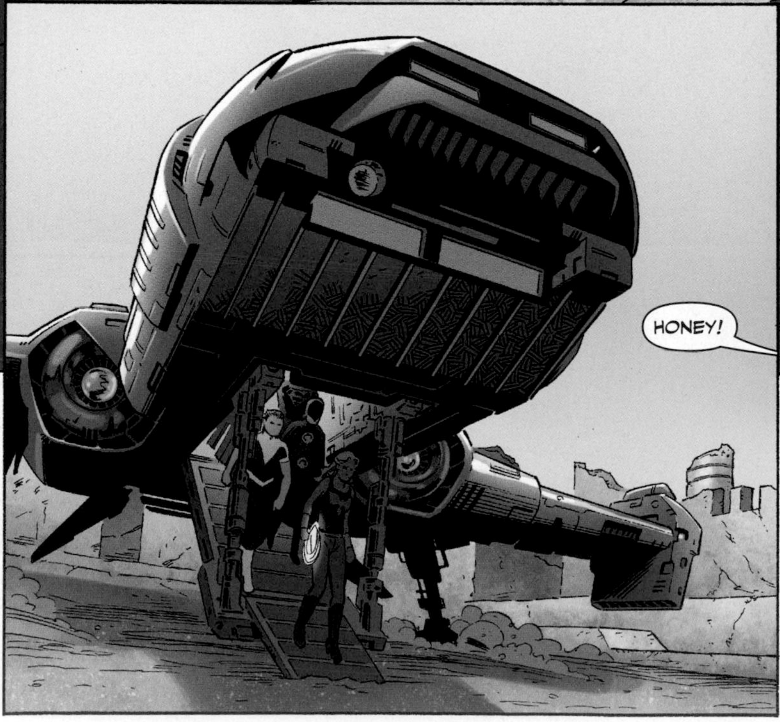
HONEY!
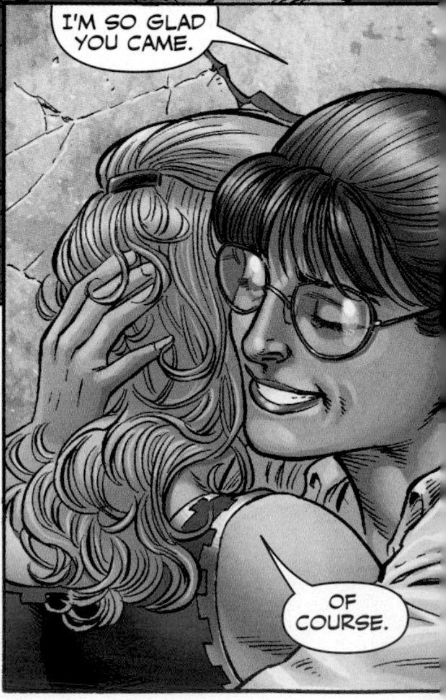
I'M SO GLAD YOU CAME.
OF COURSE.

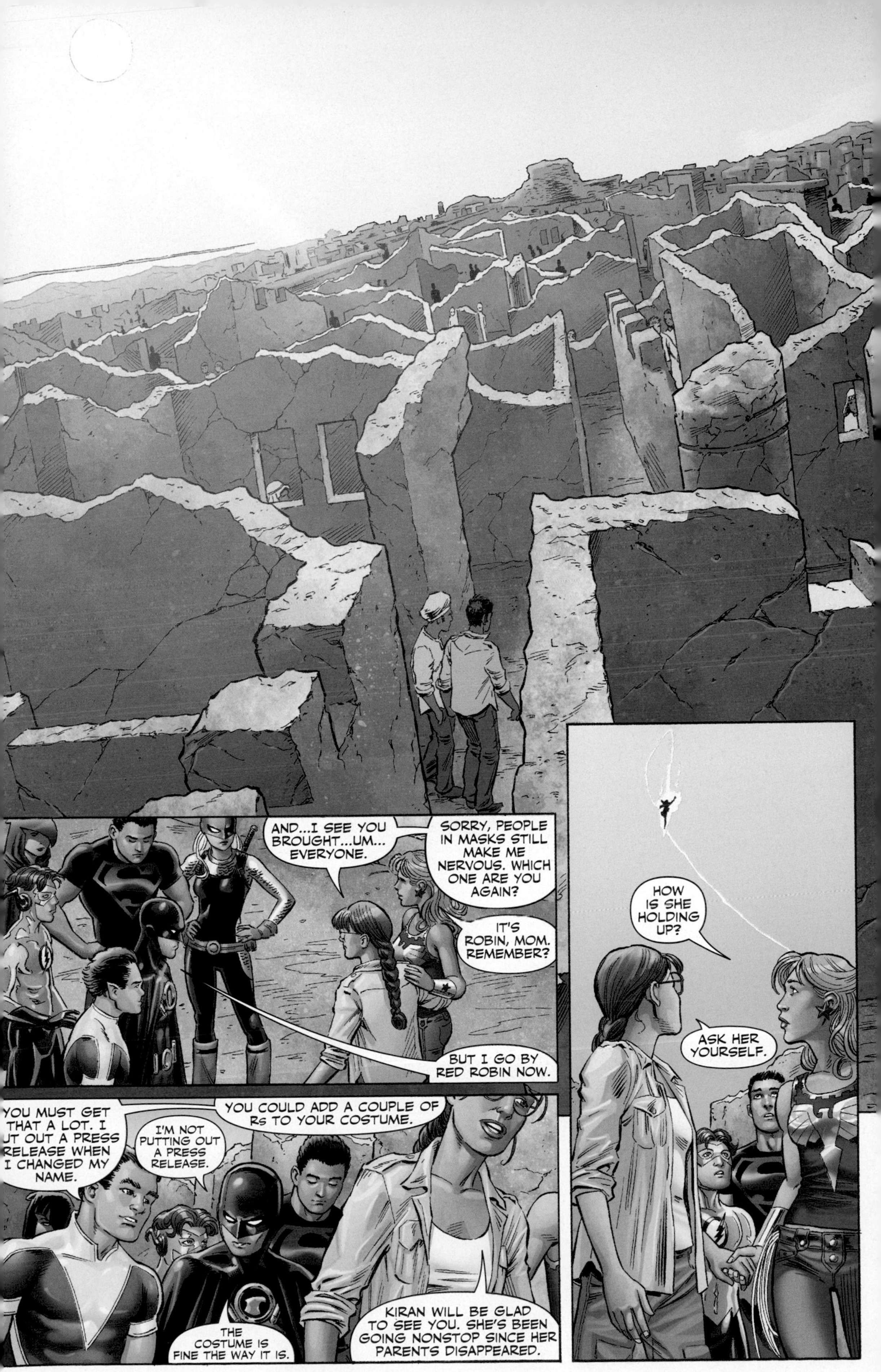
AND...I SEE YOU BROUGHT...UM... EVERYONE.
SORRY, PEOPLE IN MASKS STILL MAKE ME NERVOUS. WHICH ONE ARE YOU AGAIN?
IT'S ROBIN, MOM. REMEMBER?
BUT I GO BY RED ROBIN NOW.
YOU MUST GET THAT A LOT. I UT OUT A PRESS RELEASE WHEN I CHANGED MY NAME.
I'M NOT PUTTING OUT A PRESS RELEASE.
YOU COULD ADD A COUPLE OF Rs TO YOUR COSTUME.
THE COSTUME IS FINE THE WAY IT IS.
KIRAN WILL BE GLAD TO SEE YOU. SHE'S BEEN GOING NONSTOP SINCE HER PARENTS DISAPPEARED.
HOW IS SHE HOLDING UP?
ASK HER YOURSELF.

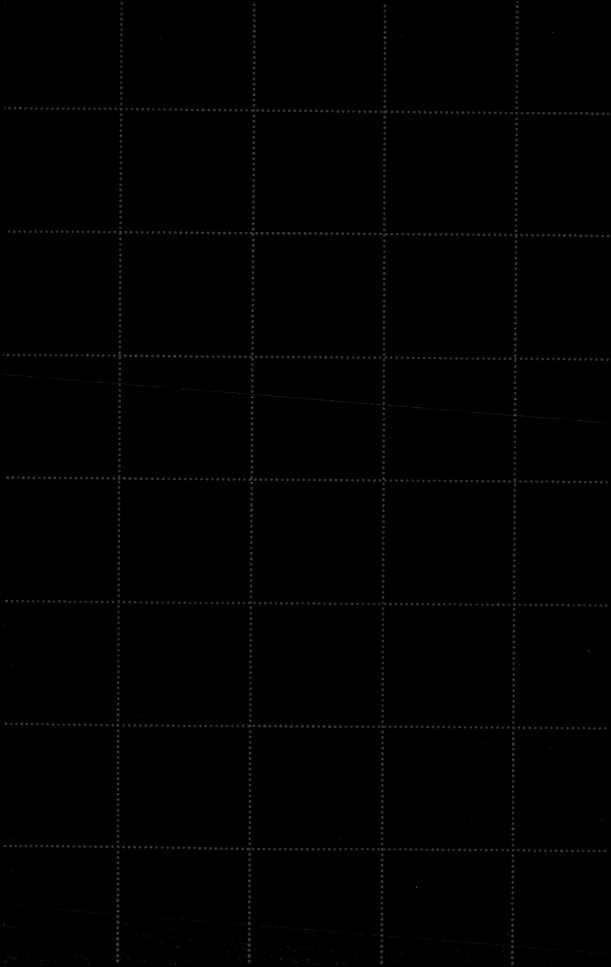

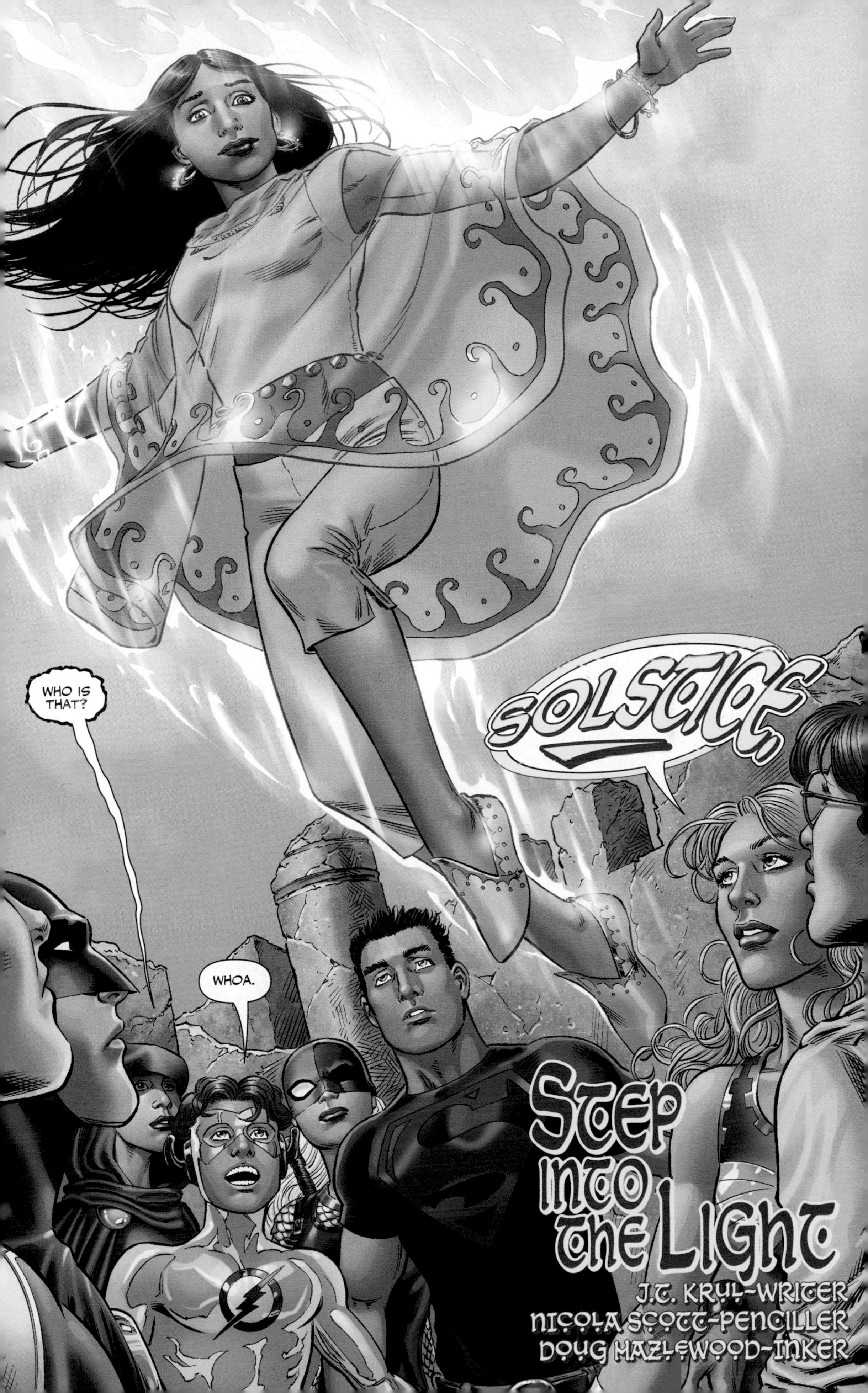
WHO IS THAT?
SOLSTICE.
WHOA.
STEP INTO THE LIGHT
J.T. KRUL-WRITER
NICOLA SCOTT-PENCILLER
DOUG HAZLEWOOD-INKER

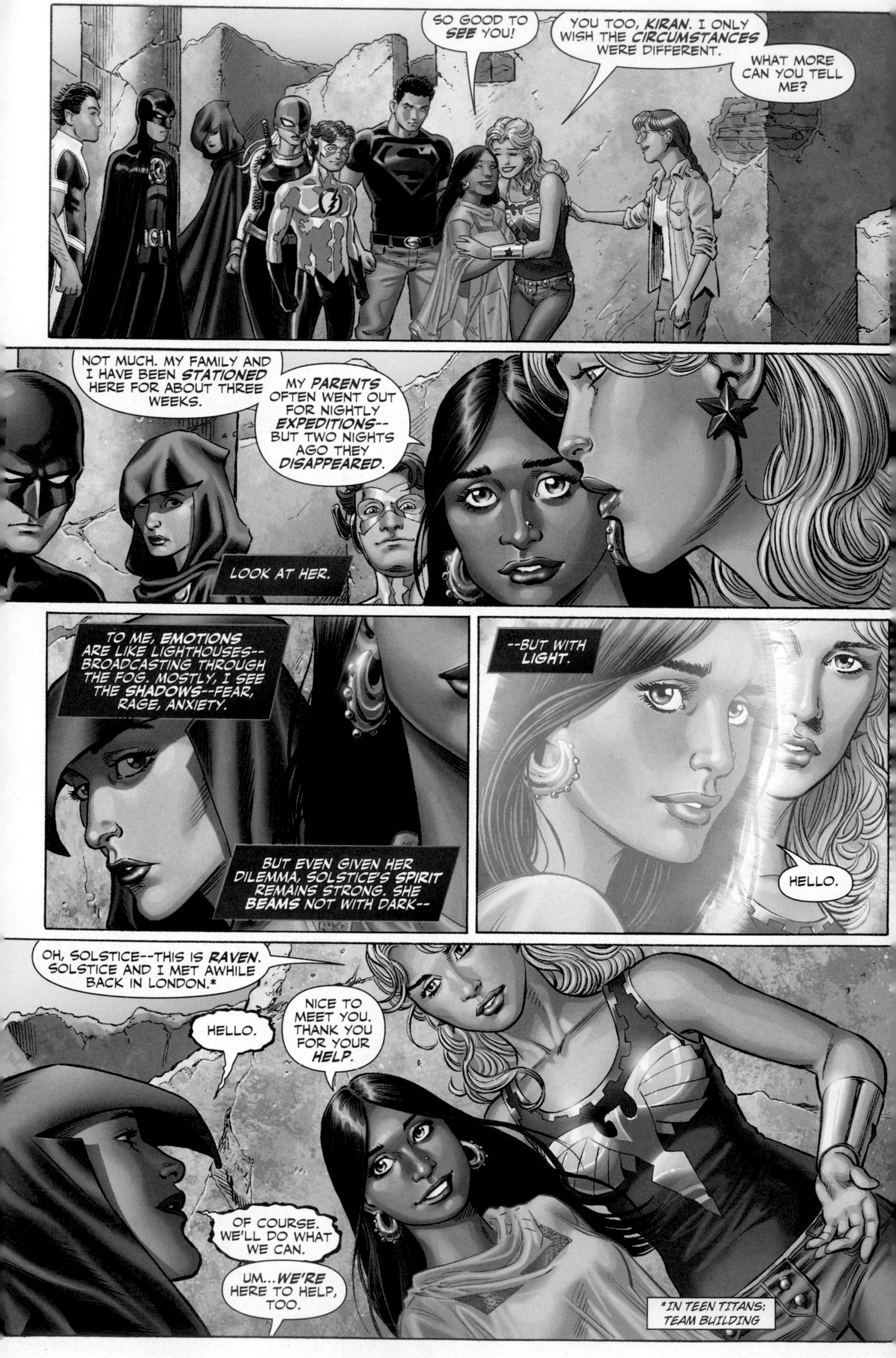
SO GOOD TO SEE YOU!
YOU TOO, KIRAN. I ONLY WISH THE CIRCUMSTANCES WERE DIFFERENT.
WHAT MORE CAN YOU TELL ME?
NOT MUCH. MY FAMILY AND I HAVE BEEN STATIONED HERE FOR ABOUT THREE WEEKS.
MY PARENTS OFTEN WENT OUT FOR NIGHTLY EXPEDITIONS--BUT TWO NIGHTS AGO THEY DISAPPEARED.
LOOK AT HER.
TO ME, EMOTIONS ARE LIKE LIGHTHOUSES--BROADCASTING THROUGH THE FOG. MOSTLY, I SEE THE SHADOWS--FEAR, RAGE, ANXIETY.
BUT EVEN GIVEN HER DILEMMA, SOLSTICE'S SPIRIT REMAINS STRONG. SHE BEAMS NOT WITH DARK--
--BUT WITH LIGHT.
HELLO.
OH, SOLSTICE--THIS IS RAVEN. SOLSTICE AND I MET AWHILE BACK IN LONDON.*
HELLO.
NICE TO MEET YOU. THANK YOU FOR YOUR HELP.
OF COURSE. WE'LL DO WHAT WE CAN.
UM...WE'RE HERE TO HELP, TOO.
*IN TEEN TITANS: TEAM BUILDING

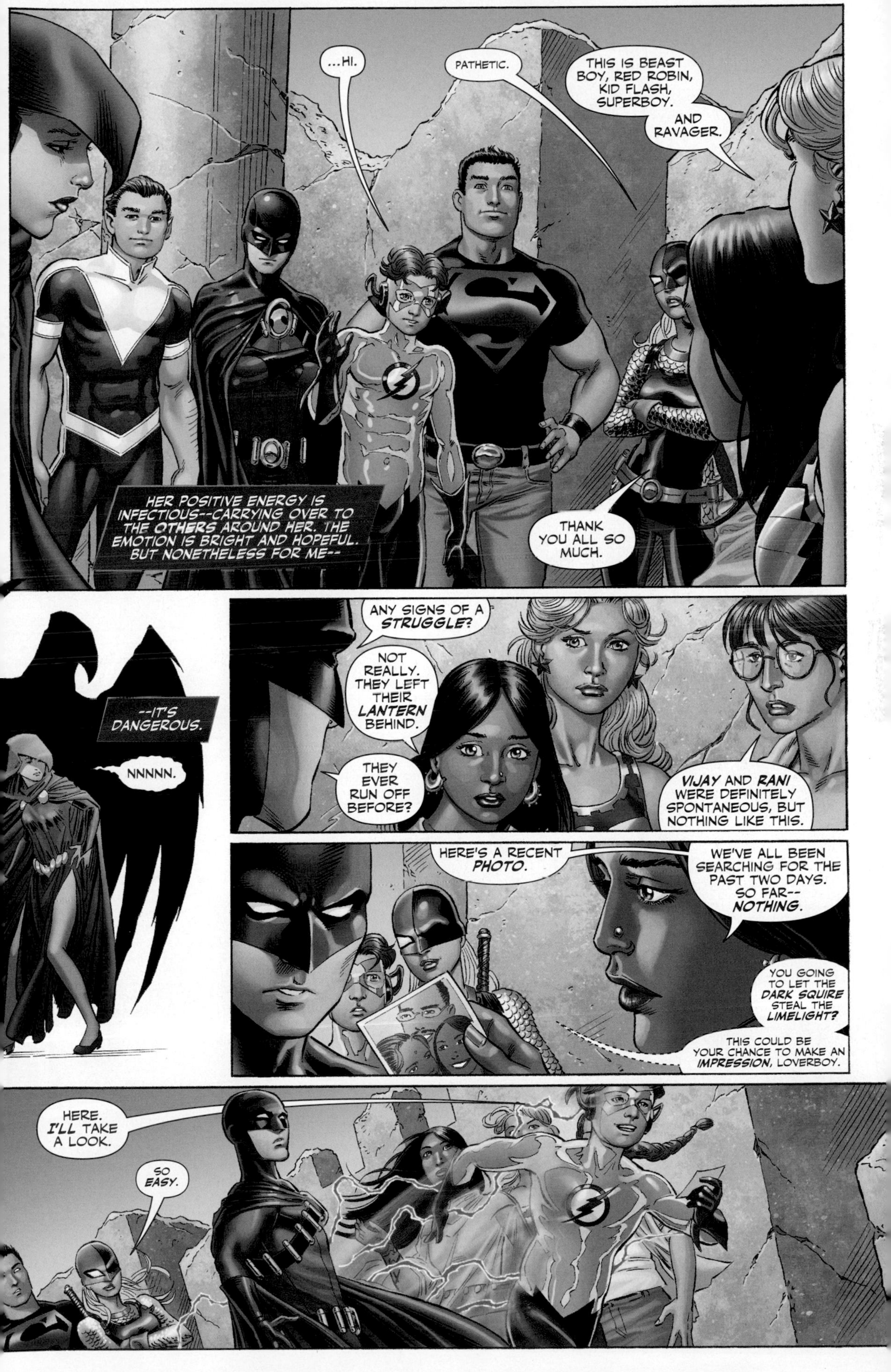
...HI.
PATHETIC.
THIS IS BEAST BOY, RED ROBIN, KID FLASH, SUPERBOY.
AND RAVAGER.
HER POSITIVE ENERGY IS INFECTIOUS--CARRYING OVER TO THE OTHERS AROUND HER. THE EMOTION IS BRIGHT AND HOPEFUL. BUT NONETHELESS FOR ME--
THANK YOU ALL SO MUCH.
--IT'S DANGEROUS.
NNNNN.
ANY SIGNS OF A STRUGGLE?
NOT REALLY. THEY LEFT THEIR LANTERN BEHIND.
THEY EVER RUN OFF BEFORE?
VIJAY AND RANI WERE DEFINITELY SPONTANEOUS, BUT NOTHING LIKE THIS.
HERE'S A RECENT PHOTO.
WE'VE ALL BEEN SEARCHING FOR THE PAST TWO DAYS. SO FAR--NOTHING.
YOU GOING TO LET THE DARK SQUIRE STEAL THE LIMELIGHT?
THIS COULD BE YOUR CHANCE TO MAKE AN IMPRESSION, LOVERBOY.
HERE. I'LL TAKE A LOOK.
SO EASY.

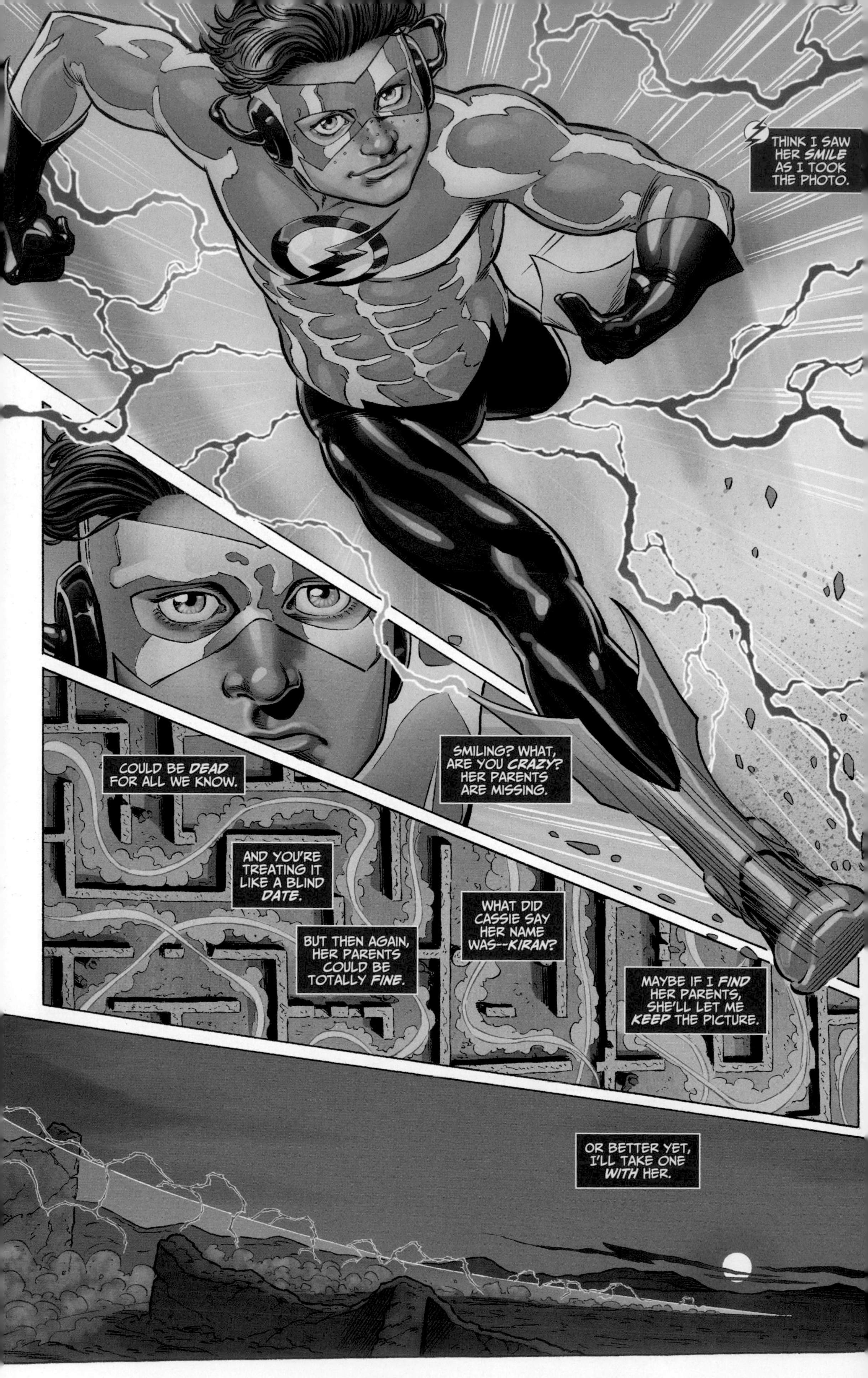
THINK I SAW HER SMILE AS I TOOK THE PHOTO.
SMILING? WHAT, ARE YOU CRAZY? HER PARENTS ARE MISSING.
COULD BE DEAD FOR ALL WE KNOW.
AND YOU'RE TREATING IT LIKE A BLIND DATE.
BUT THEN AGAIN, HER PARENTS COULD BE TOTALLY FINE.
WHAT DID CASSIE SAY HER NAME WAS--KIRAN?
MAYBE IF I FIND HER PARENTS, SHE'LL LET ME KEEP THE PICTURE.
OR BETTER YET, I'LL TAKE ONE WITH HER.

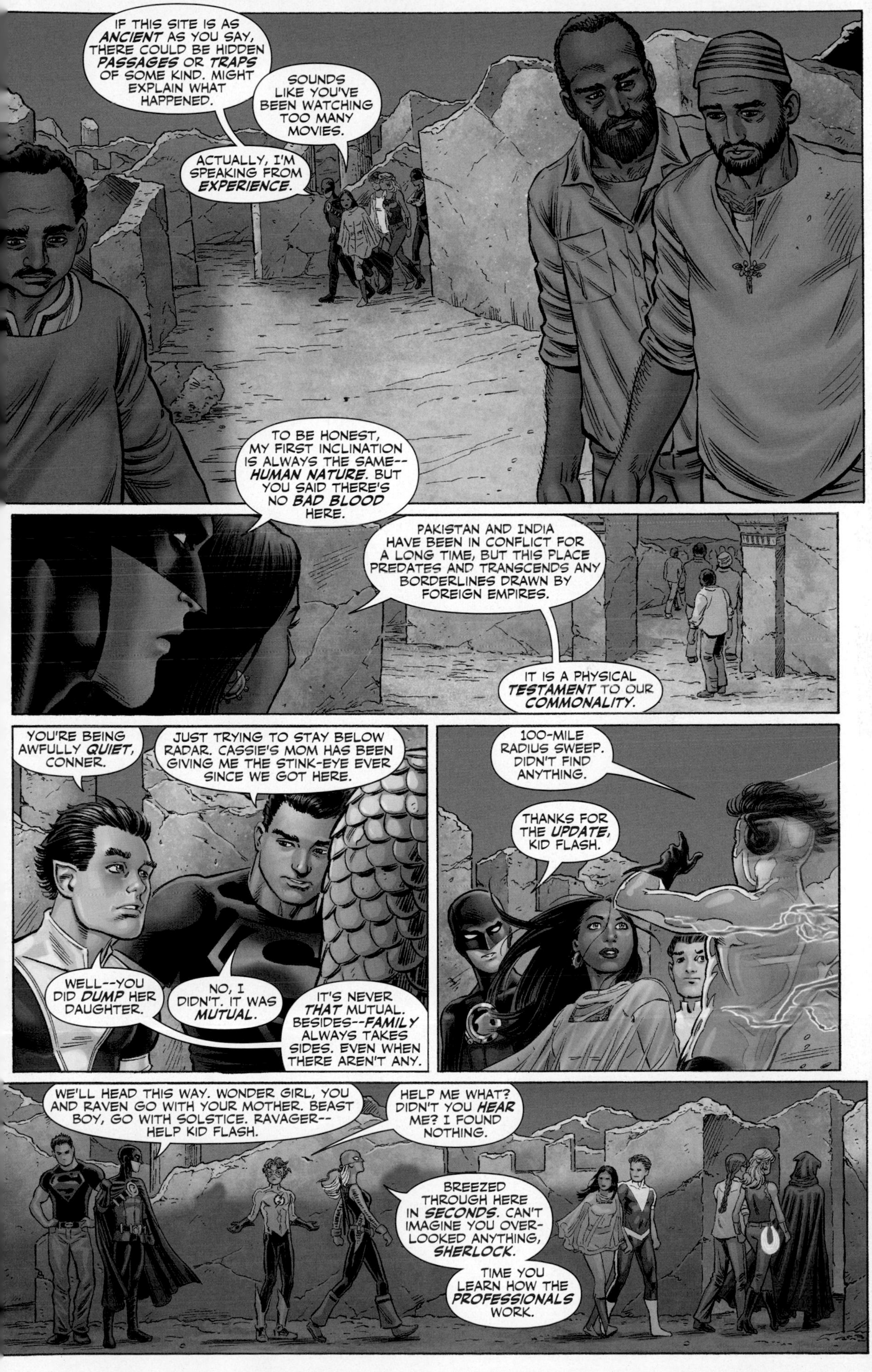
IF THIS SITE IS AS ANCIENT AS YOU SAY, THERE COULD BE HIDDEN PASSAGES OR TRAPS OF SOME KIND. MIGHT EXPLAIN WHAT HAPPENED.
SOUNDS LIKE YOU'VE BEEN WATCHING TOO MANY MOVIES.
ACTUALLY, I'M SPEAKING FROM EXPERIENCE.
TO BE HONEST, MY FIRST INCLINATION IS ALWAYS THE SAME--HUMAN NATURE. BUT YOU SAID THERE'S NO BAD BLOOD HERE.
PAKISTAN AND INDIA HAVE BEEN IN CONFLICT FOR A LONG TIME, BUT THIS PLACE PREDATES AND TRANSCENDS ANY BORDERLINES DRAWN BY FOREIGN EMPIRES.
IT IS A PHYSICAL TESTAMENT TO OUR COMMONALITY.
YOU'RE BEING AWFULLY QUIET, CONNER.
JUST TRYING TO STAY BELOW RADAR. CASSIE'S MOM HAS BEEN GIVING ME THE STINK-EYE EVER SINCE WE GOT HERE.
WELL--YOU DID DUMP HER DAUGHTER.
NO, I DIDN'T. IT WAS MUTUAL.
IT'S NEVER THAT MUTUAL. BESIDES--FAMILY ALWAYS TAKES SIDES. EVEN WHEN THERE AREN'T ANY.
100-MILE RADIUS SWEEP. DIDN'T FIND ANYTHING.
THANKS FOR THE UPDATE, KID FLASH.
WE'LL HEAD THIS WAY. WONDER GIRL, YOU AND RAVEN GO WITH YOUR MOTHER. BEAST BOY, GO WITH SOLSTICE. RAVAGER--HELP KID FLASH.
HELP ME WHAT? DIDN'T YOU HEAR ME? I FOUND NOTHING.
BREEZED THROUGH HERE IN SECONDS. CAN'T IMAGINE YOU OVER-LOOKED ANYTHING, SHERLOCK.
TIME YOU LEARN HOW THE PROFESSIONALS WORK.

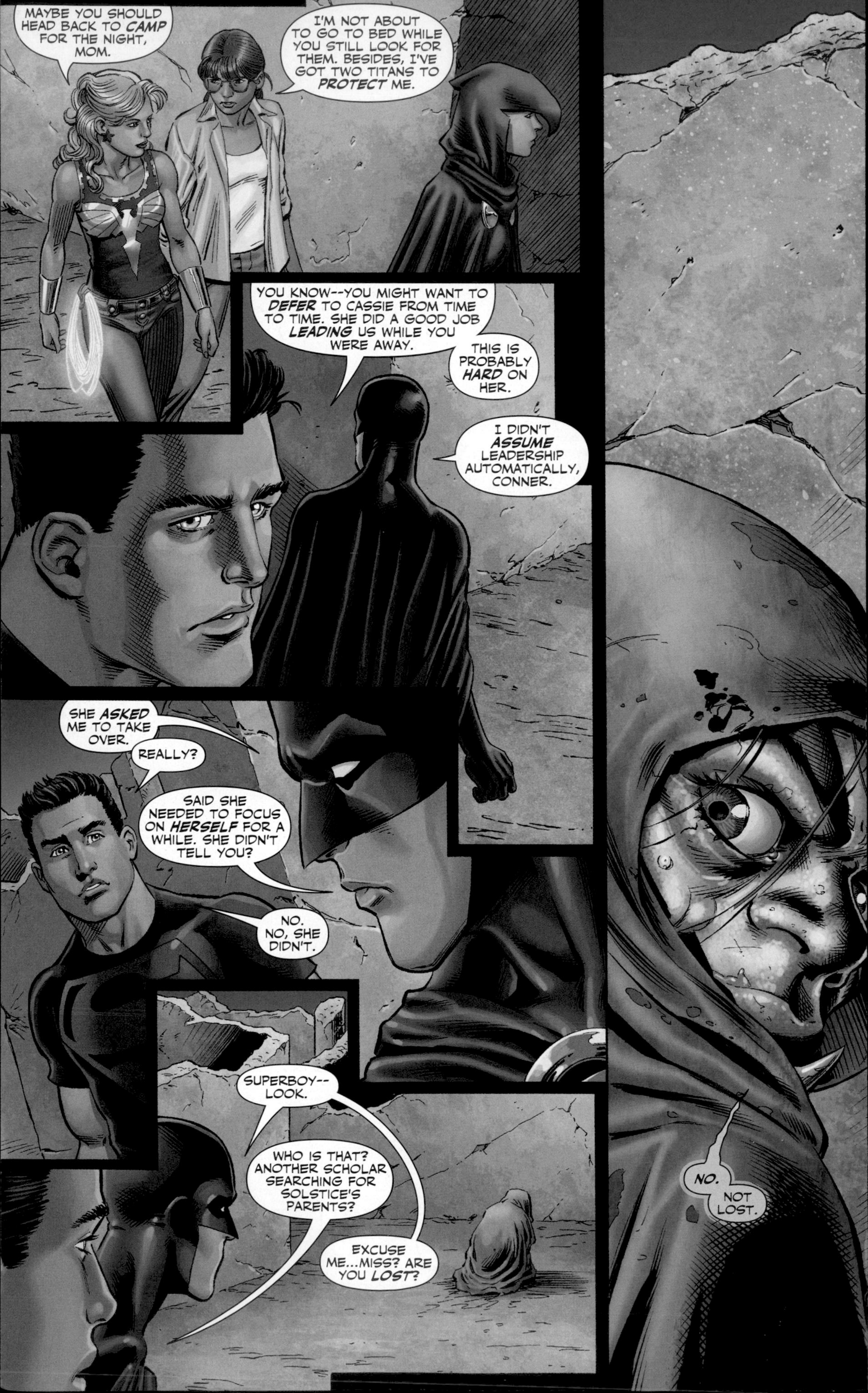
MAYBE YOU SHOULD HEAD BACK TO CAMP FOR THE NIGHT, MOM.
I'M NOT ABOUT TO GO TO BED WHILE YOU STILL LOOK FOR THEM. BESIDES, I'VE GOT TWO TITANS TO PROTECT ME.
YOU KNOW--YOU MIGHT WANT TO DEFER TO CASSIE FROM TIME TO TIME. SHE DID A GOOD JOB LEADING US WHILE YOU WERE AWAY.
THIS IS PROBABLY HARD ON HER.
I DIDN'T ASSUME LEADERSHIP AUTOMATICALLY, CONNER.
SHE ASKED ME TO TAKE OVER.
REALLY?
SAID SHE NEEDED TO FOCUS ON HERSELF FOR A WHILE. SHE DIDN'T TELL YOU?
NO. NO, SHE DIDN'T.
SUPERBOY-- LOOK.
WHO IS THAT? ANOTHER SCHOLAR SEARCHING FOR SOLSTICE'S PARENTS?
EXCUSE ME...MISS? ARE YOU LOST?
NO.
NOT LOST.

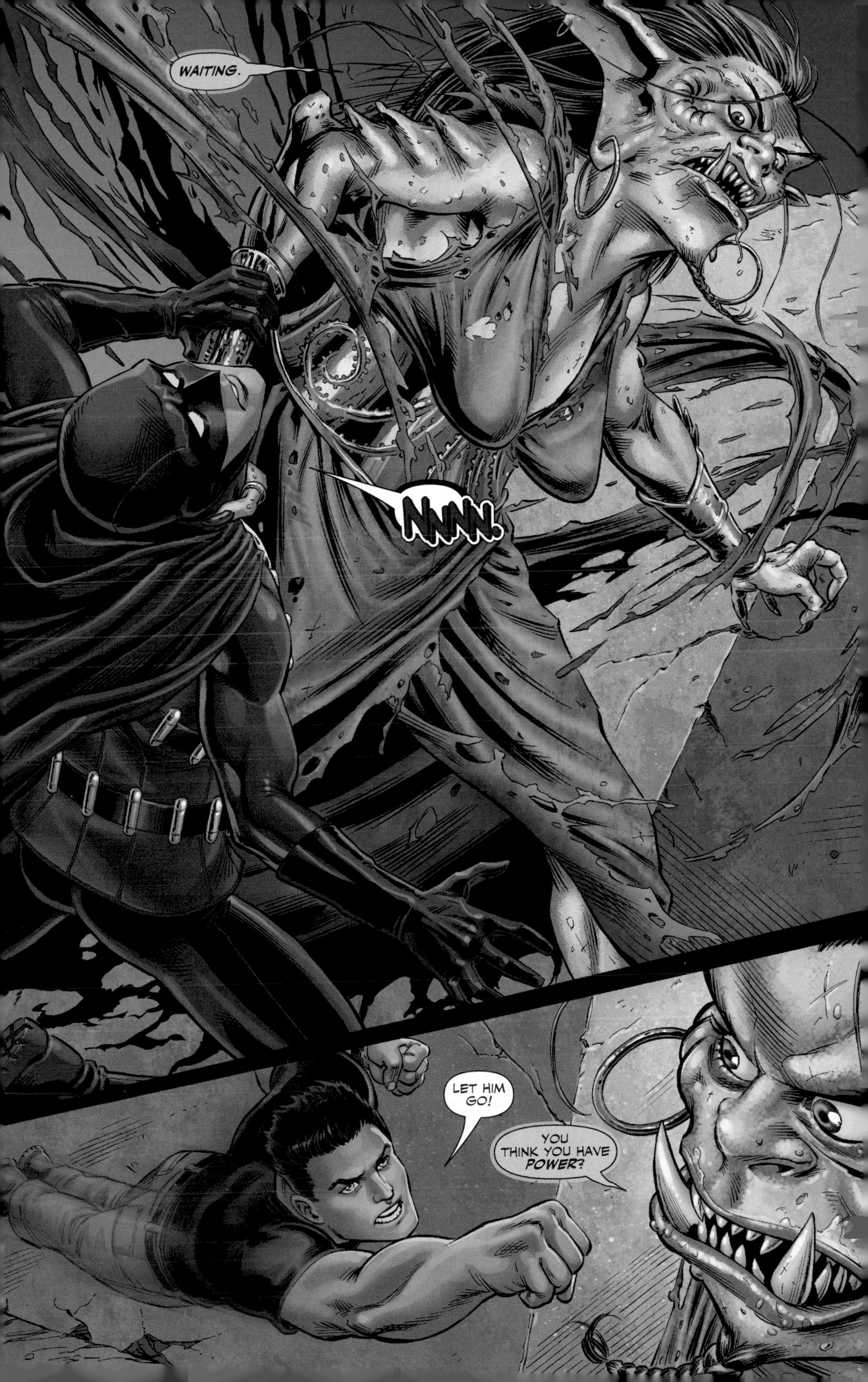
WAITING.
NNNN.
LET HIM GO!
YOU THINK YOU HAVE POWER?

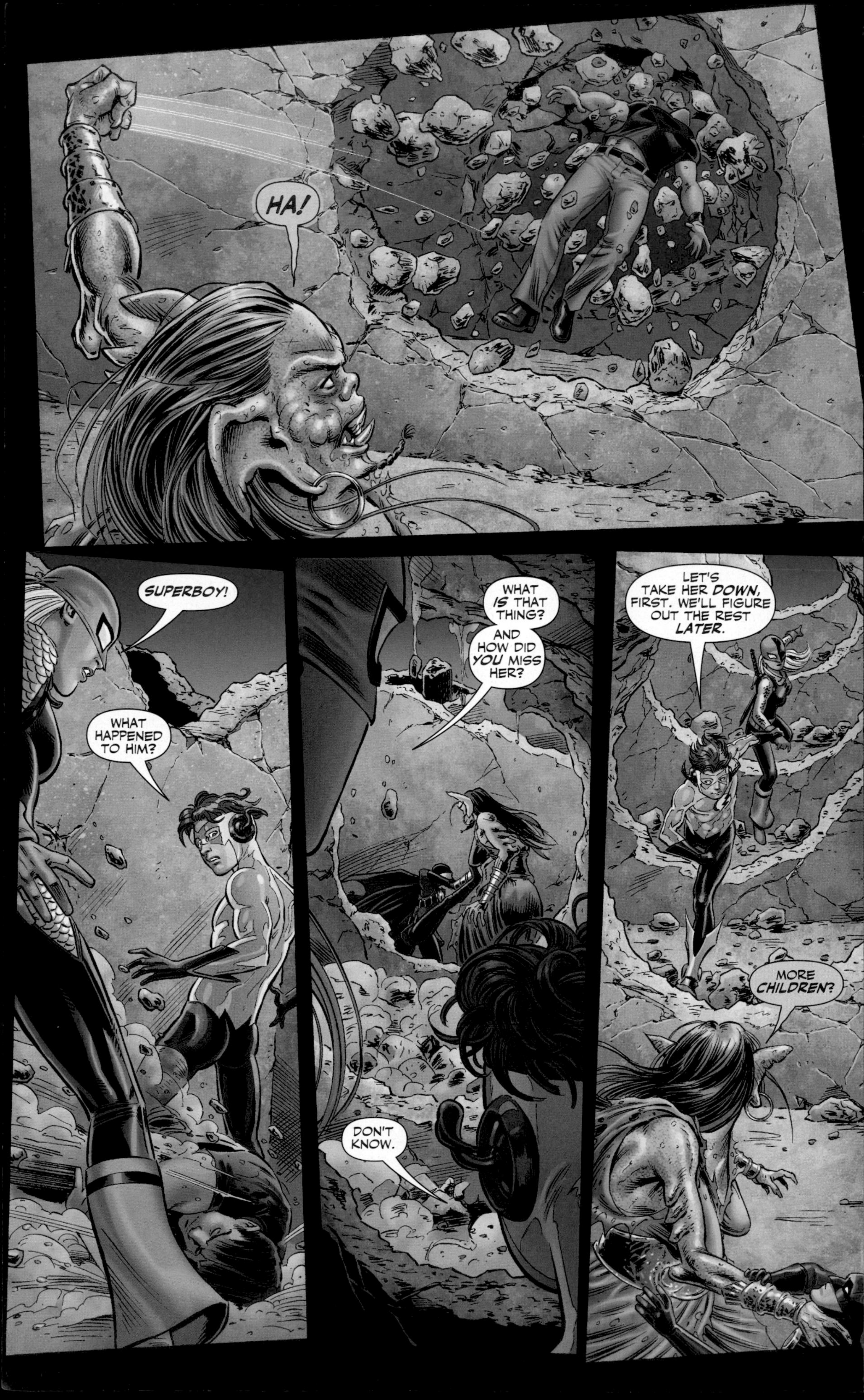
HA!
SUPERBOY!
WHAT HAPPENED TO HIM?
WHAT IS THAT THING?
AND HOW DID YOU MISS HER?
DON'T KNOW.
LET'S TAKE HER DOWN, FIRST. WE'LL FIGURE OUT THE REST LATER.
MORE CHILDREN?

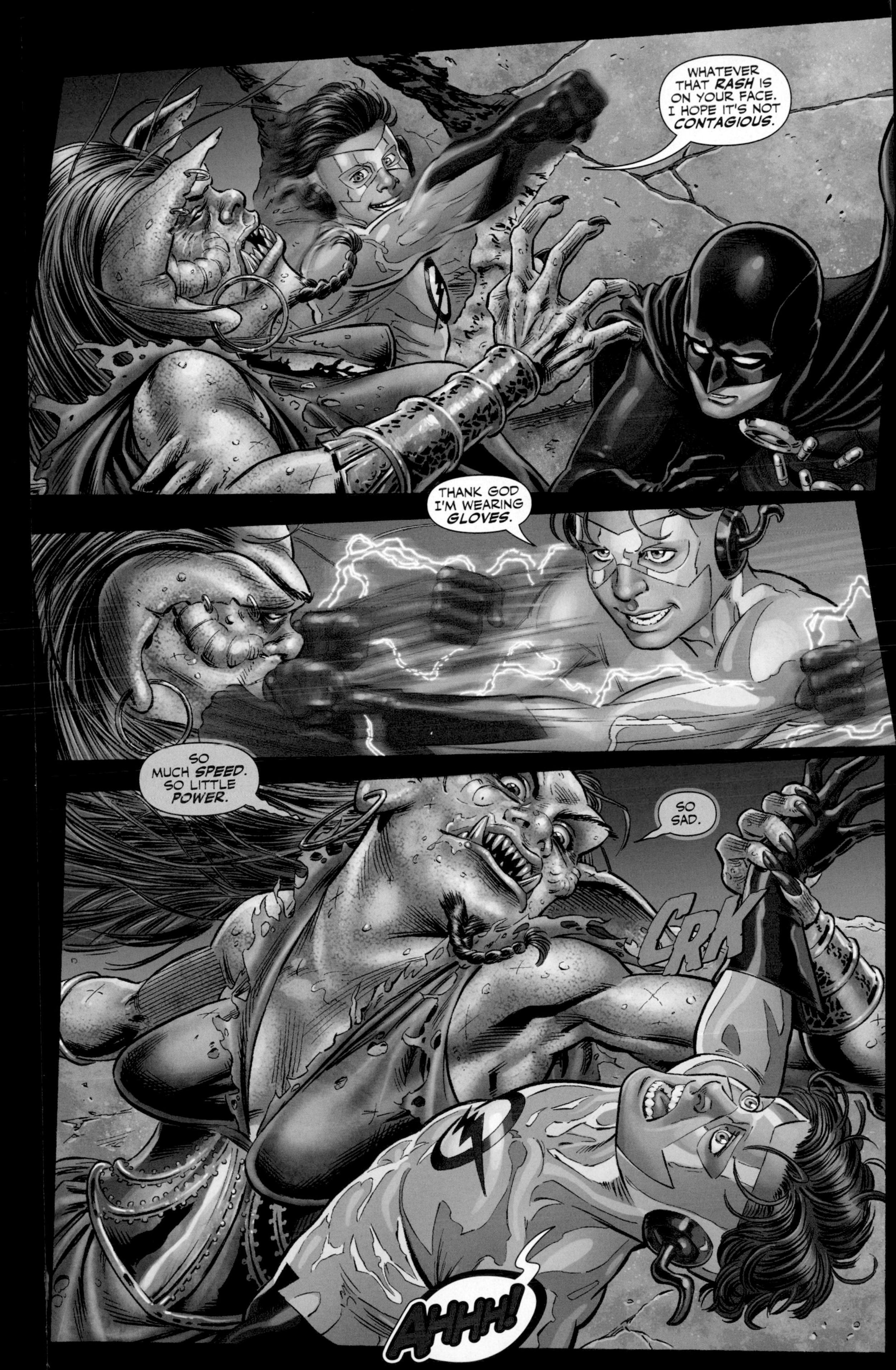
WHATEVER THAT RASH IS ON YOUR FACE. I HOPE IT'S NOT CONTAGIOUS.
THANK GOD I'M WEARING GLOVES.
SO MUCH SPEED. SO LITTLE POWER.
SO SAD.
CRK
AHHH!

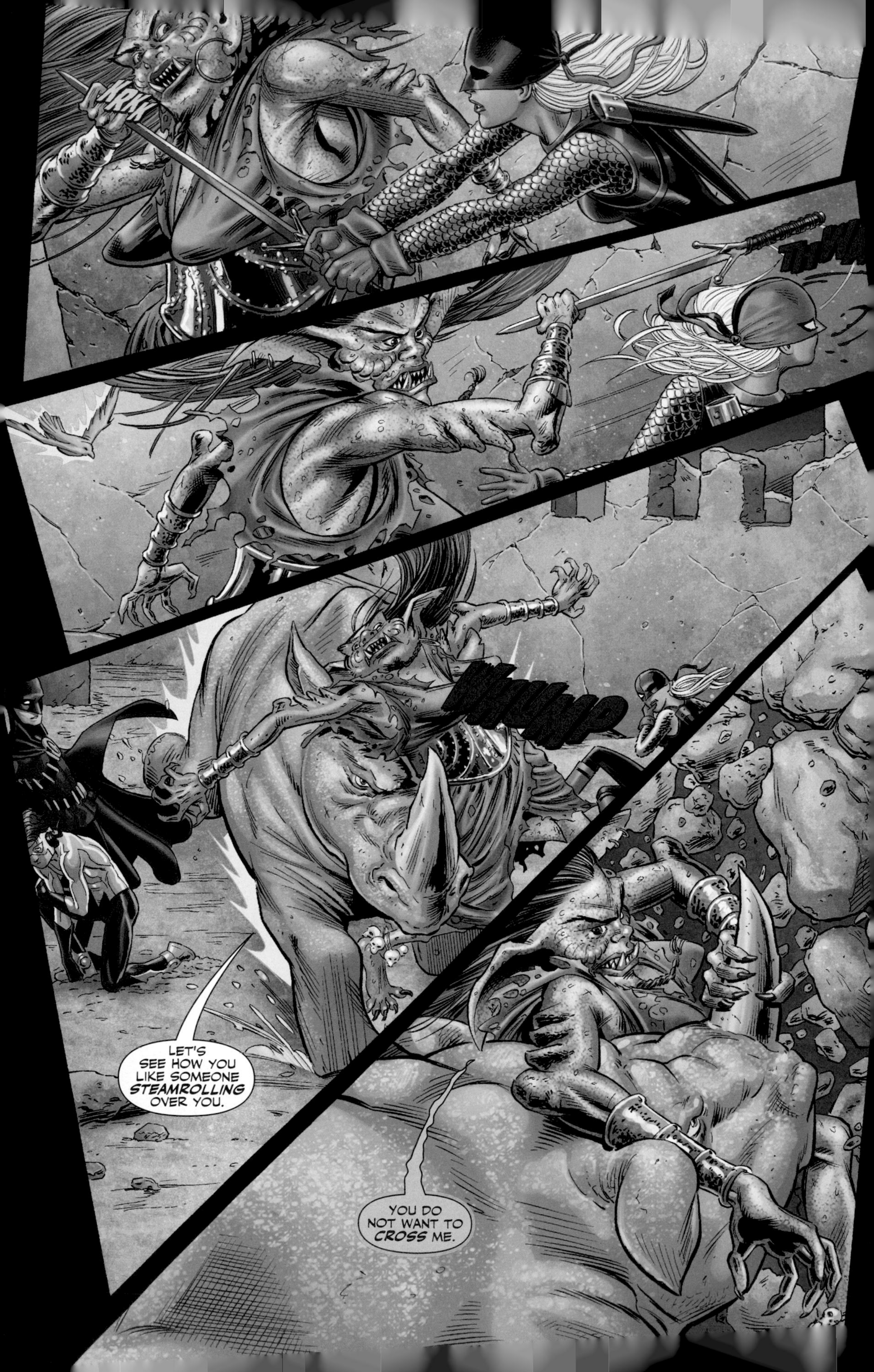
KRKK
THWUP
WHUMP
LET'S SEE HOW YOU LIKE SOMEONE STEAMROLLING OVER YOU.
YOU DO NOT WANT TO CROSS ME.

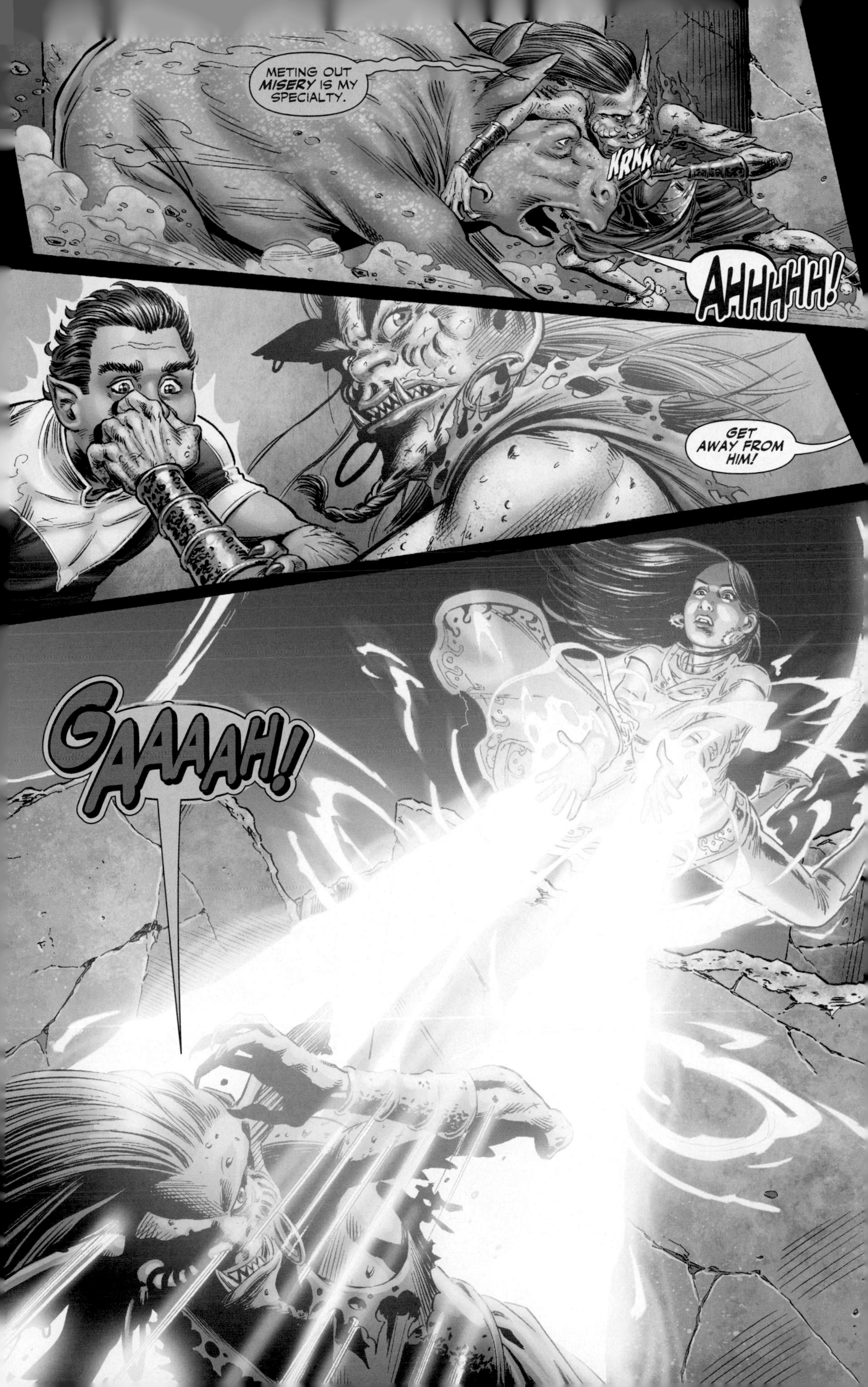
MEETING OUT MISERY IS MY SPECIALTY.
KRKK
AHHHHH!
GET AWAY FROM HIM!
GAAAAH!

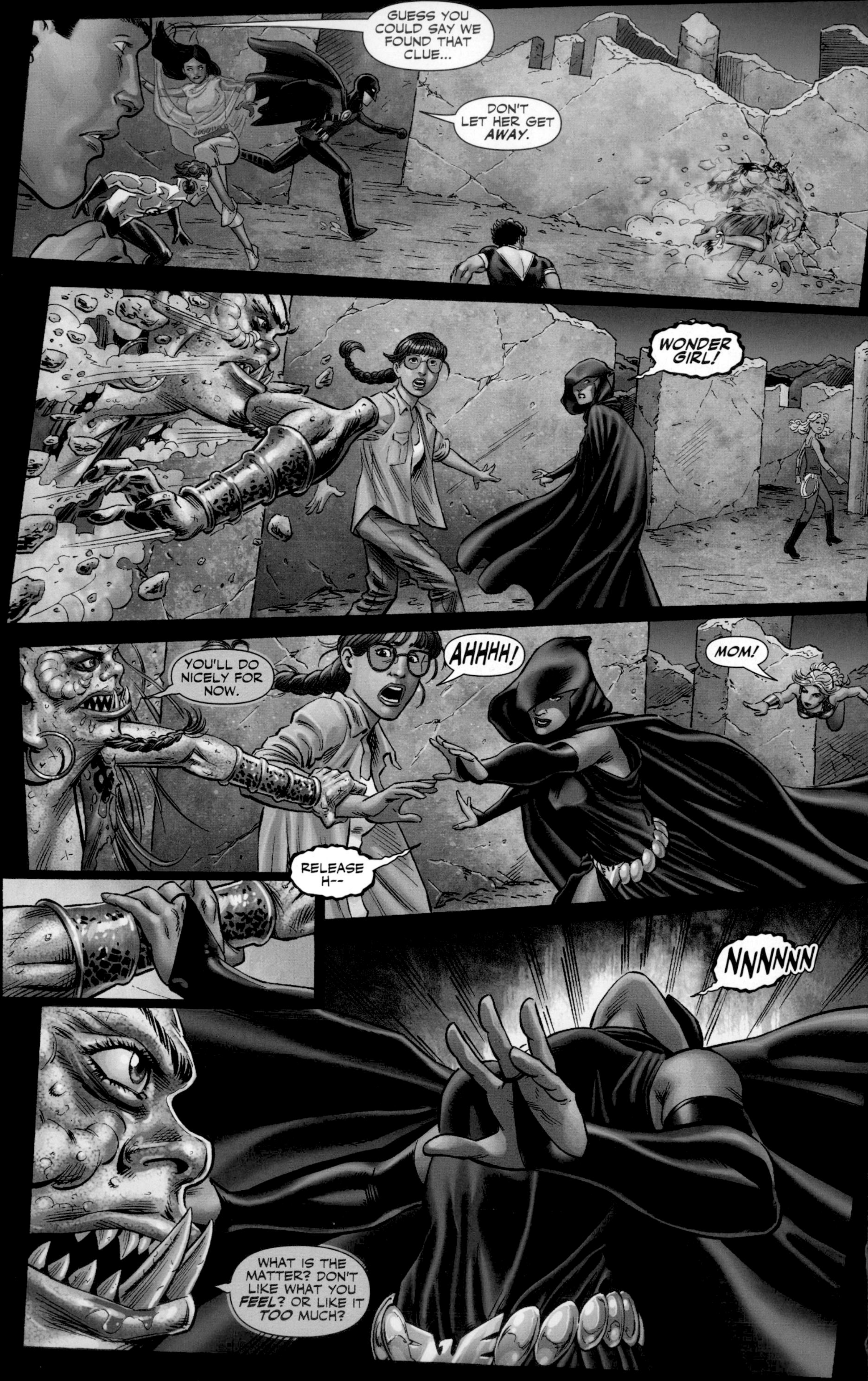
GUESS YOU COULD SAY WE FOUND THAT CLUE...
DON'T LET HER GET AWAY.
WONDER GIRL!
YOU'LL DO NICELY FOR NOW.
AHHHH!
MOM!
RELEASE H--
NNNNNN
WHAT IS THE MATTER? DON'T LIKE WHAT YOU FEEL? OR LIKE IT TOO MUCH?

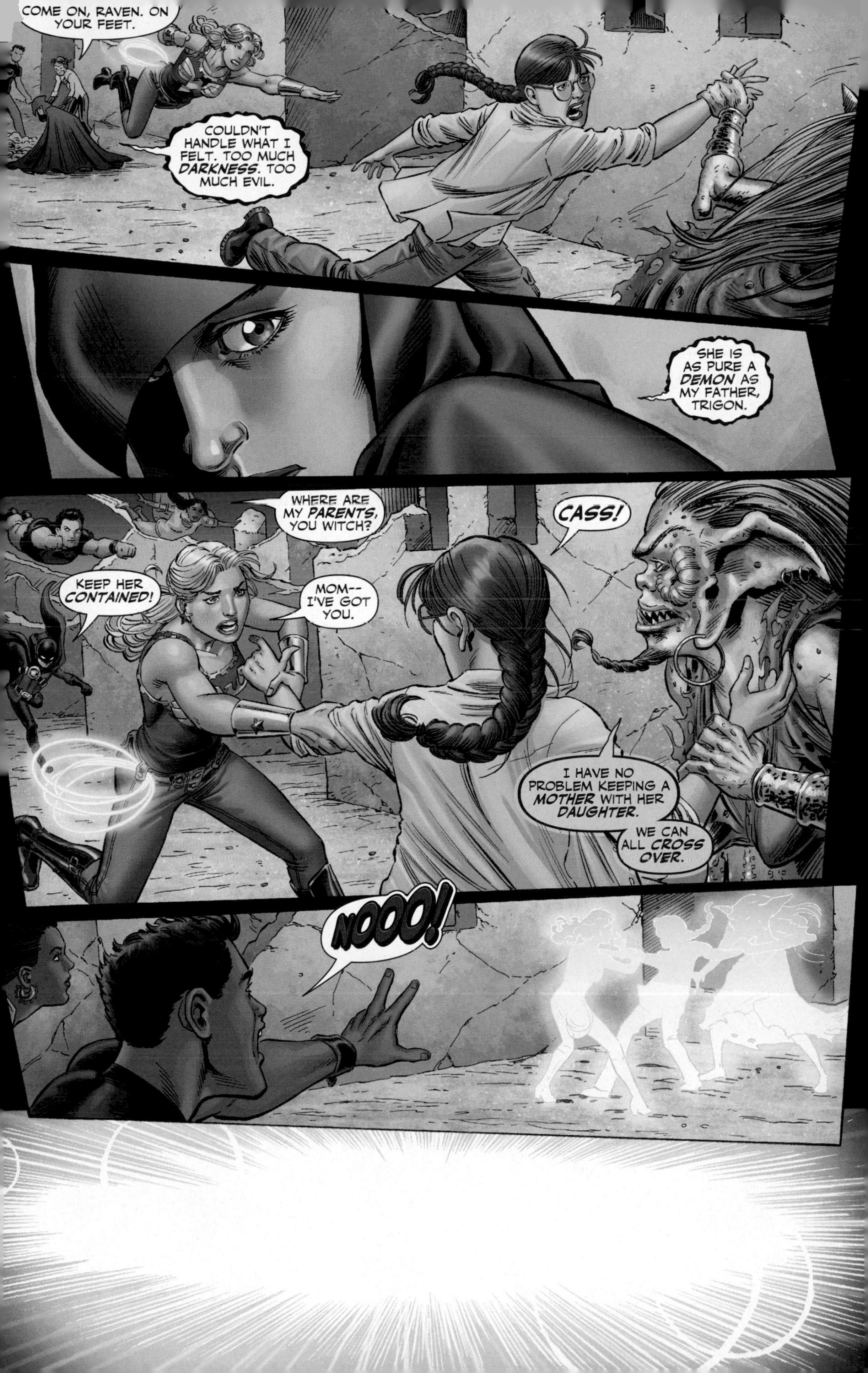
COME ON, RAVEN. ON YOUR FEET.
COULDN'T HANDLE WHAT I FELT. TOO MUCH DARKNESS. TOO MUCH EVIL.
SHE IS AS PURE A DEMON AS MY FATHER, TRIGON.
WHERE ARE MY PARENTS, YOU WITCH?
CASS!
KEEP HER CONTAINED!
MOM-- I'VE GOT YOU.
I HAVE NO PROBLEM KEEPING A MOTHER WITH HER DAUGHTER.
WE CAN ALL CROSS OVER.
NOOO!

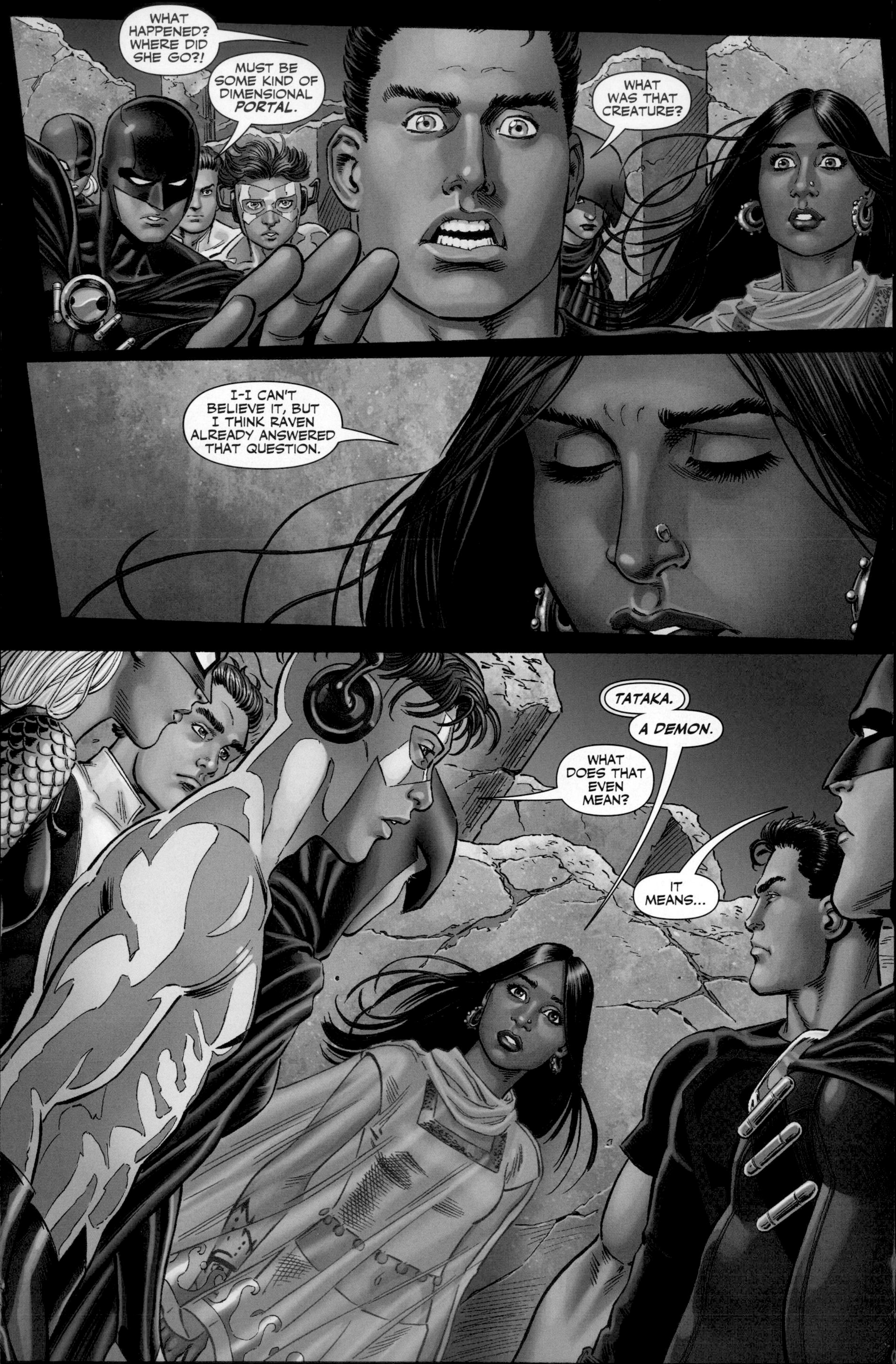
WHAT HAPPENED? WHERE DID SHE GO?!
MUST BE SOME KIND OF DIMENSIONAL PORTAL.
WHAT WAS THAT CREATURE?
I-I CAN'T BELIEVE IT, BUT I THINK RAVEN ALREADY ANSWERED THAT QUESTION.
TATAKA.
A DEMON.
WHAT DOES THAT EVEN MEAN?
IT MEANS...

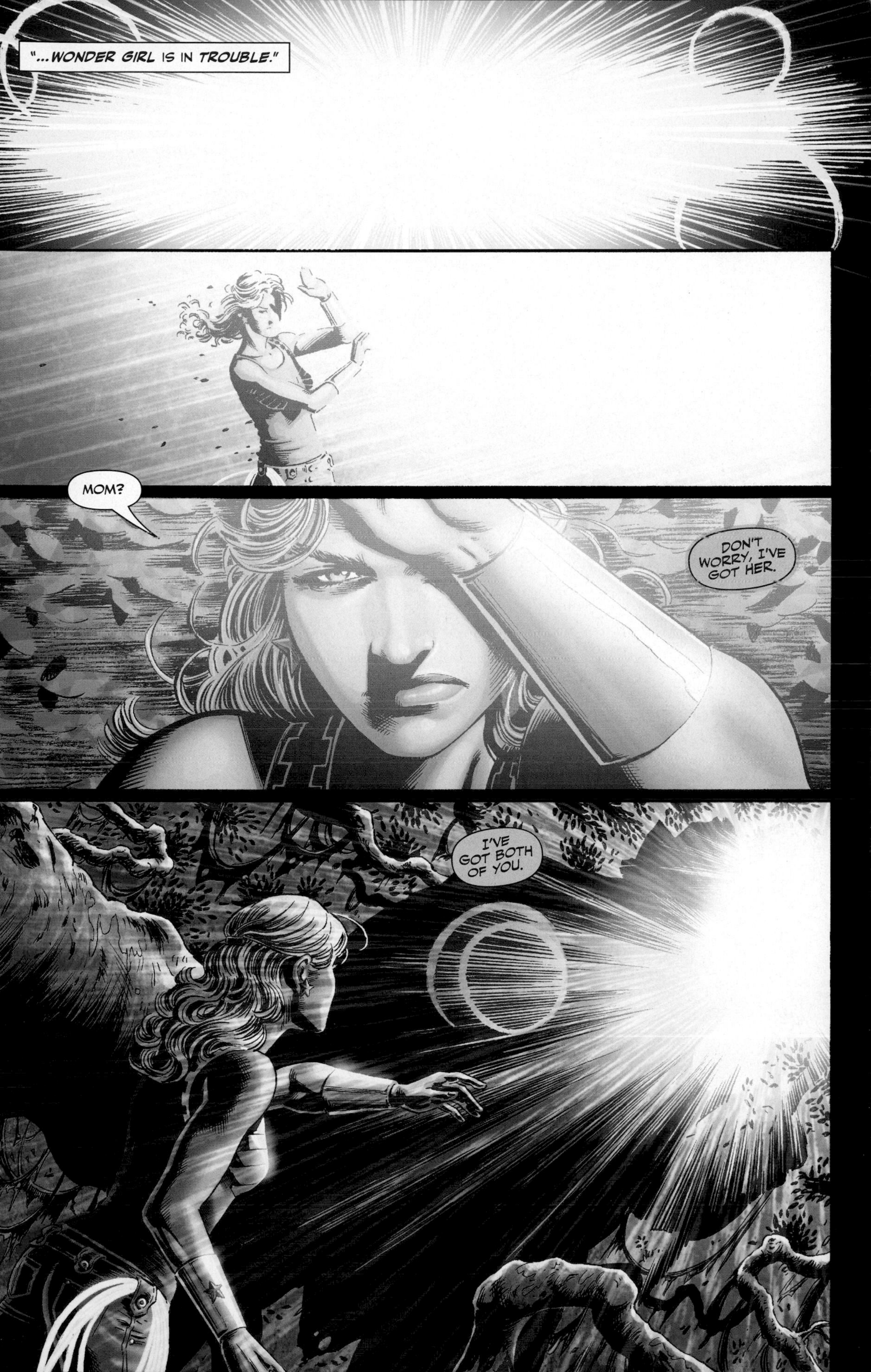
"...WONDER GIRL IS IN TROUBLE."
MOM?
DON'T WORRY, I'VE GOT HER.
I'VE GOT BOTH OF YOU.

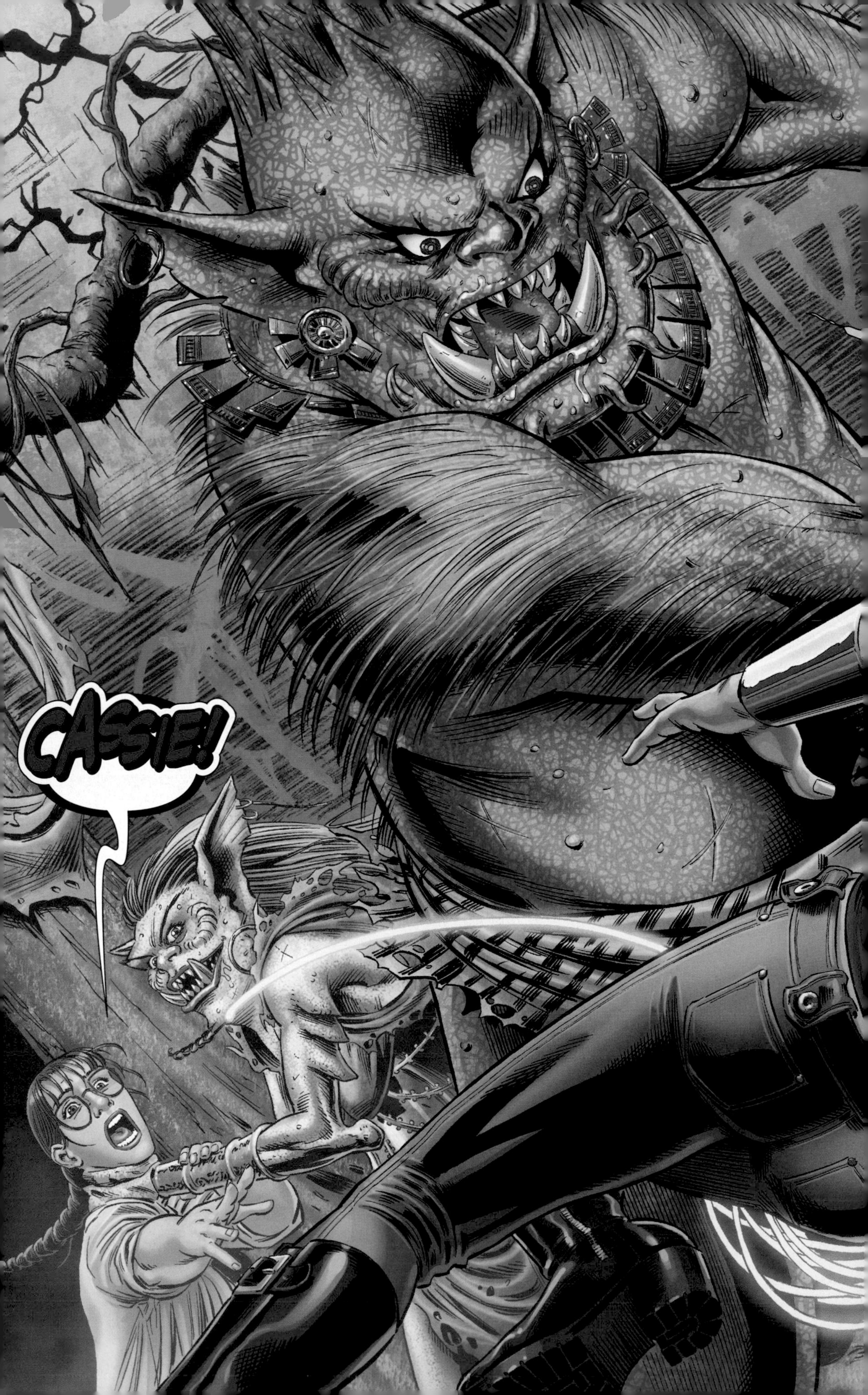
CASSIE!

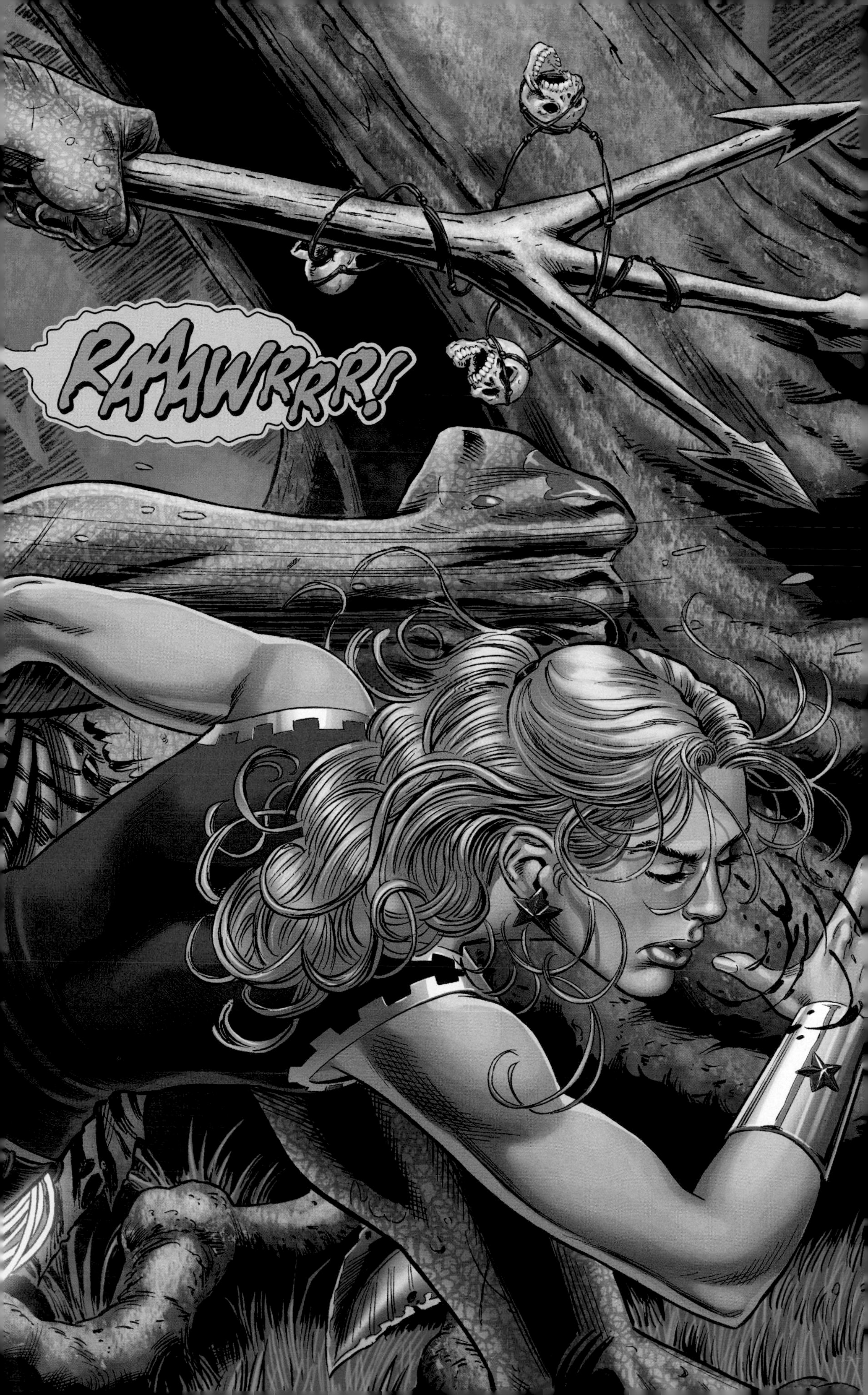
RAAAWRRRR!

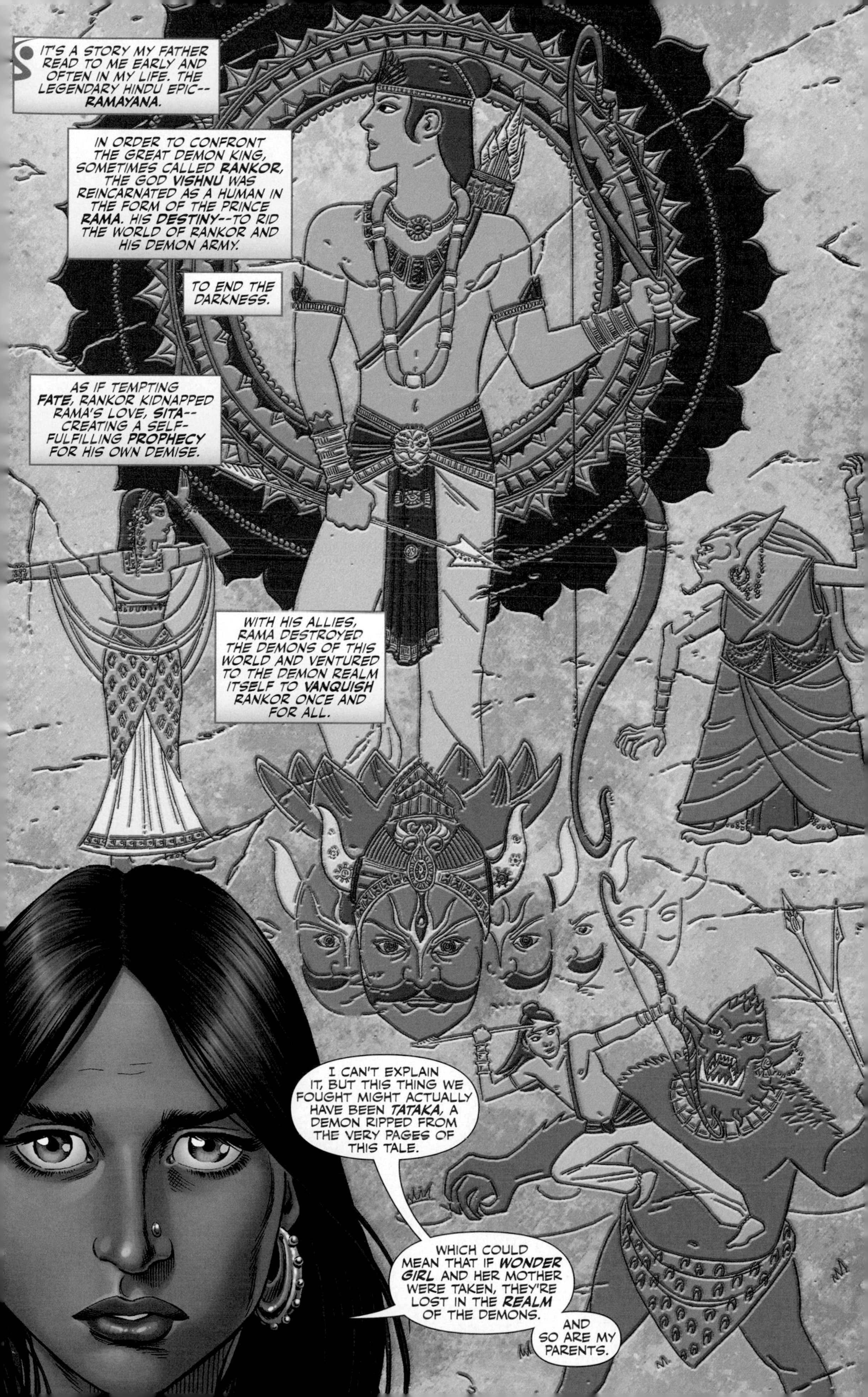
IT'S A STORY MY FATHER READ TO ME EARLY AND OFTEN IN MY LIFE. THE LEGENDARY HINDU EPIC-- **RAMAYANA.**
IN ORDER TO CONFRONT THE GREAT DEMON KING, SOMETIMES CALLED **RANKOR,** THE GOD **VISHNU** WAS REINCARNATED AS A HUMAN IN THE FORM OF THE PRINCE **RAMA.** HIS **DESTINY**--TO RID THE WORLD OF RANKOR AND HIS DEMON ARMY.
TO END THE DARKNESS.
AS IF TEMPTING **FATE,** RANKOR KIDNAPPED RAMA'S LOVE, **SITA**-- CREATING A SELF-FULFILLING **PROPHECY** FOR HIS OWN DEMISE.
WITH HIS ALLIES, RAMA DESTROYED THE DEMONS OF THIS WORLD AND VENTURED TO THE DEMON REALM ITSELF TO **VANQUISH** RANKOR ONCE AND FOR ALL.
I CAN'T EXPLAIN IT, BUT THIS THING WE FOUGHT MIGHT ACTUALLY HAVE BEEN ***TATAKA,*** A DEMON RIPPED FROM THE VERY PAGES OF THIS TALE.
WHICH COULD MEAN THAT IF ***WONDER GIRL*** AND HER MOTHER WERE TAKEN, THEY'RE LOST IN THE ***REALM*** OF THE DEMONS.
AND SO ARE MY PARENTS.

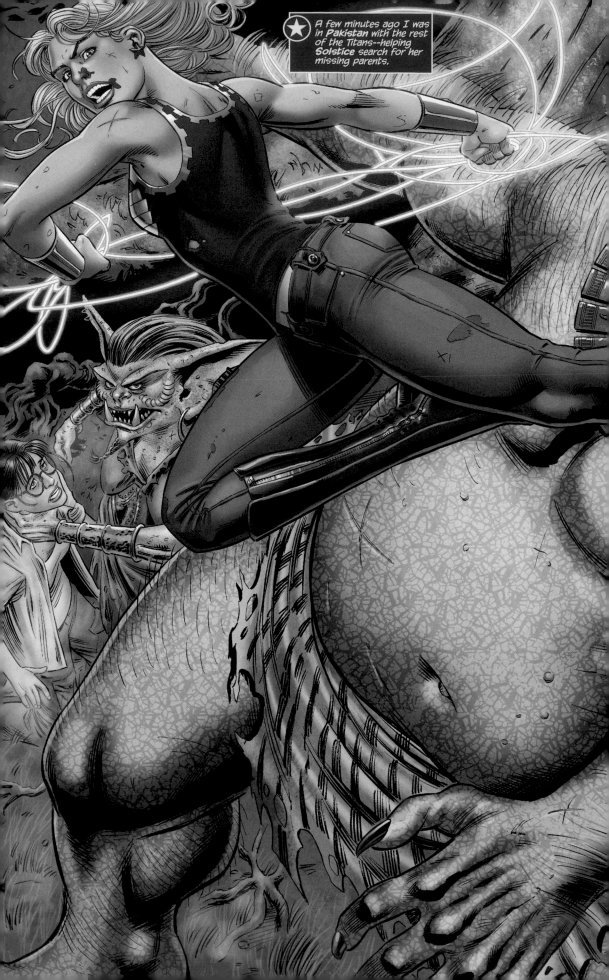

A few minutes ago I was in **Pakistan** with the rest of the Titans--helping **Solstice** search for her missing parents.

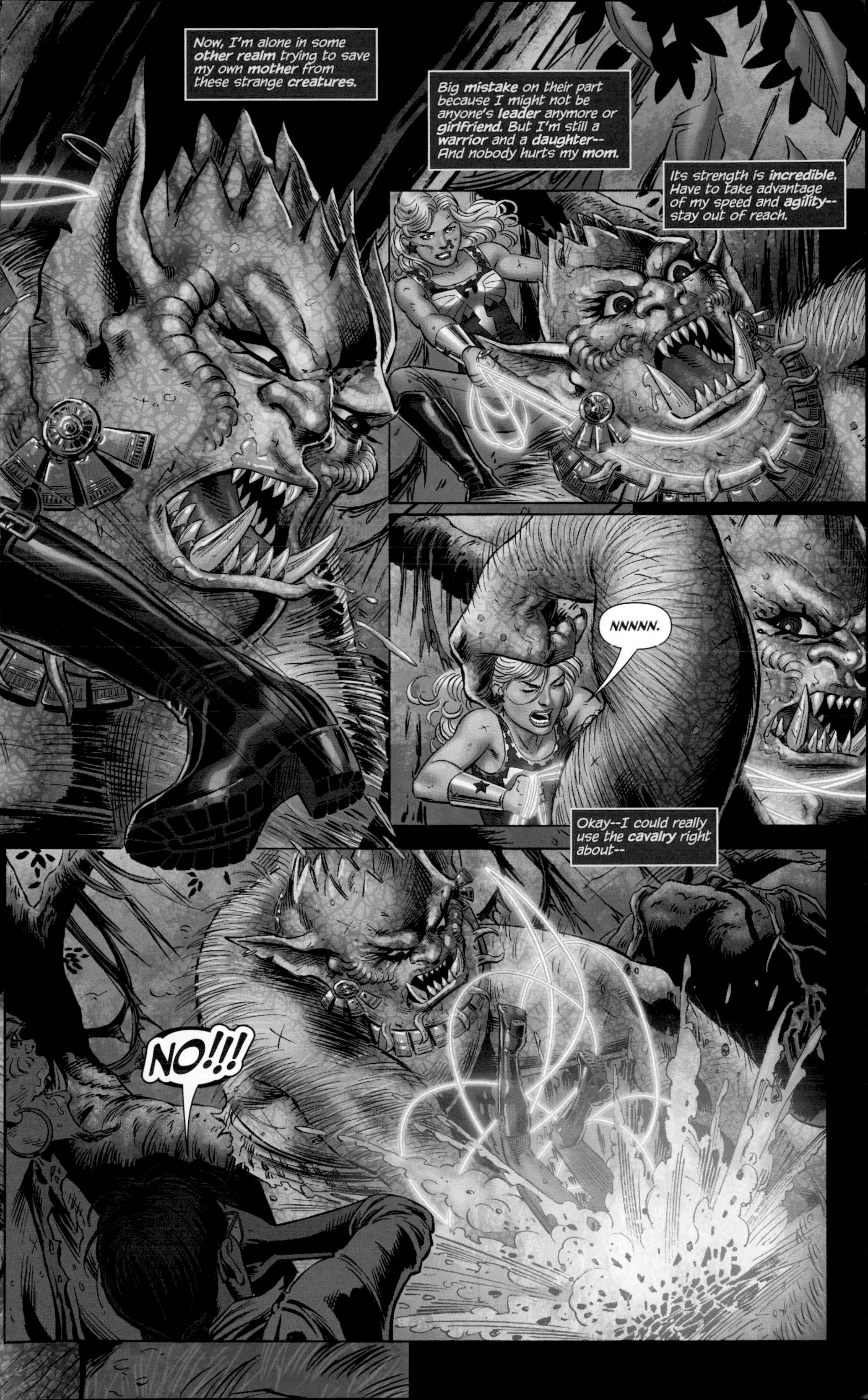
Now, I'm alone in some other realm trying to save my own mother from these strange creatures.
Big mistake on their part because I might not be anyone's leader anymore or girlfriend. But I'm still a warrior and a daughter-- And nobody hurts my mom.
Its strength is incredible. Have to take advantage of my speed and agility-- stay out of reach.
NNNNN.
Okay--I could really use the cavalry right about--
NO!!!

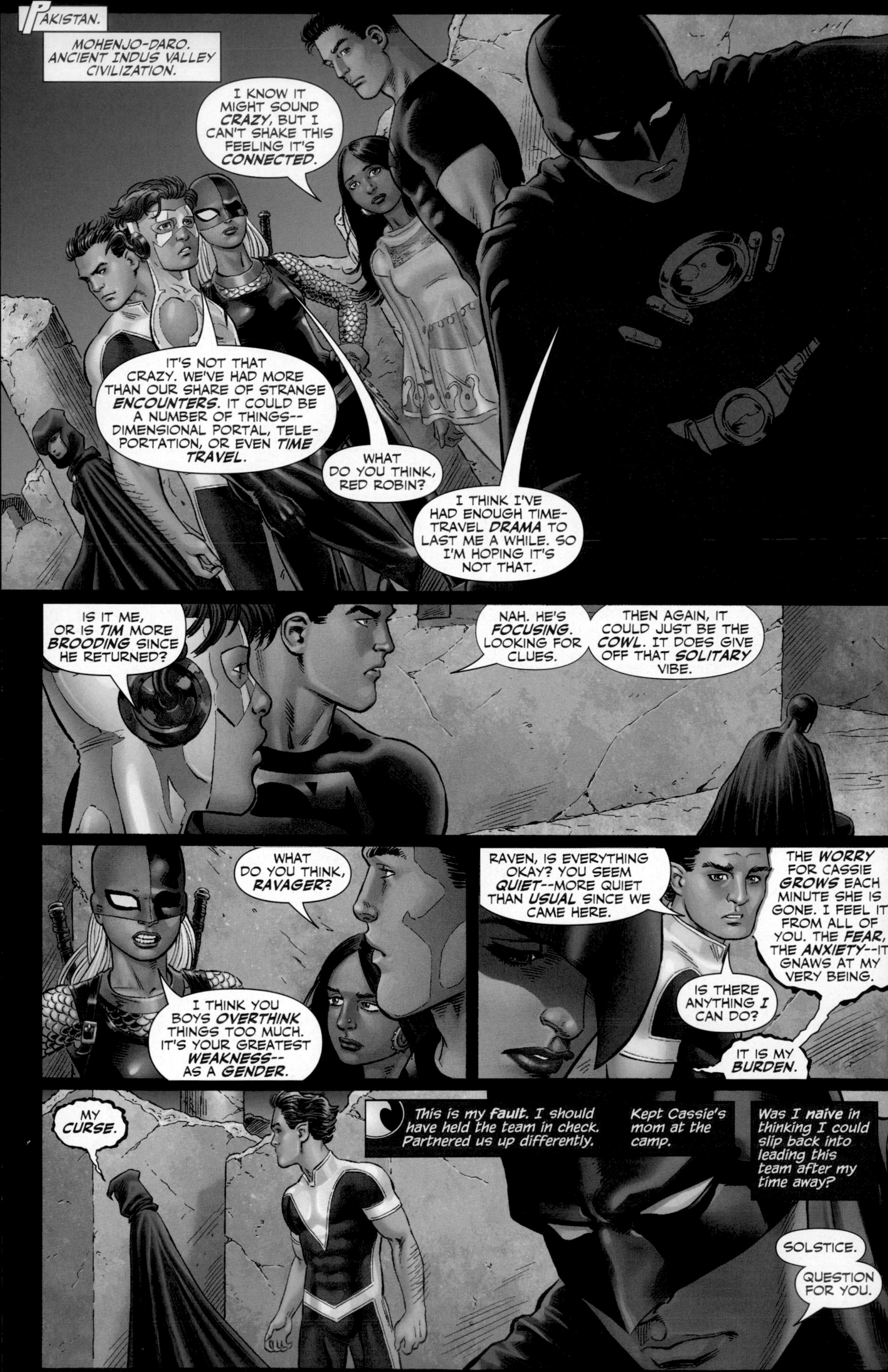
PAKISTAN.
MOHENJO-DARO. ANCIENT INDUS VALLEY CIVILIZATION.
I KNOW IT MIGHT SOUND CRAZY, BUT I CAN'T SHAKE THIS FEELING IT'S CONNECTED.
IT'S NOT THAT CRAZY. WE'VE HAD MORE THAN OUR SHARE OF STRANGE ENCOUNTERS. IT COULD BE A NUMBER OF THINGS-- DIMENSIONAL PORTAL, TELE-PORTATION, OR EVEN TIME TRAVEL.
WHAT DO YOU THINK, RED ROBIN?
I THINK I'VE HAD ENOUGH TIME-TRAVEL DRAMA TO LAST ME A WHILE. SO I'M HOPING IT'S NOT THAT.
IS IT ME, OR IS TIM MORE BROODING SINCE HE RETURNED?
NAH. HE'S FOCUSING. LOOKING FOR CLUES.
THEN AGAIN, IT COULD JUST BE THE COWL. IT DOES GIVE OFF THAT SOLITARY VIBE.
WHAT DO YOU THINK, RAVAGER?
I THINK YOU BOYS OVERTHINK THINGS TOO MUCH. IT'S YOUR GREATEST WEAKNESS-- AS A GENDER.
RAVEN, IS EVERYTHING OKAY? YOU SEEM QUIET--MORE QUIET THAN USUAL SINCE WE CAME HERE.
THE WORRY FOR CASSIE GROWS EACH MINUTE SHE IS GONE. I FEEL IT FROM ALL OF YOU. THE FEAR, THE ANXIETY--IT GNAWS AT MY VERY BEING.
IS THERE ANYTHING I CAN DO?
IT IS MY BURDEN.
MY CURSE.
This is my fault. I should have held the team in check. Partnered us up differently.
Kept Cassie's mom at the camp.
Was I naive in thinking I could slip back into leading this team after my time away?
SOLSTICE.
QUESTION FOR YOU.

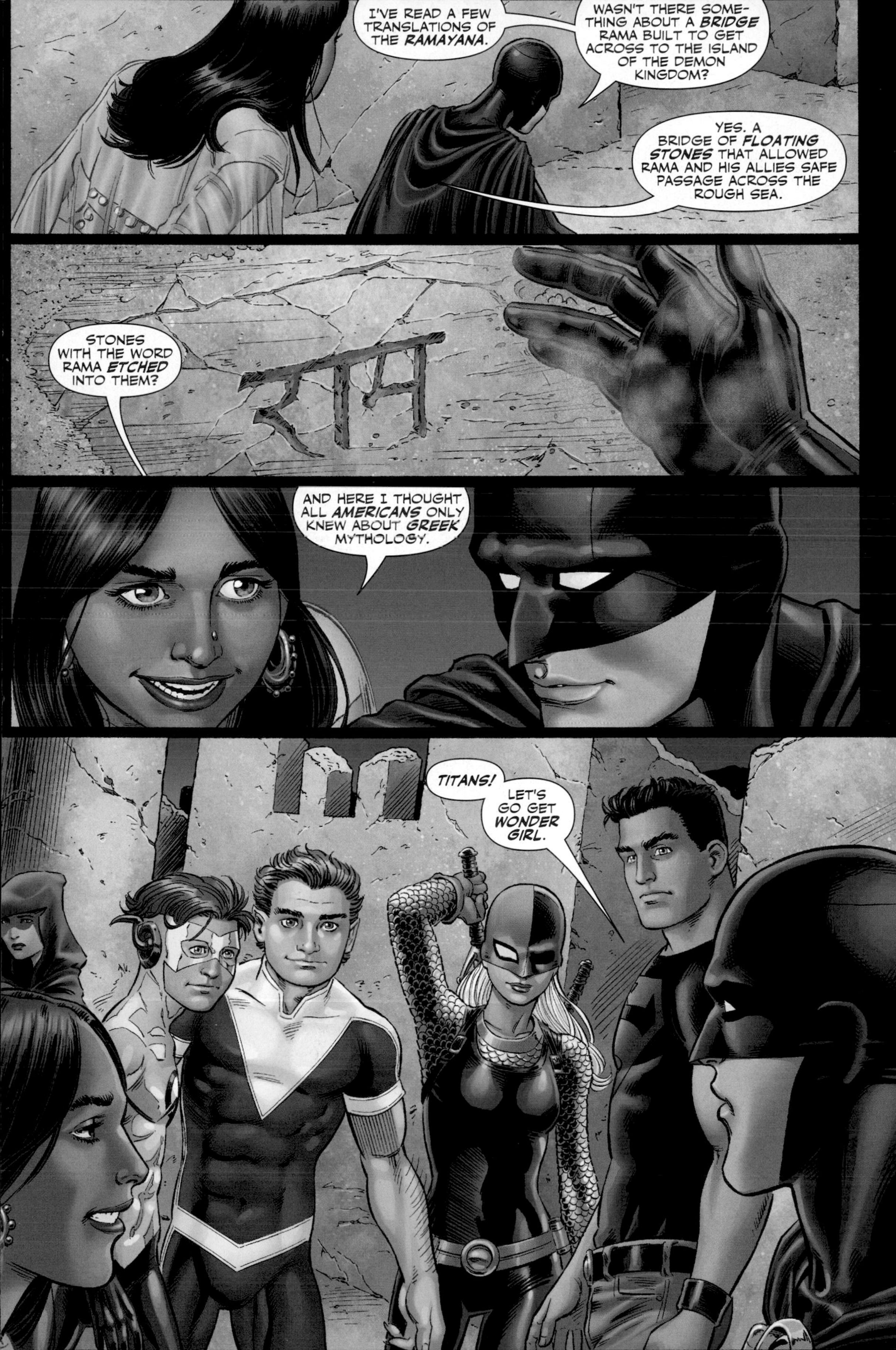
I'VE READ A FEW TRANSLATIONS OF THE RAMAYANA.
WASN'T THERE SOME-THING ABOUT A BRIDGE RAMA BUILT TO GET ACROSS TO THE ISLAND OF THE DEMON KINGDOM?
YES. A BRIDGE OF FLOATING STONES THAT ALLOWED RAMA AND HIS ALLIES SAFE PASSAGE ACROSS THE ROUGH SEA.
STONES WITH THE WORD RAMA ETCHED INTO THEM?
राम
AND HERE I THOUGHT ALL AMERICANS ONLY KNEW ABOUT GREEK MYTHOLOGY.
TITANS!
LET'S GO GET WONDER GIRL.

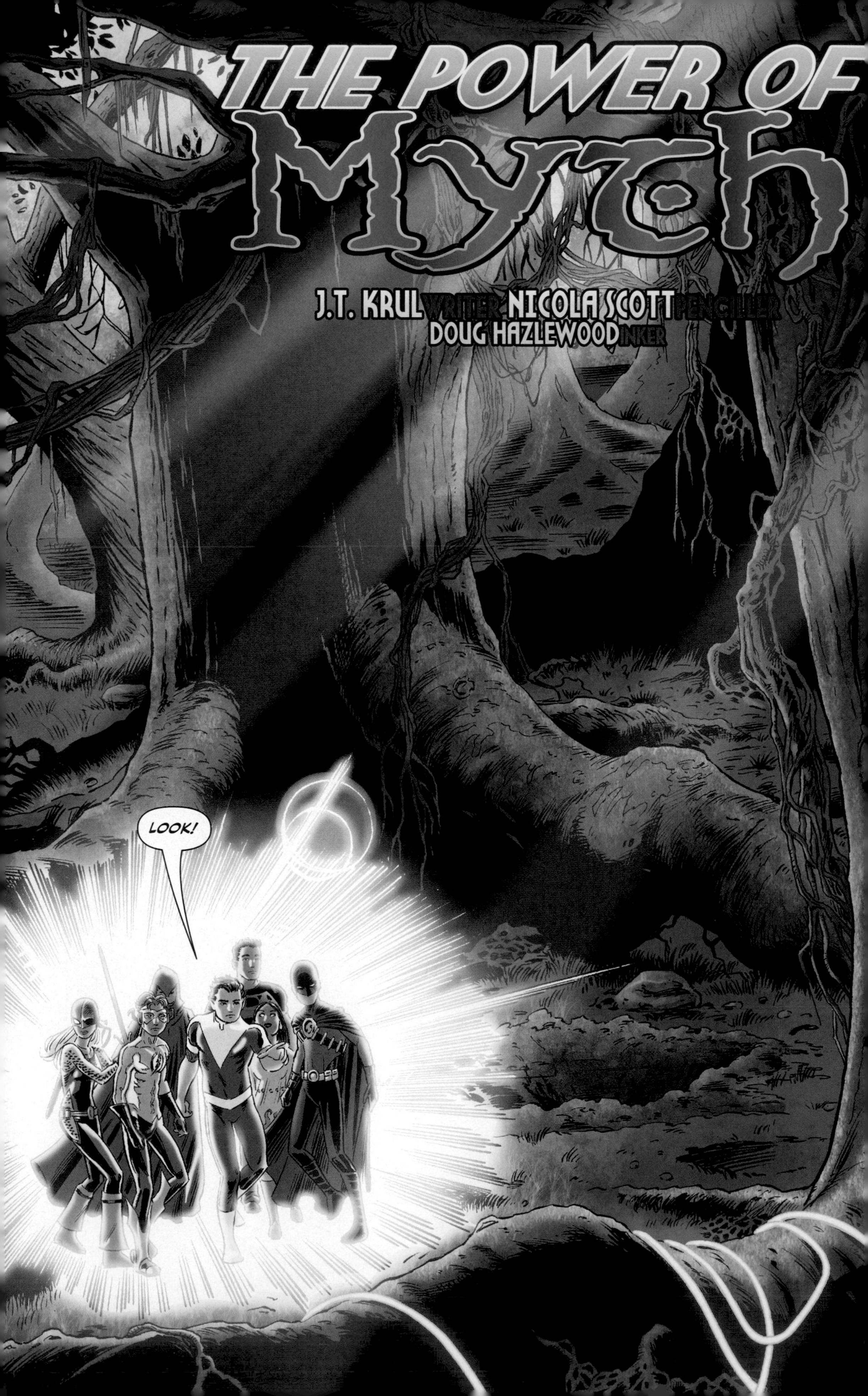
THE POWER OF
Myth
J.T. KRUL WRITER NICOLA SCOTT PENCILLER
DOUG HAZLEWOOD INKER
LOOK!

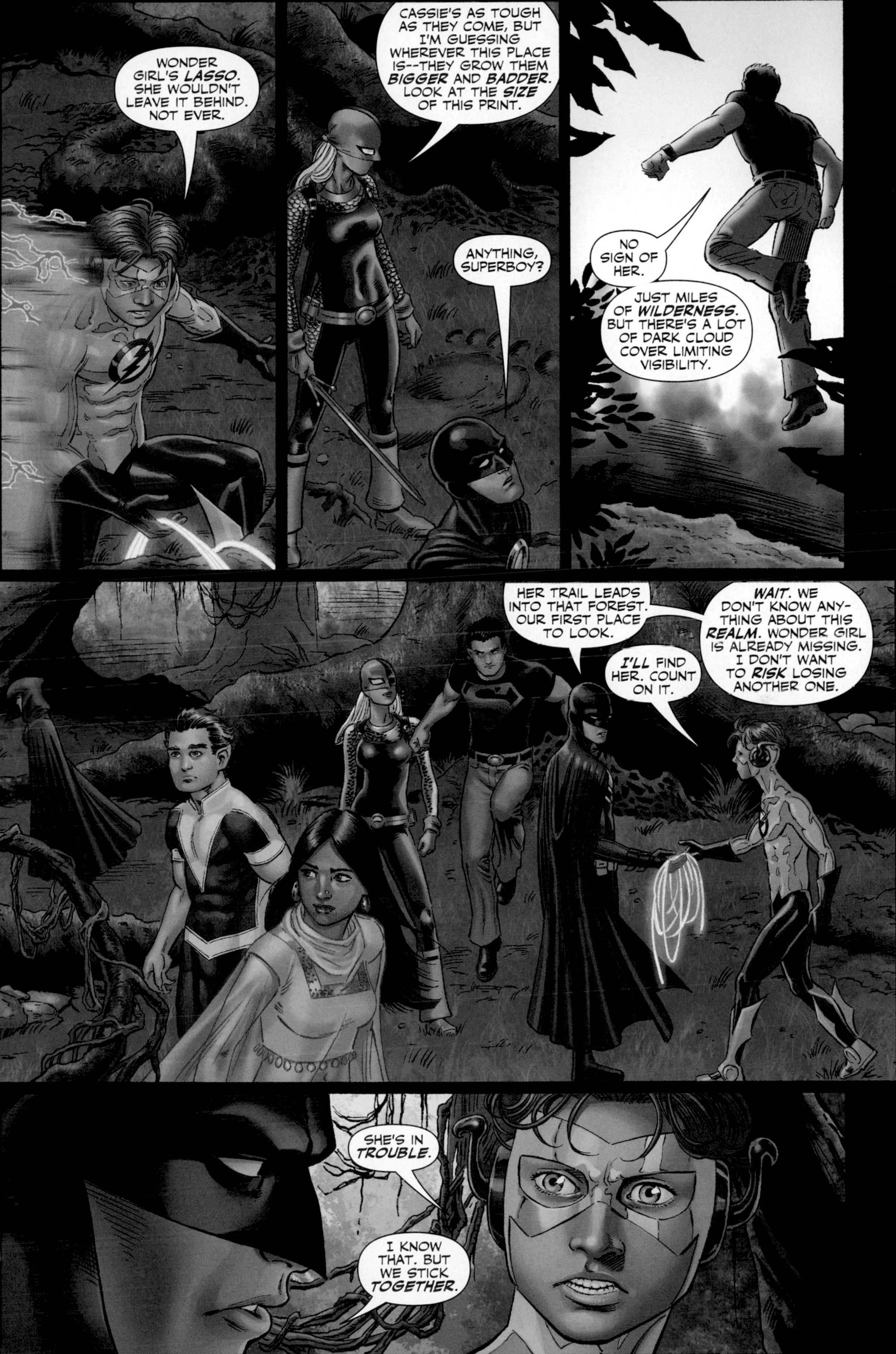
WONDER GIRL'S LASSO. SHE WOULDN'T LEAVE IT BEHIND. NOT EVER.
CASSIE'S AS TOUGH AS THEY COME, BUT I'M GUESSING WHEREVER THIS PLACE IS--THEY GROW THEM BIGGER AND BADDER. LOOK AT THE SIZE OF THIS PRINT.
ANYTHING, SUPERBOY?
NO SIGN OF HER.
JUST MILES OF WILDERNESS. BUT THERE'S A LOT OF DARK CLOUD COVER LIMITING VISIBILITY.
HER TRAIL LEADS INTO THAT FOREST. OUR FIRST PLACE TO LOOK.
I'LL FIND HER. COUNT ON IT.
WAIT. WE DON'T KNOW ANY-THING ABOUT THIS REALM. WONDER GIRL IS ALREADY MISSING. I DON'T WANT TO RISK LOSING ANOTHER ONE.
SHE'S IN TROUBLE.
I KNOW THAT. BUT WE STICK TOGETHER.

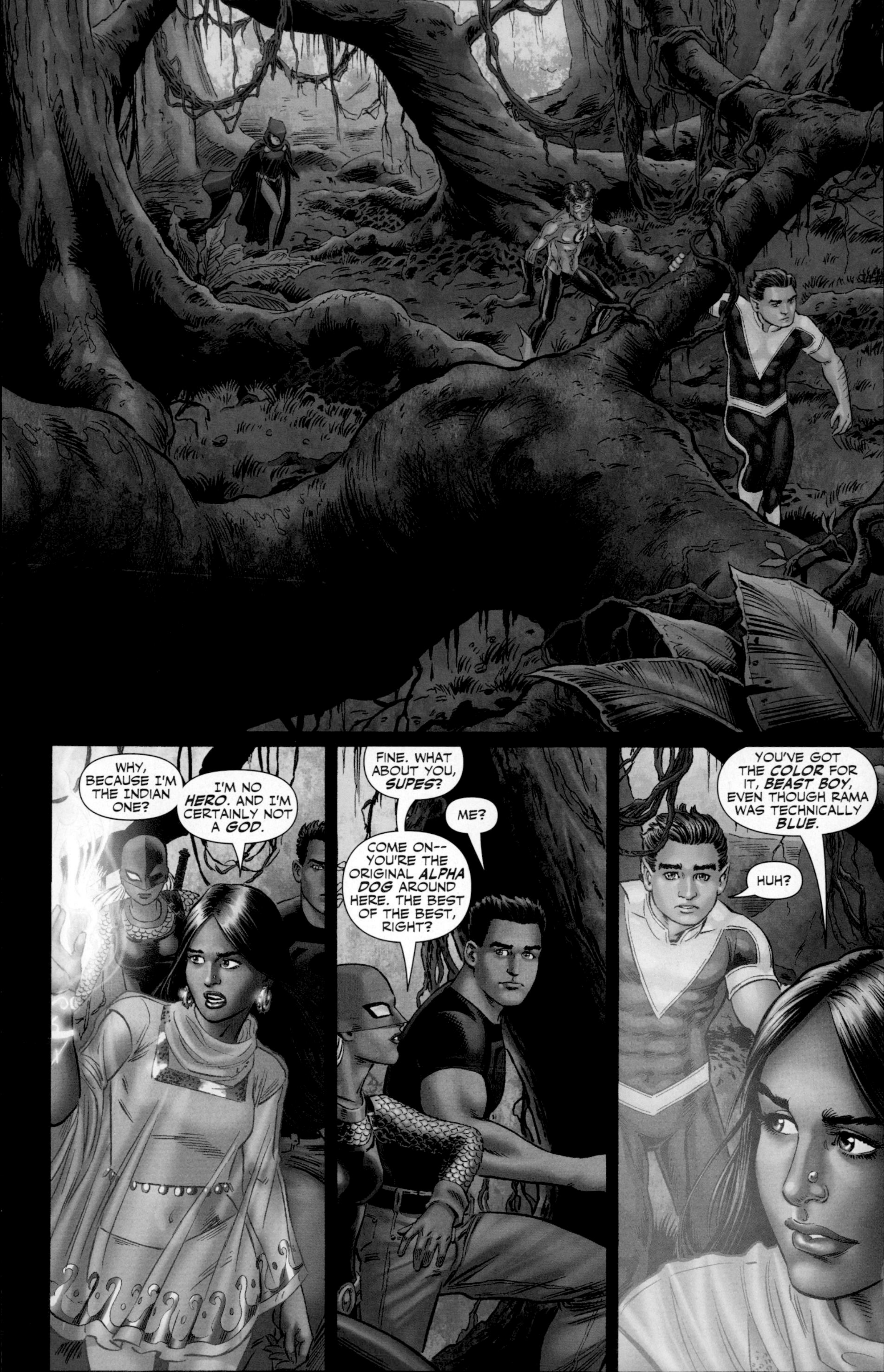
WHY, BECAUSE I'M THE INDIAN ONE?
I'M NO *HERO*. AND I'M CERTAINLY NOT A *GOD*.
FINE. WHAT ABOUT YOU, *SUPES*?
ME?
COME ON-- YOU'RE THE ORIGINAL *ALPHA DOG* AROUND HERE. THE BEST OF THE BEST, RIGHT?
YOU'VE GOT THE *COLOR* FOR IT, *BEAST BOY*, EVEN THOUGH RAMA WAS TECHNICALLY *BLUE*.
HUH?

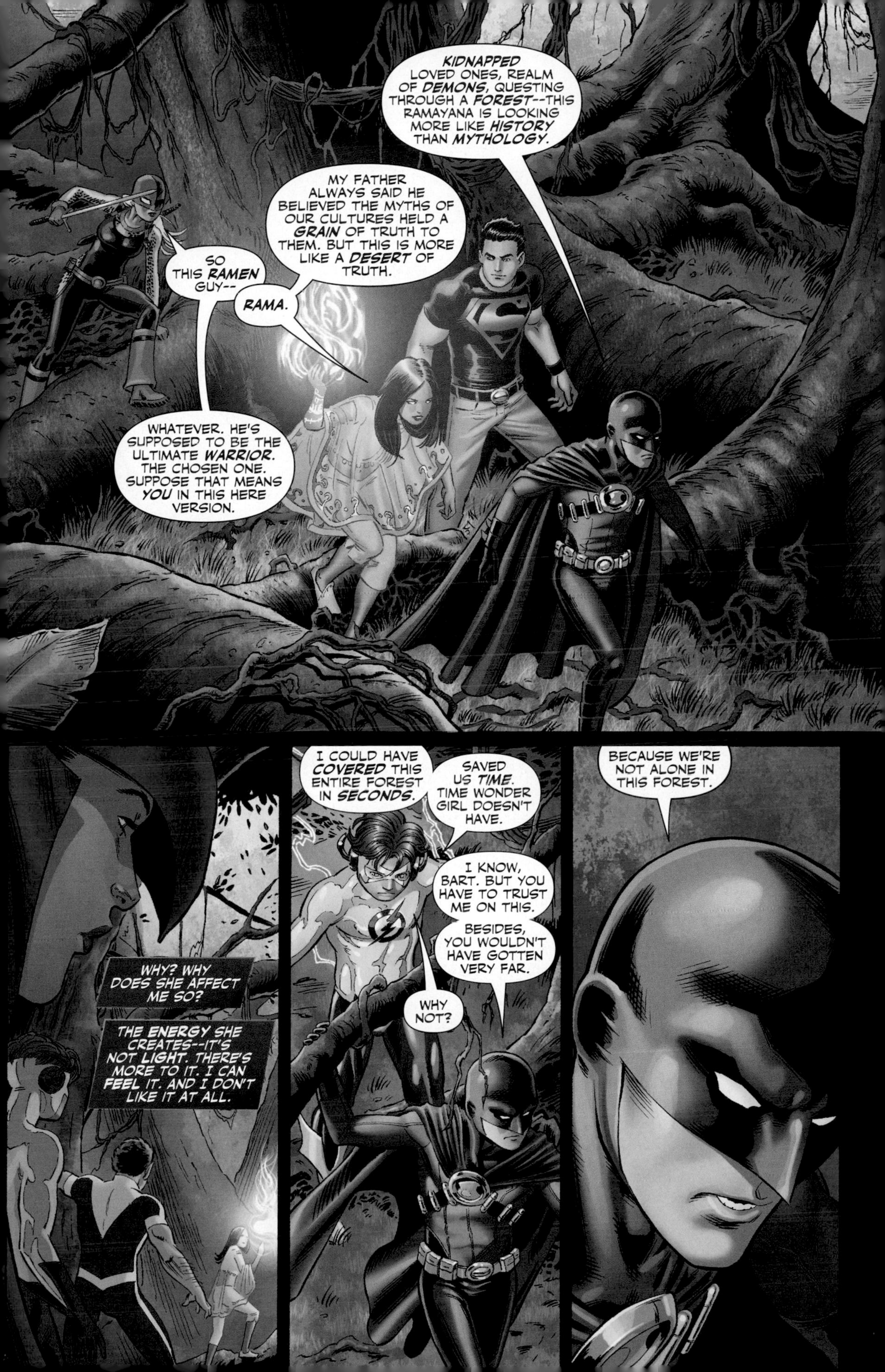

KIDNAPPED LOVED ONES, REALM OF DEMONS, QUESTING THROUGH A FOREST--THIS RAMAYANA IS LOOKING MORE LIKE HISTORY THAN MYTHOLOGY.
SO THIS RAMEN GUY--
RAMA.
MY FATHER ALWAYS SAID HE BELIEVED THE MYTHS OF OUR CULTURES HELD A GRAIN OF TRUTH TO THEM. BUT THIS IS MORE LIKE A DESERT OF TRUTH.
WHATEVER. HE'S SUPPOSED TO BE THE ULTIMATE WARRIOR. THE CHOSEN ONE. SUPPOSE THAT MEANS YOU IN THIS HERE VERSION.
WHY? WHY DOES SHE AFFECT ME SO?
THE ENERGY SHE CREATES--IT'S NOT LIGHT. THERE'S MORE TO IT. I CAN FEEL IT. AND I DON'T LIKE IT AT ALL.
I COULD HAVE COVERED THIS ENTIRE FOREST IN SECONDS.
SAVED US TIME. TIME WONDER GIRL DOESN'T HAVE.
I KNOW, BART. BUT YOU HAVE TO TRUST ME ON THIS.
BESIDES, YOU WOULDN'T HAVE GOTTEN VERY FAR.
WHY NOT?
BECAUSE WE'RE NOT ALONE IN THIS FOREST.

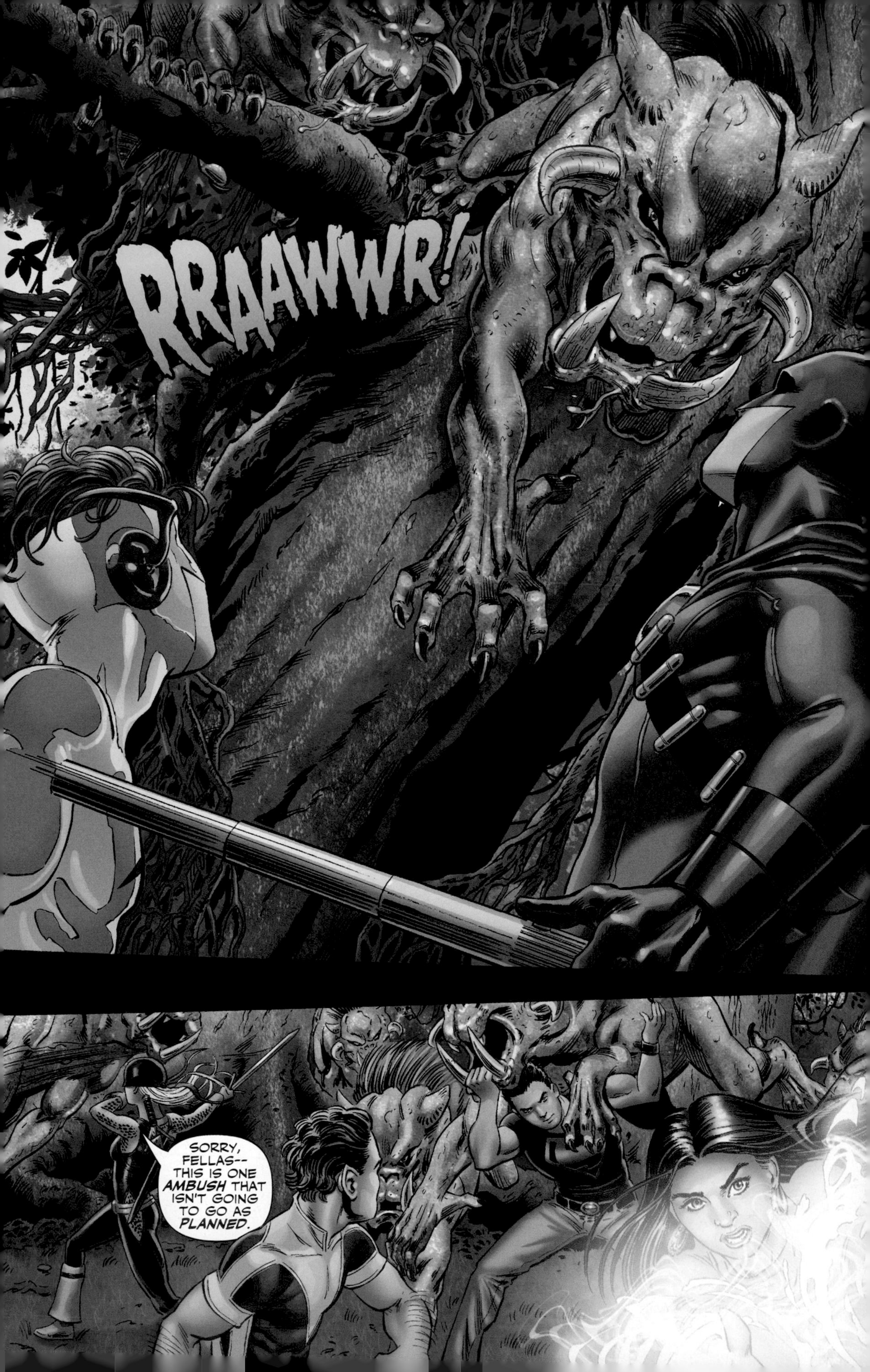
RRAAWWR!
SORRY, FELLAS-- THIS IS ONE AMBUSH THAT ISN'T GOING TO GO AS PLANNED.

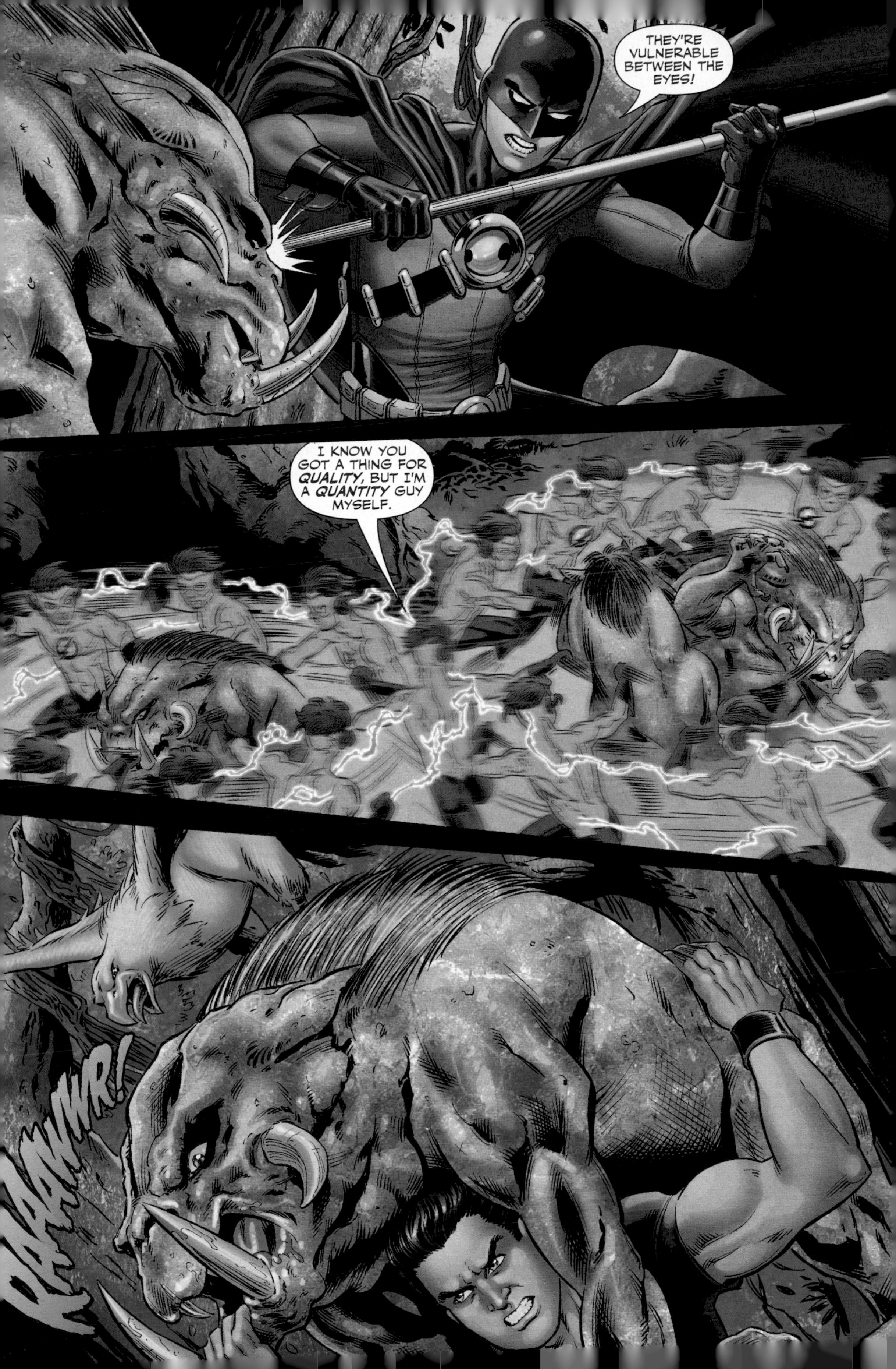
THEY'RE VULNERABLE BETWEEN THE EYES!
I KNOW YOU GOT A THING FOR *QUALITY*, BUT I'M A *QUANTITY* GUY MYSELF.
RAAAWR!

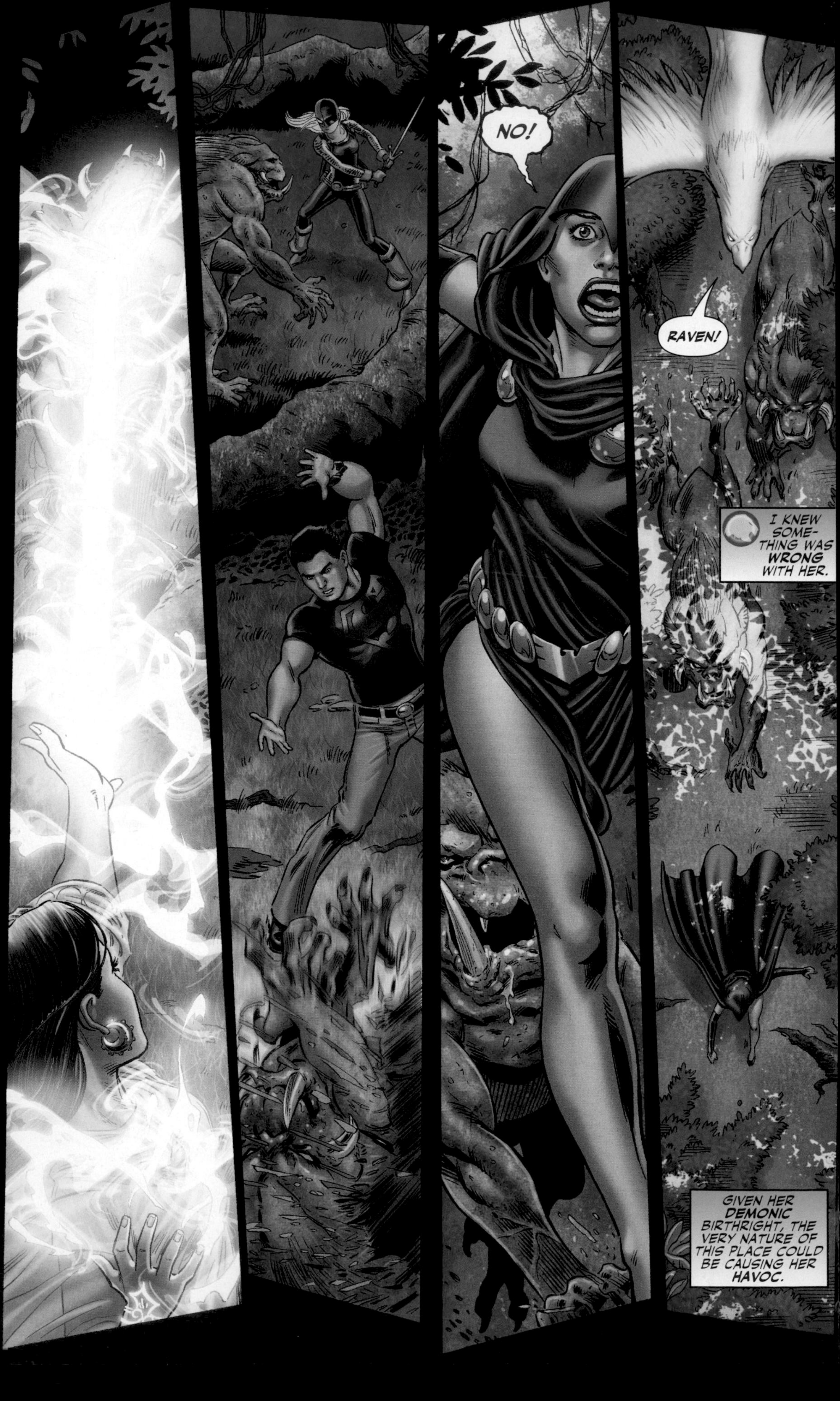

NO!
RAVEN!
I KNEW SOME-THING WAS WRONG WITH HER.
GIVEN HER DEMONIC BIRTHRIGHT, THE VERY NATURE OF THIS PLACE COULD BE CAUSING HER HAVOC.

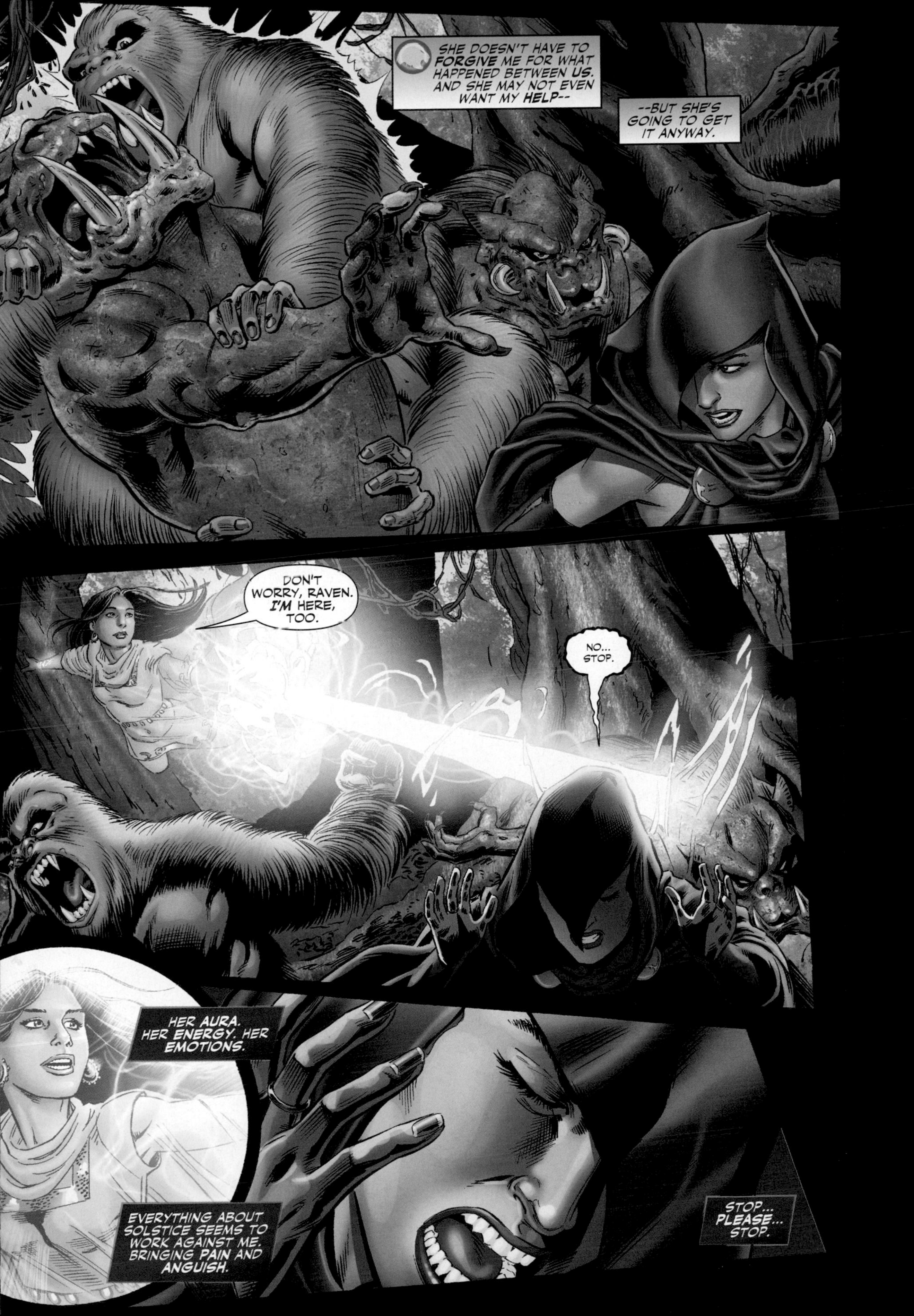
SHE DOESN'T HAVE TO FORGIVE ME FOR WHAT HAPPENED BETWEEN US. AND SHE MAY NOT EVEN WANT MY HELP--
--BUT SHE'S GOING TO GET IT ANYWAY.
DON'T WORRY, RAVEN. I'M HERE, TOO.
NO... STOP.
HER AURA. HER ENERGY. HER EMOTIONS.
EVERYTHING ABOUT SOLSTICE SEEMS TO WORK AGAINST ME. BRINGING PAIN AND ANGUISH.
STOP... PLEASE... STOP.

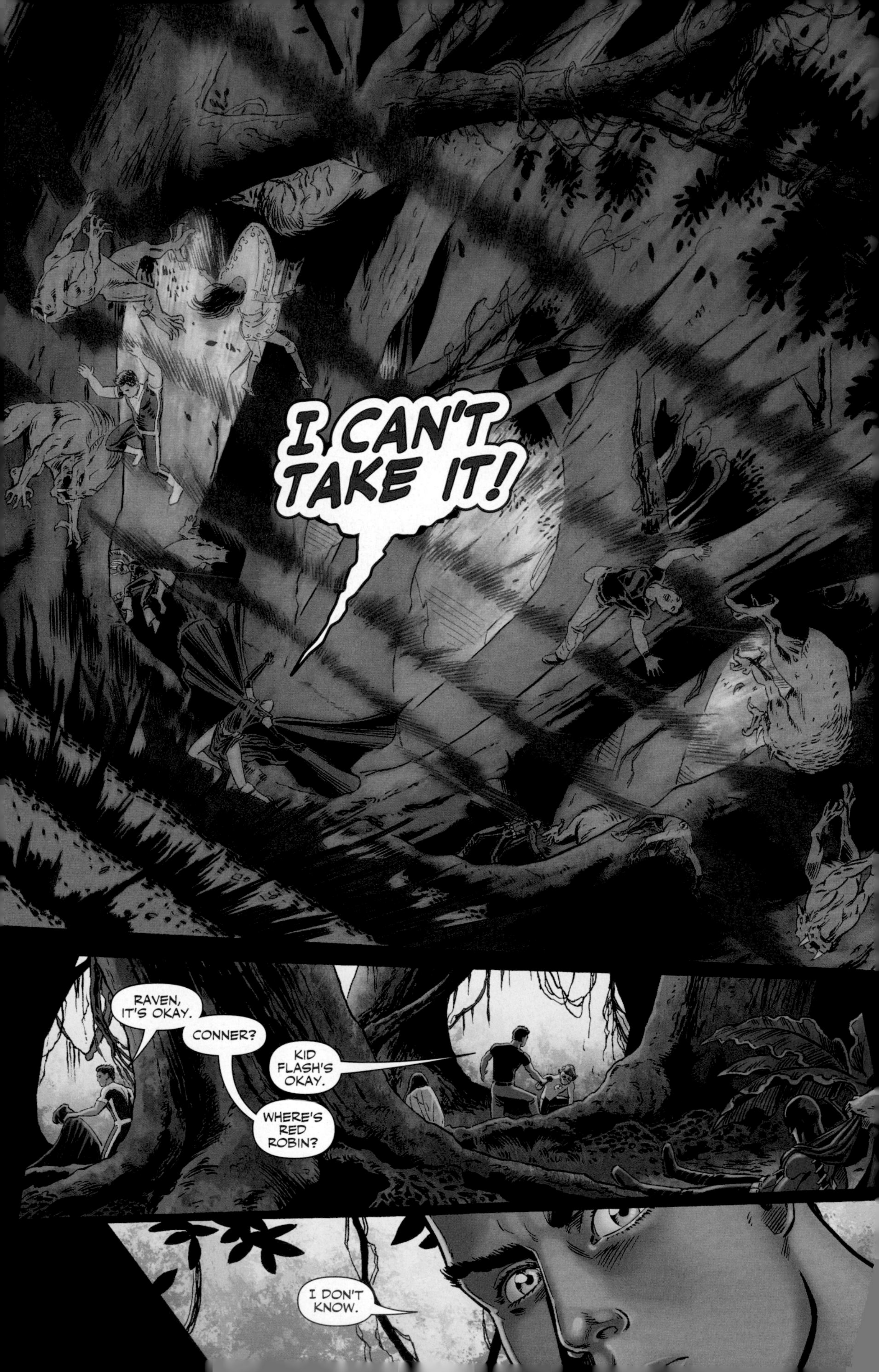

I CAN'T TAKE IT!
RAVEN, IT'S OKAY.
CONNER?
KID FLASH'S OKAY.
WHERE'S RED ROBIN?
I DON'T KNOW.

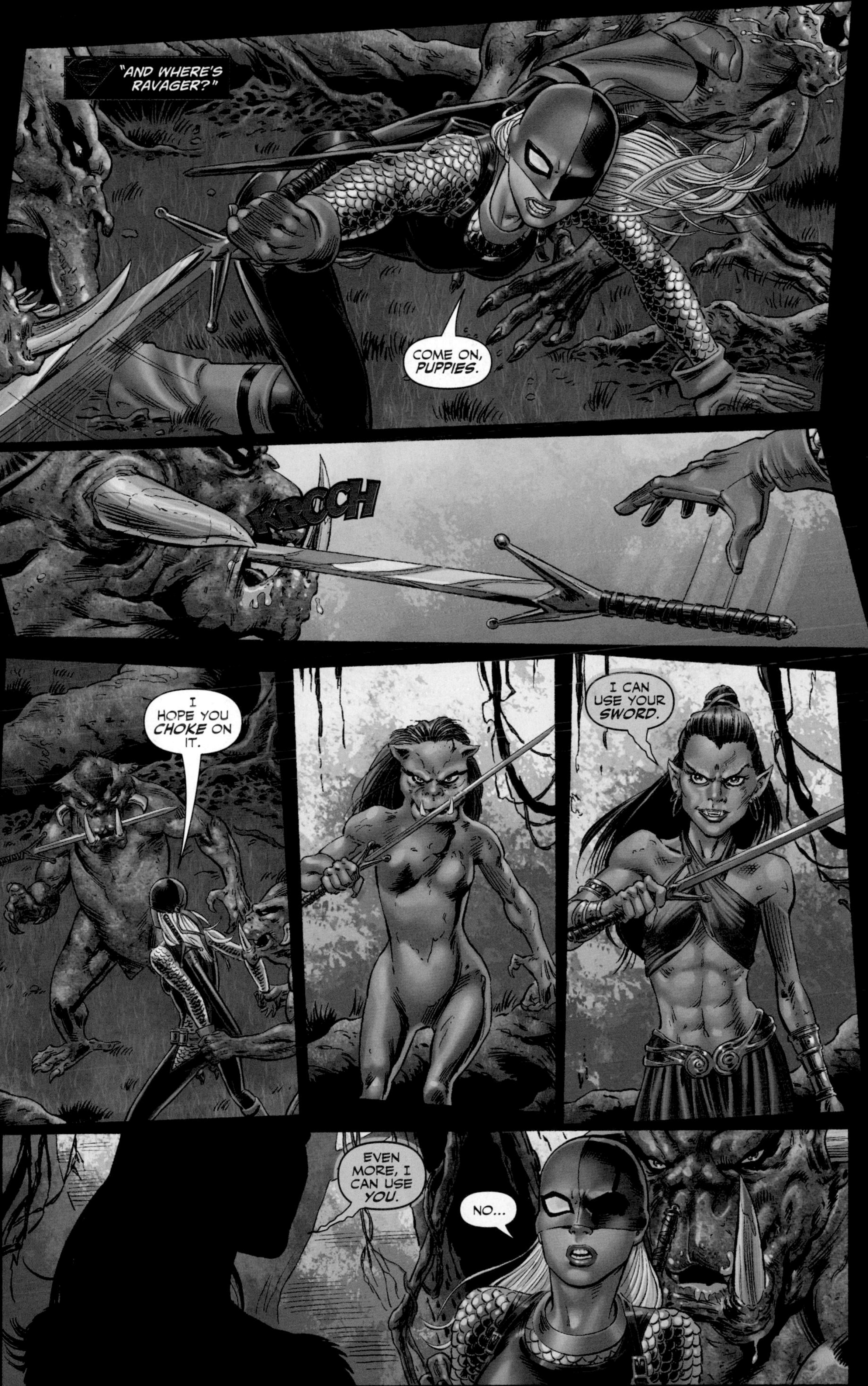
"AND WHERE'S RAVAGER?"
COME ON, PUPPIES.
KRCCH
I HOPE YOU CHOKE ON IT.
I CAN USE YOUR SWORD.
EVEN MORE, I CAN USE YOU.
NO...

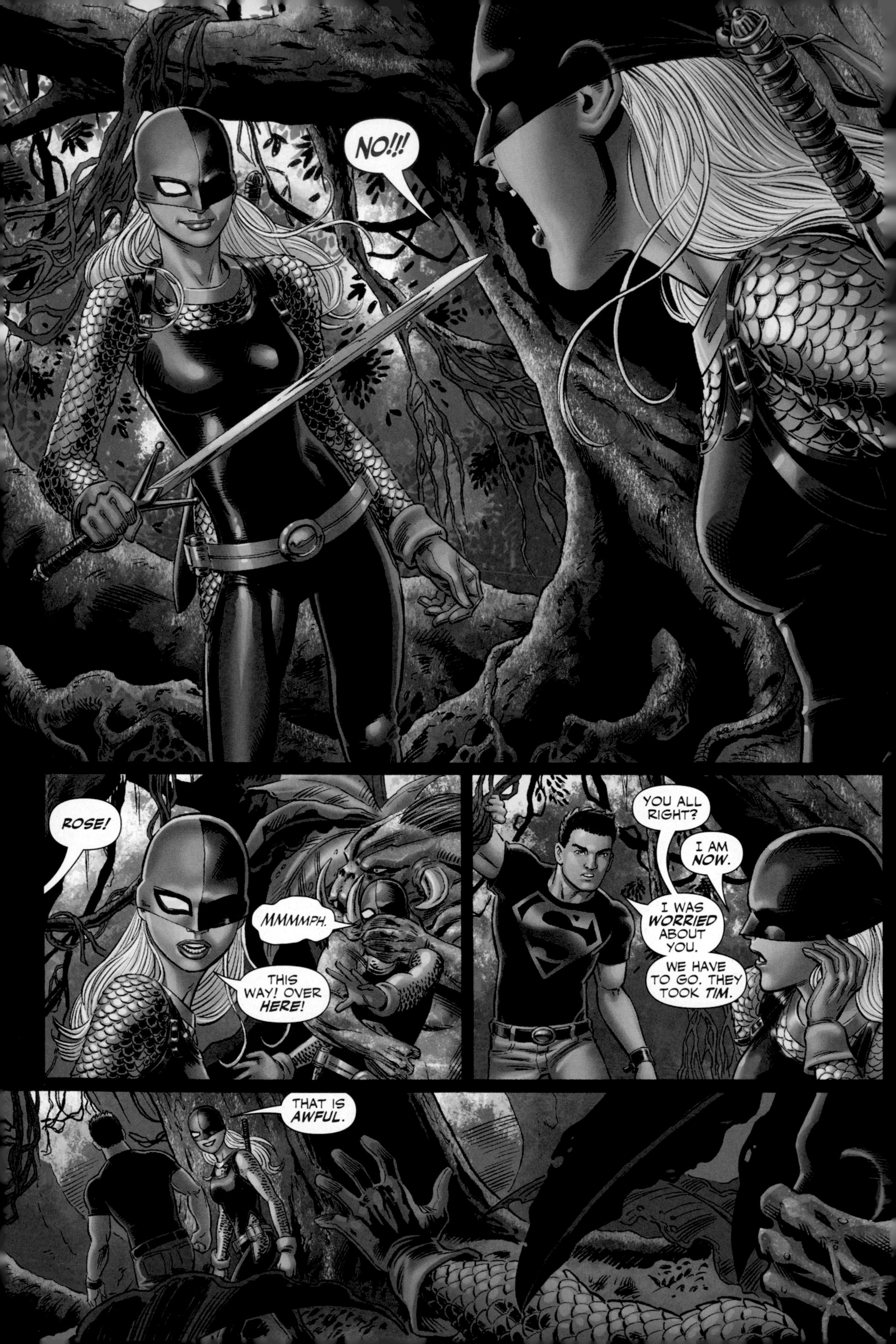
NO!!!
ROSE!
MMMMPH.
THIS WAY! OVER HERE!
YOU ALL RIGHT?
I AM NOW.
I WAS WORRIED ABOUT YOU.
WE HAVE TO GO. THEY TOOK TIM.
THAT IS AWFUL.

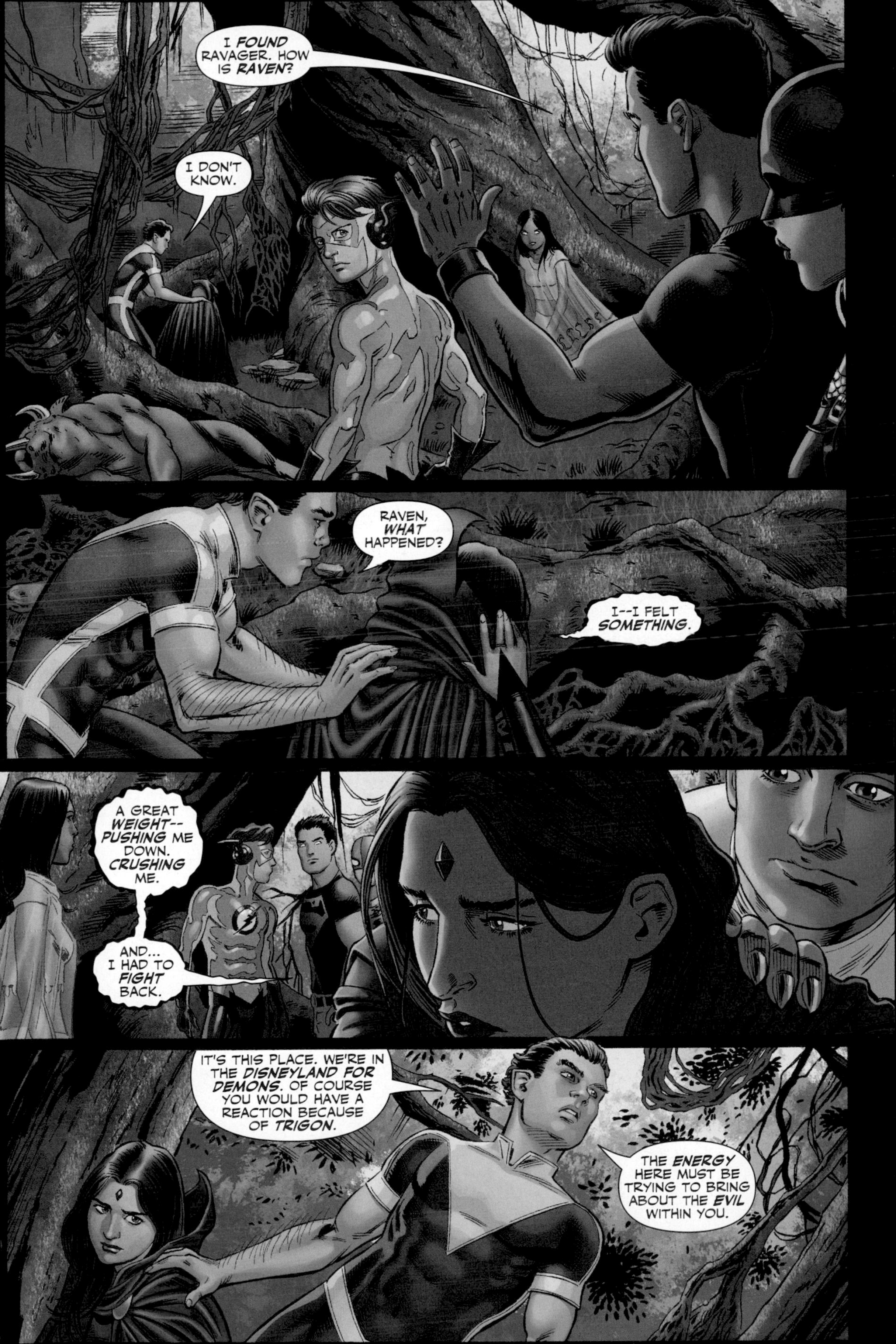
I FOUND RAVAGER. HOW IS RAVEN?
I DON'T KNOW.
RAVEN, WHAT HAPPENED?
I--I FELT SOMETHING.
A GREAT WEIGHT--PUSHING ME DOWN. CRUSHING ME.
AND... I HAD TO FIGHT BACK.
IT'S THIS PLACE. WE'RE IN THE DISNEYLAND FOR DEMONS. OF COURSE YOU WOULD HAVE A REACTION BECAUSE OF TRIGON.
THE ENERGY HERE MUST BE TRYING TO BRING ABOUT THE EVIL WITHIN YOU.

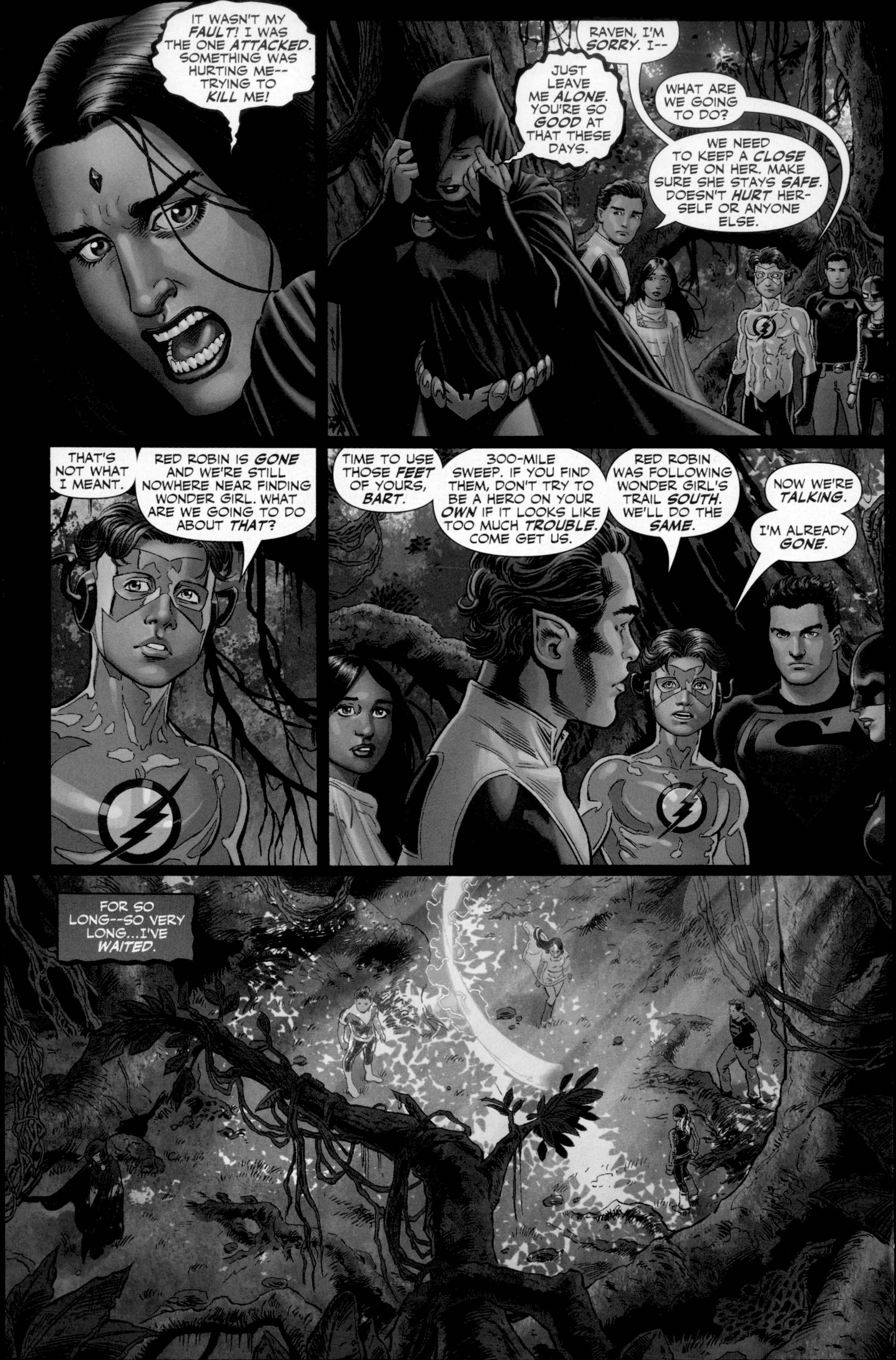
IT WASN'T MY FAULT! I WAS THE ONE ATTACKED. SOMETHING WAS HURTING ME-- TRYING TO KILL ME!
RAVEN, I'M SORRY. I--
JUST LEAVE ME ALONE. YOU'RE SO GOOD AT THAT THESE DAYS.
WHAT ARE WE GOING TO DO?
WE NEED TO KEEP A CLOSE EYE ON HER. MAKE SURE SHE STAYS SAFE. DOESN'T HURT HER-SELF OR ANYONE ELSE.
THAT'S NOT WHAT I MEANT.
RED ROBIN IS GONE AND WE'RE STILL NOWHERE NEAR FINDING WONDER GIRL. WHAT ARE WE GOING TO DO ABOUT THAT?
TIME TO USE THOSE FEET OF YOURS, BART.
300-MILE SWEEP. IF YOU FIND THEM, DON'T TRY TO BE A HERO ON YOUR OWN IF IT LOOKS LIKE TOO MUCH TROUBLE. COME GET US.
RED ROBIN WAS FOLLOWING WONDER GIRL'S TRAIL SOUTH. WE'LL DO THE SAME.
NOW WE'RE TALKING.
I'M ALREADY GONE.
FOR SO LONG--SO VERY LONG...I'VE WAITED.

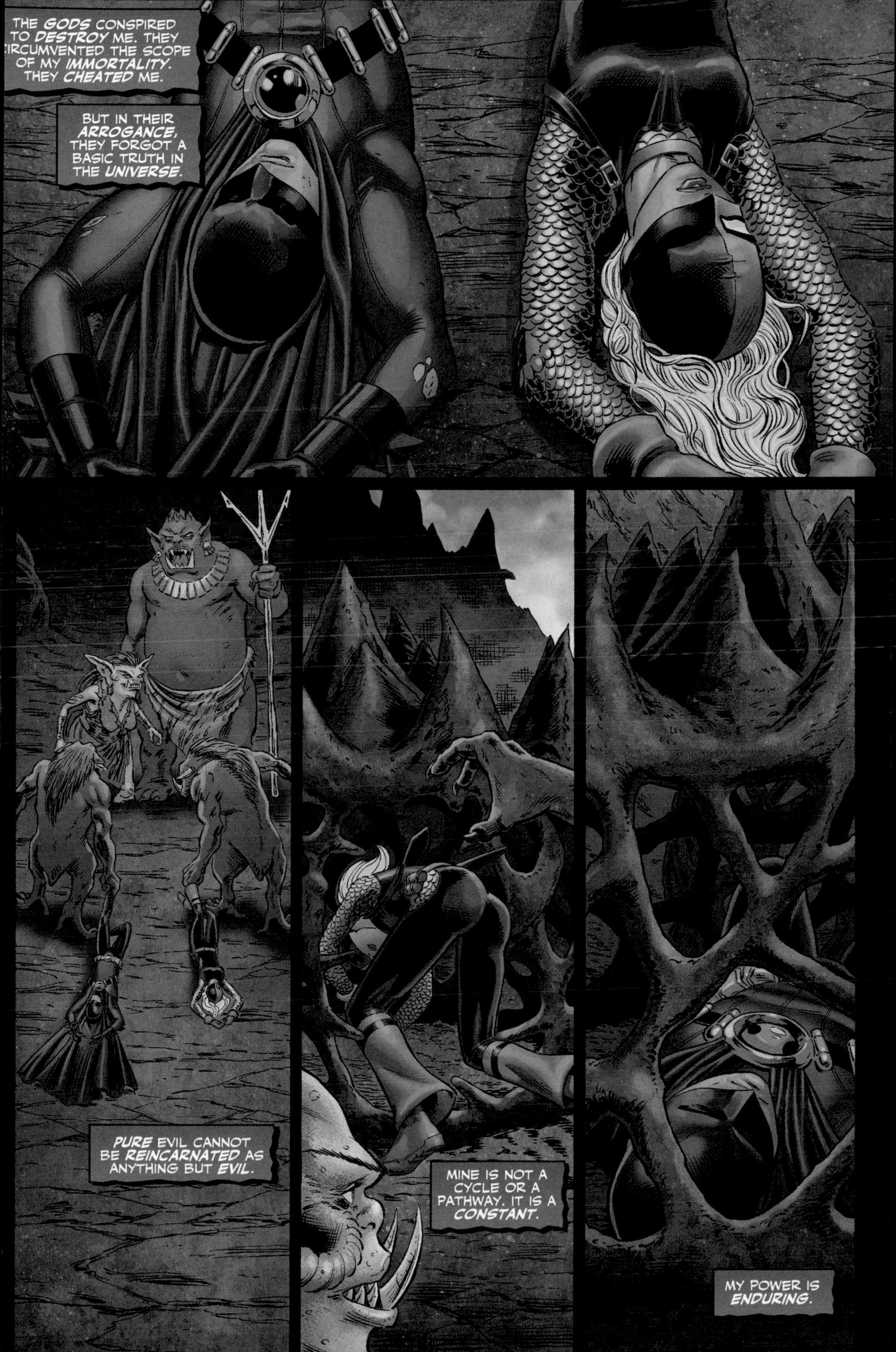
THE GODS CONSPIRED TO DESTROY ME. THEY CIRCUMVENTED THE SCOPE OF MY IMMORTALITY. THEY CHEATED ME.
BUT IN THEIR ARROGANCE, THEY FORGOT A BASIC TRUTH IN THE UNIVERSE.
PURE EVIL CANNOT BE REINCARNATED AS ANYTHING BUT EVIL.
MINE IS NOT A CYCLE OR A PATHWAY. IT IS A CONSTANT.
MY POWER IS ENDURING.

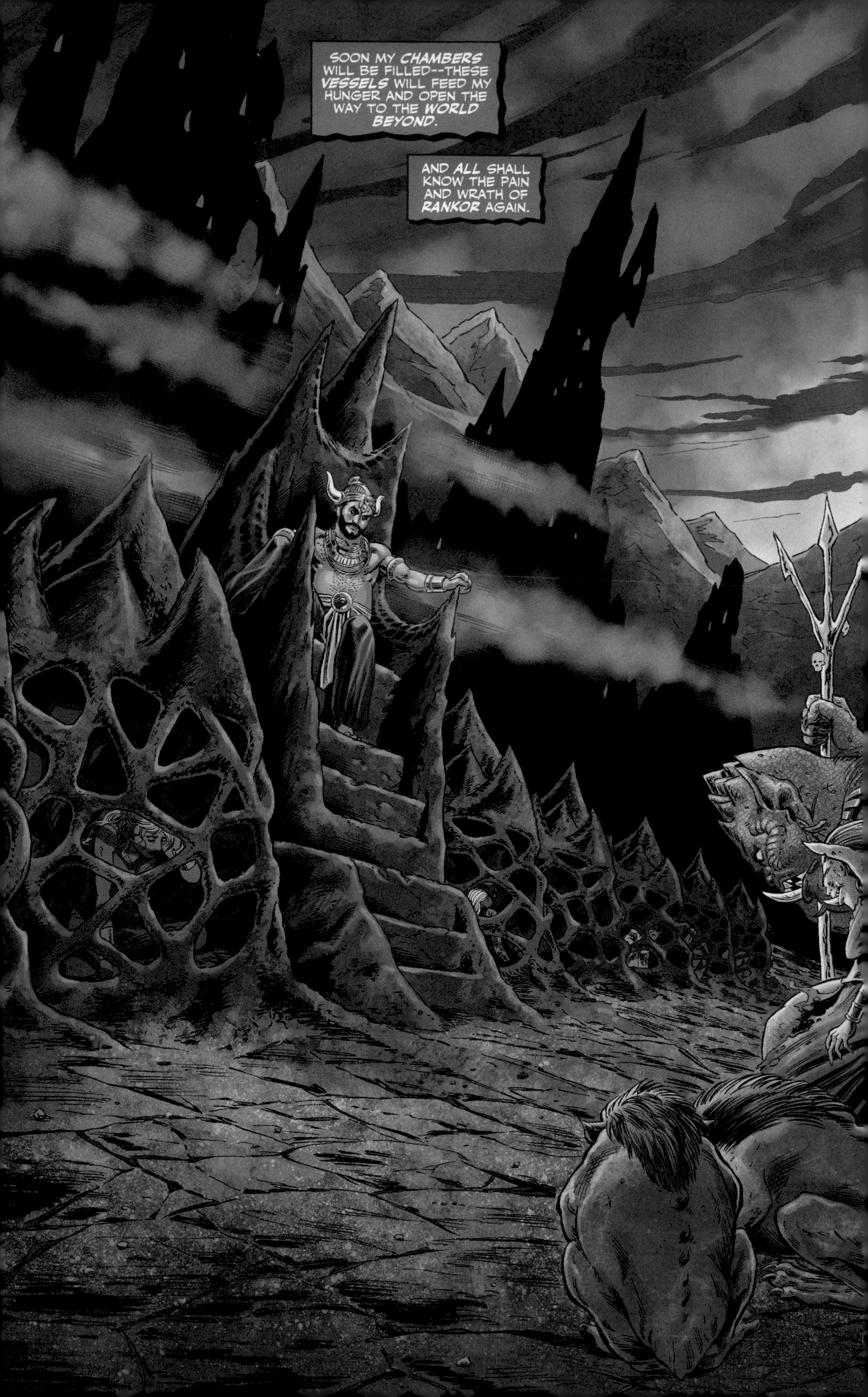
SOON MY CHAMBERS WILL BE FILLED--THESE VESSELS WILL FEED MY HUNGER AND OPEN THE WAY TO THE WORLD BEYOND.
AND ALL SHALL KNOW THE PAIN AND WRATH OF RANKOR AGAIN.

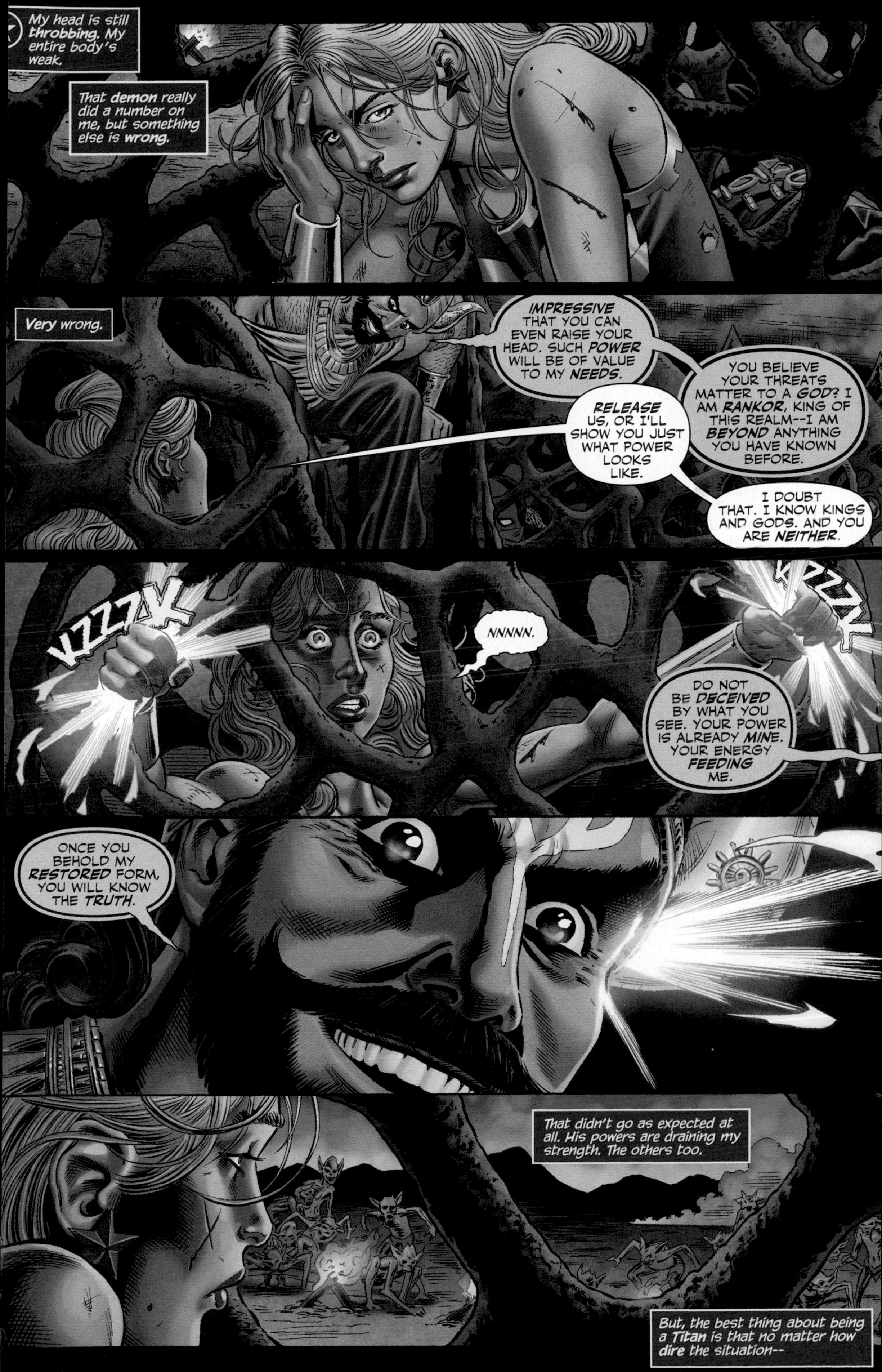

My head is still throbbing. My entire body's weak.
That demon really did a number on me, but something else is wrong.
Very wrong.
IMPRESSIVE THAT YOU CAN EVEN RAISE YOUR HEAD. SUCH POWER WILL BE OF VALUE TO MY NEEDS.
RELEASE US, OR I'LL SHOW YOU JUST WHAT POWER LOOKS LIKE.
YOU BELIEVE YOUR THREATS MATTER TO A GOD? I AM RANKOR, KING OF THIS REALM--I AM BEYOND ANYTHING YOU HAVE KNOWN BEFORE.
I DOUBT THAT. I KNOW KINGS AND GODS. AND YOU ARE NEITHER.
VZZZK
NNNNN.
VZZZK
DO NOT BE DECEIVED BY WHAT YOU SEE. YOUR POWER IS ALREADY MINE. YOUR ENERGY FEEDING ME.
ONCE YOU BEHOLD MY RESTORED FORM, YOU WILL KNOW THE TRUTH.
That didn't go as expected at all. His powers are draining my strength. The others too.
But, the best thing about being a Titan is that no matter how dire the situation--

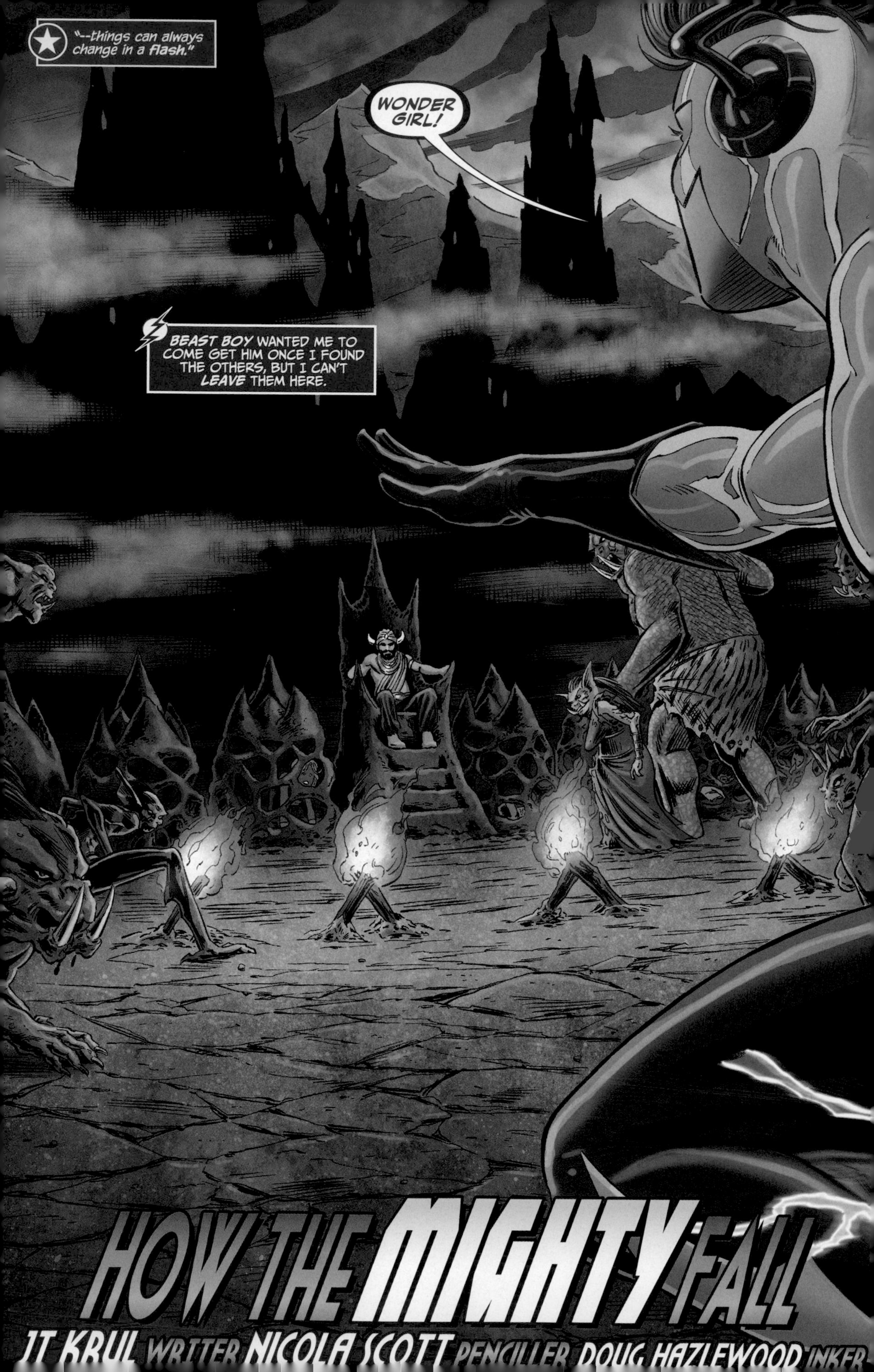
"--things can always change in a flash."
WONDER GIRL!
BEAST BOY WANTED ME TO COME GET HIM ONCE I FOUND THE OTHERS, BUT I CAN'T LEAVE THEM HERE.
HOW THE MIGHTY FALL
JT KRUL WRITER NICOLA SCOTT PENCILLER DOUG HAZLEWOOD INKER

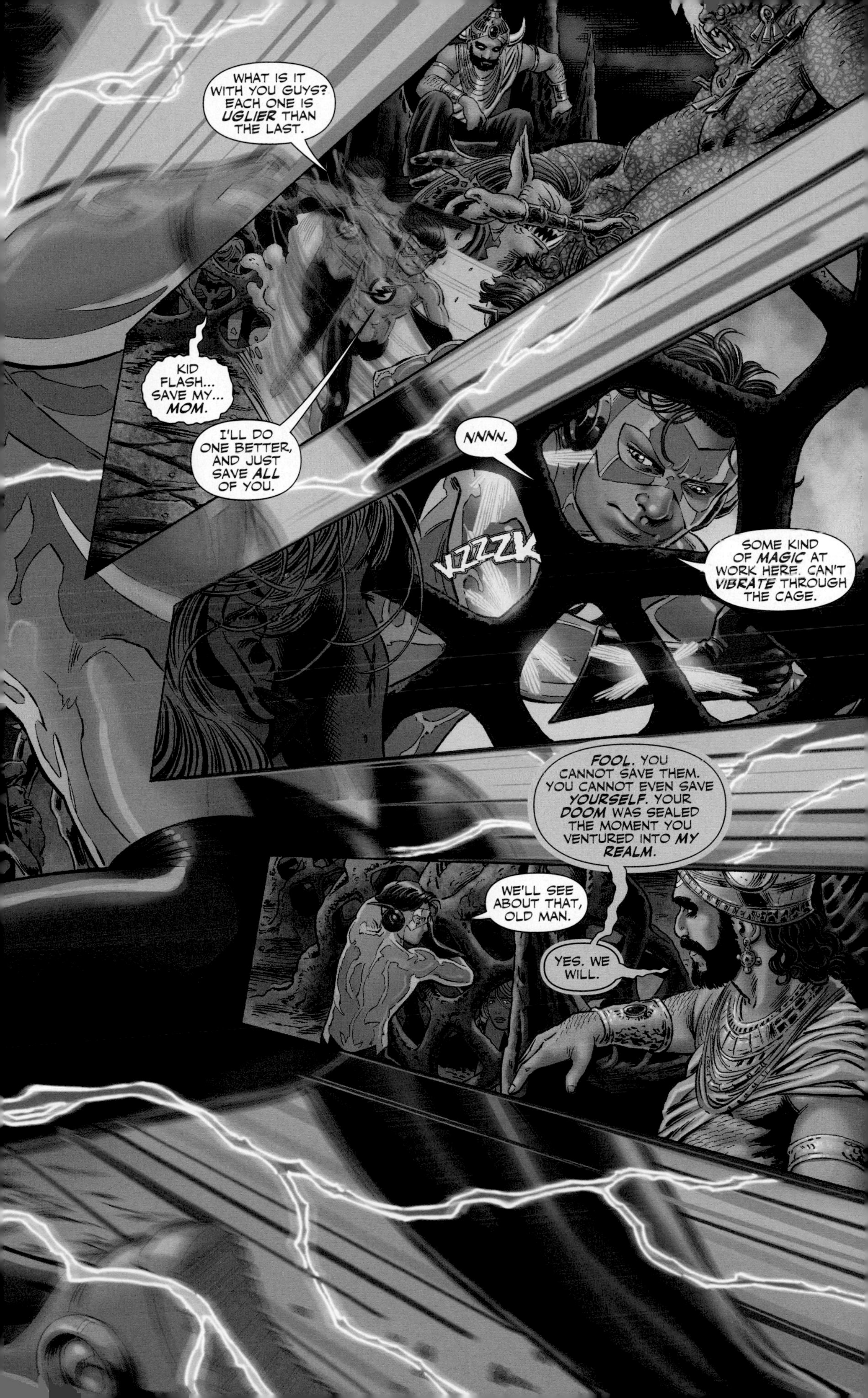
WHAT IS IT WITH YOU GUYS? EACH ONE IS UGLIER THAN THE LAST.
KID FLASH... SAVE MY... MOM.
I'LL DO ONE BETTER, AND JUST SAVE ALL OF YOU.
NNNN.
VZZZZK
SOME KIND OF MAGIC AT WORK HERE. CAN'T VIBRATE THROUGH THE CAGE.
FOOL. YOU CANNOT SAVE THEM. YOU CANNOT EVEN SAVE YOURSELF. YOUR DOOM WAS SEALED THE MOMENT YOU VENTURED INTO MY REALM.
WE'LL SEE ABOUT THAT, OLD MAN.
YES. WE WILL.

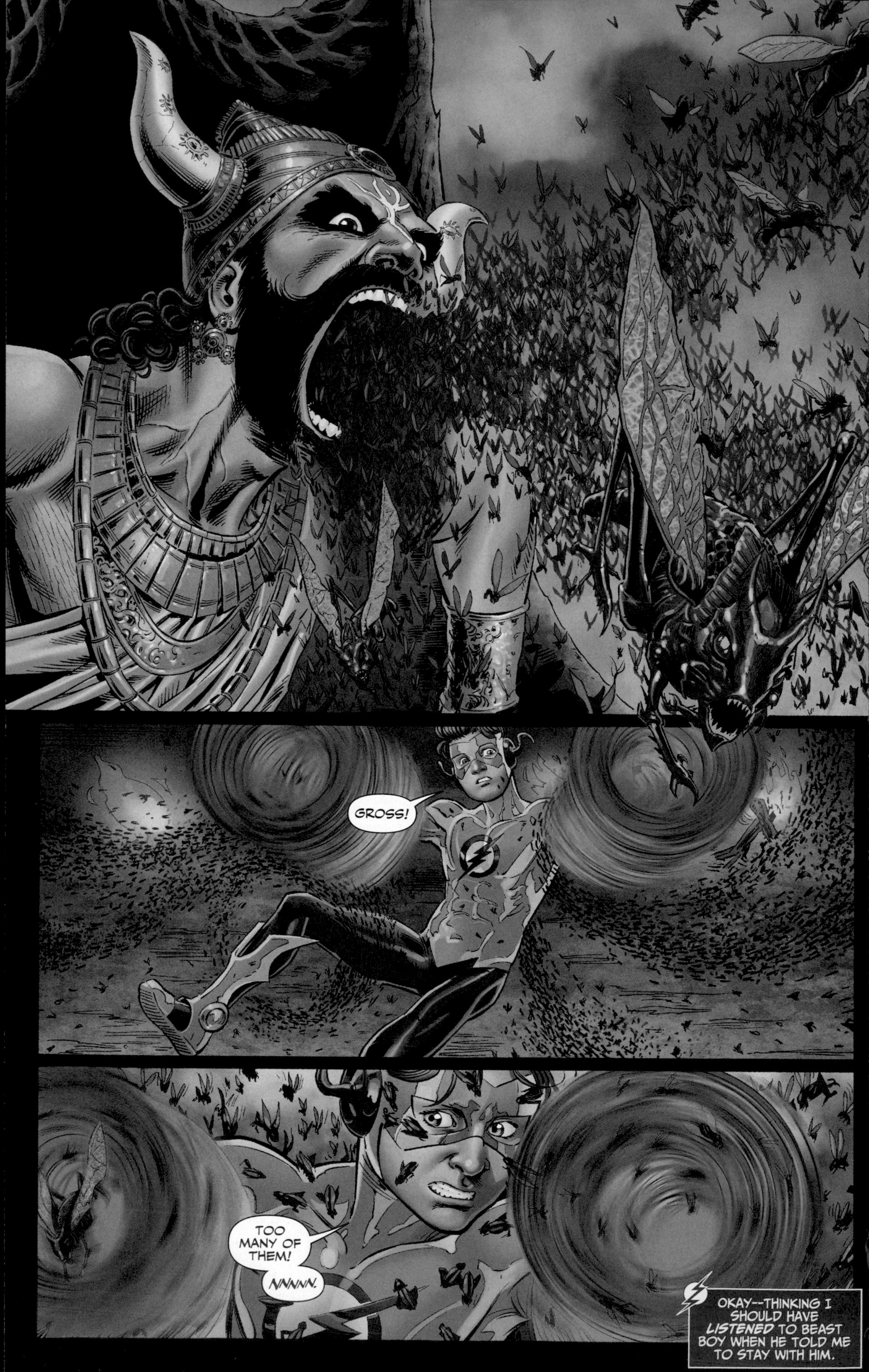
GROSS!
TOO MANY OF THEM!
NNNNN.
OKAY--THINKING I SHOULD HAVE LISTENED TO BEAST BOY WHEN HE TOLD ME TO STAY WITH HIM.

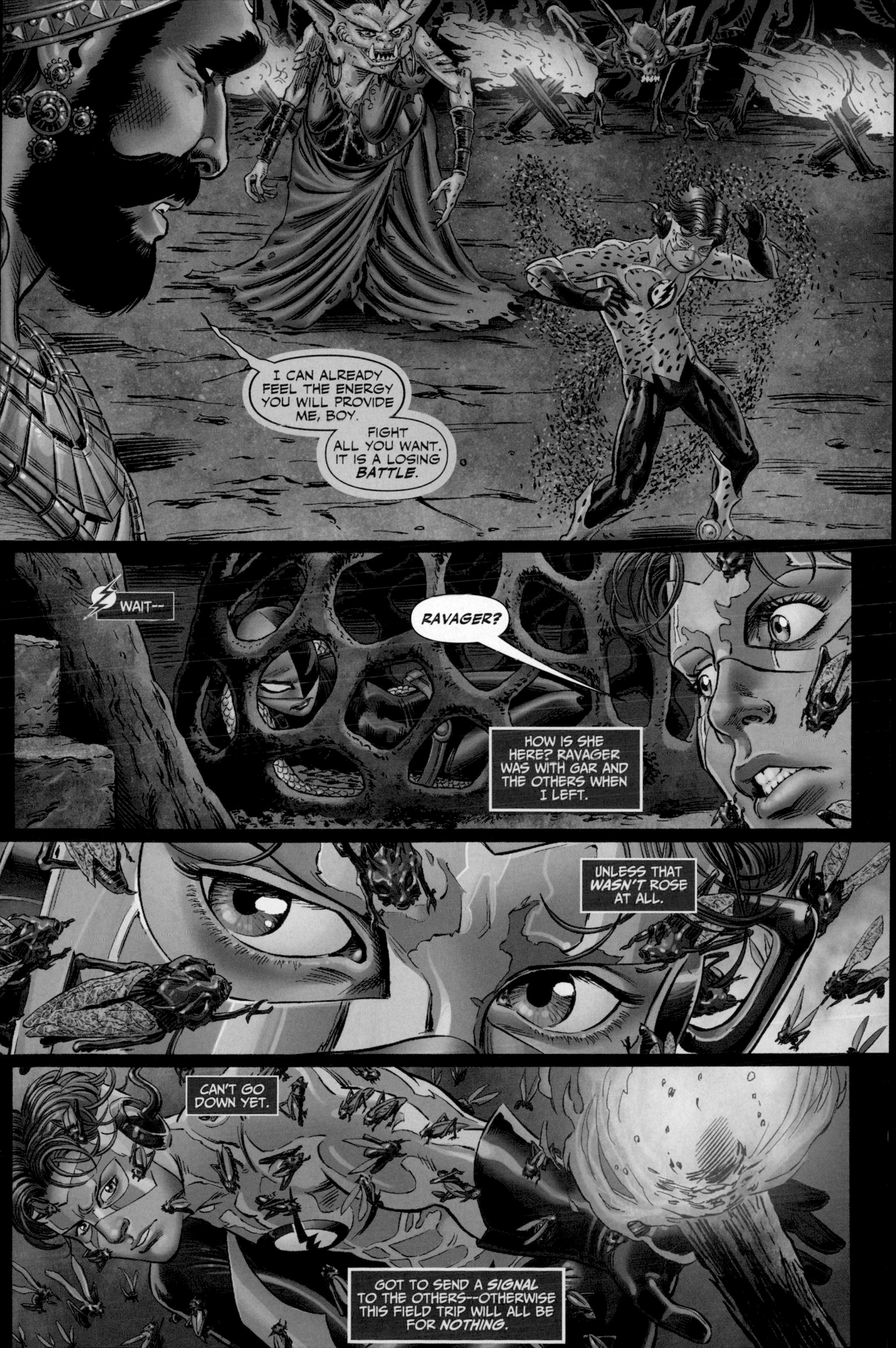

I CAN ALREADY FEEL THE ENERGY YOU WILL PROVIDE ME, BOY.
FIGHT ALL YOU WANT. IT IS A LOSING BATTLE.
WAIT--
RAVAGER?
HOW IS SHE HERE? RAVAGER WAS WITH GAR AND THE OTHERS WHEN I LEFT.
UNLESS THAT WASN'T ROSE AT ALL.
CAN'T GO DOWN YET.
GOT TO SEND A SIGNAL TO THE OTHERS--OTHERWISE THIS FIELD TRIP WILL ALL BE FOR NOTHING.

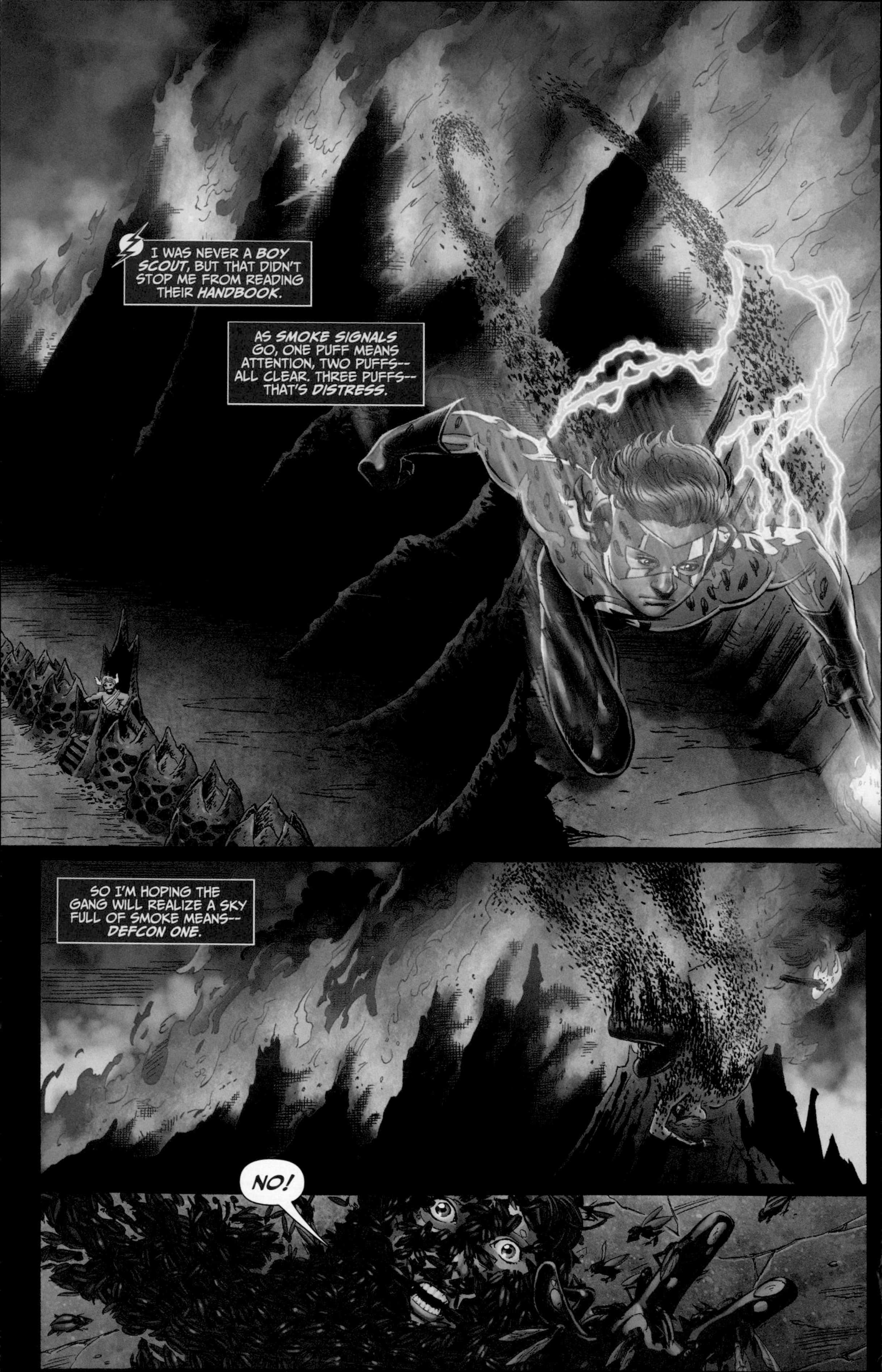
I WAS NEVER A *BOY SCOUT*, BUT THAT DIDN'T STOP ME FROM READING THEIR *HANDBOOK*.
AS *SMOKE SIGNALS* GO, ONE PUFF MEANS ATTENTION, TWO PUFFS-- ALL CLEAR. THREE PUFFS-- THAT'S *DISTRESS*.
SO I'M HOPING THE GANG WILL REALIZE A SKY FULL OF SMOKE MEANS-- *DEFCON ONE*.
NO!

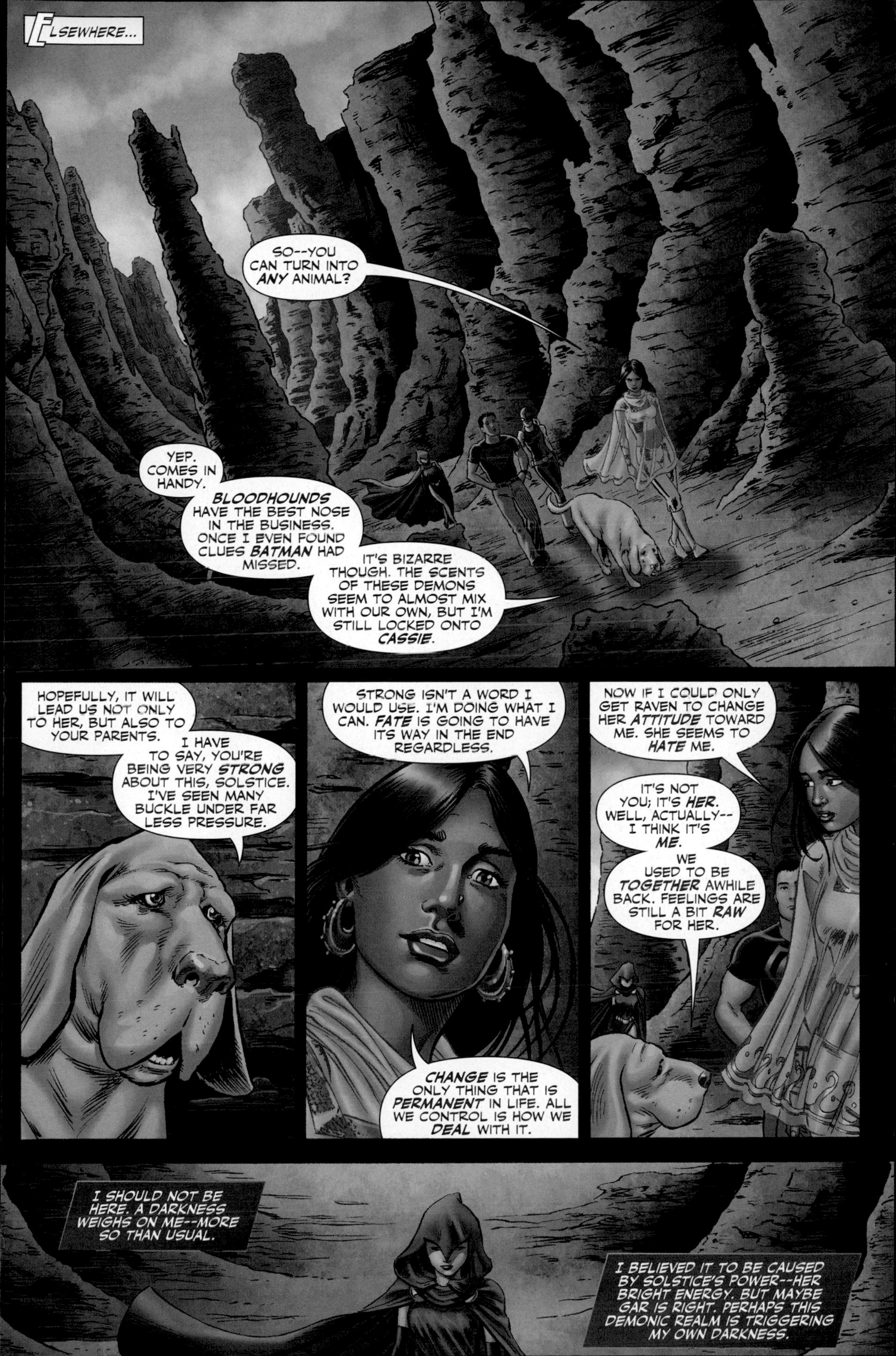
ELSEWHERE...
SO--YOU CAN TURN INTO ANY ANIMAL?
YEP. COMES IN HANDY. BLOODHOUNDS HAVE THE BEST NOSE IN THE BUSINESS. ONCE I EVEN FOUND CLUES BATMAN HAD MISSED.
IT'S BIZARRE THOUGH. THE SCENTS OF THESE DEMONS SEEM TO ALMOST MIX WITH OUR OWN, BUT I'M STILL LOCKED ONTO CASSIE.
HOPEFULLY, IT WILL LEAD US NOT ONLY TO HER, BUT ALSO TO YOUR PARENTS.
I HAVE TO SAY, YOU'RE BEING VERY STRONG ABOUT THIS, SOLSTICE. I'VE SEEN MANY BUCKLE UNDER FAR LESS PRESSURE.
STRONG ISN'T A WORD I WOULD USE. I'M DOING WHAT I CAN. FATE IS GOING TO HAVE ITS WAY IN THE END REGARDLESS.
CHANGE IS THE ONLY THING THAT IS PERMANENT IN LIFE. ALL WE CONTROL IS HOW WE DEAL WITH IT.
NOW IF I COULD ONLY GET RAVEN TO CHANGE HER ATTITUDE TOWARD ME. SHE SEEMS TO HATE ME.
IT'S NOT YOU; IT'S HER. WELL, ACTUALLY-- I THINK IT'S ME.
WE USED TO BE TOGETHER AWHILE BACK. FEELINGS ARE STILL A BIT RAW FOR HER.
I SHOULD NOT BE HERE. A DARKNESS WEIGHS ON ME--MORE SO THAN USUAL.
I BELIEVED IT TO BE CAUSED BY SOLSTICE'S POWER--HER BRIGHT ENERGY. BUT MAYBE GAR IS RIGHT. PERHAPS THIS DEMONIC REALM IS TRIGGERING MY OWN DARKNESS.

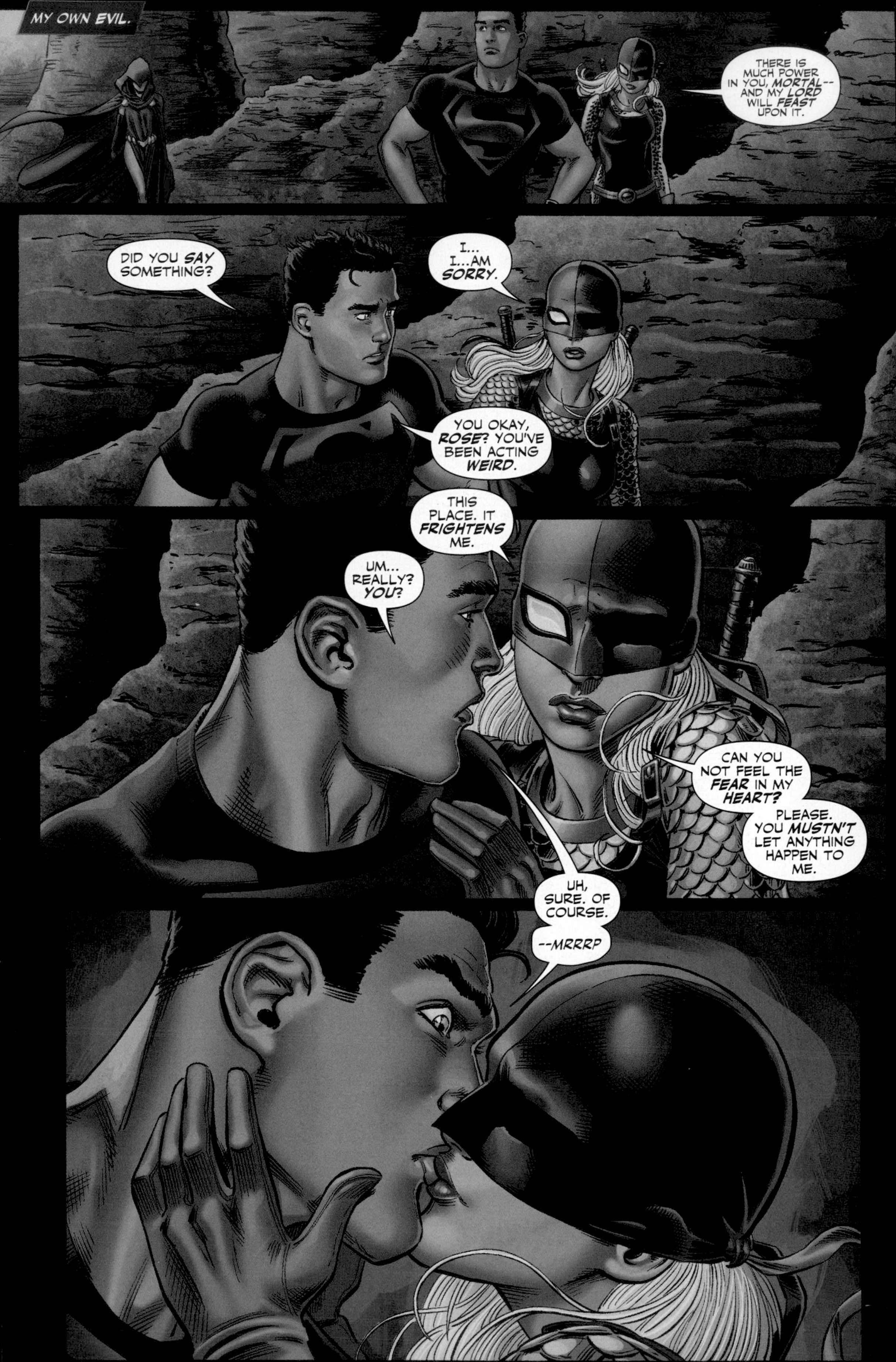
MY OWN EVIL.
THERE IS MUCH POWER IN YOU, MORTAL-- AND MY LORD WILL FEAST UPON IT.
DID YOU SAY SOMETHING?
I... I...AM SORRY.
YOU OKAY, ROSE? YOU'VE BEEN ACTING WEIRD.
THIS PLACE. IT FRIGHTENS ME.
UM... REALLY? YOU?
CAN YOU NOT FEEL THE FEAR IN MY HEART?
PLEASE. YOU MUSTN'T LET ANYTHING HAPPEN TO ME.
UH, SURE. OF COURSE.
--MRRRP

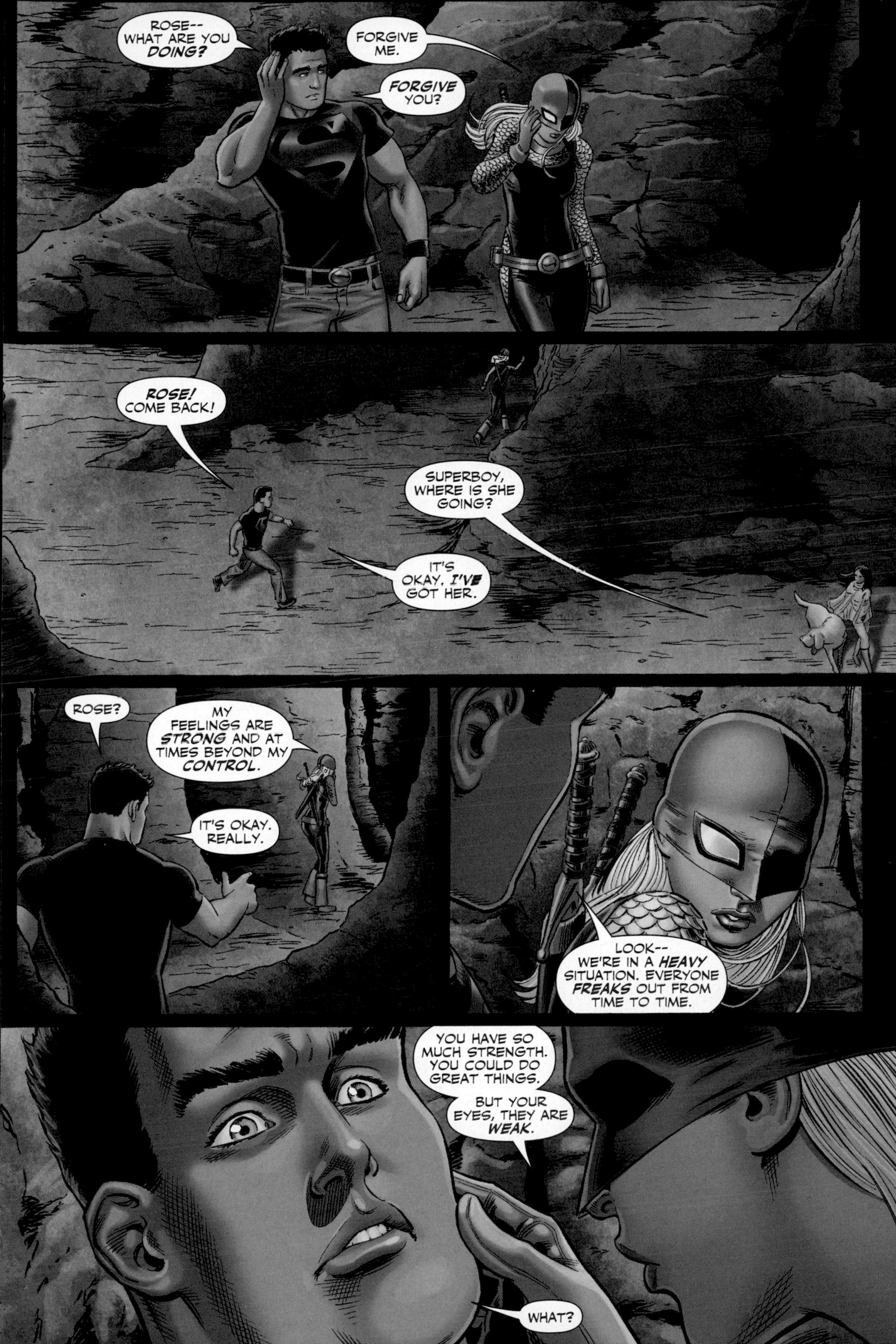
ROSE-- WHAT ARE YOU *DOING?*
FORGIVE ME.
FORGIVE YOU?
ROSE! COME BACK!
SUPERBOY, WHERE IS SHE GOING?
IT'S OKAY. *I'VE* GOT HER.
ROSE?
MY FEELINGS ARE *STRONG* AND AT TIMES BEYOND MY *CONTROL*.
IT'S OKAY. REALLY.
LOOK-- WE'RE IN A *HEAVY* SITUATION. EVERYONE *FREAKS* OUT FROM TIME TO TIME.
YOU HAVE SO MUCH STRENGTH. YOU COULD DO GREAT THINGS.
BUT YOUR EYES, THEY ARE *WEAK*.
WHAT?

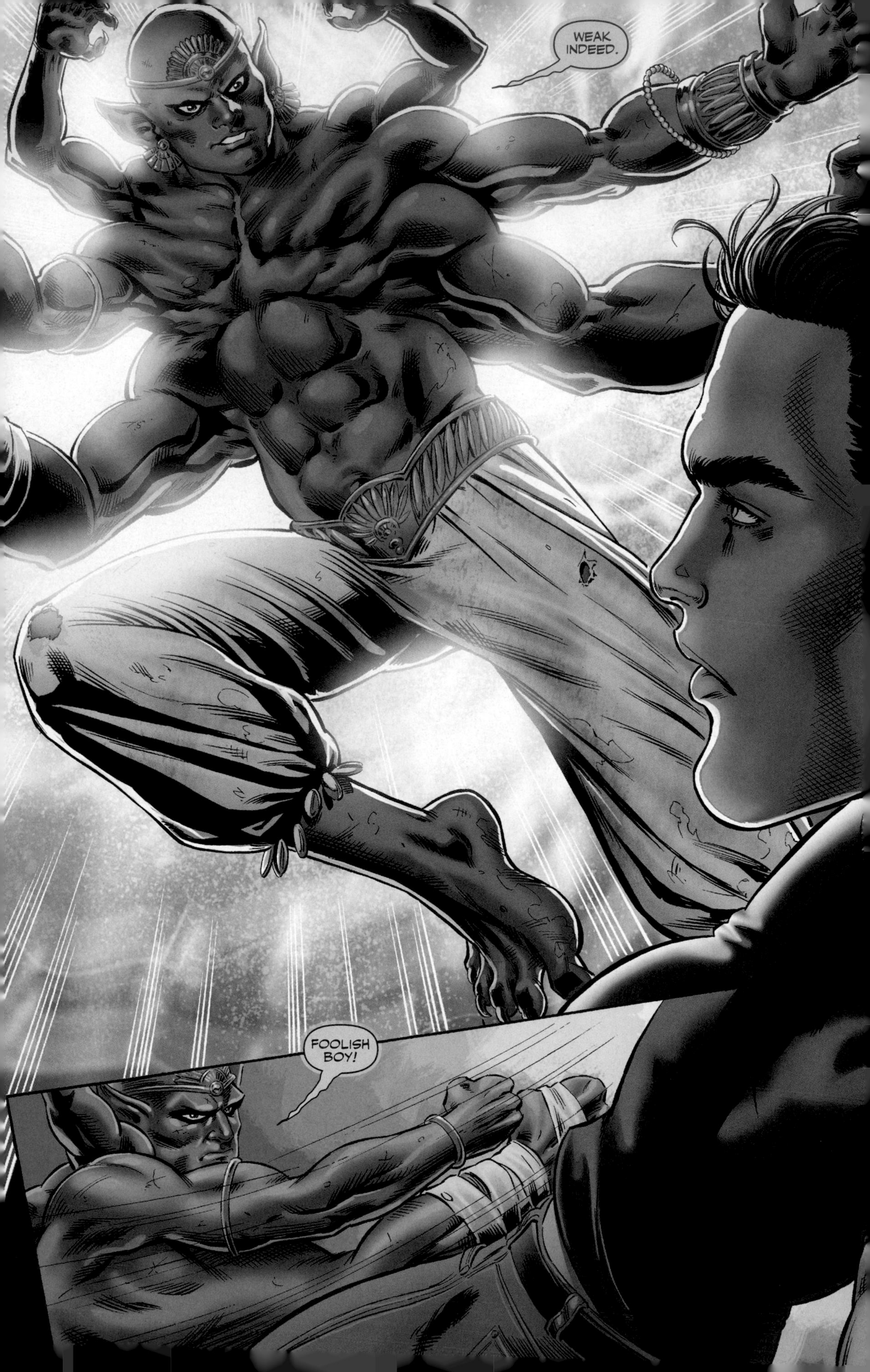
WEAK INDEED.
FOOLISH BOY!

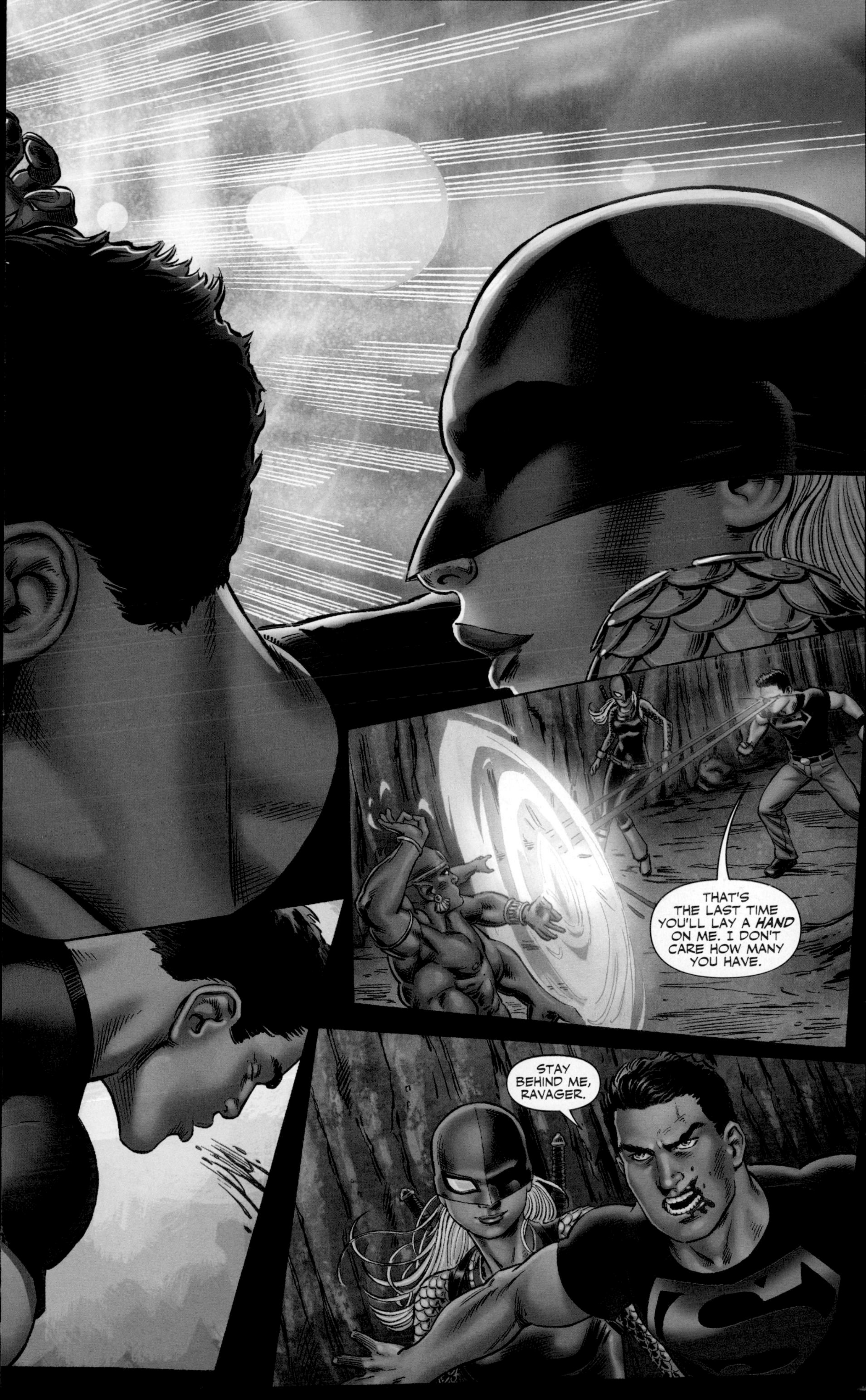
THAT'S THE LAST TIME YOU'LL LAY A *HAND* ON ME. I DON'T CARE HOW MANY YOU HAVE.
STAY BEHIND ME, RAVAGER.

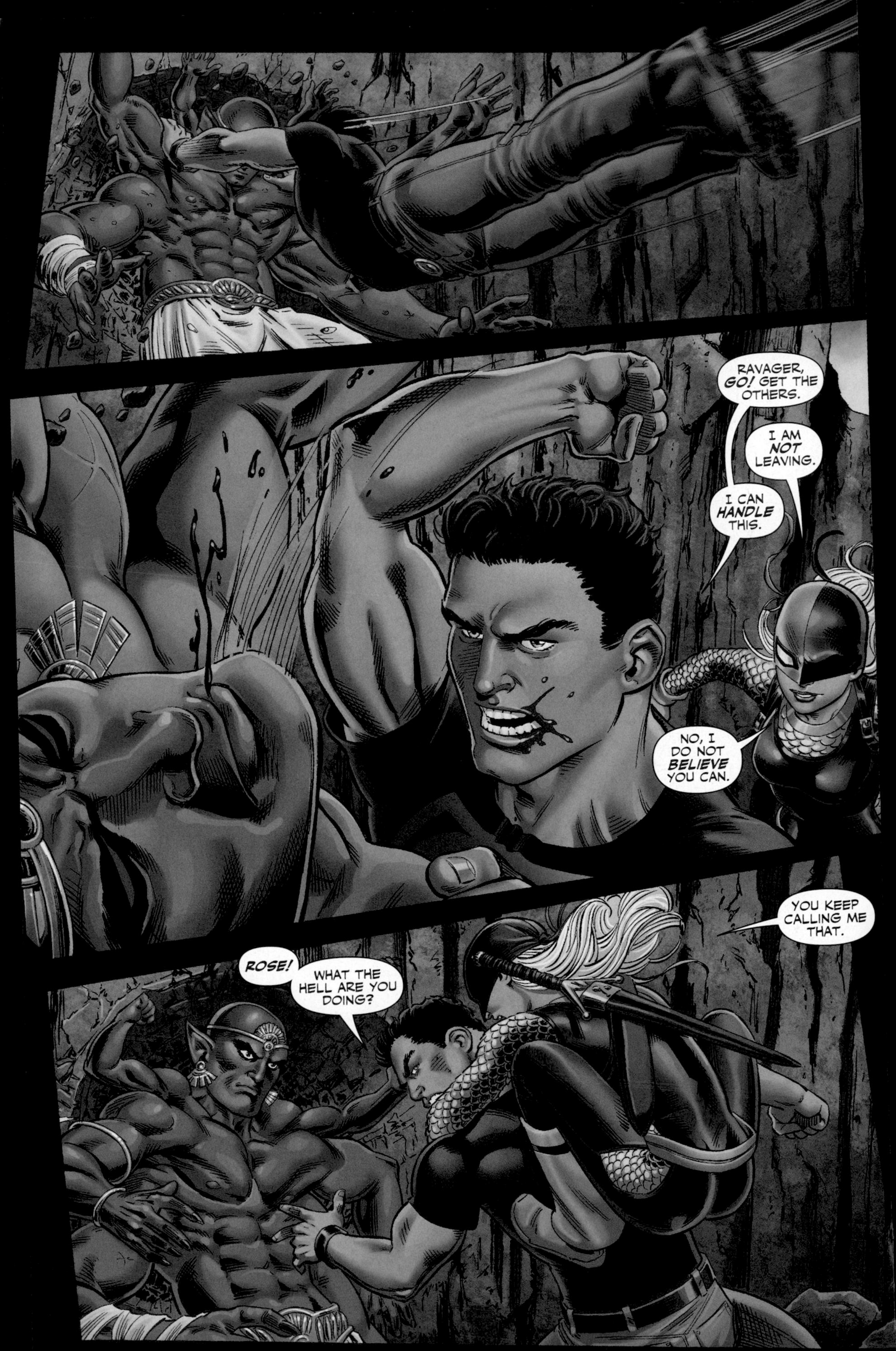
RAVAGER, GO! GET THE OTHERS.
I AM NOT LEAVING.
I CAN HANDLE THIS.
NO, I DO NOT BELIEVE YOU CAN.
YOU KEEP CALLING ME THAT.
ROSE!
WHAT THE HELL ARE YOU DOING?

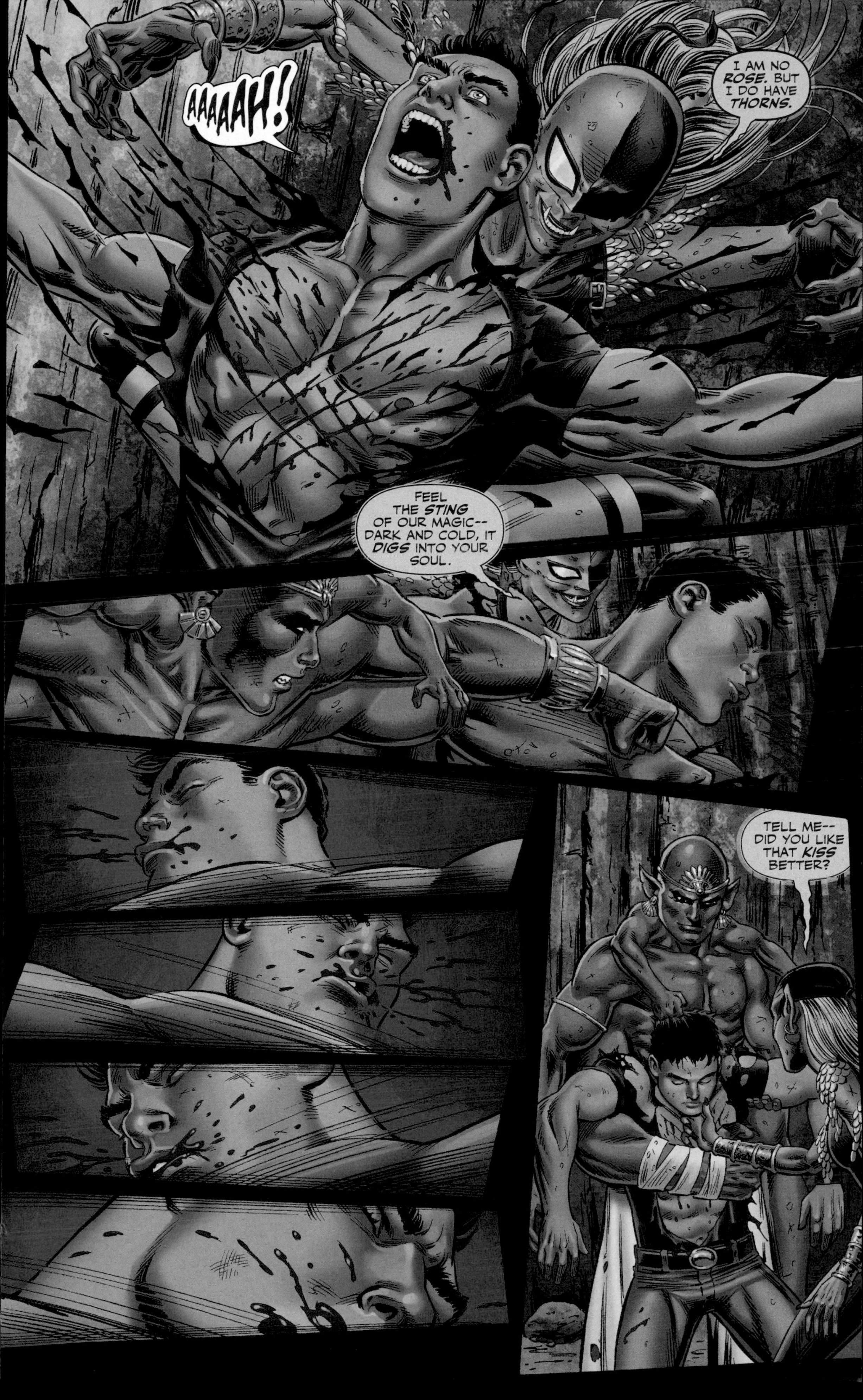
AAAAAH!
I AM NO ROSE. BUT I DO HAVE THORNS.
FEEL THE STING OF OUR MAGIC-- DARK AND COLD, IT DIGS INTO YOUR SOUL.
TELL ME-- DID YOU LIKE THAT KISS BETTER?

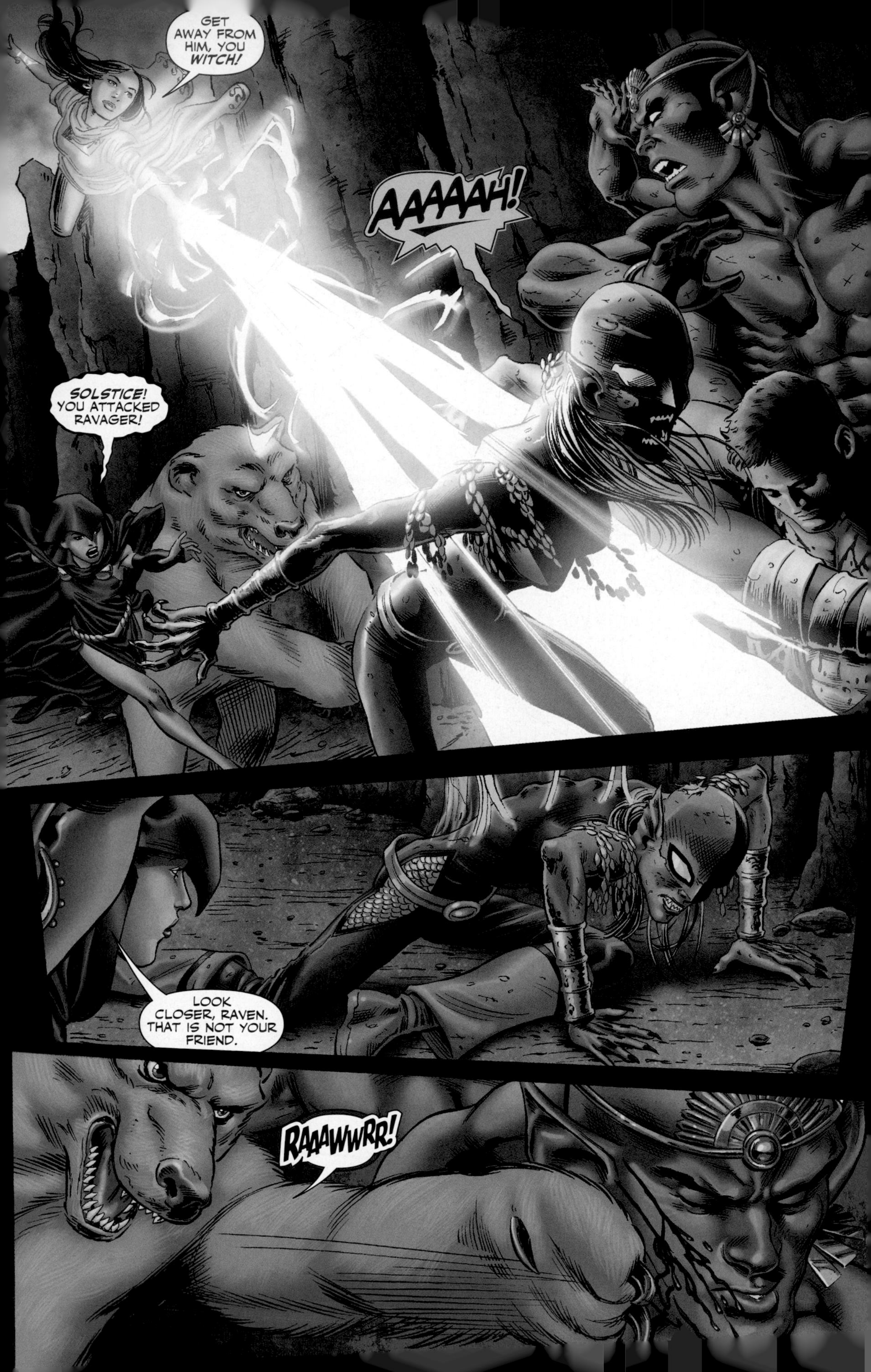
GET AWAY FROM HIM, YOU WITCH!
AAAAAH!
SOLSTICE! YOU ATTACKED RAVAGER!
LOOK CLOSER, RAVEN. THAT IS NOT YOUR FRIEND.
RAAAWWRR!

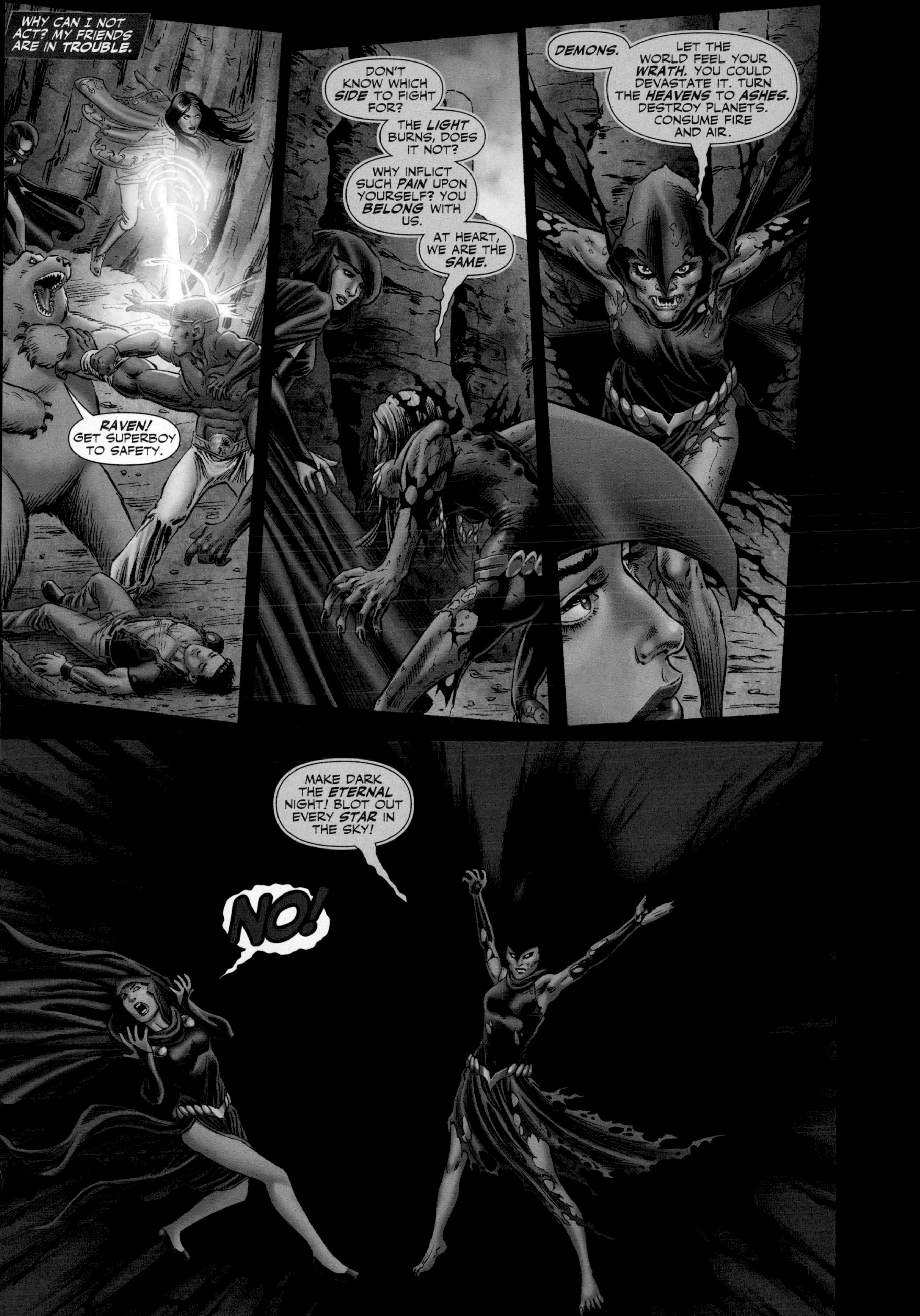
WHY CAN I NOT ACT? MY FRIENDS ARE IN TROUBLE.
RAVEN! GET SUPERBOY TO SAFETY.
DON'T KNOW WHICH SIDE TO FIGHT FOR?
THE LIGHT BURNS, DOES IT NOT?
WHY INFLICT SUCH PAIN UPON YOURSELF? YOU BELONG WITH US.
AT HEART, WE ARE THE SAME.
DEMONS.
LET THE WORLD FEEL YOUR WRATH. YOU COULD DEVASTATE IT. TURN THE HEAVENS TO ASHES. DESTROY PLANETS. CONSUME FIRE AND AIR.
MAKE DARK THE ETERNAL NIGHT! BLOT OUT EVERY STAR IN THE SKY!
NO!

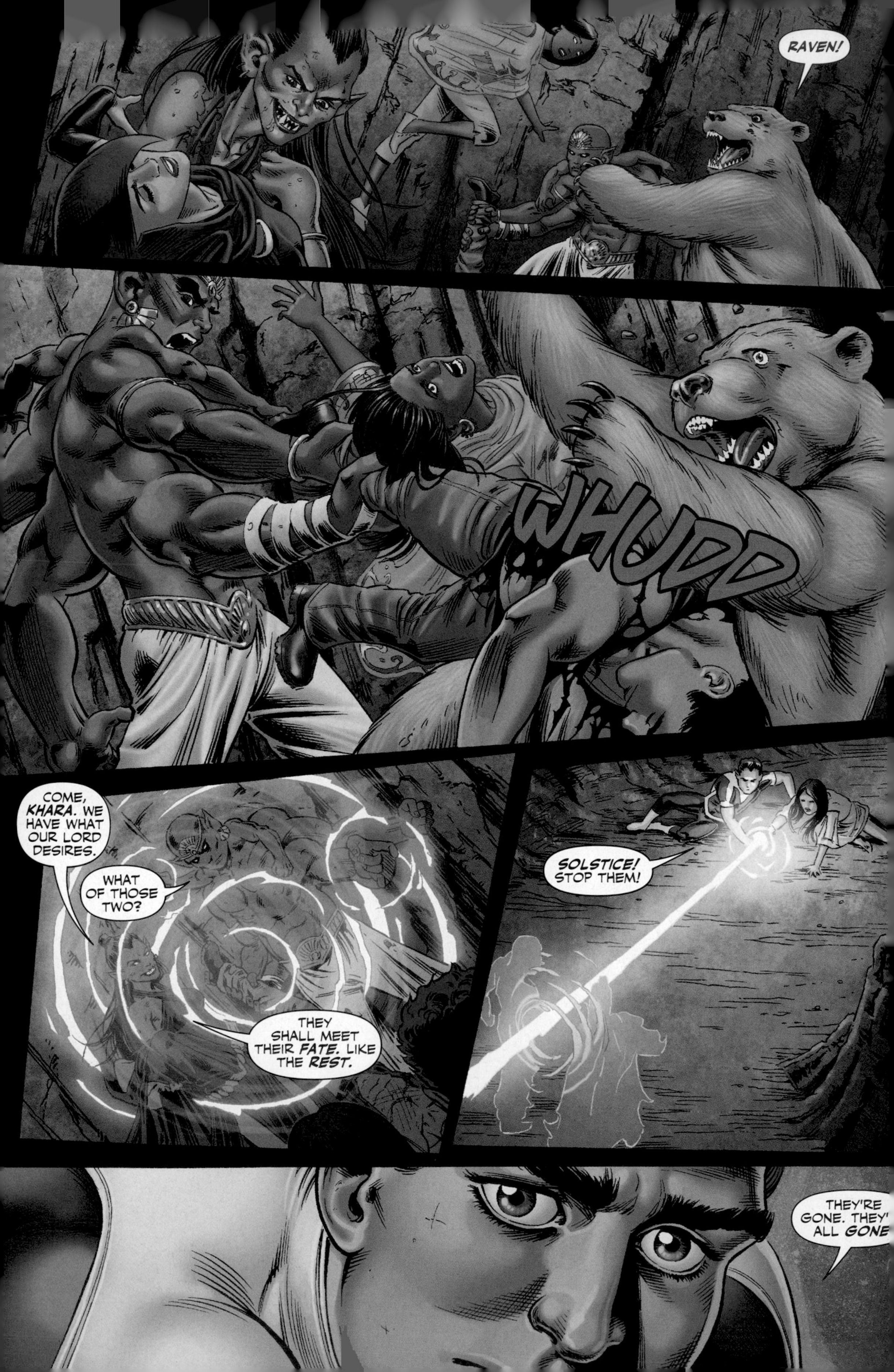
RAVEN!
WHUDD
COME, KHARA. WE HAVE WHAT OUR LORD DESIRES.
WHAT OF THOSE TWO?
THEY SHALL MEET THEIR FATE. LIKE THE REST.
SOLSTICE! STOP THEM!
THEY'RE GONE. THEY' ALL GONE

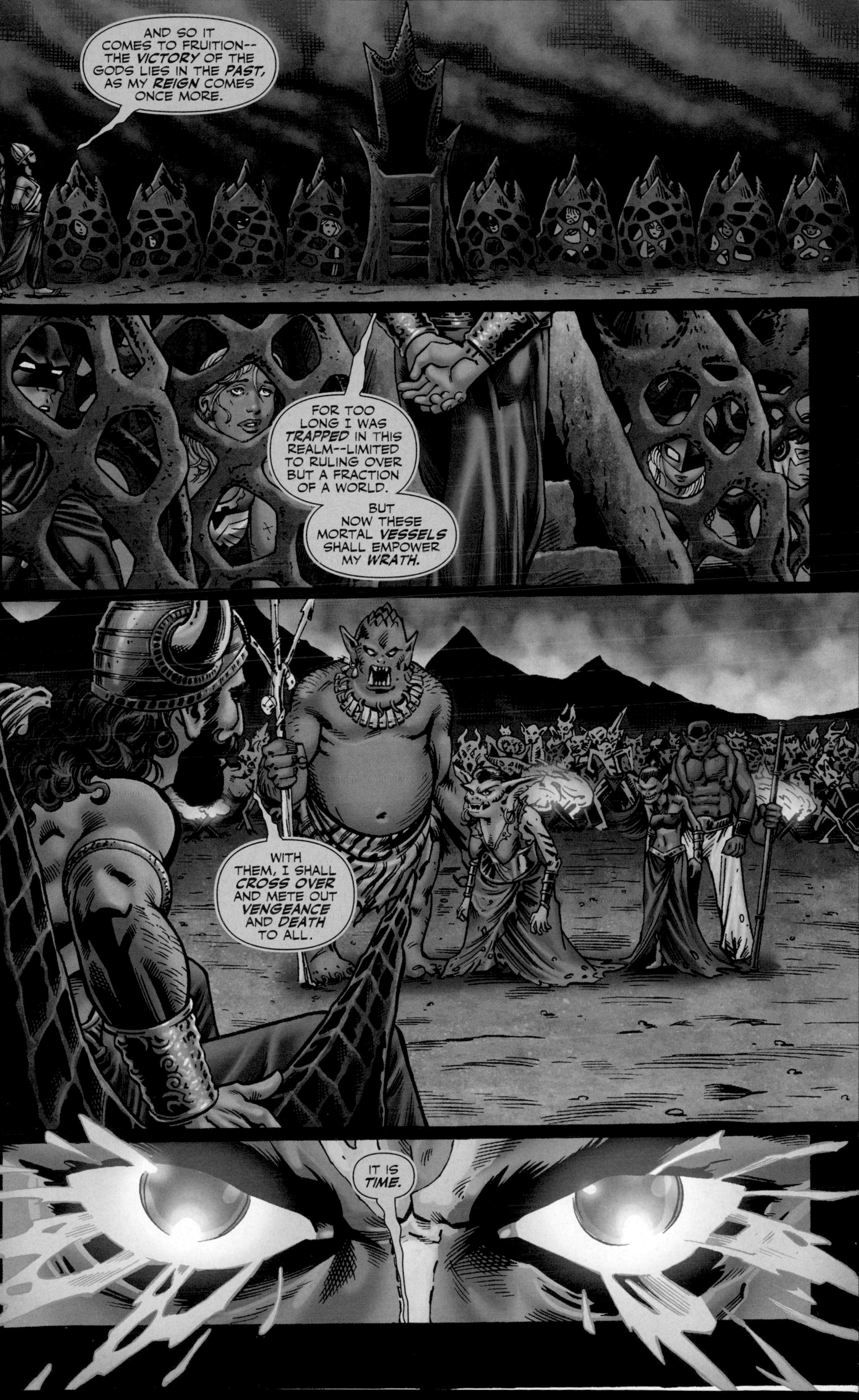
AND SO IT COMES TO FRUITION-- THE VICTORY OF THE GODS LIES IN THE PAST, AS MY REIGN COMES ONCE MORE.
FOR TOO LONG I WAS TRAPPED IN THIS REALM--LIMITED TO RULING OVER BUT A FRACTION OF A WORLD.
BUT NOW THESE MORTAL VESSELS SHALL EMPOWER MY WRATH.
WITH THEM, I SHALL CROSS OVER AND METE OUT VENGEANCE AND DEATH TO ALL.
IT IS TIME.

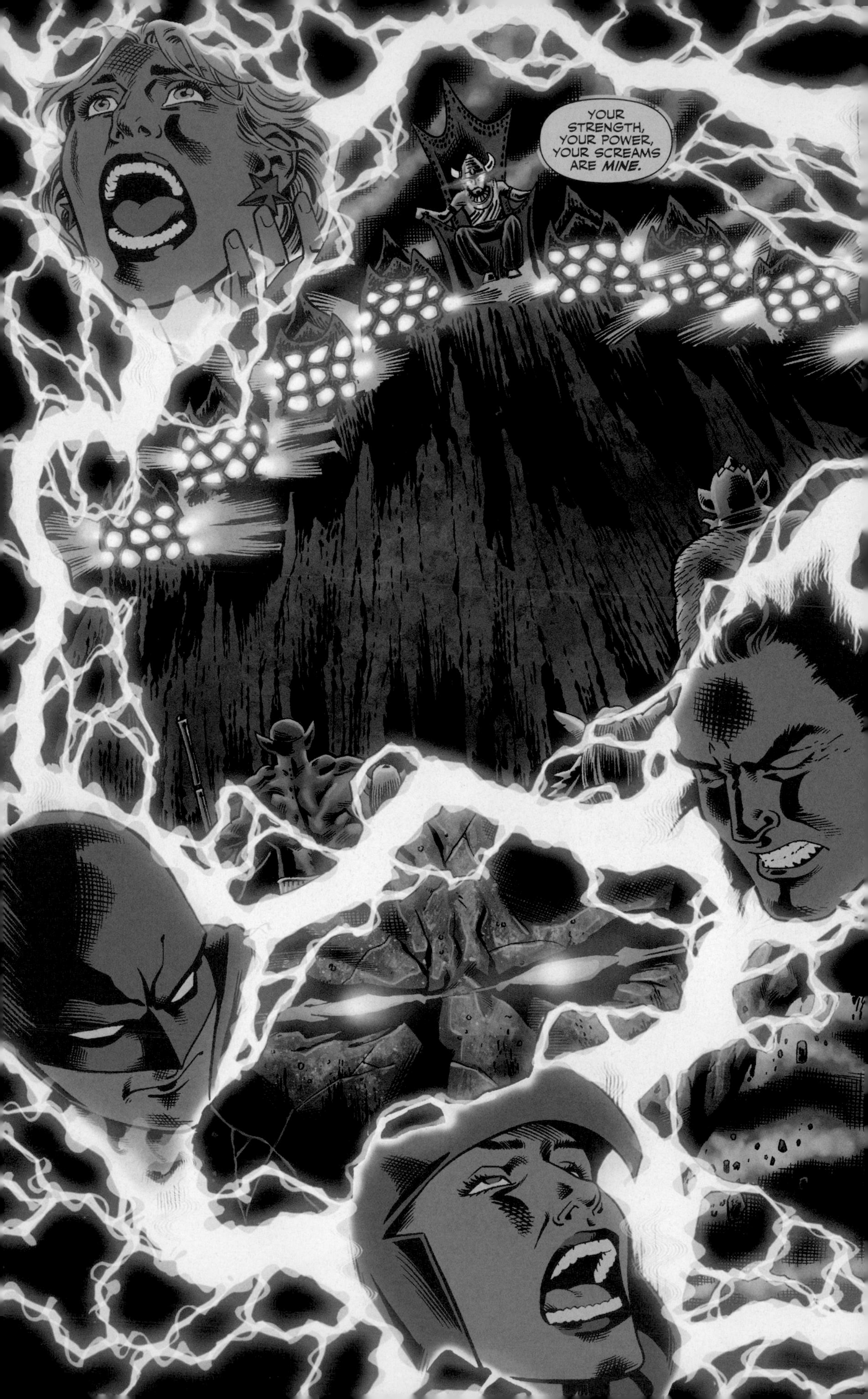
YOUR STRENGTH, YOUR POWER, YOUR SCREAMS ARE *MINE.*

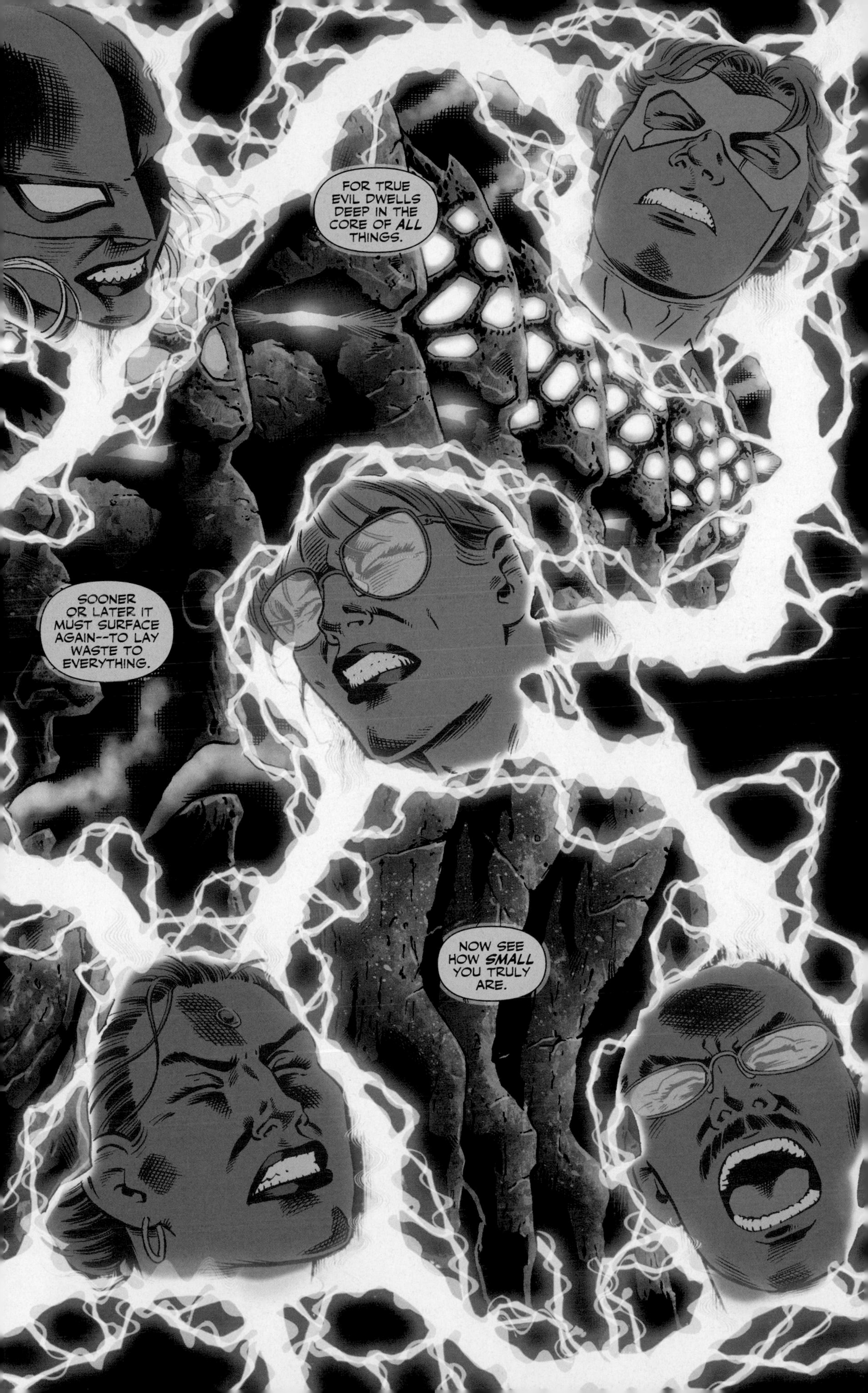
FOR TRUE EVIL DWELLS DEEP IN THE CORE OF ALL THINGS.
SOONER OR LATER IT MUST SURFACE AGAIN--TO LAY WASTE TO EVERYTHING.
NOW SEE HOW SMALL YOU TRULY ARE.

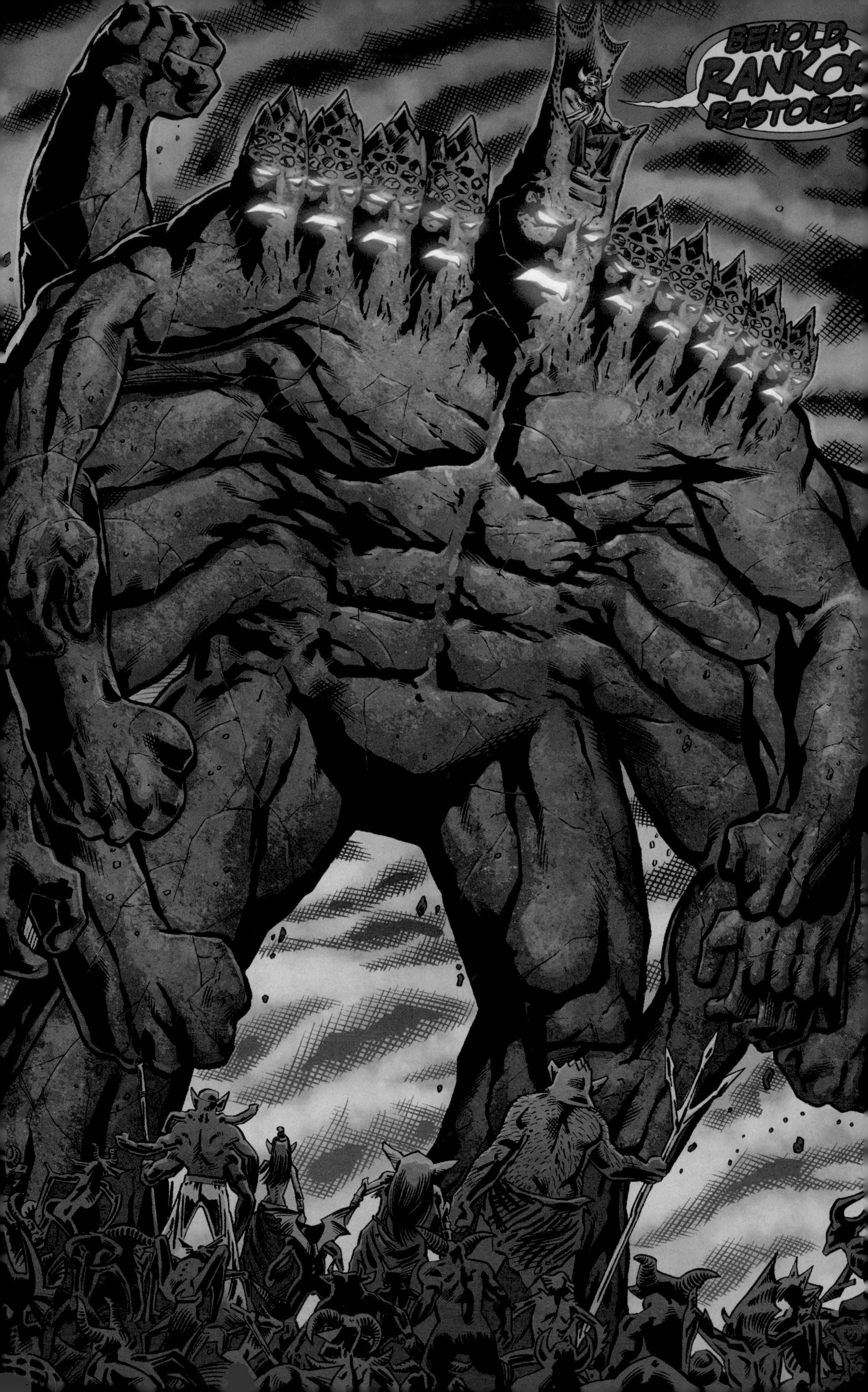
BEHOLD, RANKOR RESTORED

AT HIS THRONE SAT THE **LORD** OF **DARKNESS. RANKOR** WAS--IN A WORD-- A **MONSTER.** A DEMON WITH **TEN HEADS**--EACH ONE MORE EVIL THAN THE NEXT. HIS POWER WAS **EPIC.** HIS WRATH **LIMITLESS.**

THE GREAT **RAMA** SENSED ANXIETY IN HIS **HEART** AS RANKOR'S GAZE BURNED WITH **HATRED.** BUT RAMA FOUND **STRENGTH** IN HIS ALLY, THE MONKEY KING **HANUMAN.** HE HELD HIS GROUND, STEELING HIS RESOLVE. HIS **LIGHT** WOULD **ENDURE.**

DAD, IF RAMA WAS SO **SCARED** OF RANKOR, WHY DID HE STAY AND **FIGHT** HIM?

HE HAD NO CHOICE, KIRAN.

BECAUSE RANKOR HAD KIDNAPPED HIS PRINCESS, **SITA?**

YES, BUT **MORE** THAN THAT.

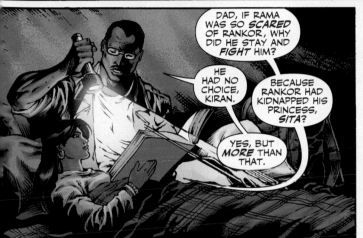

RAMA KNEW EARLY ON THAT FACING RANKOR WAS HIS **FATE**--THE PATH THAT WAS **CHOSEN** FOR HIM BEFORE HE WAS EVEN BORN.

HE COULD NO MORE **CHANGE** HIS PATH THAN A **RIVER** COULD DECIDE TO TURN BACK UPSTREAM. TURN ANY WAY IT LIKES, IT'LL ALWAYS END UP AT THE **OCEAN**--WHERE IT BELONGS.

DADDY, DO YOU THINK RAMA KNEW HE WOULD WIN?

I BELIEVE HE HAD **FAITH.**

FAITH IN HIMSELF?

FAITH IN THE LIGHT OVERCOMING THE DARKNESS.

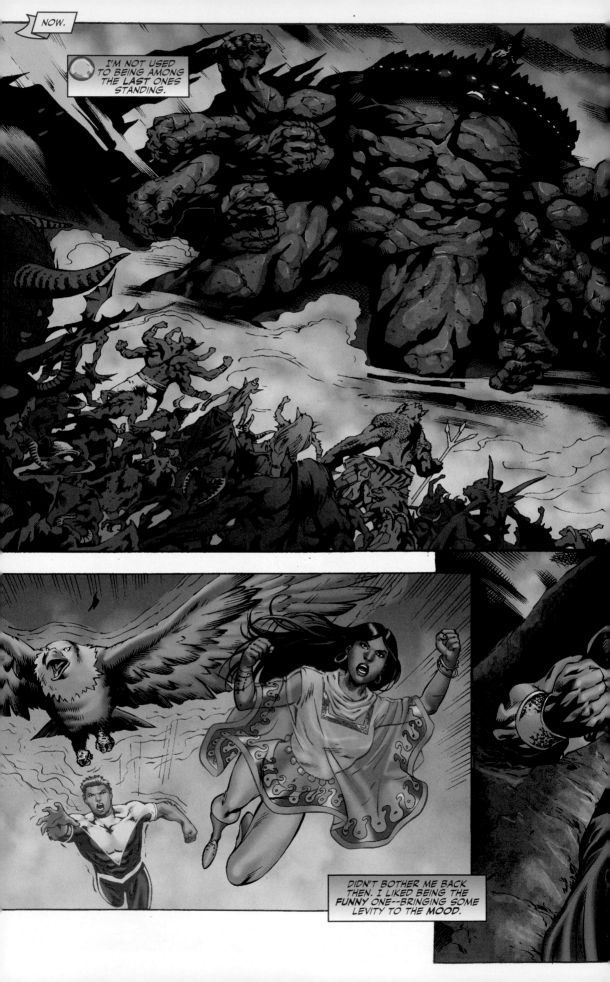

NOW.

I'M NOT USED TO BEING AMONG THE *LAST ONES STANDING.*

DIDN'T BOTHER ME BACK THEN. I LIKED BEING THE *FUNNY ONE*--BRINGING SOME *LEVITY* TO THE MOOD.

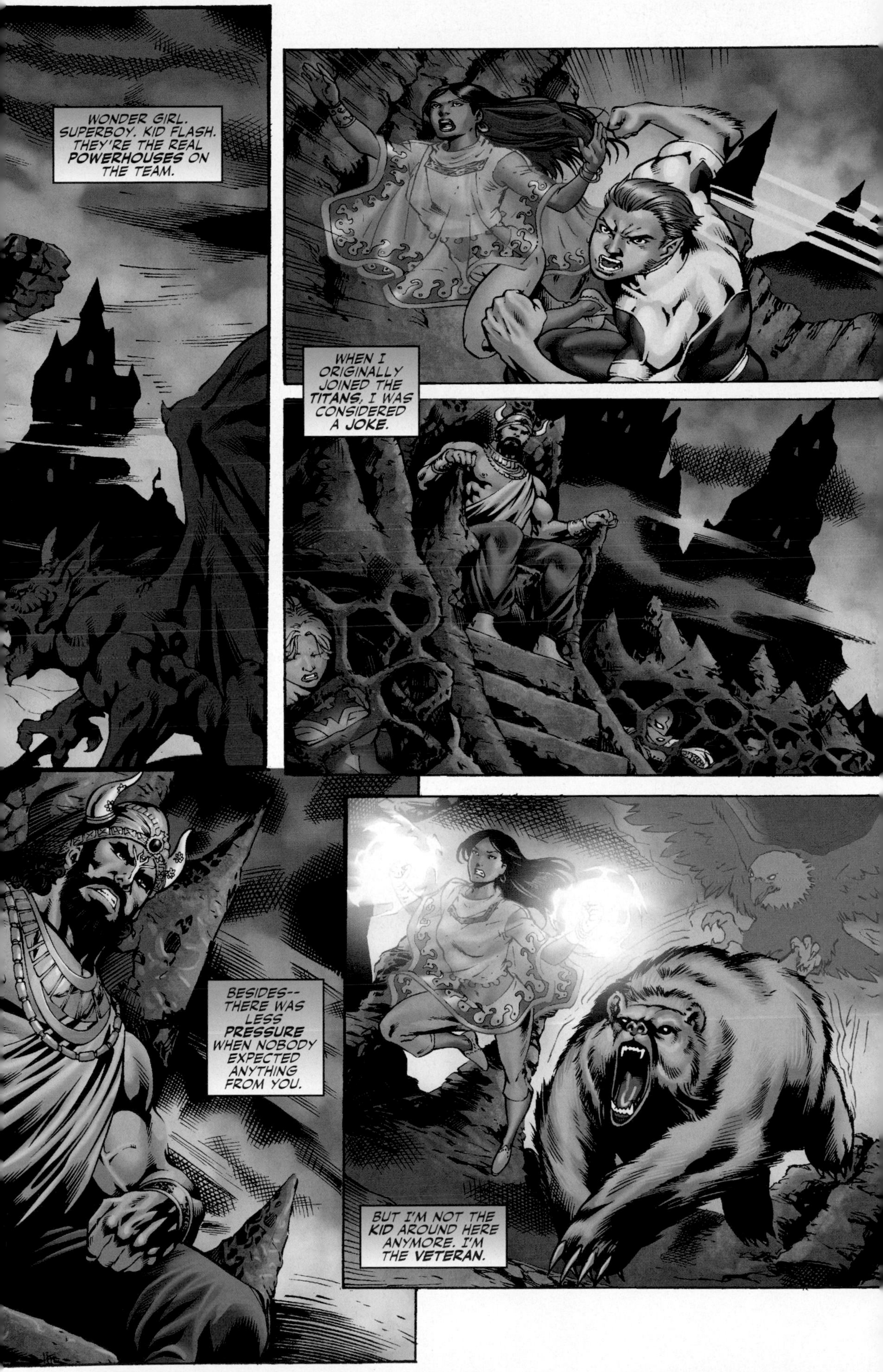
WONDER GIRL. SUPERBOY. KID FLASH. THEY'RE THE REAL POWERHOUSES ON THE TEAM.
WHEN I ORIGINALLY JOINED THE TITANS, I WAS CONSIDERED A JOKE.
BESIDES-- THERE WAS LESS PRESSURE WHEN NOBODY EXPECTED ANYTHING FROM YOU.
BUT I'M NOT THE KID AROUND HERE ANYMORE. I'M THE VETERAN.

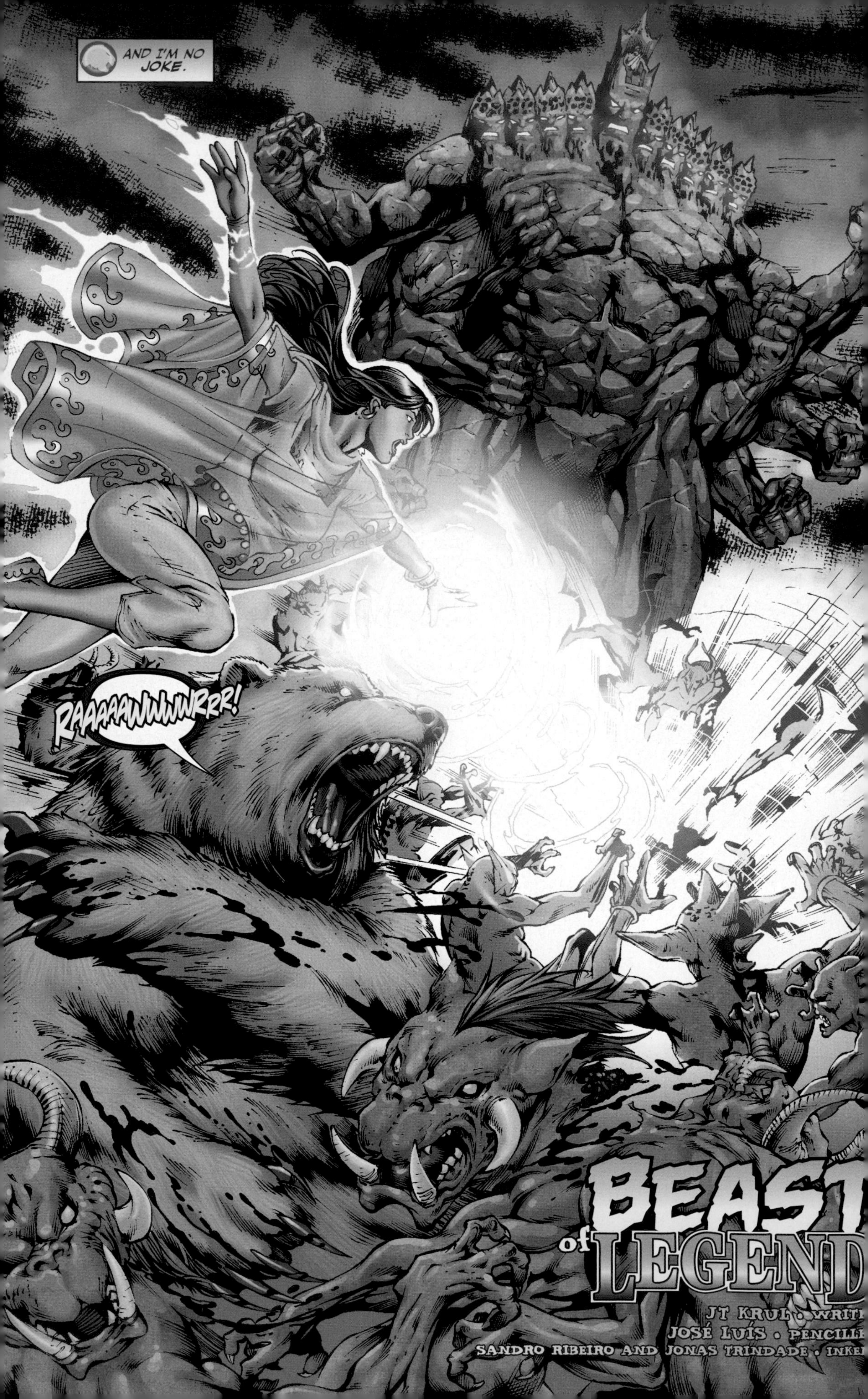
AND I'M NO JOKE.
RAAAAAWWWWRRR!
BEAST of LEGEND
JT KRUL • WRIT
JOSÉ LUÍS • PENCILL
SANDRO RIBEIRO AND JONAS TRINDADE • INKE

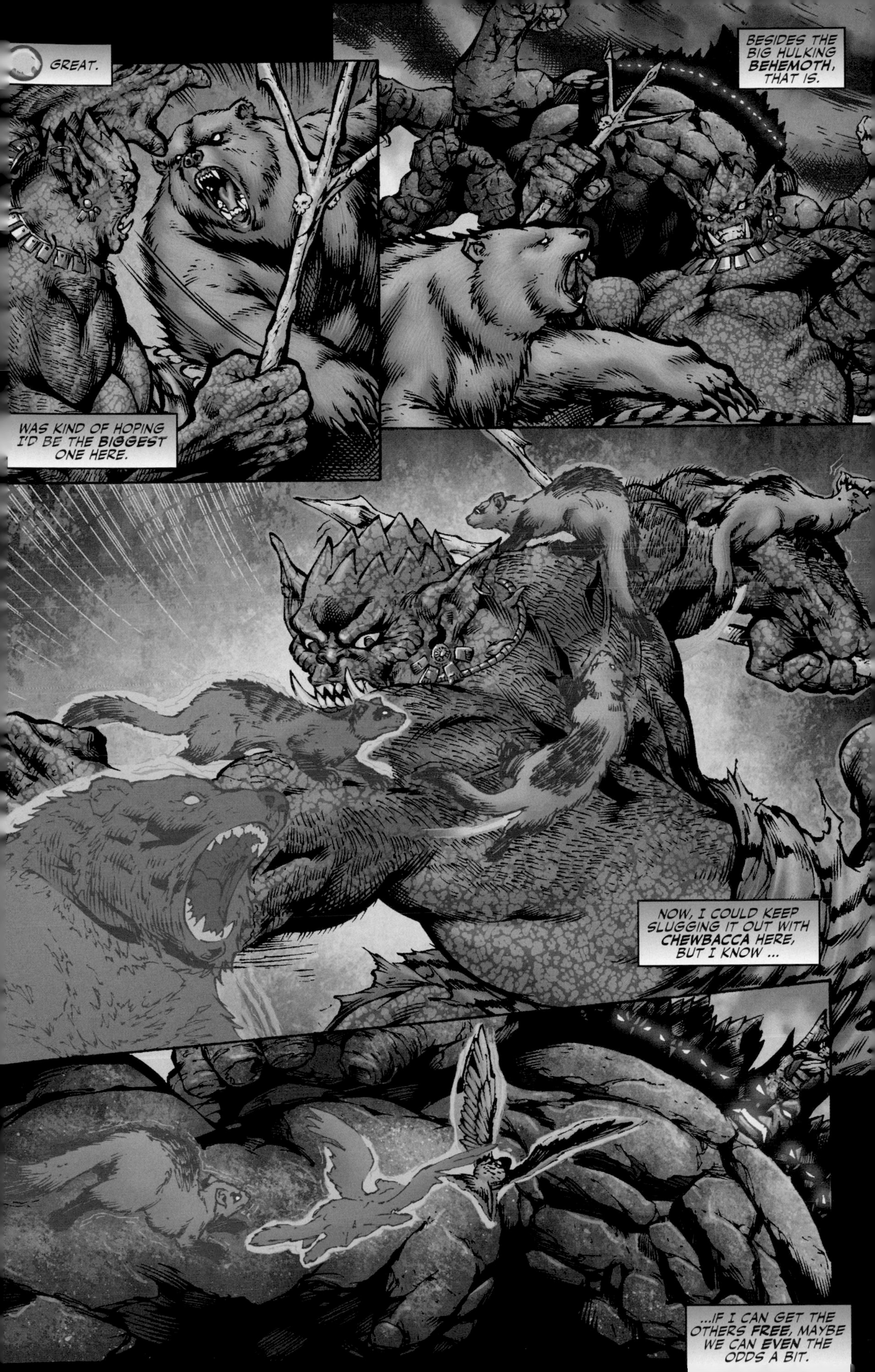
GREAT.
BESIDES THE BIG HULKING BEHEMOTH, THAT IS.
WAS KIND OF HOPING I'D BE THE BIGGEST ONE HERE.
NOW, I COULD KEEP SLUGGING IT OUT WITH CHEWBACCA HERE, BUT I KNOW ...
...IF I CAN GET THE OTHERS FREE, MAYBE WE CAN EVEN THE ODDS A BIT.

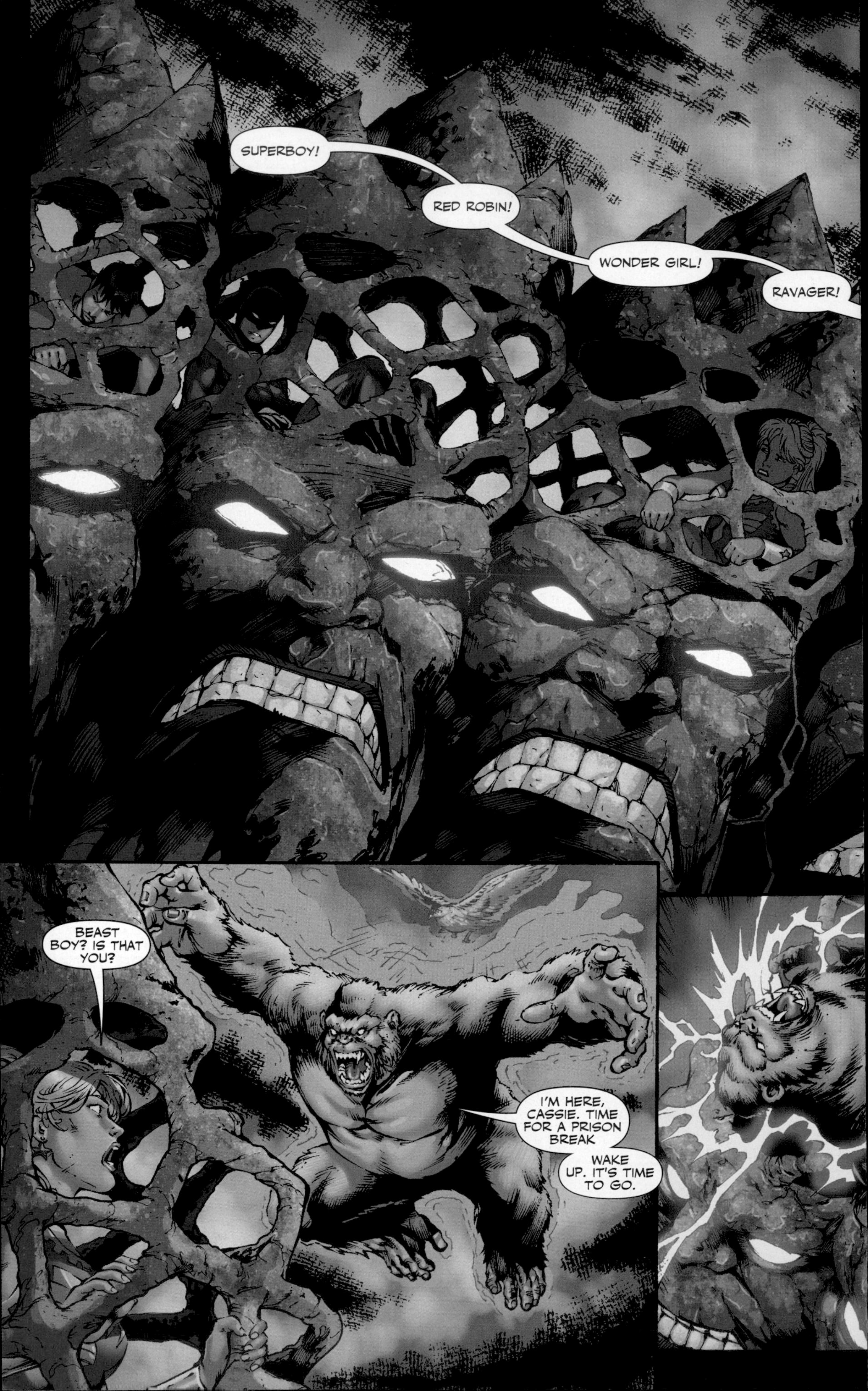
SUPERBOY!
RED ROBIN!
WONDER GIRL!
RAVAGER!
BEAST BOY? IS THAT YOU?
I'M HERE, CASSIE. TIME FOR A PRISON BREAK
WAKE UP. IT'S TIME TO GO.

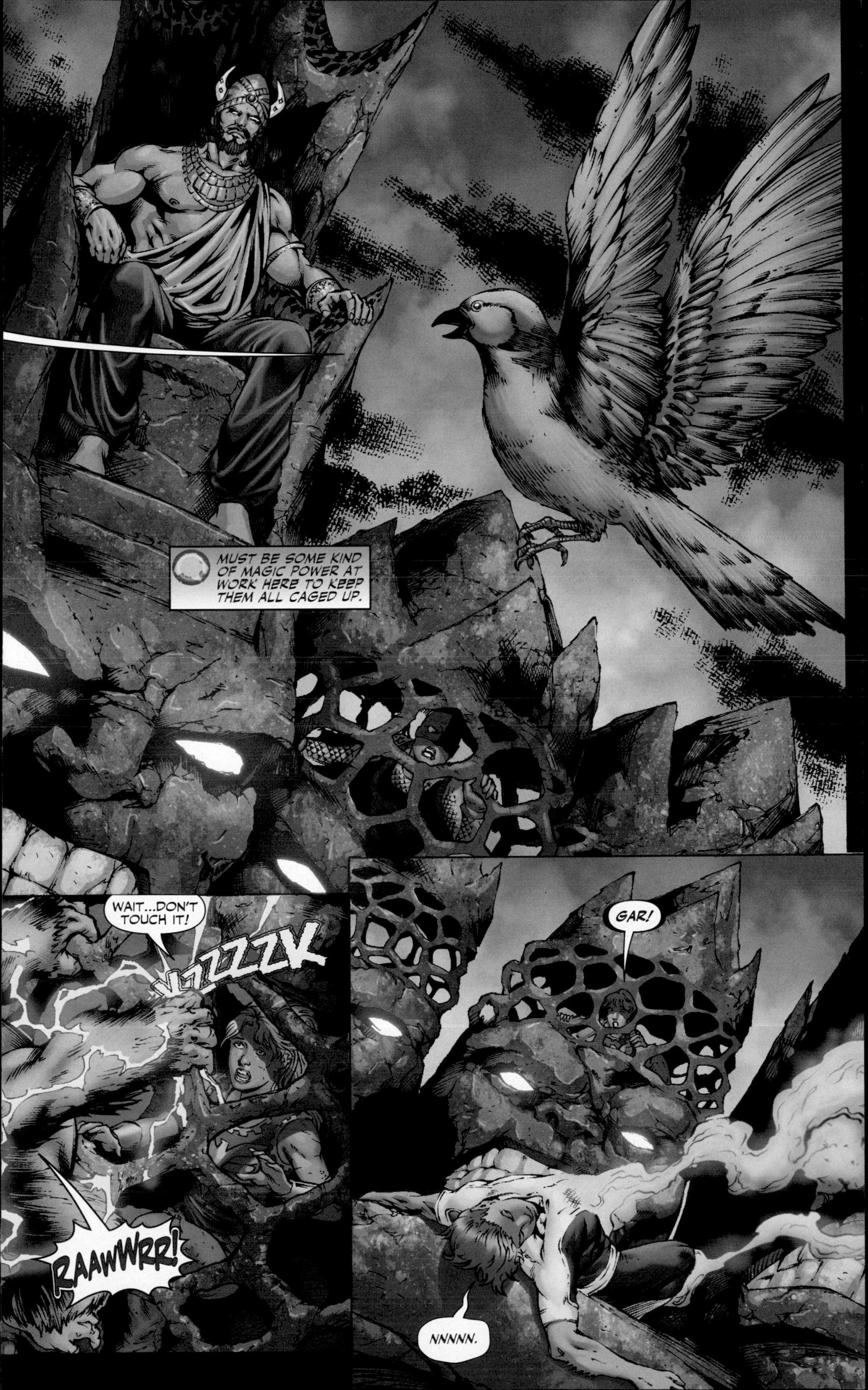
MUST BE SOME KIND OF MAGIC POWER AT WORK HERE TO KEEP THEM ALL CAGED UP.
WAIT...DON'T TOUCH IT!
VZZZZZK
RAAWWRR!
GAR!
NNNNN.

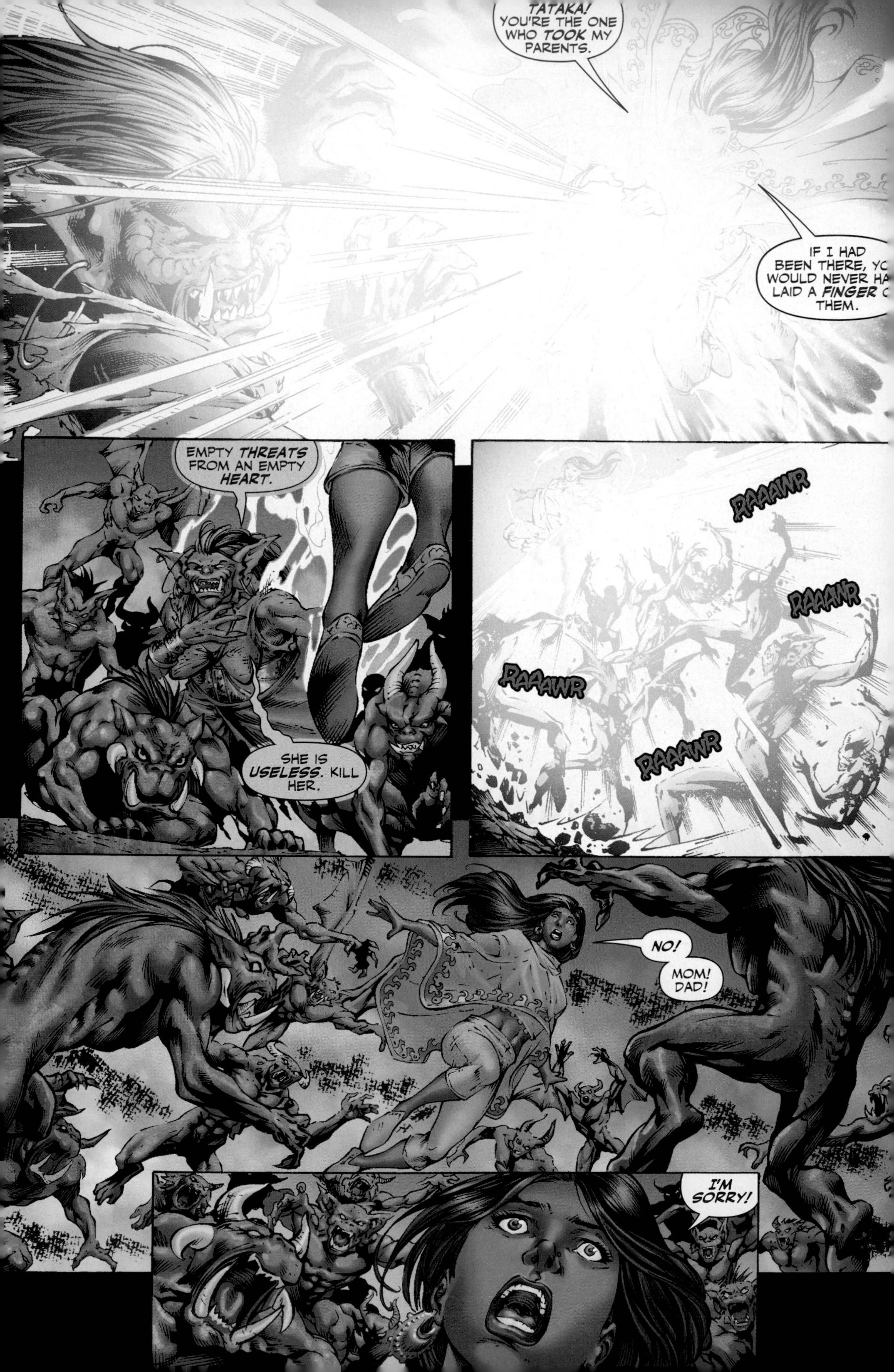

TATAKA! YOU'RE THE ONE WHO TOOK MY PARENTS.
IF I HAD BEEN THERE, YO WOULD NEVER HA LAID A FINGER O THEM.
EMPTY THREATS FROM AN EMPTY HEART.
SHE IS USELESS. KILL HER.
RAAAWR
RAAAWR
RAAAWR
RAAAWR
NO!
MOM! DAD!
I'M SORRY!

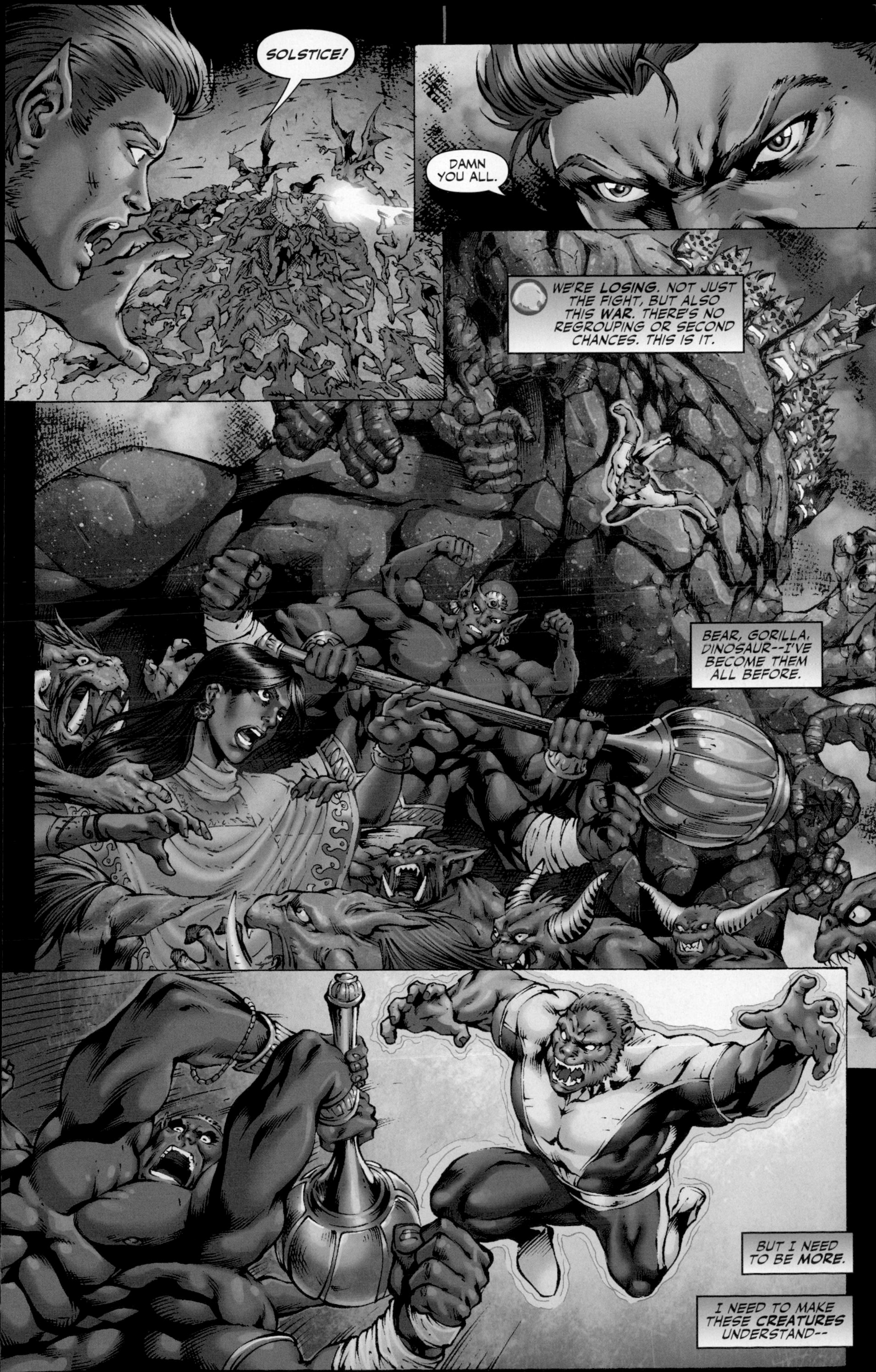
SOLSTICE!
DAMN YOU ALL.
WE'RE LOSING. NOT JUST THE FIGHT, BUT ALSO THIS WAR. THERE'S NO REGROUPING OR SECOND CHANCES. THIS IS IT.
BEAR, GORILLA, DINOSAUR--I'VE BECOME THEM ALL BEFORE.
BUT I NEED TO BE MORE.
I NEED TO MAKE THESE CREATURES UNDERSTAND--

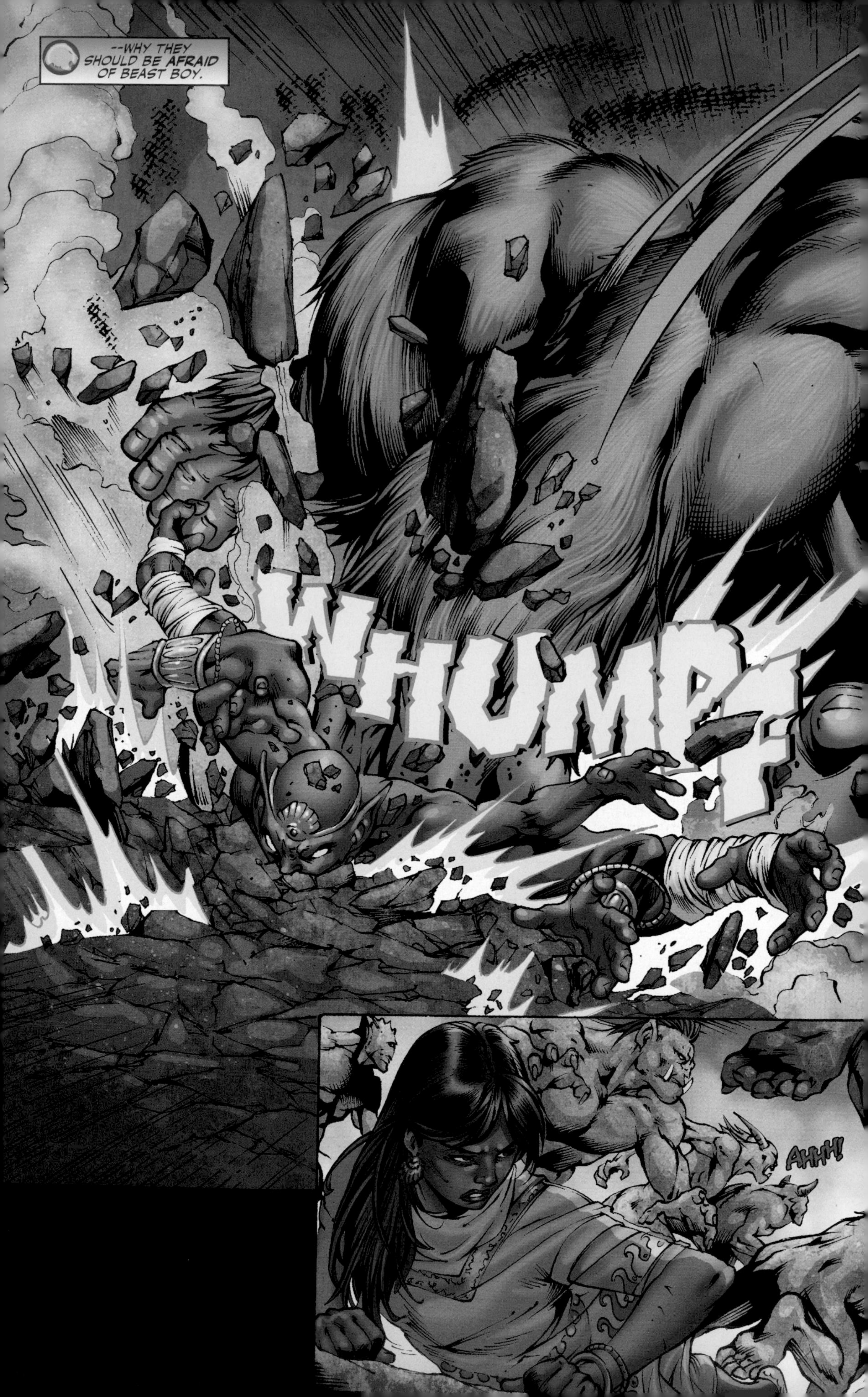
--WHY THEY SHOULD BE AFRAID OF BEAST BOY.
WHUMPF
AHHH!

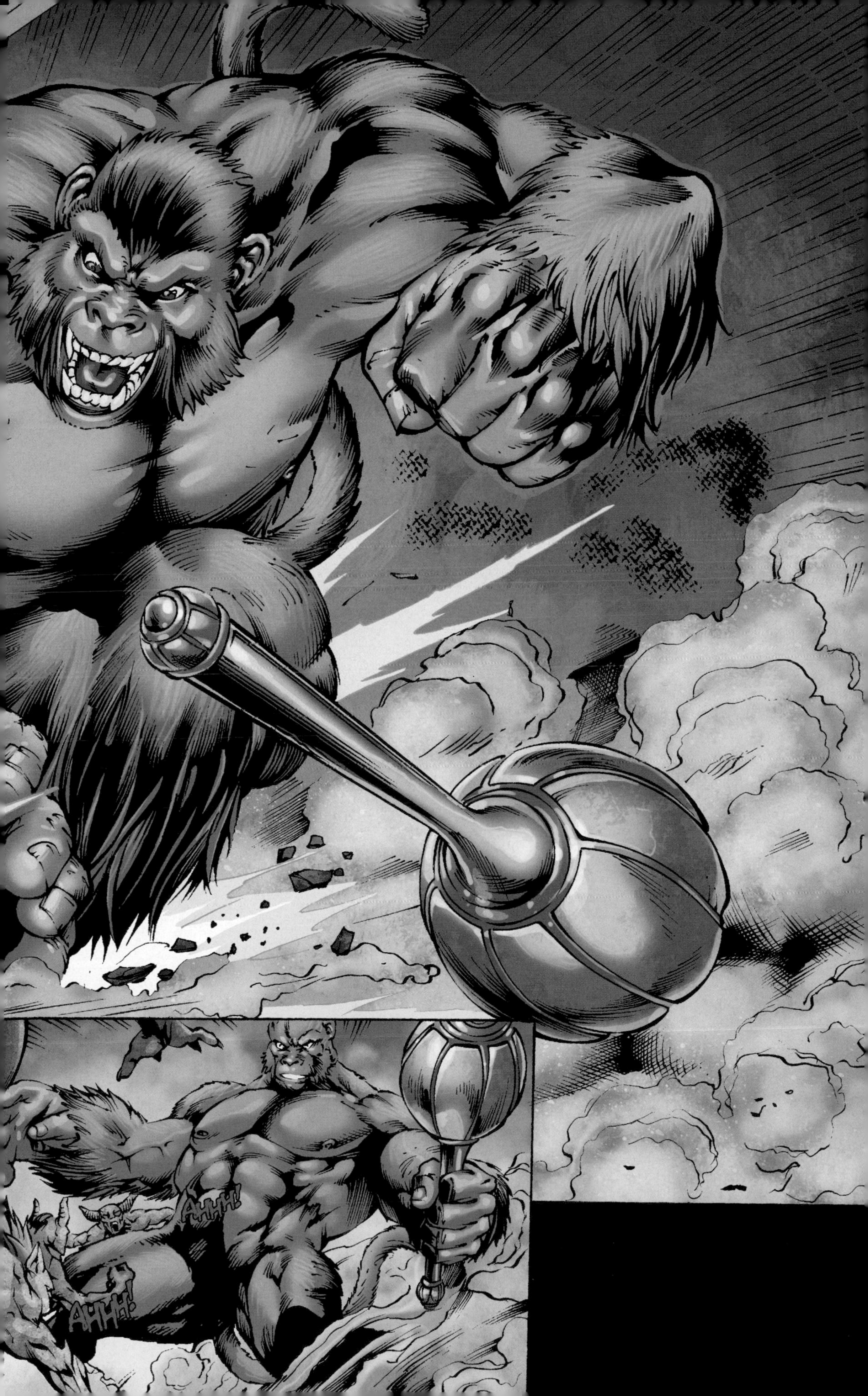
AHHH!
AHHH!

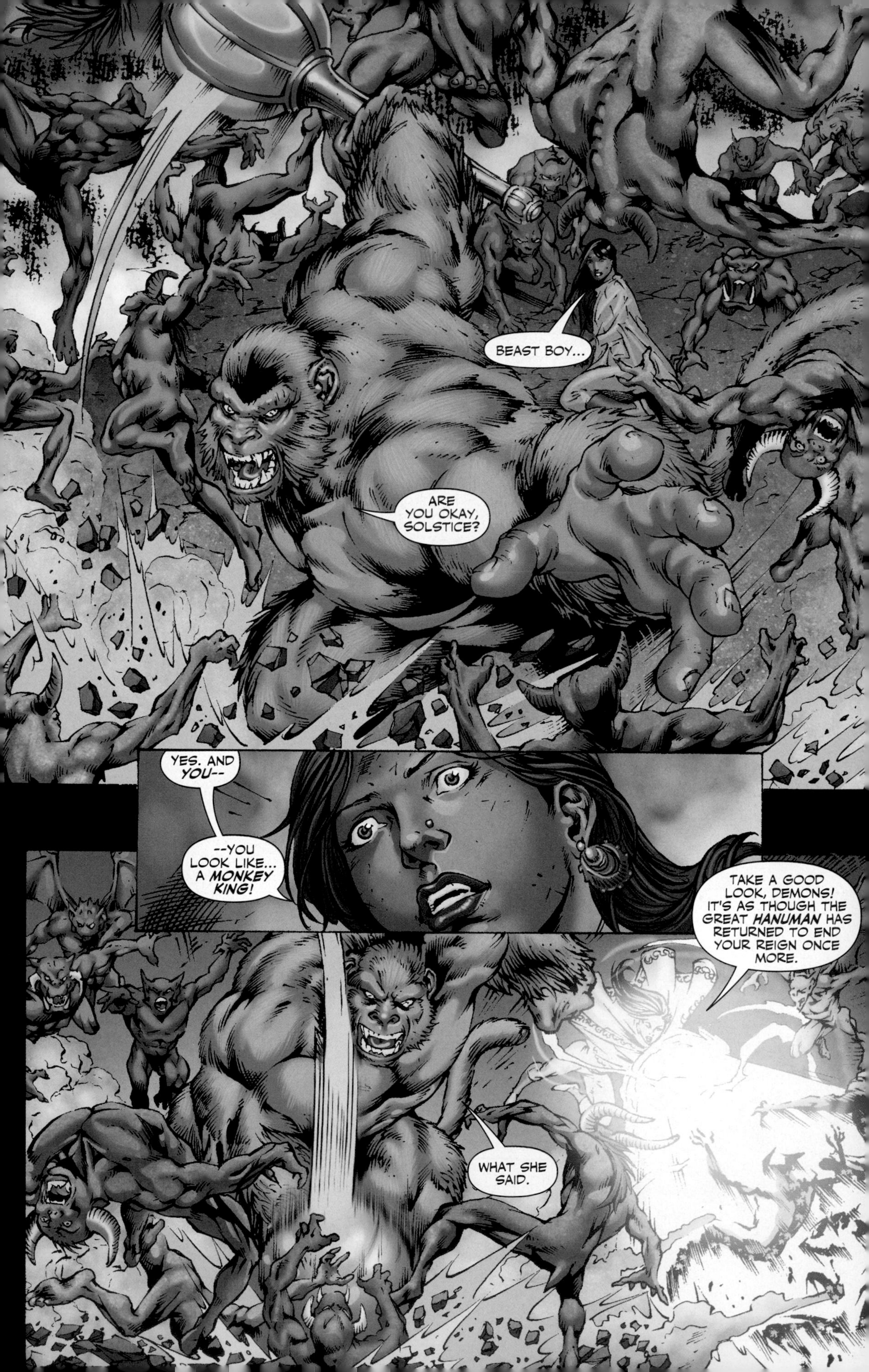
BEAST BOY...
ARE YOU OKAY, SOLSTICE?
YES. AND *YOU*--
--YOU LOOK LIKE... A *MONKEY KING!*
TAKE A GOOD LOOK, DEMONS! IT'S AS THOUGH THE GREAT *HANUMAN* HAS RETURNED TO END YOUR REIGN ONCE MORE.
WHAT SHE SAID.

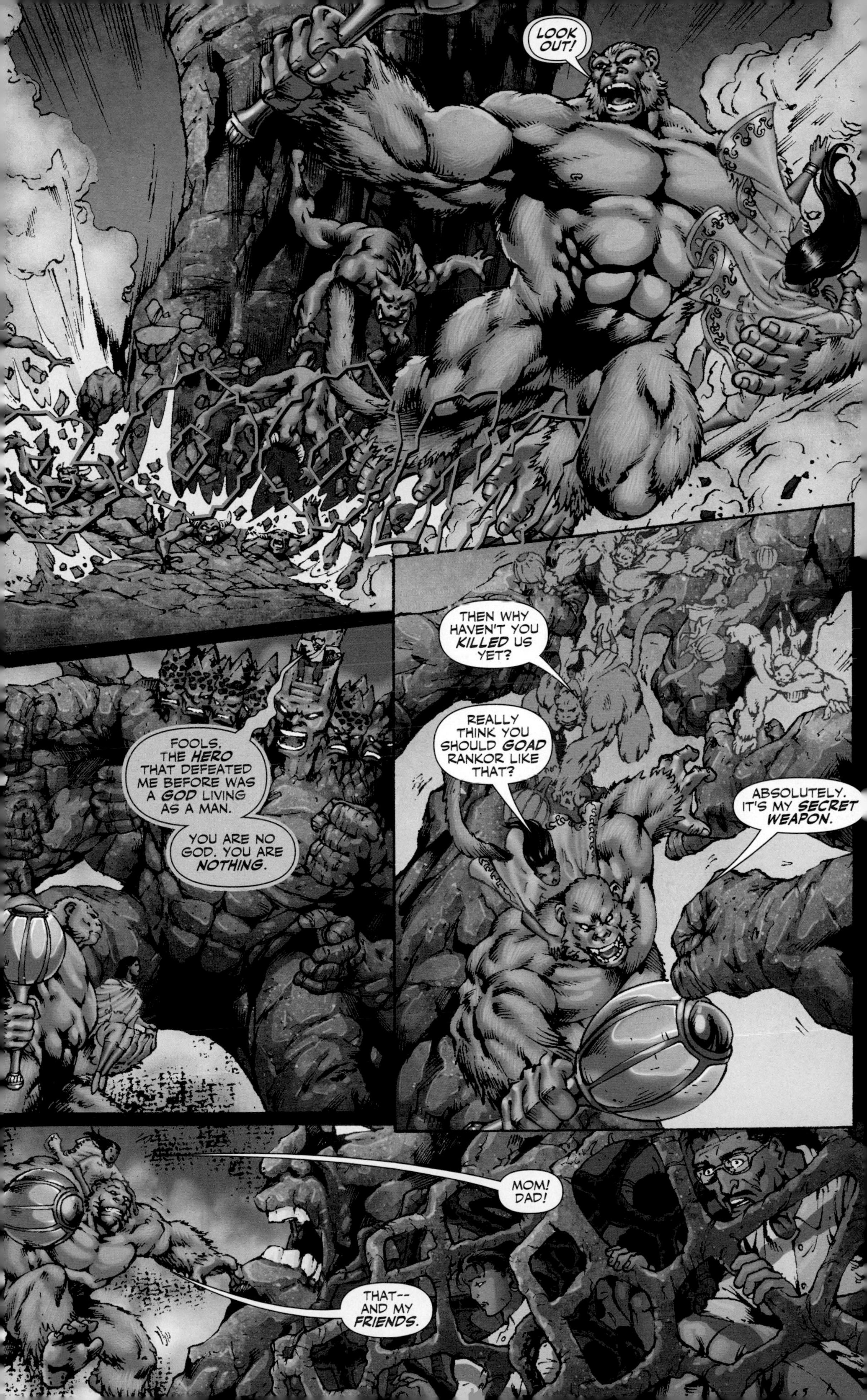
LOOK OUT!
THEN WHY HAVEN'T YOU KILLED US YET?
FOOLS. THE HERO THAT DEFEATED ME BEFORE WAS A GOD LIVING AS A MAN.
YOU ARE NO GOD. YOU ARE NOTHING.
REALLY THINK YOU SHOULD GOAD RANKOR LIKE THAT?
ABSOLUTELY. IT'S MY SECRET WEAPON.
MOM! DAD!
THAT-- AND MY FRIENDS.

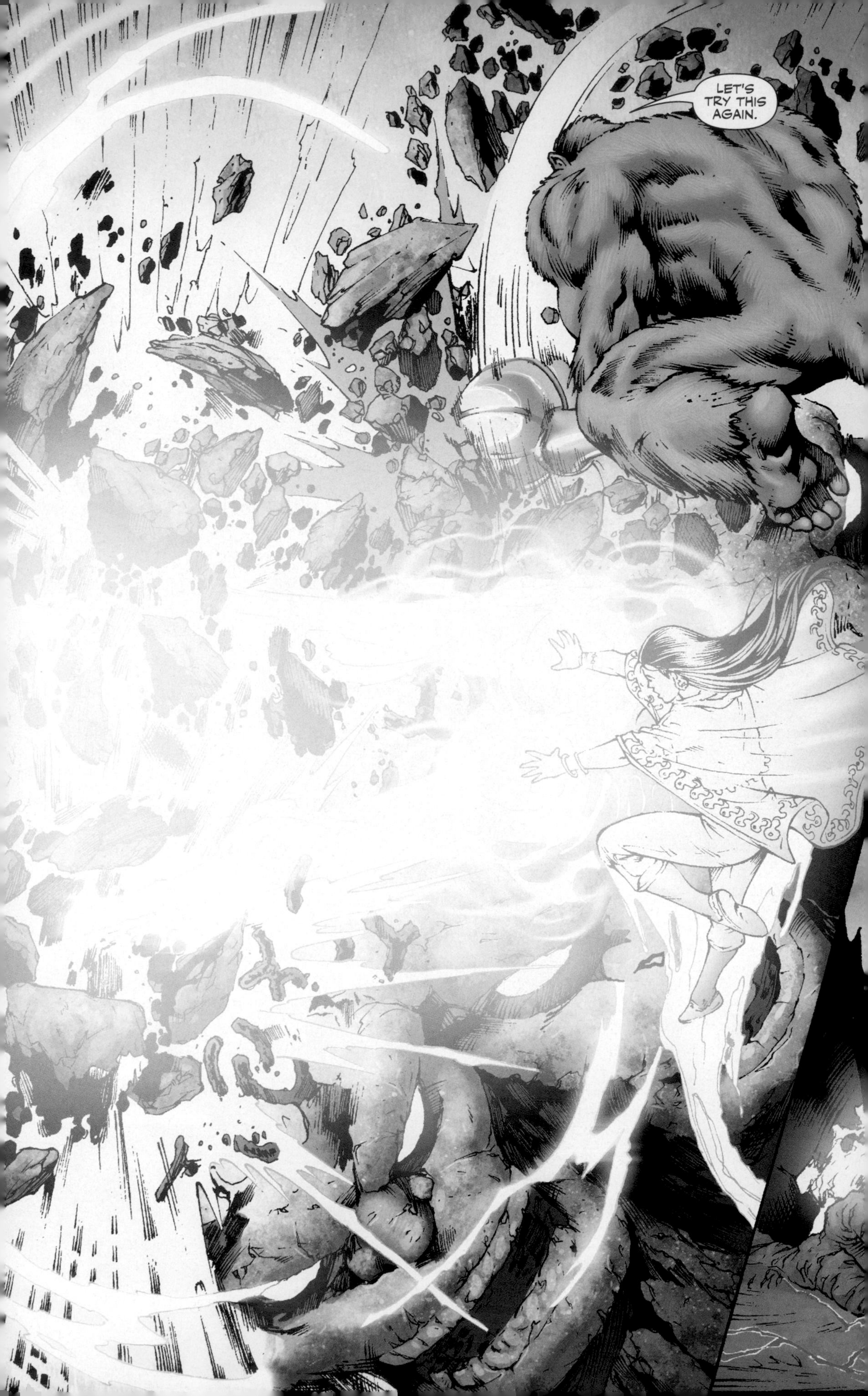
LET'S TRY THIS AGAIN.

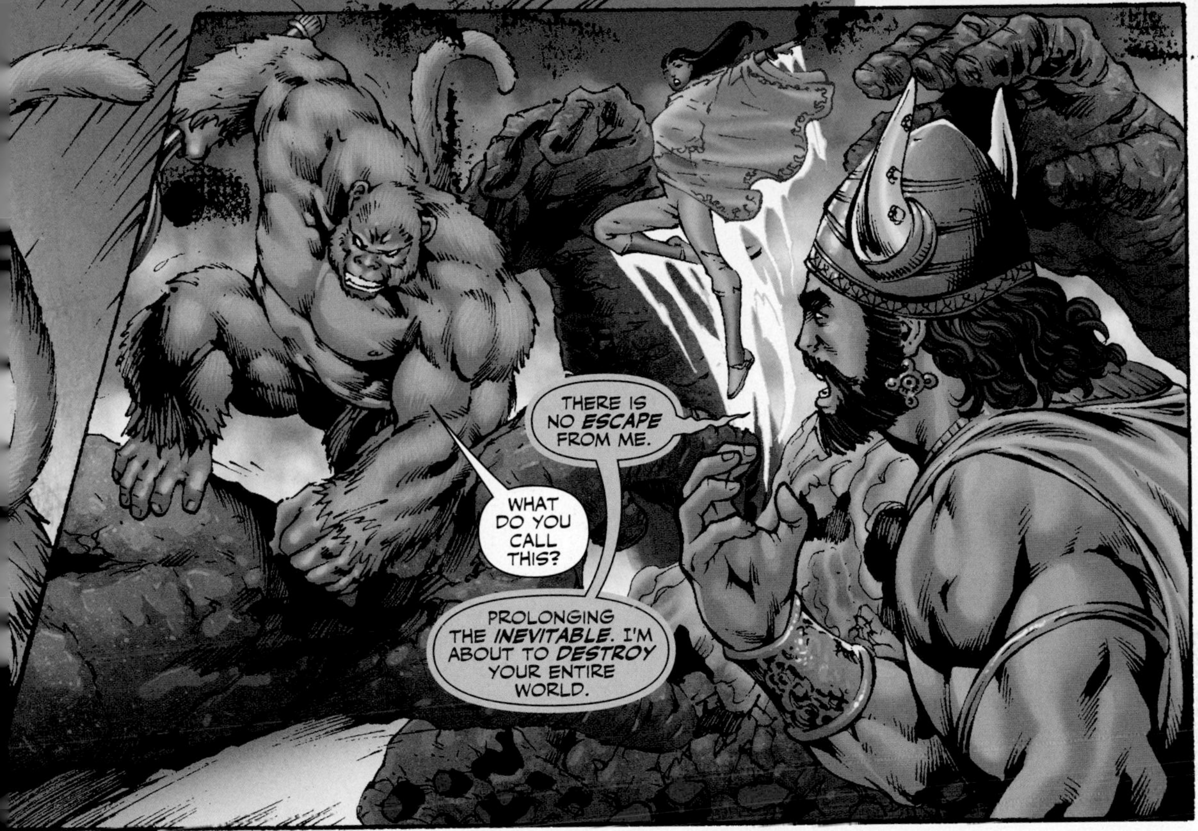
THERE IS NO ESCAPE FROM ME.
WHAT DO YOU CALL THIS?
PROLONGING THE INEVITABLE. I'M ABOUT TO DESTROY YOUR ENTIRE WORLD.

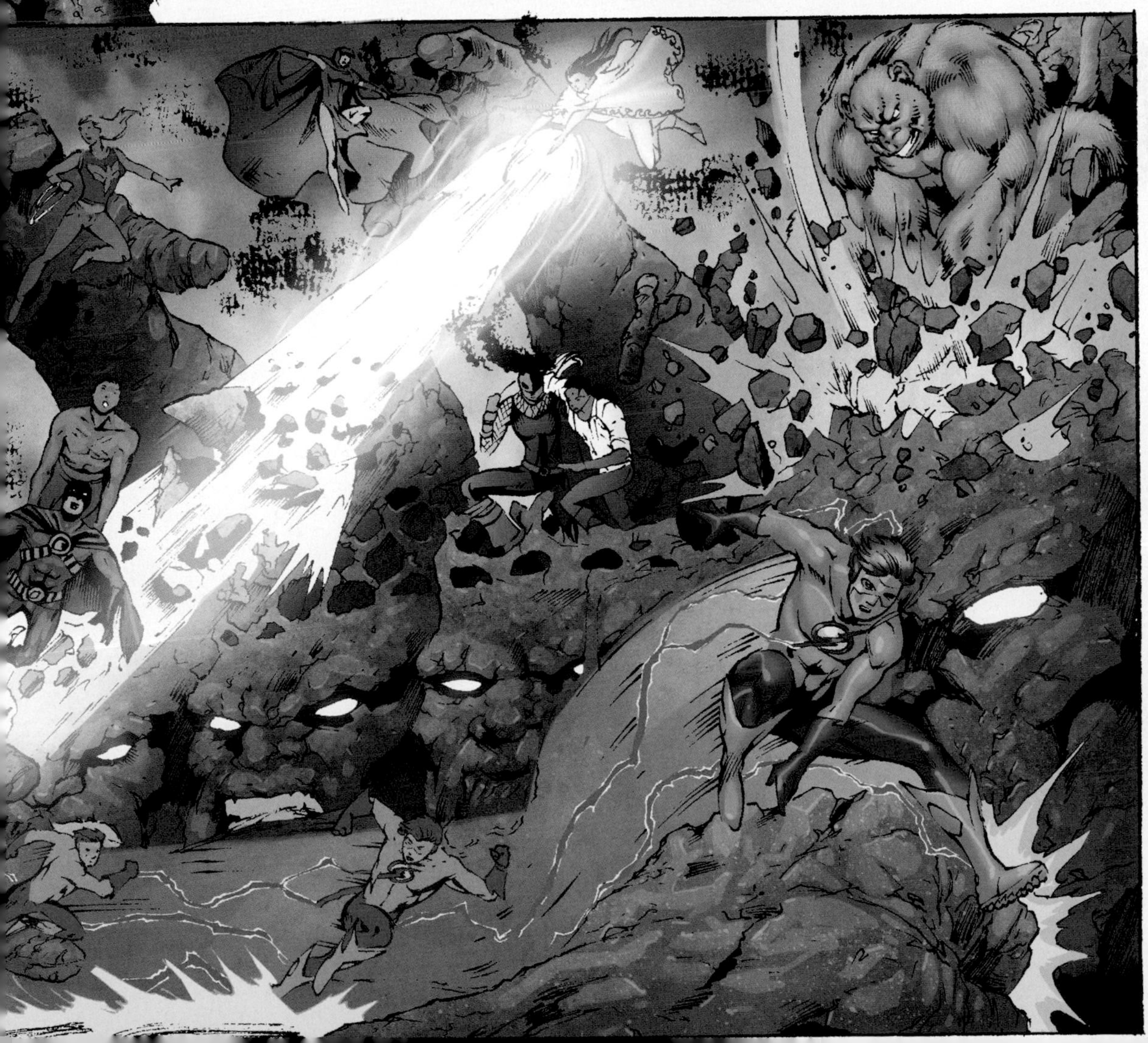

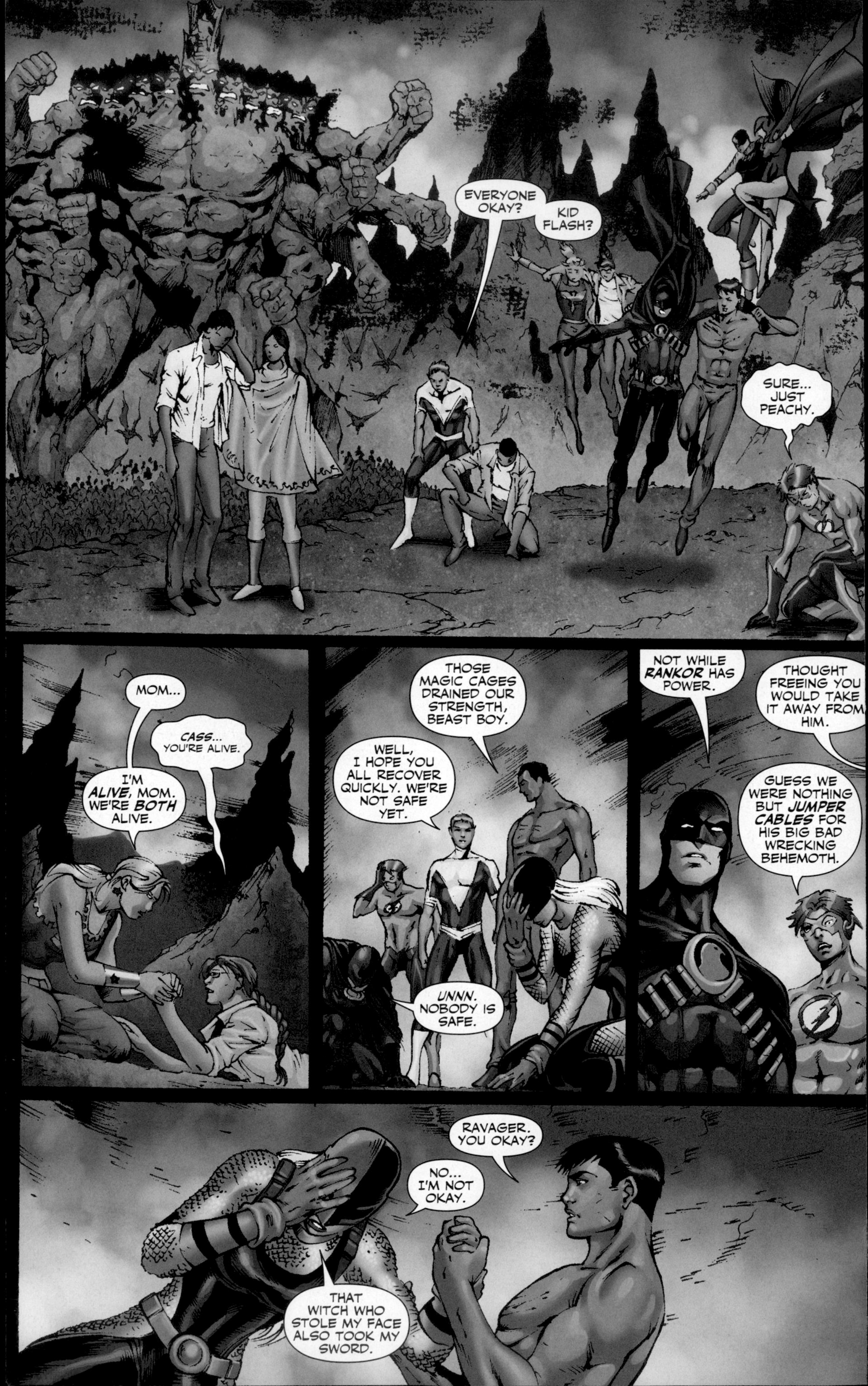
EVERYONE OKAY?
KID FLASH?
SURE... JUST PEACHY.
MOM...
CASS... YOU'RE ALIVE.
I'M ALIVE, MOM. WE'RE BOTH ALIVE.
THOSE MAGIC CAGES DRAINED OUR STRENGTH, BEAST BOY.
WELL, I HOPE YOU ALL RECOVER QUICKLY. WE'RE NOT SAFE YET.
UNNN. NOBODY IS SAFE.
NOT WHILE RANKOR HAS POWER.
THOUGHT FREEING YOU WOULD TAKE IT AWAY FROM HIM.
GUESS WE WERE NOTHING BUT JUMPER CABLES FOR HIS BIG BAD WRECKING BEHEMOTH.
RAVAGER. YOU OKAY?
NO... I'M NOT OKAY.
THAT WITCH WHO STOLE MY FACE ALSO TOOK MY SWORD.

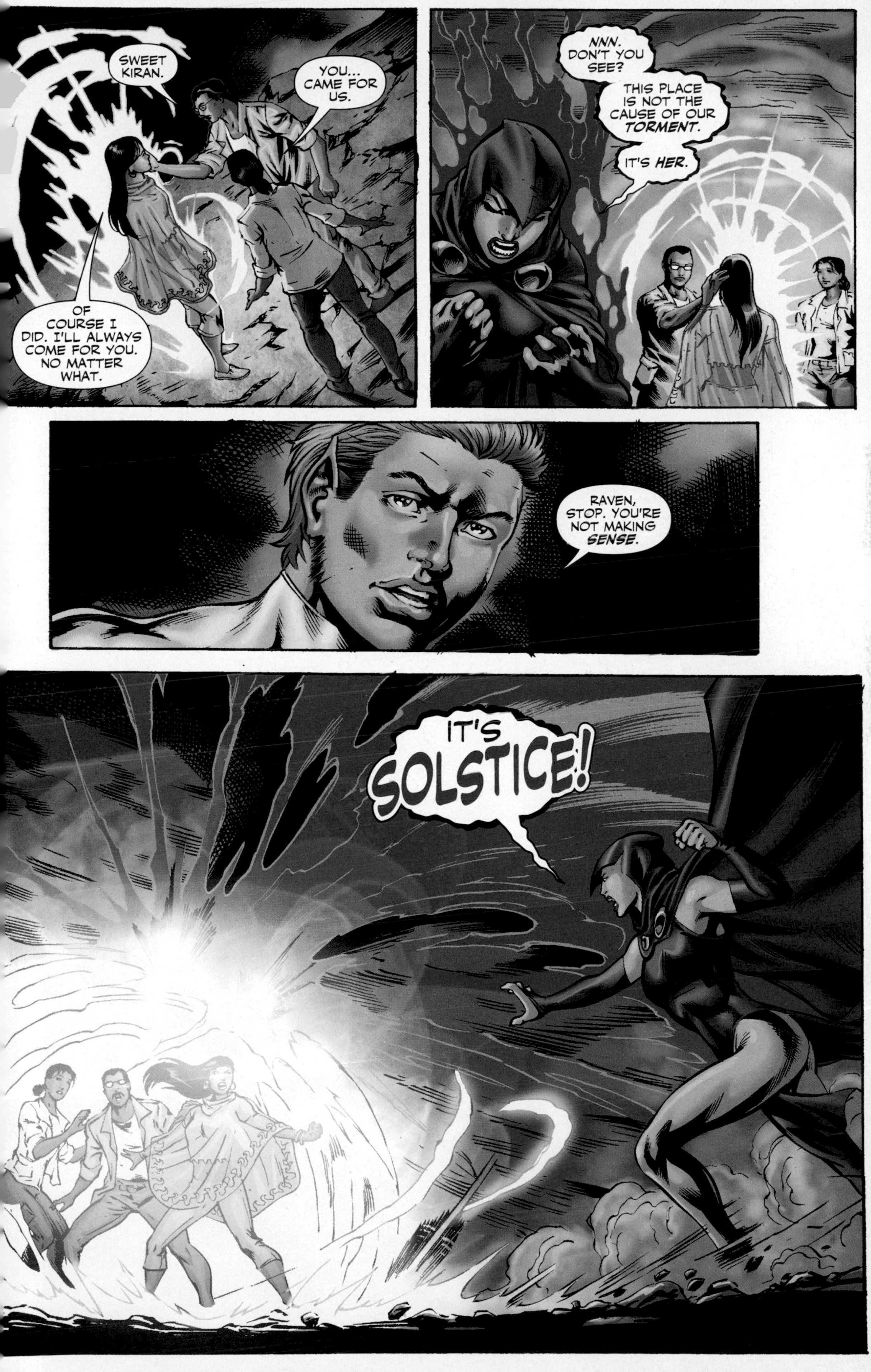
SWEET KIRAN.
YOU... CAME FOR US.
OF COURSE I DID. I'LL ALWAYS COME FOR YOU. NO MATTER WHAT.
NNN. DON'T YOU SEE?
THIS PLACE IS NOT THE CAUSE OF OUR TORMENT.
IT'S HER.
RAVEN, STOP. YOU'RE NOT MAKING SENSE.
IT'S SOLSTICE!

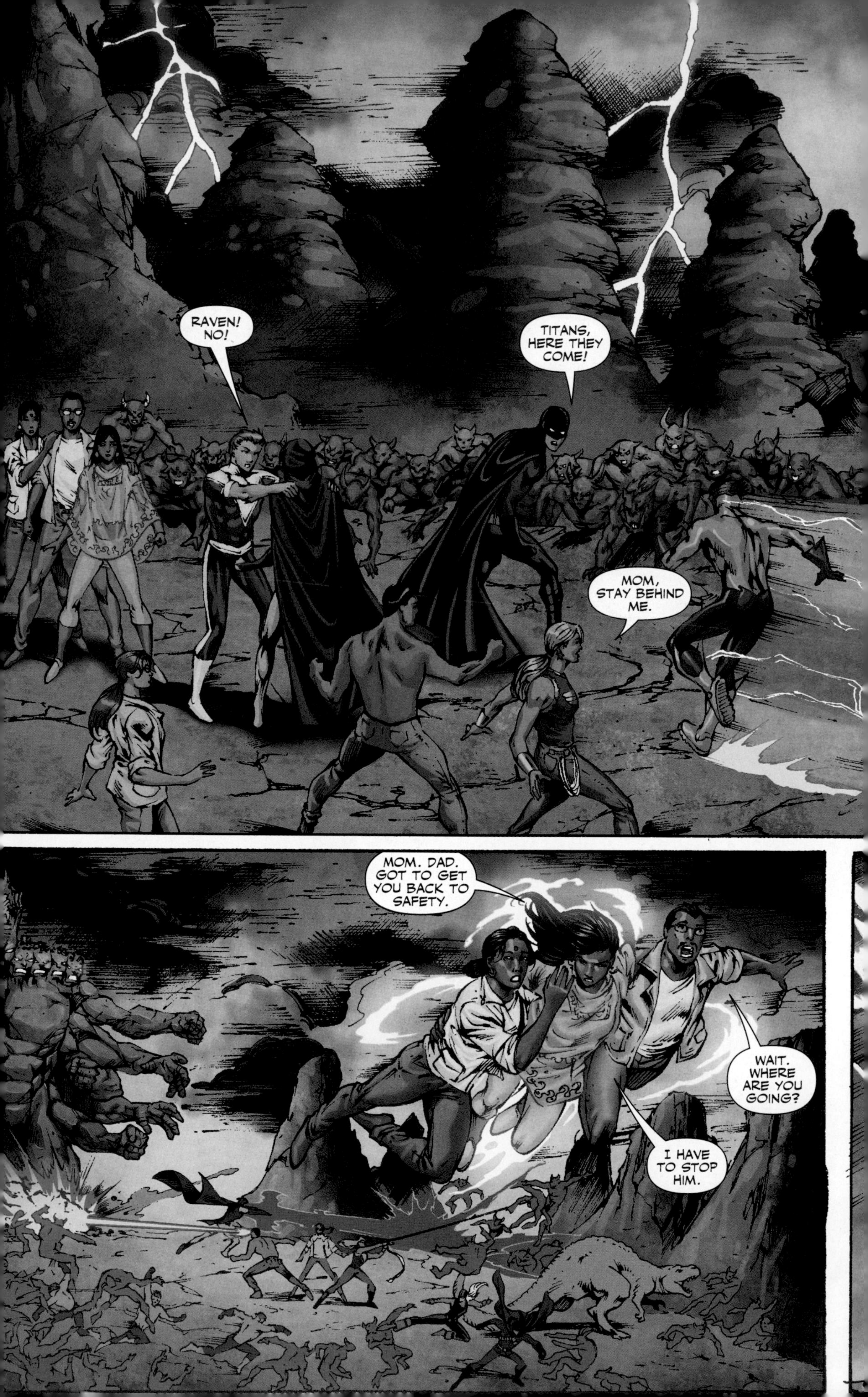
RAVEN! NO!
TITANS, HERE THEY COME!
MOM, STAY BEHIND ME.
MOM. DAD. GOT TO GET YOU BACK TO SAFETY.
WAIT. WHERE ARE YOU GOING?
I HAVE TO STOP HIM.

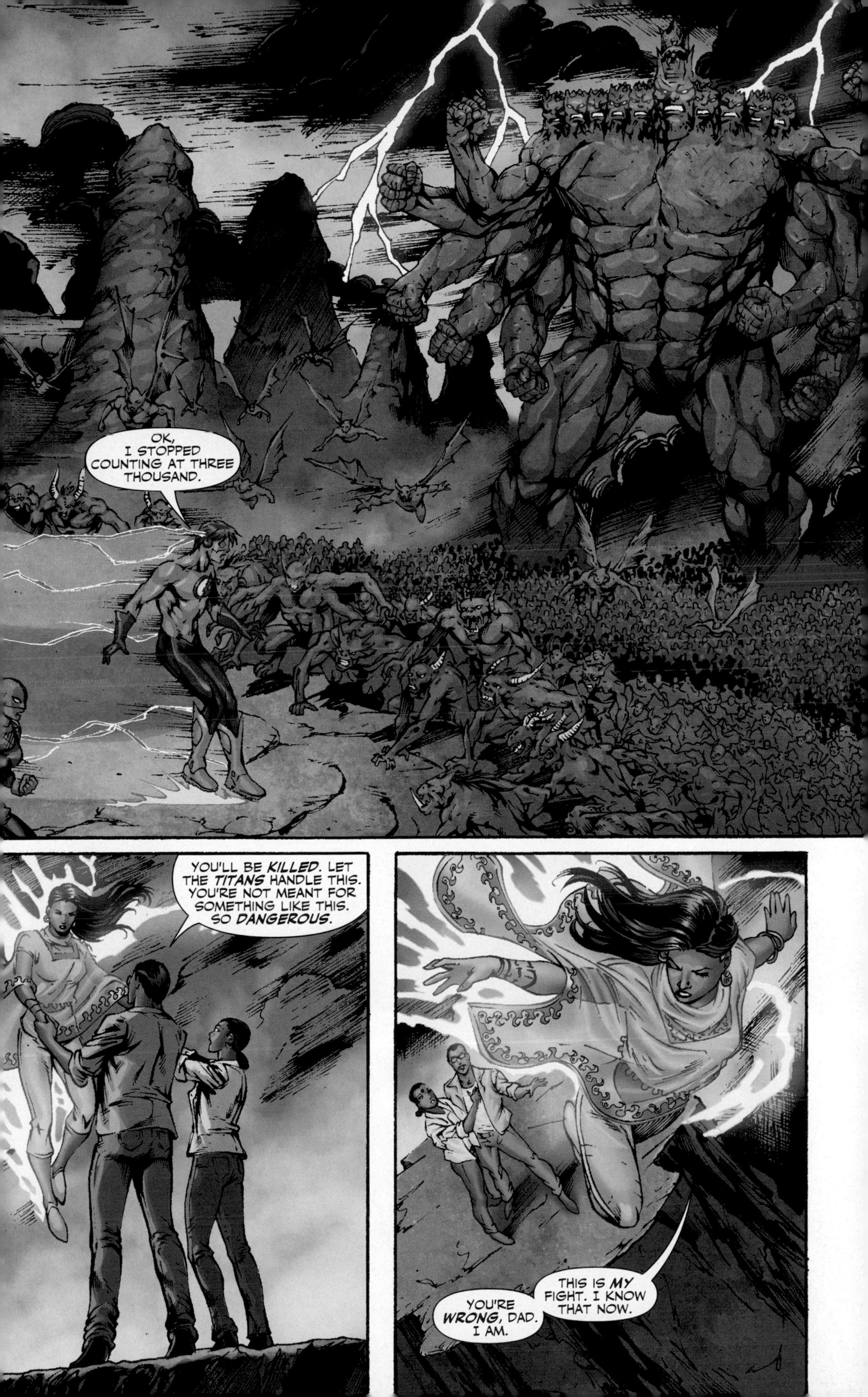
OK, I STOPPED COUNTING AT THREE THOUSAND.
YOU'LL BE KILLED. LET THE TITANS HANDLE THIS. YOU'RE NOT MEANT FOR SOMETHING LIKE THIS. SO DANGEROUS.
THIS IS MY FIGHT. I KNOW THAT NOW.
YOU'RE WRONG, DAD. I AM.

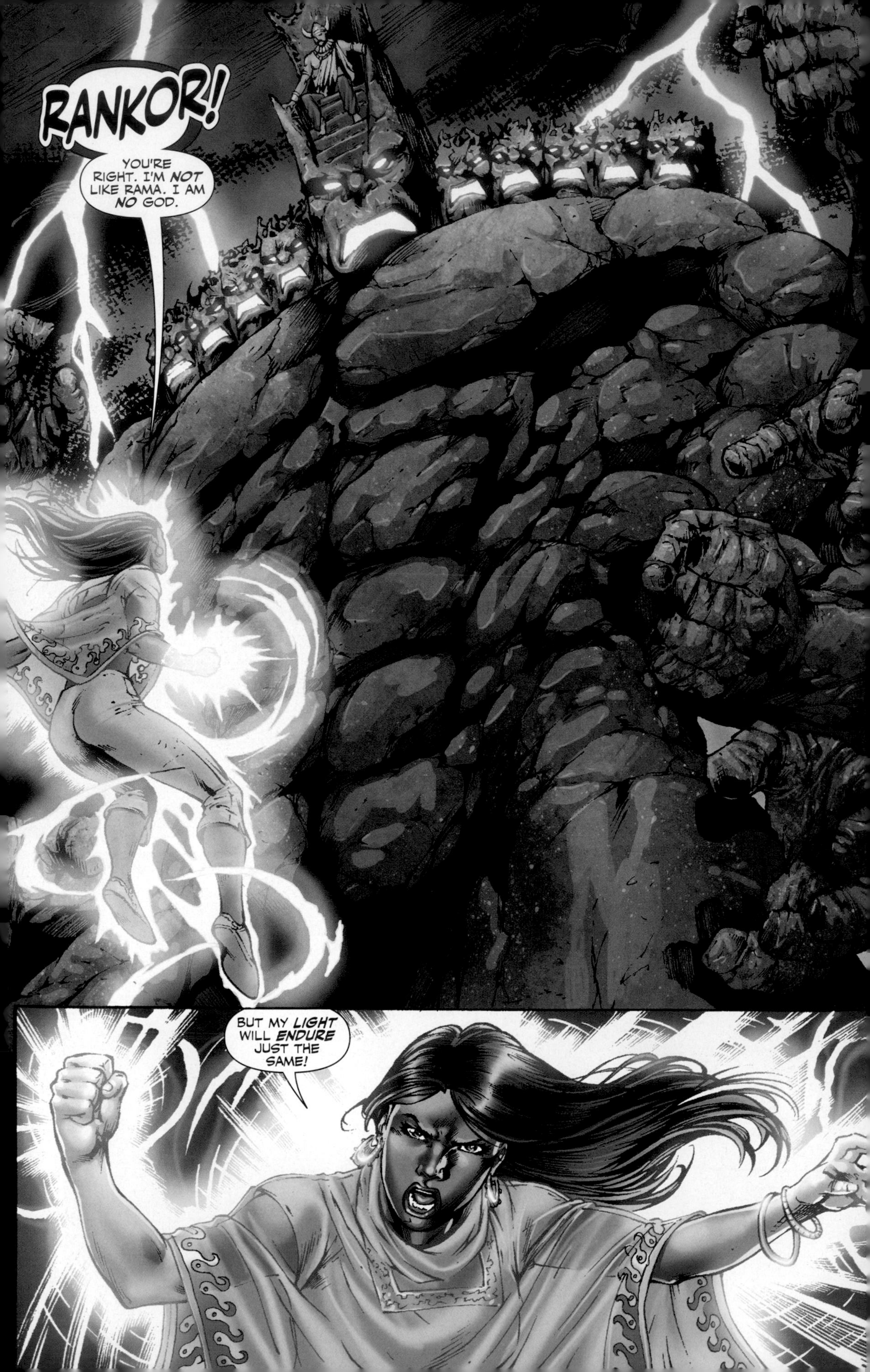
RANKOR!
YOU'RE RIGHT. I'M NOT LIKE RAMA. I AM NO GOD.
BUT MY LIGHT WILL ENDURE JUST THE SAME!

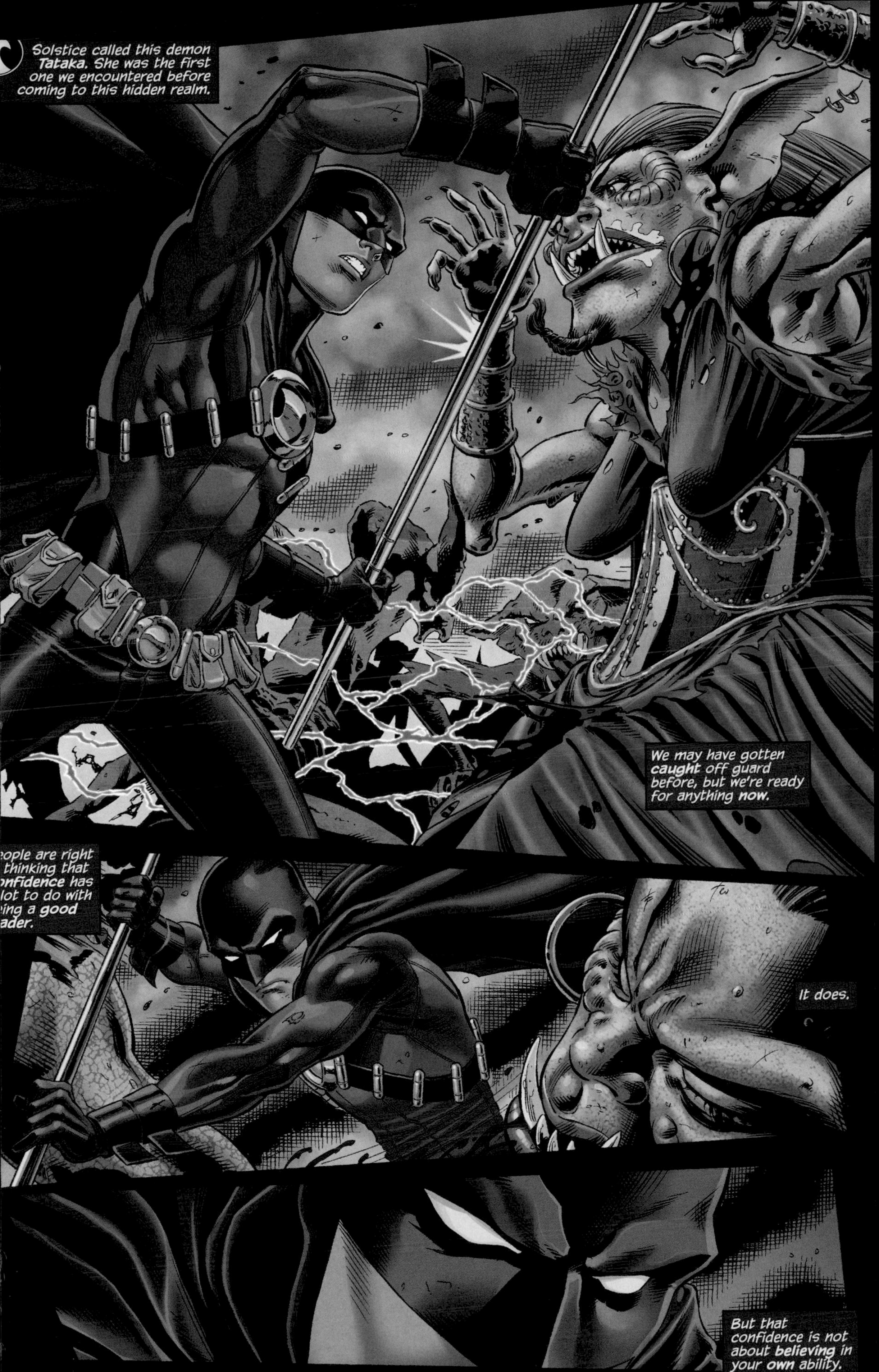
Solstice called this demon **Tataka**. She was the first one we encountered before coming to this hidden realm.
We may have gotten **caught** off guard before, but we're ready for anything **now**.
eople are right thinking that onfidence has lot to do with ing a **good** ader.
It does.
But that confidence is not about **believing** in your **own** ability.

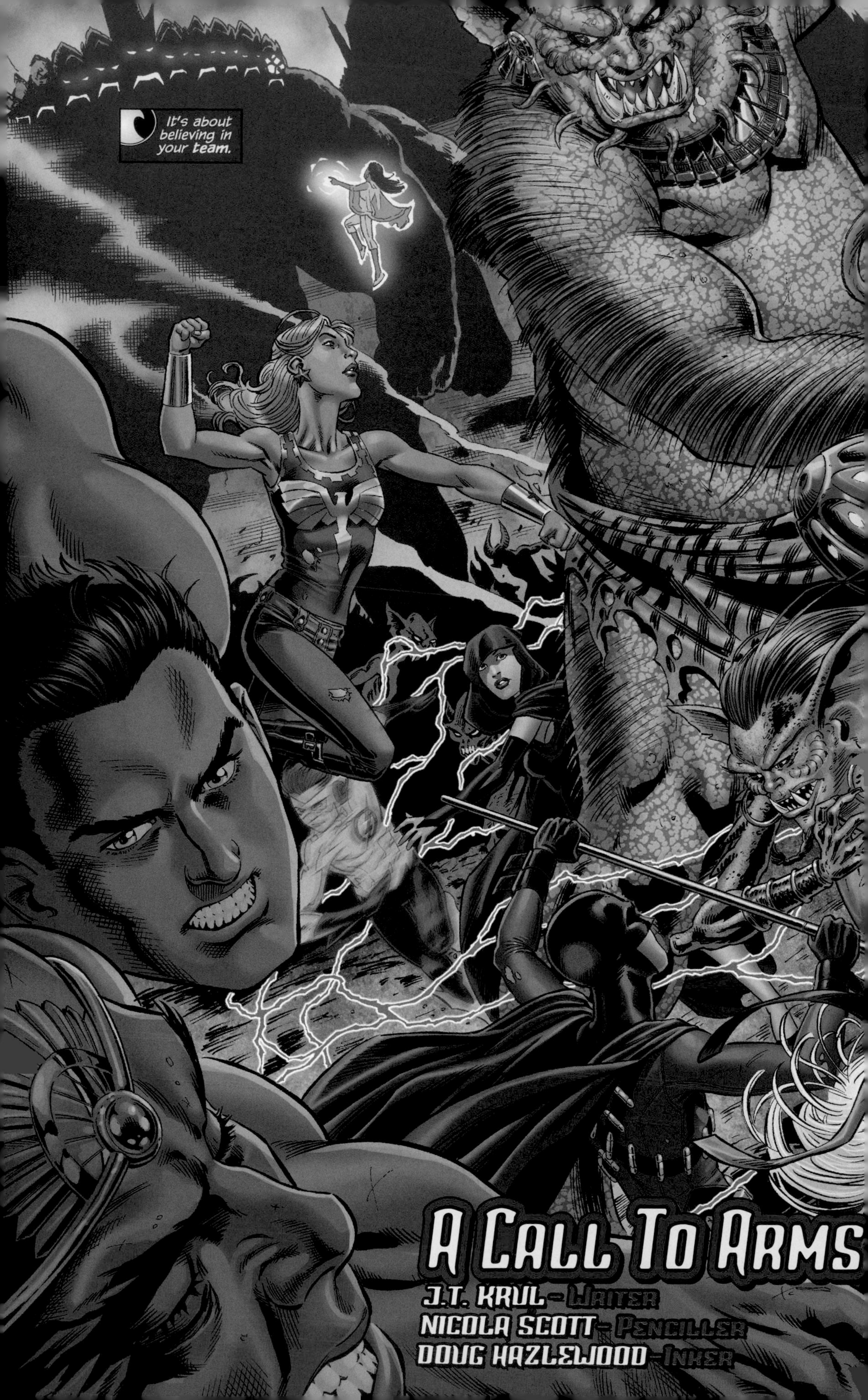
It's about believing in your team.
A CALL TO ARMS
J.T. KRUL - WRITER
NICOLA SCOTT - PENCILLER
DOUG HAZLEWOOD - INKER

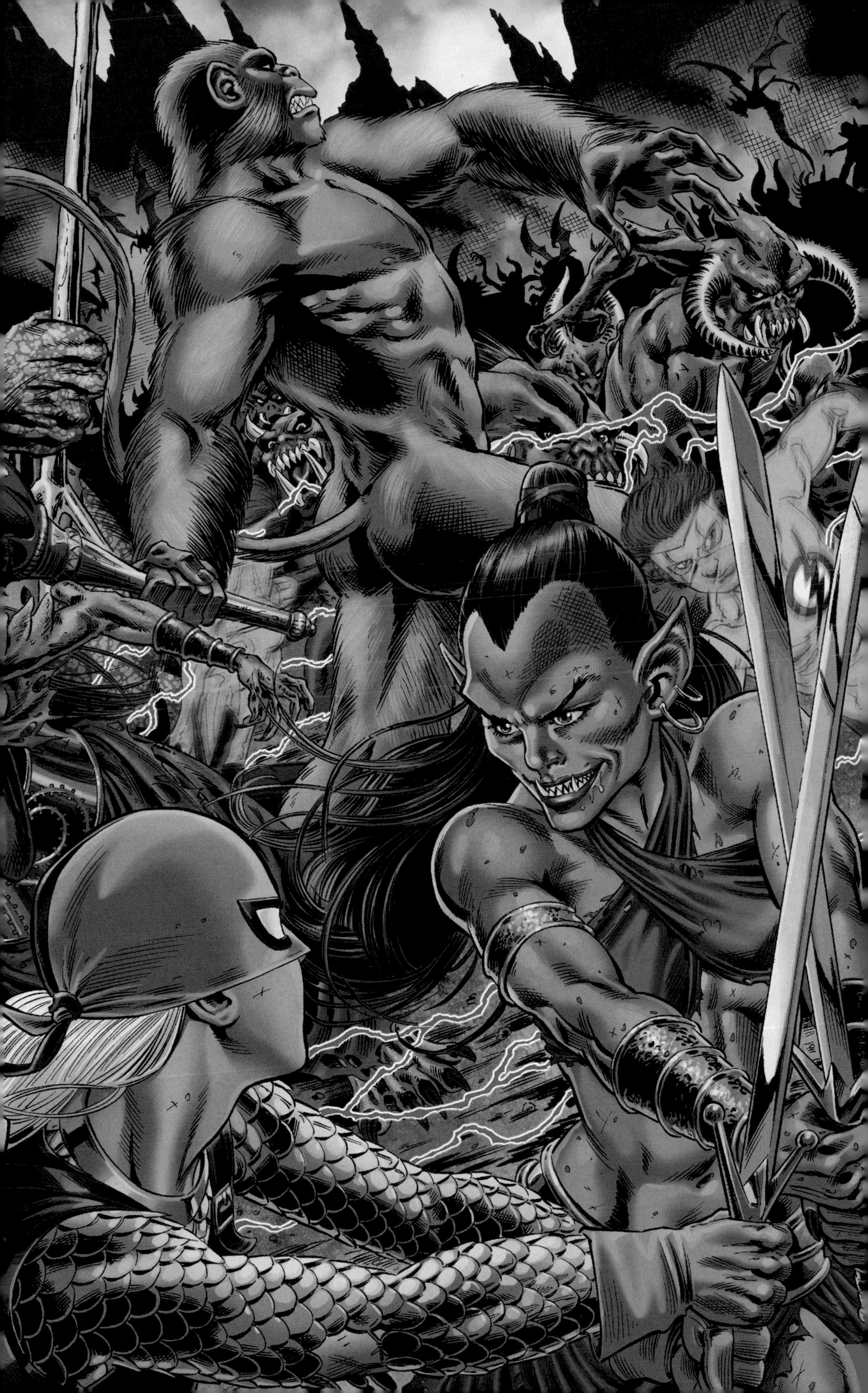

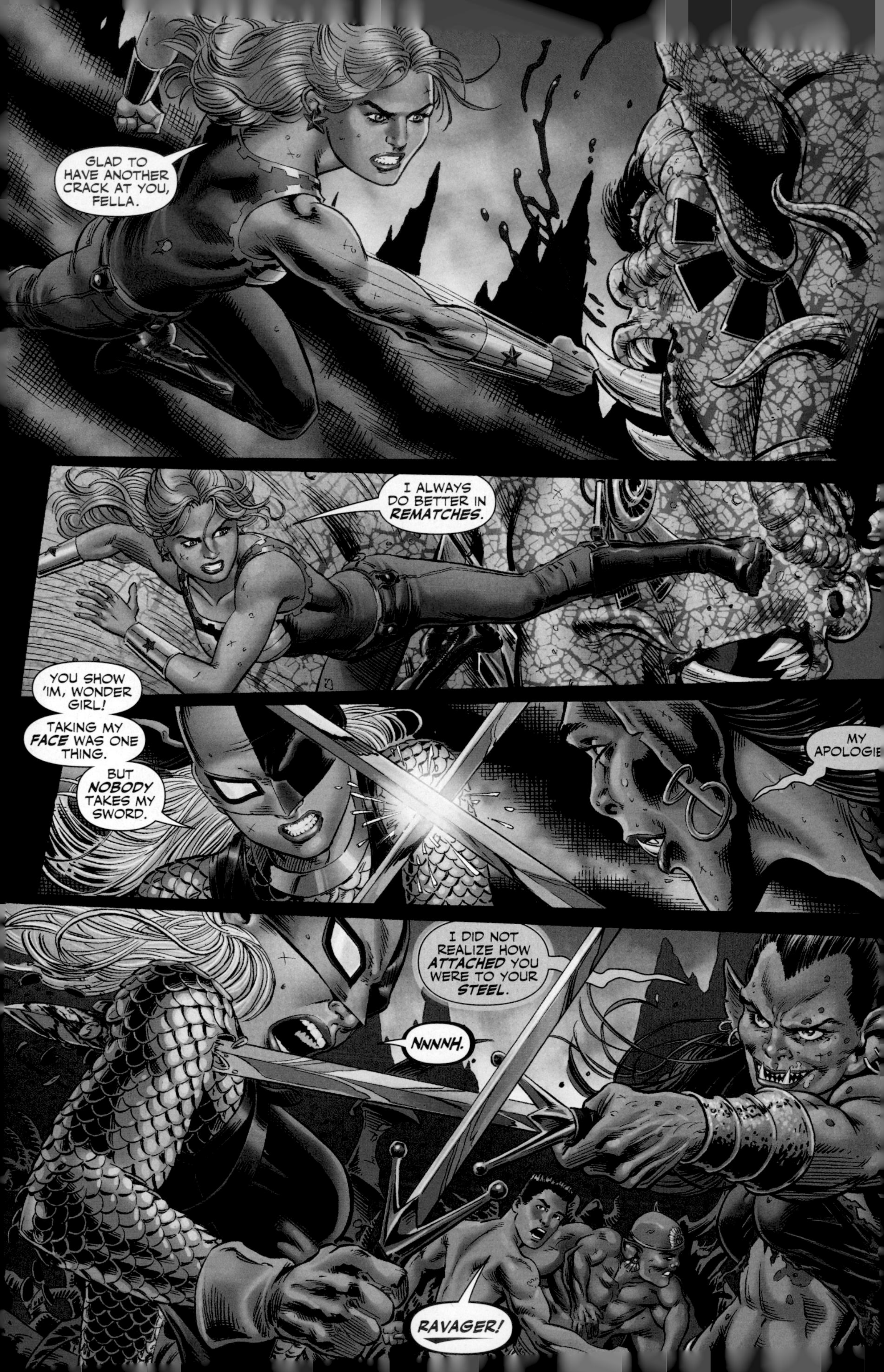
GLAD TO HAVE ANOTHER CRACK AT YOU, FELLA.
I ALWAYS DO BETTER IN REMATCHES.
YOU SHOW 'IM, WONDER GIRL!
TAKING MY FACE WAS ONE THING.
BUT NOBODY TAKES MY SWORD.
MY APOLOGIE
I DID NOT REALIZE HOW ATTACHED YOU WERE TO YOUR STEEL.
NNNNH.
RAVAGER!

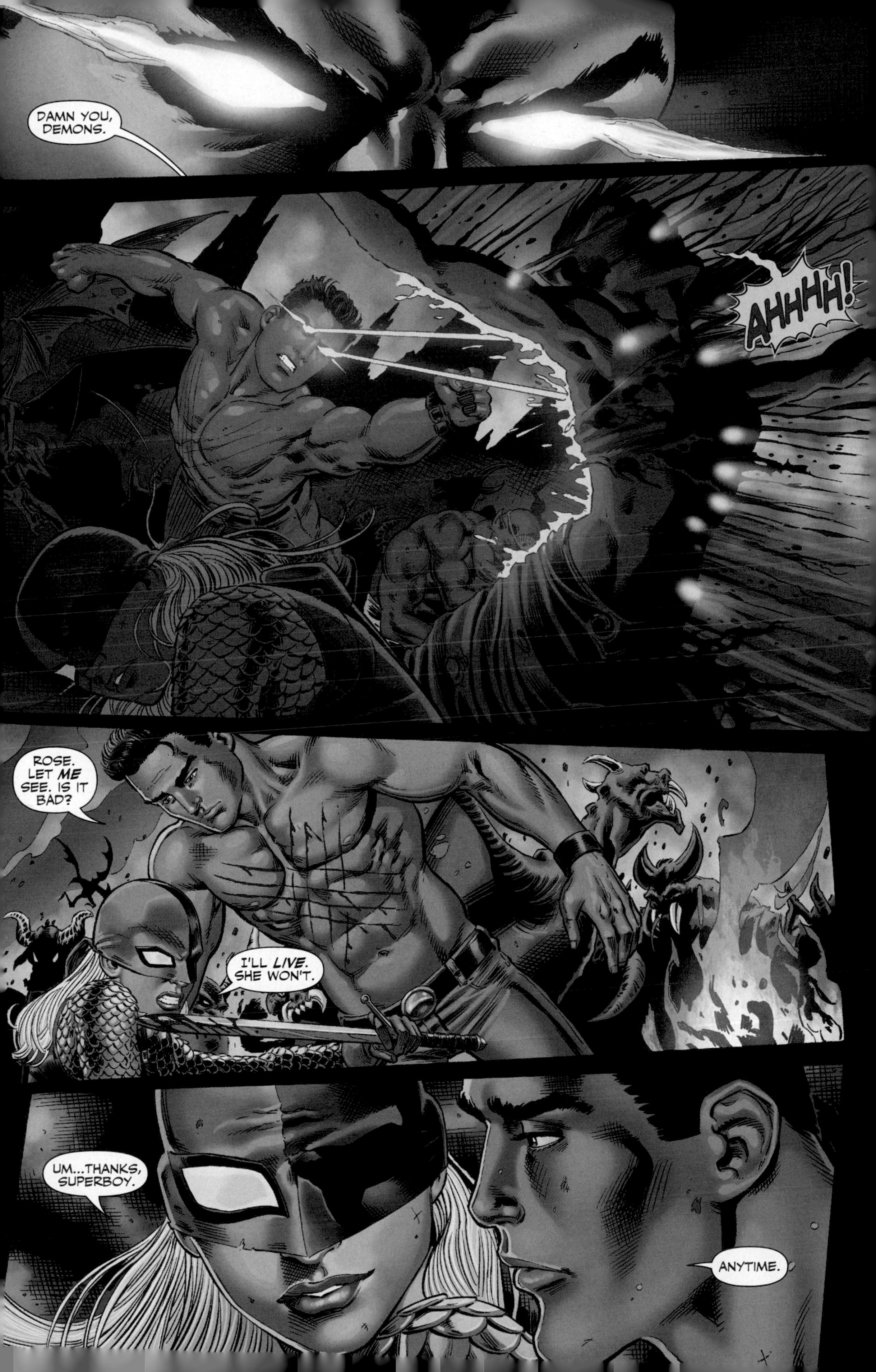
DAMN YOU, DEMONS.
AHHHH!
ROSE. LET ME SEE. IS IT BAD?
I'LL LIVE. SHE WON'T.
UM...THANKS, SUPERBOY.
ANYTIME.

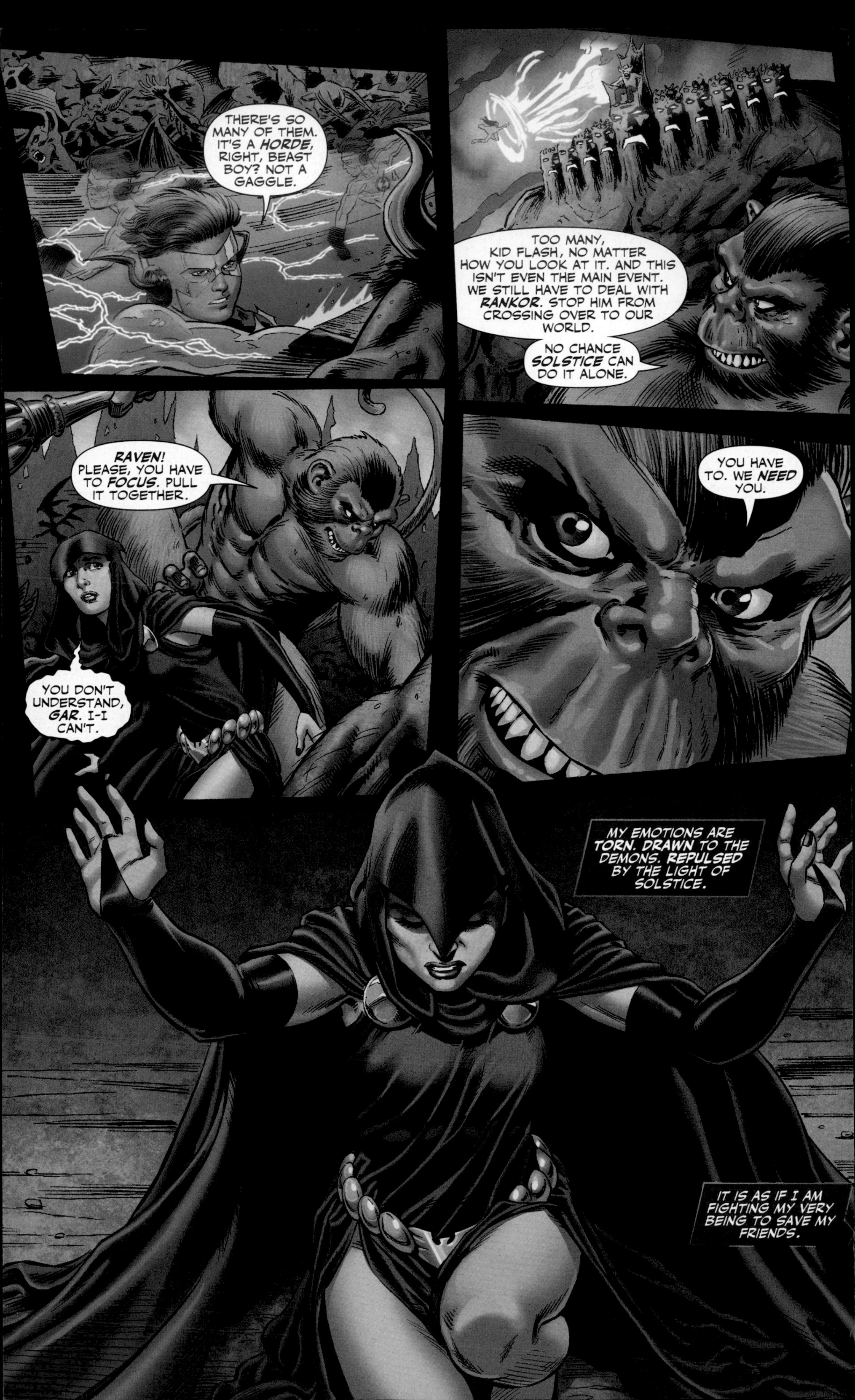
THERE'S SO MANY OF THEM. IT'S A HORDE, RIGHT, BEAST BOY? NOT A GAGGLE.
TOO MANY, KID FLASH, NO MATTER HOW YOU LOOK AT IT. AND THIS ISN'T EVEN THE MAIN EVENT. WE STILL HAVE TO DEAL WITH RANKOR. STOP HIM FROM CROSSING OVER TO OUR WORLD.
NO CHANCE SOLSTICE CAN DO IT ALONE.
RAVEN! PLEASE, YOU HAVE TO FOCUS. PULL IT TOGETHER.
YOU DON'T UNDERSTAND, GAR. I-I CAN'T.
YOU HAVE TO. WE NEED YOU.
MY EMOTIONS ARE TORN. DRAWN TO THE DEMONS. REPULSED BY THE LIGHT OF SOLSTICE.
IT IS AS IF I AM FIGHTING MY VERY BEING TO SAVE MY FRIENDS.

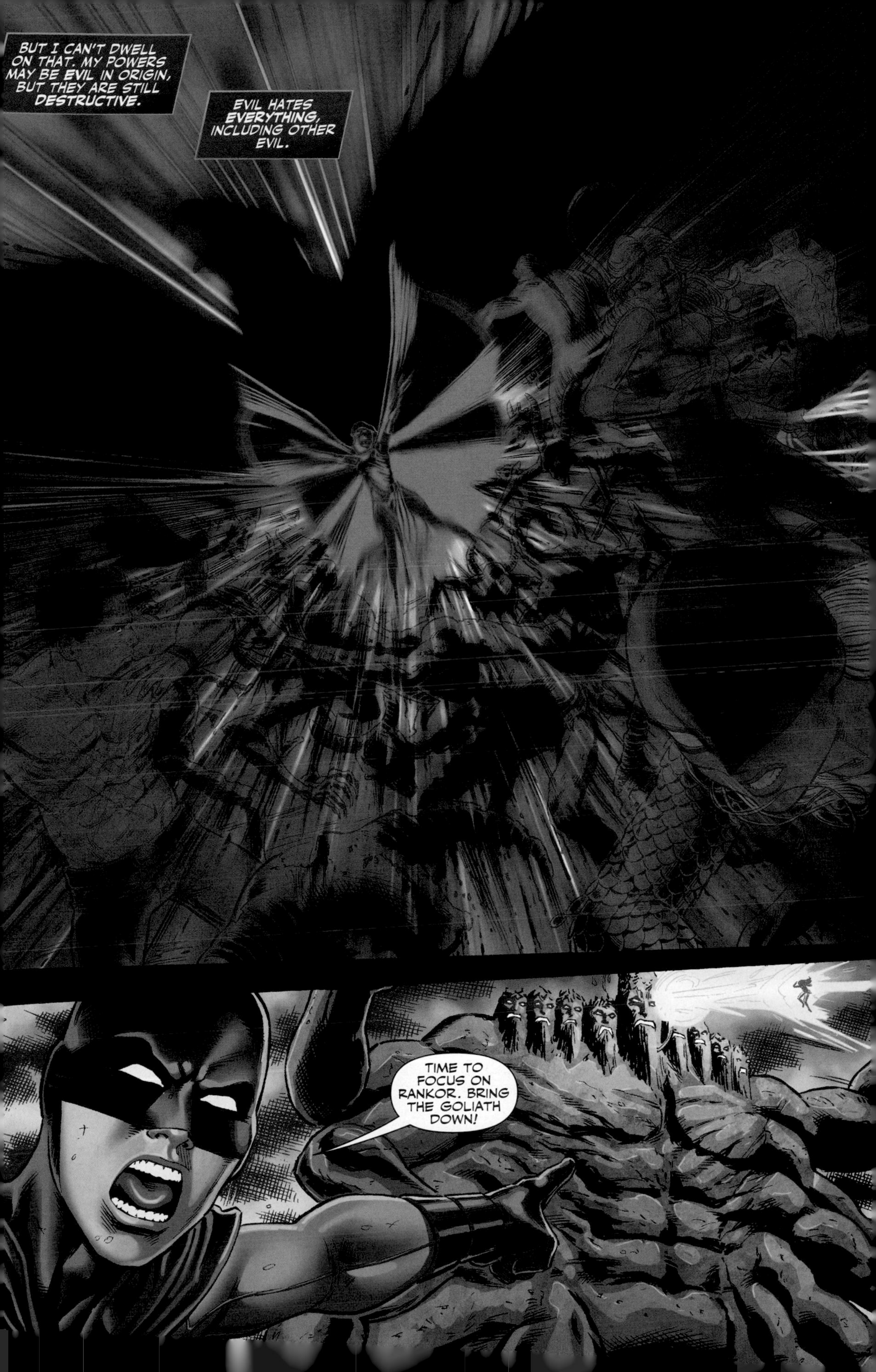
BUT I CAN'T DWELL ON THAT. MY POWERS MAY BE EVIL IN ORIGIN, BUT THEY ARE STILL DESTRUCTIVE.
EVIL HATES EVERYTHING, INCLUDING OTHER EVIL.
TIME TO FOCUS ON RANKOR. BRING THE GOLIATH DOWN!

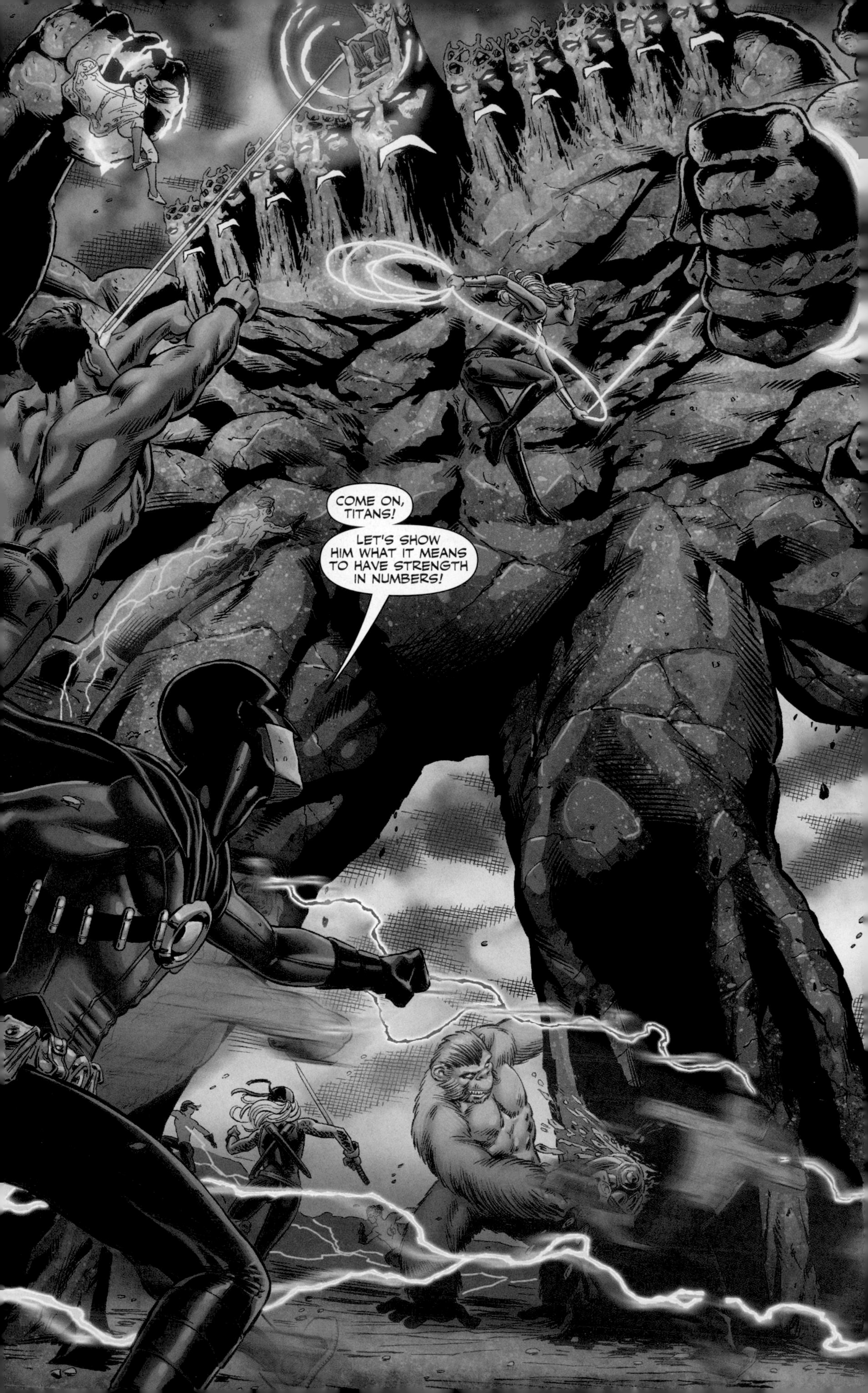
COME ON, TITANS!
LET'S SHOW HIM WHAT IT MEANS TO HAVE STRENGTH IN NUMBERS!

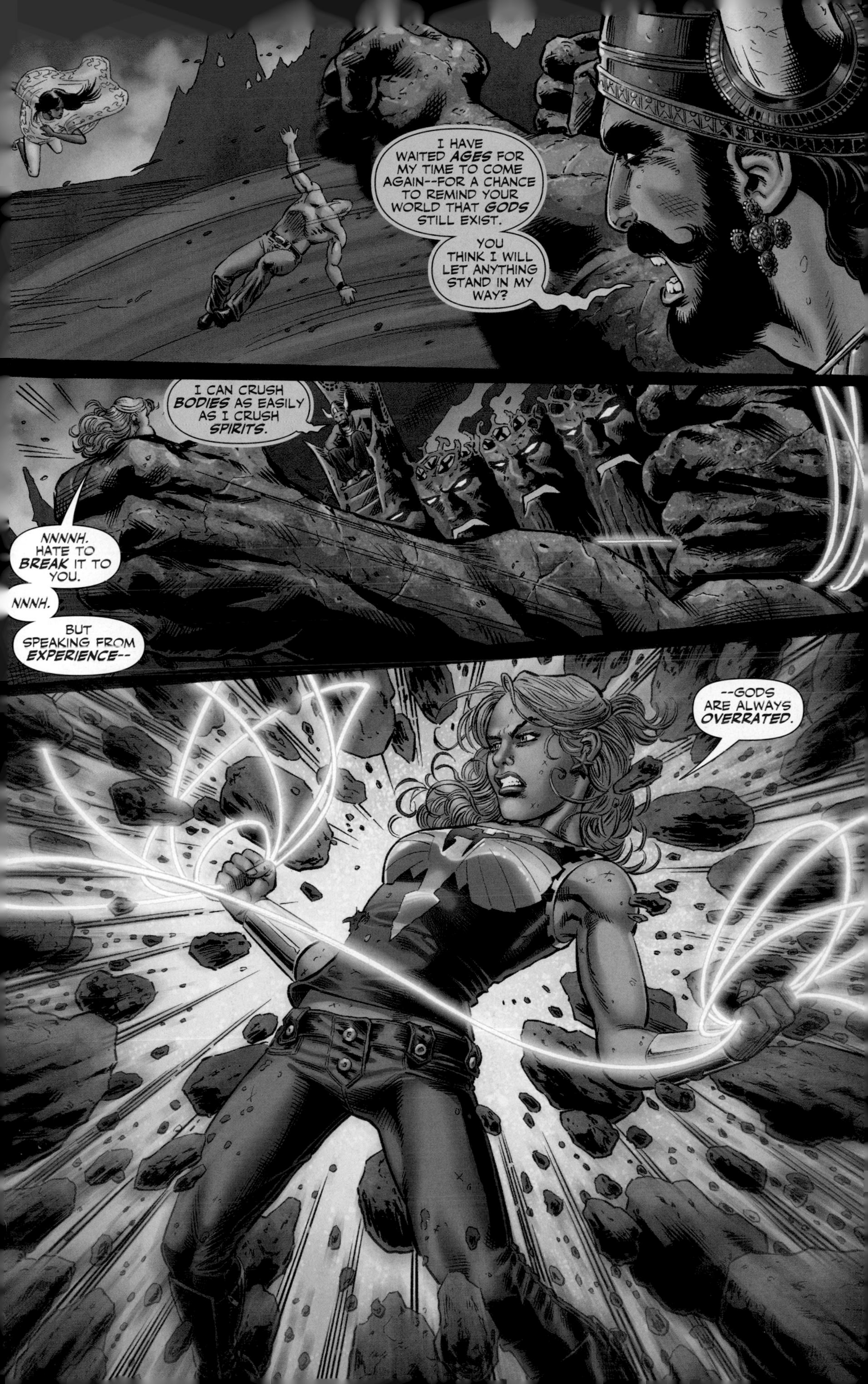
I HAVE WAITED AGES FOR MY TIME TO COME AGAIN--FOR A CHANCE TO REMIND YOUR WORLD THAT GODS STILL EXIST.
YOU THINK I WILL LET ANYTHING STAND IN MY WAY?
I CAN CRUSH BODIES AS EASILY AS I CRUSH SPIRITS.
NNNNH. HATE TO BREAK IT TO YOU.
NNNH.
BUT SPEAKING FROM EXPERIENCE--
--GODS ARE ALWAYS OVERRATED.

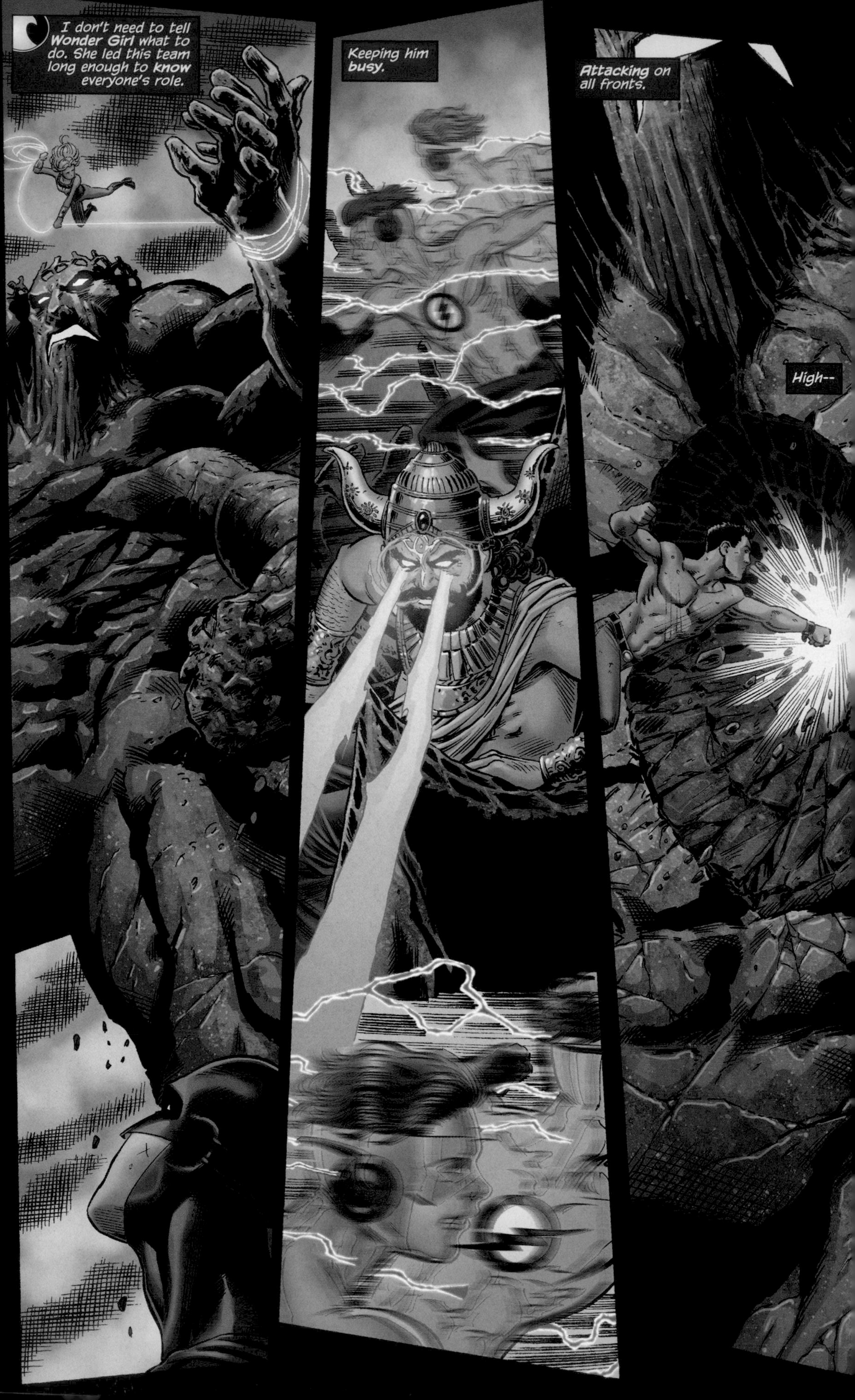
I don't need to tell Wonder Girl what to do. She led this team long enough to know everyone's role.
Keeping him busy.
Attacking on all fronts.
High--

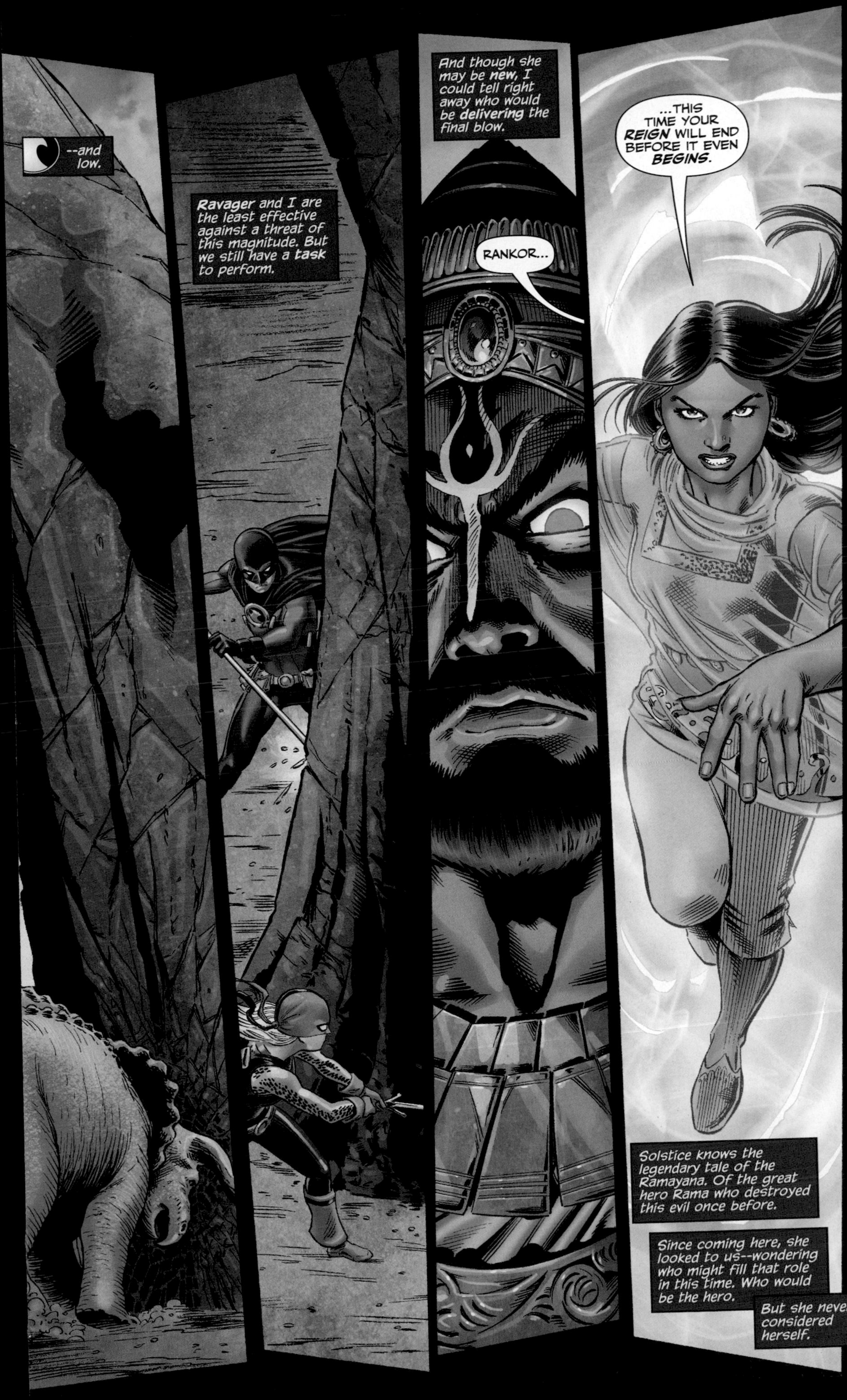

--and low.
Ravager and I are the least effective against a threat of this magnitude. But we still have a task to perform.
And though she may be new, I could tell right away who would be delivering the final blow.
RANKOR...
...THIS TIME YOUR REIGN WILL END BEFORE IT EVEN BEGINS.
Solstice knows the legendary tale of the Ramayana. Of the great hero Rama who destroyed this evil once before.
Since coming here, she looked to us--wondering who might fill that role in this time. Who would be the hero.
But she never considered herself.

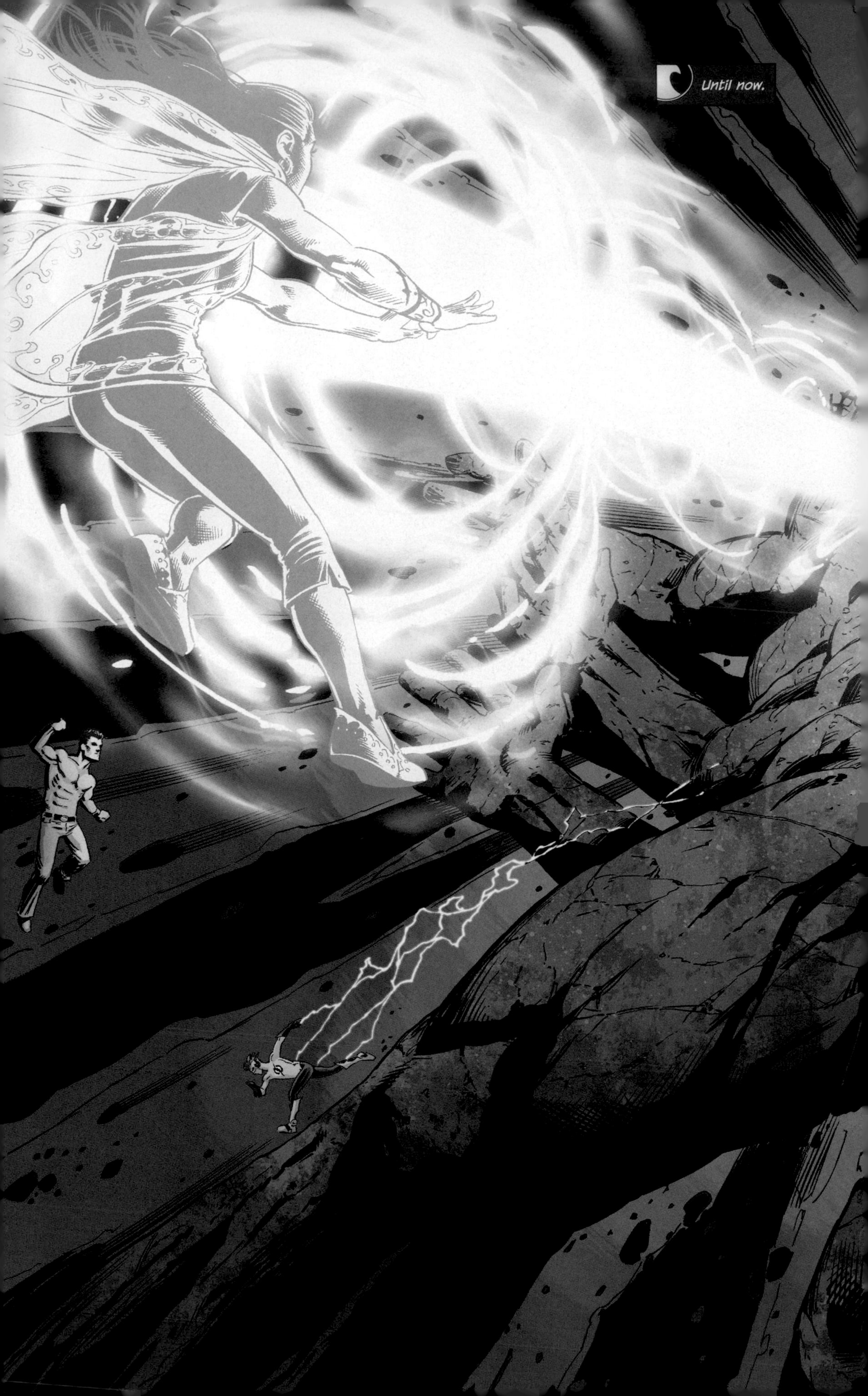
Until now.

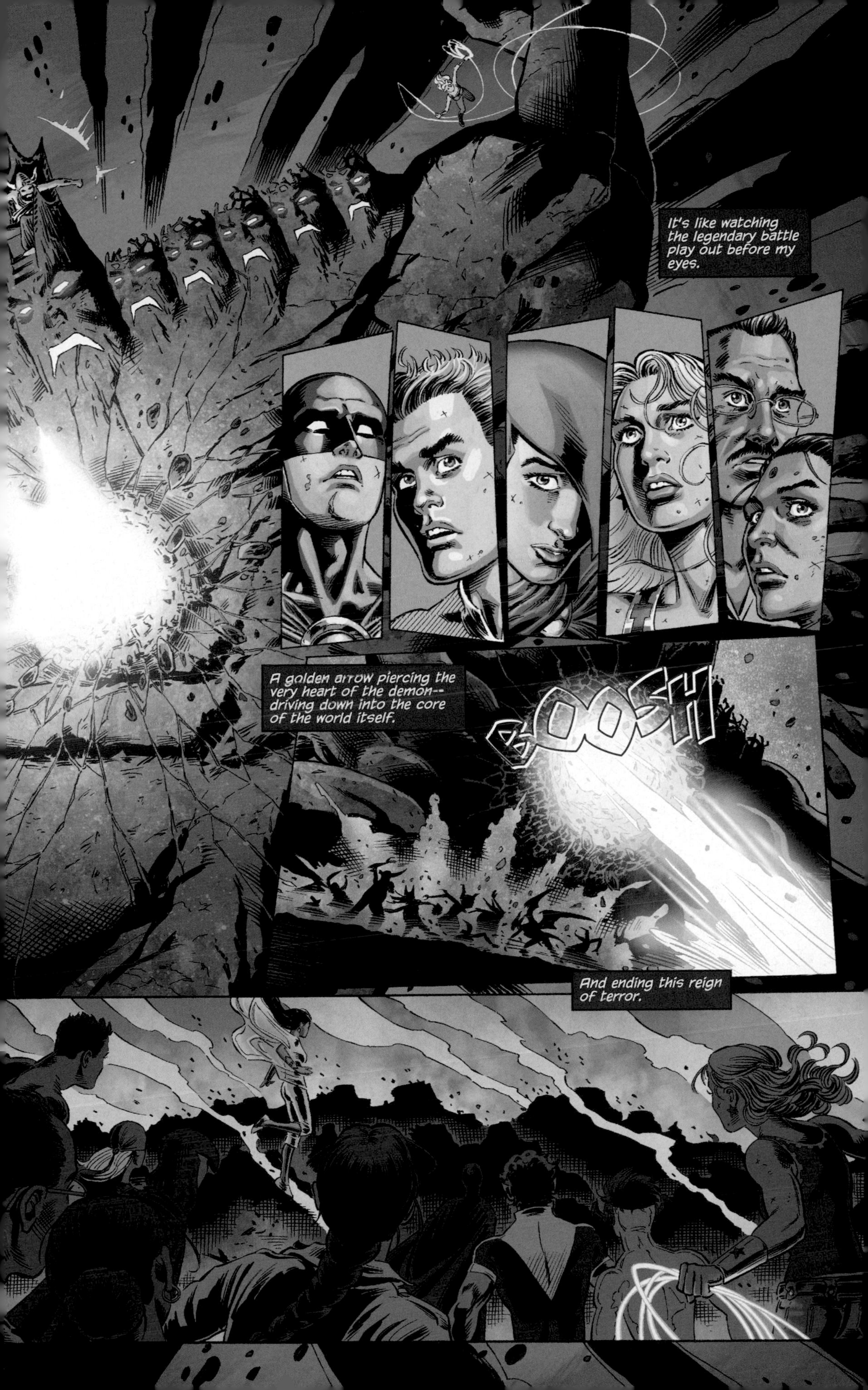
It's like watching the legendary battle play out before my eyes.
A golden arrow piercing the very heart of the demon--driving down into the core of the world itself.
BOOSH
And ending this reign of terror.

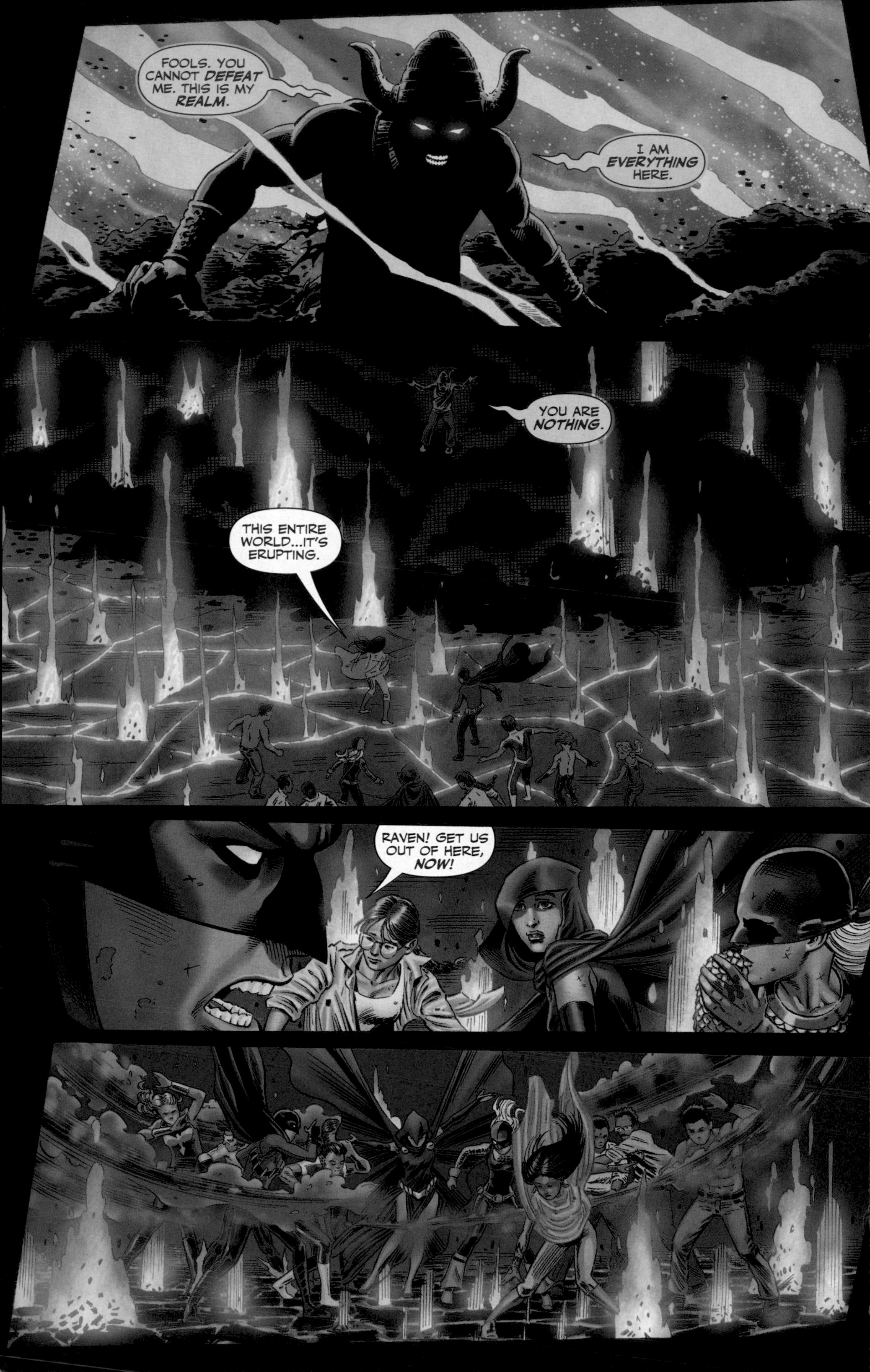
FOOLS. YOU CANNOT DEFEAT ME. THIS IS MY REALM.
I AM EVERYTHING HERE.
YOU ARE NOTHING.
THIS ENTIRE WORLD...IT'S ERUPTING.
RAVEN! GET US OUT OF HERE, NOW!

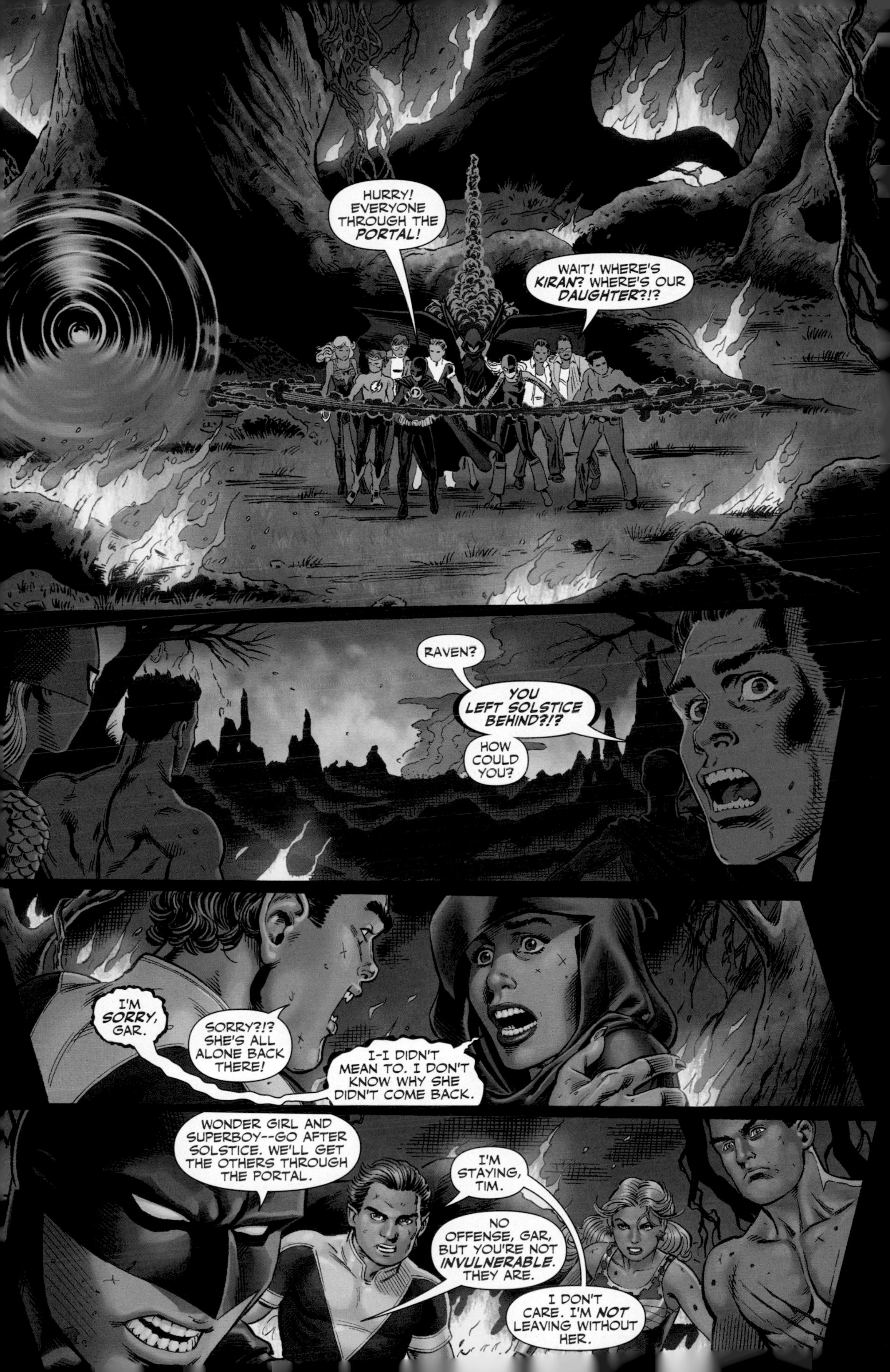
HURRY! EVERYONE THROUGH THE PORTAL!
WAIT! WHERE'S KIRAN? WHERE'S OUR DAUGHTER?!?
RAVEN?
YOU LEFT SOLSTICE BEHIND?!?
HOW COULD YOU?
I'M SORRY, GAR.
SORRY?!? SHE'S ALL ALONE BACK THERE!
I-I DIDN'T MEAN TO. I DON'T KNOW WHY SHE DIDN'T COME BACK.
WONDER GIRL AND SUPERBOY--GO AFTER SOLSTICE. WE'LL GET THE OTHERS THROUGH THE PORTAL.
I'M STAYING, TIM.
NO OFFENSE, GAR, BUT YOU'RE NOT INVULNERABLE. THEY ARE.
I DON'T CARE. I'M NOT LEAVING WITHOUT HER.

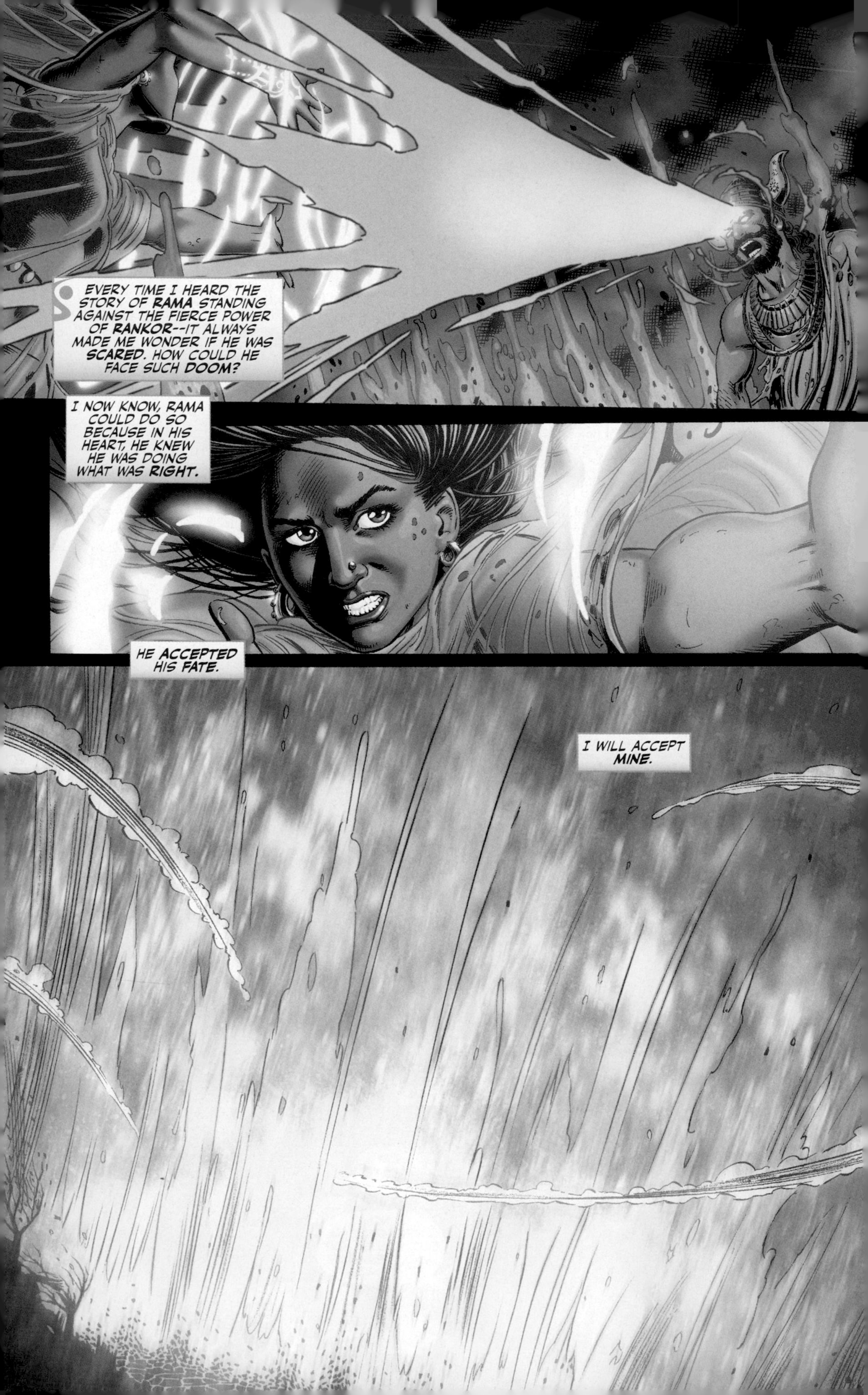
EVERY TIME I HEARD THE STORY OF RAMA STANDING AGAINST THE FIERCE POWER OF RANKOR--IT ALWAYS MADE ME WONDER IF HE WAS SCARED. HOW COULD HE FACE SUCH DOOM?
I NOW KNOW, RAMA COULD DO SO BECAUSE IN HIS HEART, HE KNEW HE WAS DOING WHAT WAS RIGHT.
HE ACCEPTED HIS FATE.
I WILL ACCEPT MINE.

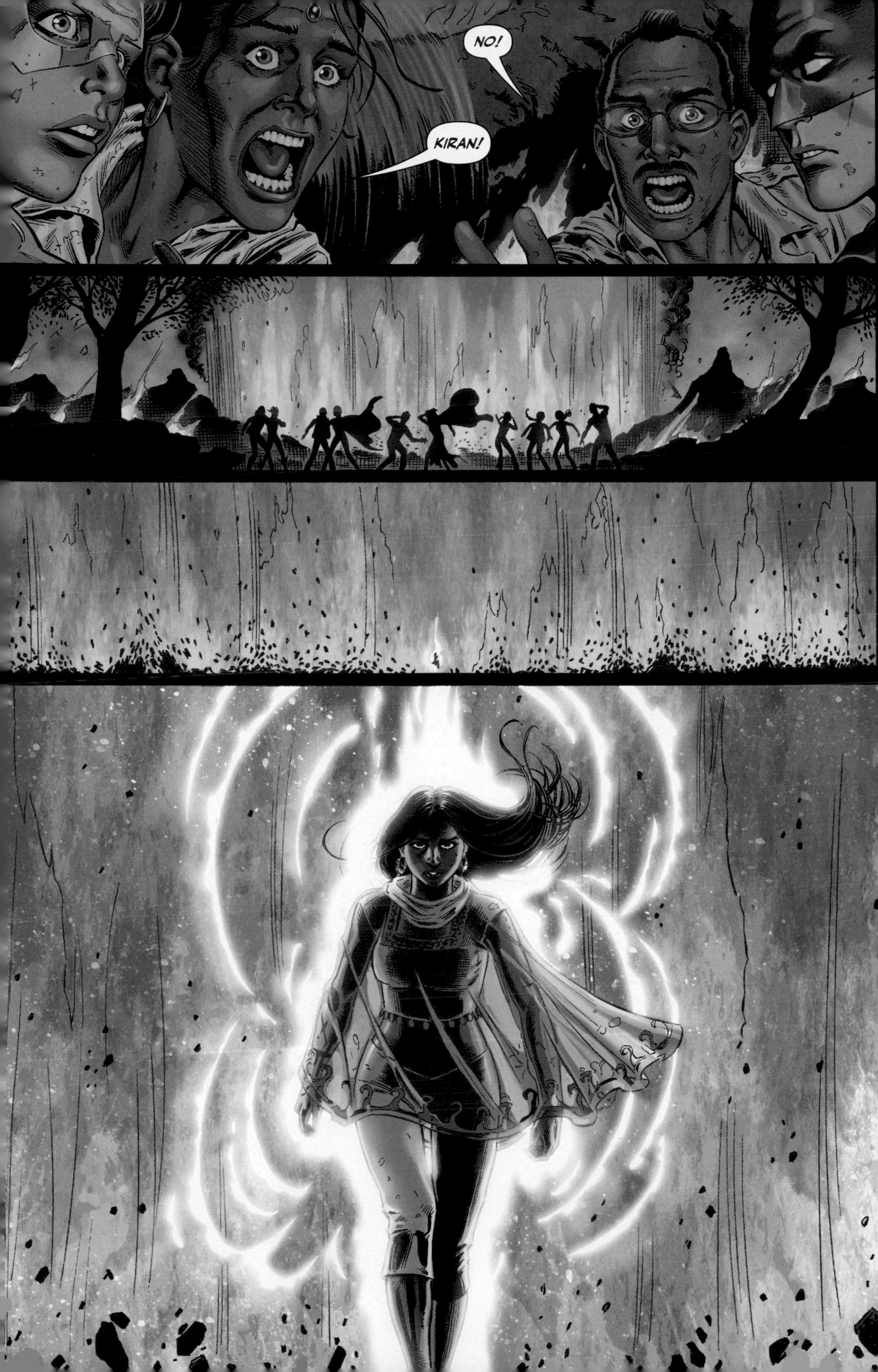
NO!
KIRAN!

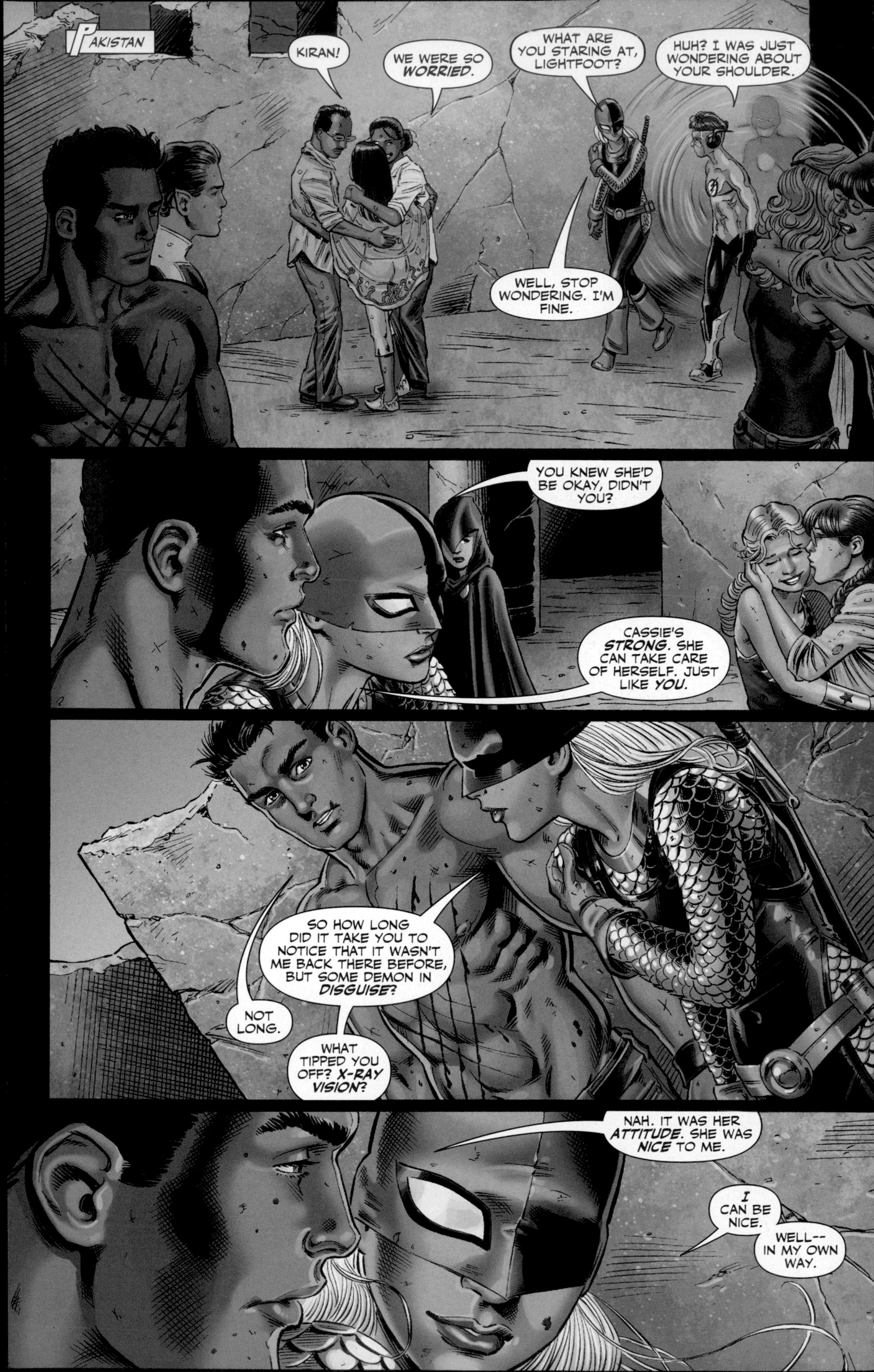
PAKISTAN
KIRAN!
WE WERE SO WORRIED.
WHAT ARE YOU STARING AT, LIGHTFOOT?
HUH? I WAS JUST WONDERING ABOUT YOUR SHOULDER.
WELL, STOP WONDERING. I'M FINE.
YOU KNEW SHE'D BE OKAY, DIDN'T YOU?
CASSIE'S STRONG. SHE CAN TAKE CARE OF HERSELF. JUST LIKE YOU.
SO HOW LONG DID IT TAKE YOU TO NOTICE THAT IT WASN'T ME BACK THERE BEFORE, BUT SOME DEMON IN DISGUISE?
NOT LONG.
WHAT TIPPED YOU OFF? X-RAY VISION?
NAH. IT WAS HER ATTITUDE. SHE WAS NICE TO ME.
I CAN BE NICE.
WELL-- IN MY OWN WAY.

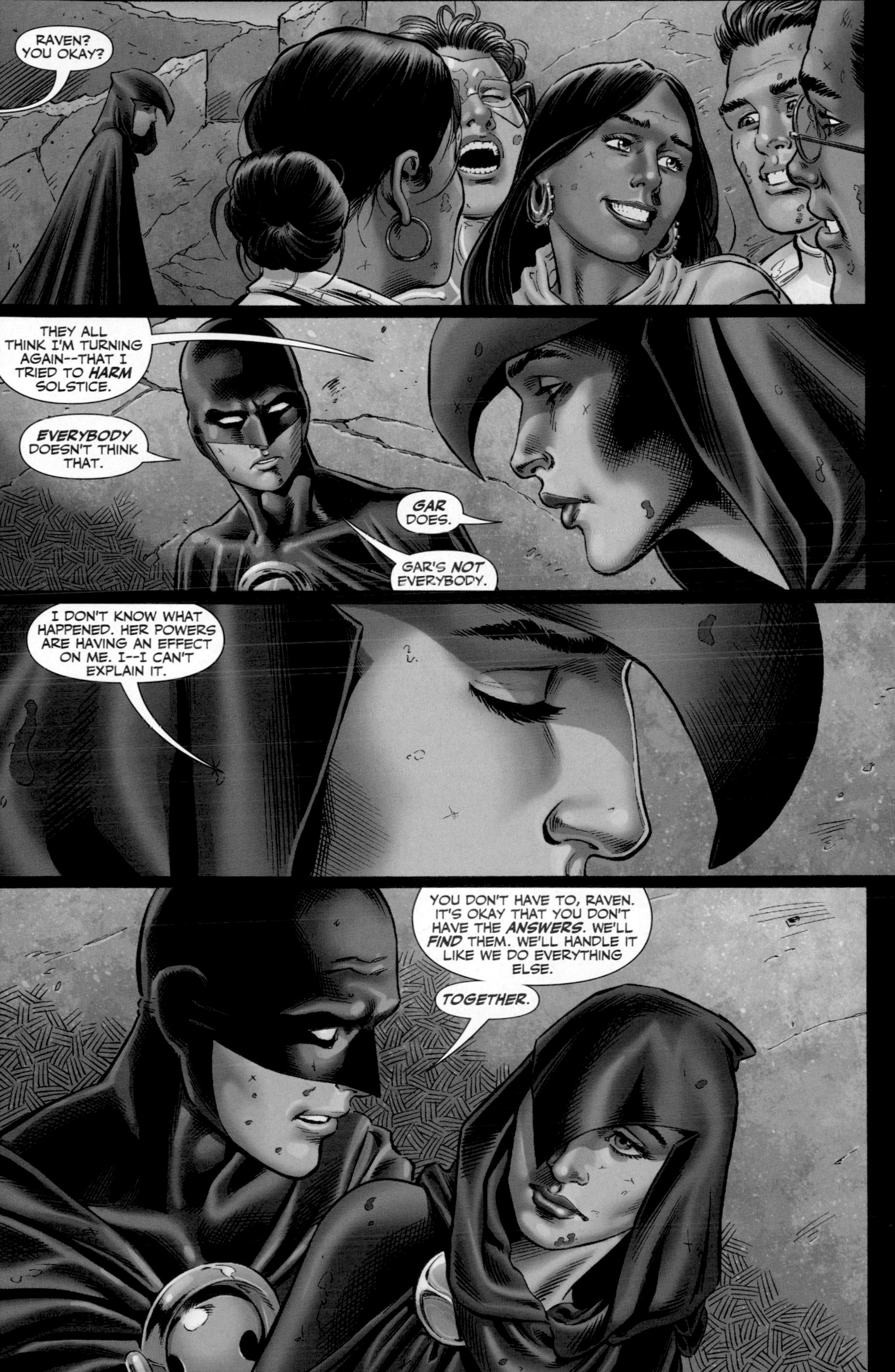
RAVEN? YOU OKAY?
THEY ALL THINK I'M TURNING AGAIN--THAT I TRIED TO HARM SOLSTICE.
EVERYBODY DOESN'T THINK THAT.
GAR DOES.
GAR'S NOT EVERYBODY.
I DON'T KNOW WHAT HAPPENED. HER POWERS ARE HAVING AN EFFECT ON ME. I--I CAN'T EXPLAIN IT.
YOU DON'T HAVE TO, RAVEN. IT'S OKAY THAT YOU DON'T HAVE THE ANSWERS. WE'LL FIND THEM. WE'LL HANDLE IT LIKE WE DO EVERYTHING ELSE.
TOGETHER.

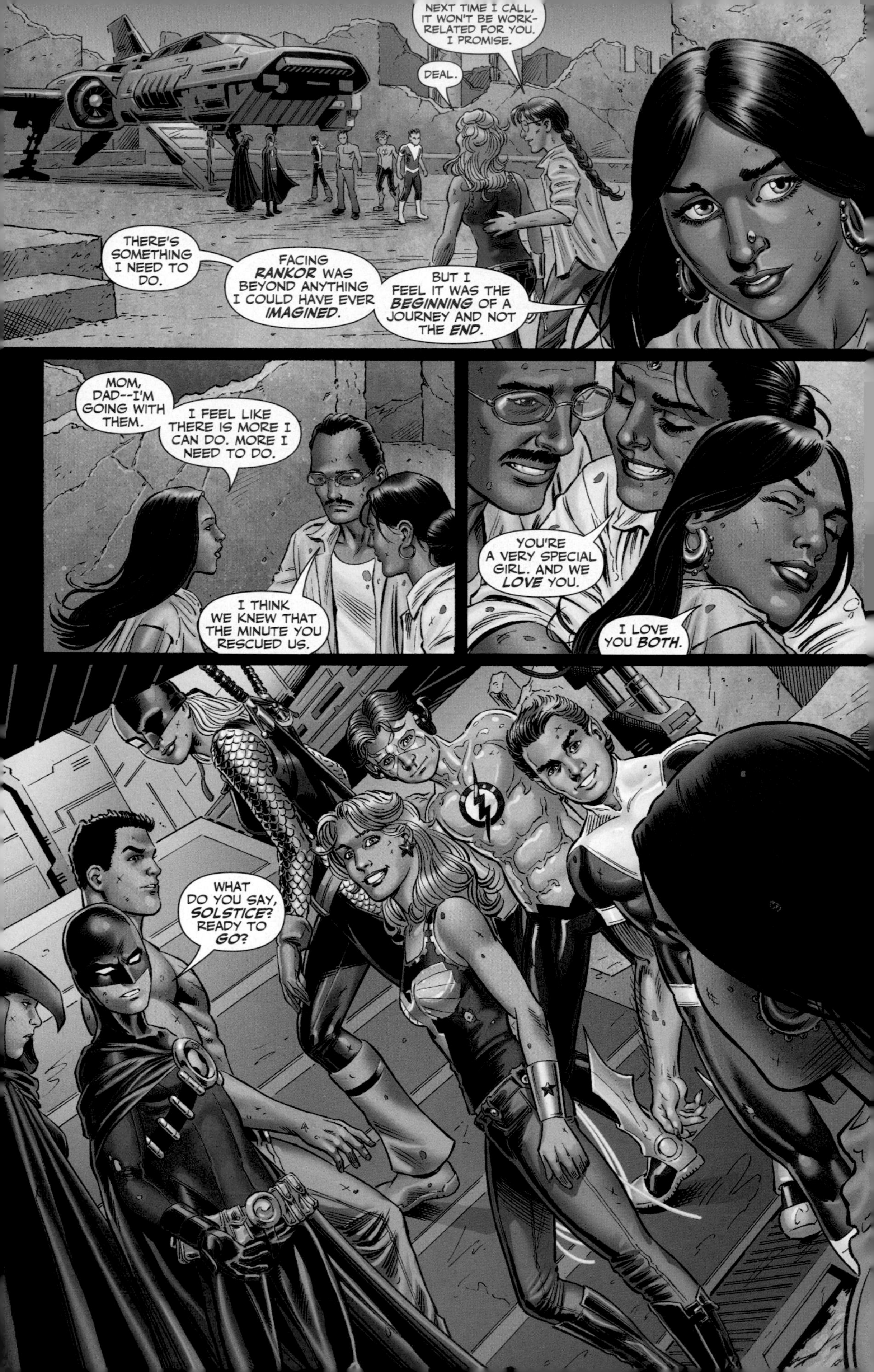
NEXT TIME I CALL, IT WON'T BE WORK-RELATED FOR YOU. I PROMISE.
DEAL.
THERE'S SOMETHING I NEED TO DO.
FACING RANKOR WAS BEYOND ANYTHING I COULD HAVE EVER IMAGINED.
BUT I FEEL IT WAS THE BEGINNING OF A JOURNEY AND NOT THE END.
MOM, DAD--I'M GOING WITH THEM.
I FEEL LIKE THERE IS MORE I CAN DO. MORE I NEED TO DO.
I THINK WE KNEW THAT THE MINUTE YOU RESCUED US.
YOU'RE A VERY SPECIAL GIRL. AND WE LOVE YOU.
I LOVE YOU BOTH.
WHAT DO YOU SAY, SOLSTICE? READY TO GO?

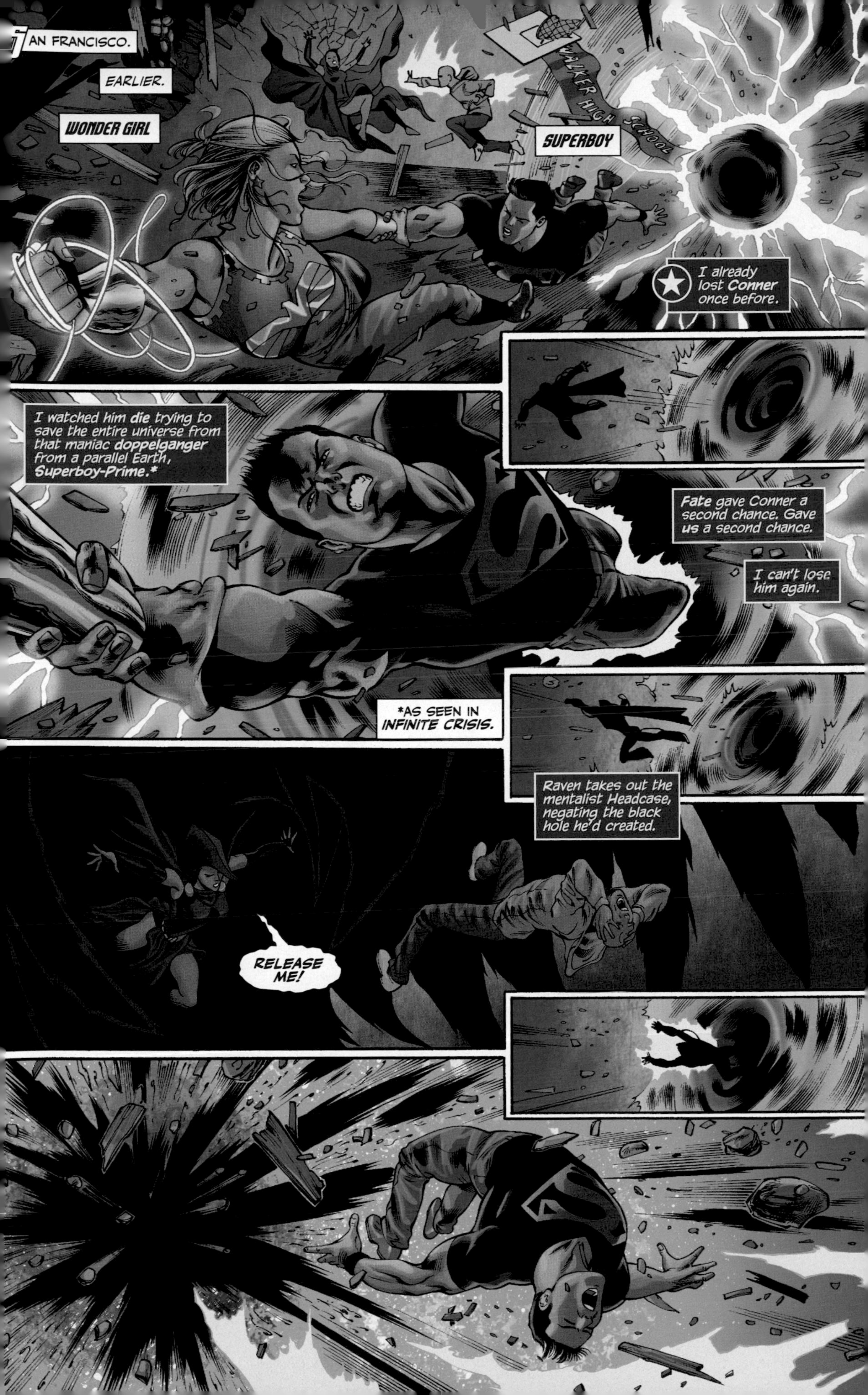
SAN FRANCISCO.
EARLIER.
WONDER GIRL
WALKER HIGH SCHOOL
SUPERBOY
I already lost Conner once before.
I watched him die trying to save the entire universe from that maniac doppelganger from a parallel Earth, Superboy-Prime.*
Fate gave Conner a second chance. Gave us a second chance.
I can't lose him again.
*AS SEEN IN INFINITE CRISIS.
Raven takes out the mentalist Headcase, negating the black hole he'd created.
RELEASE ME!

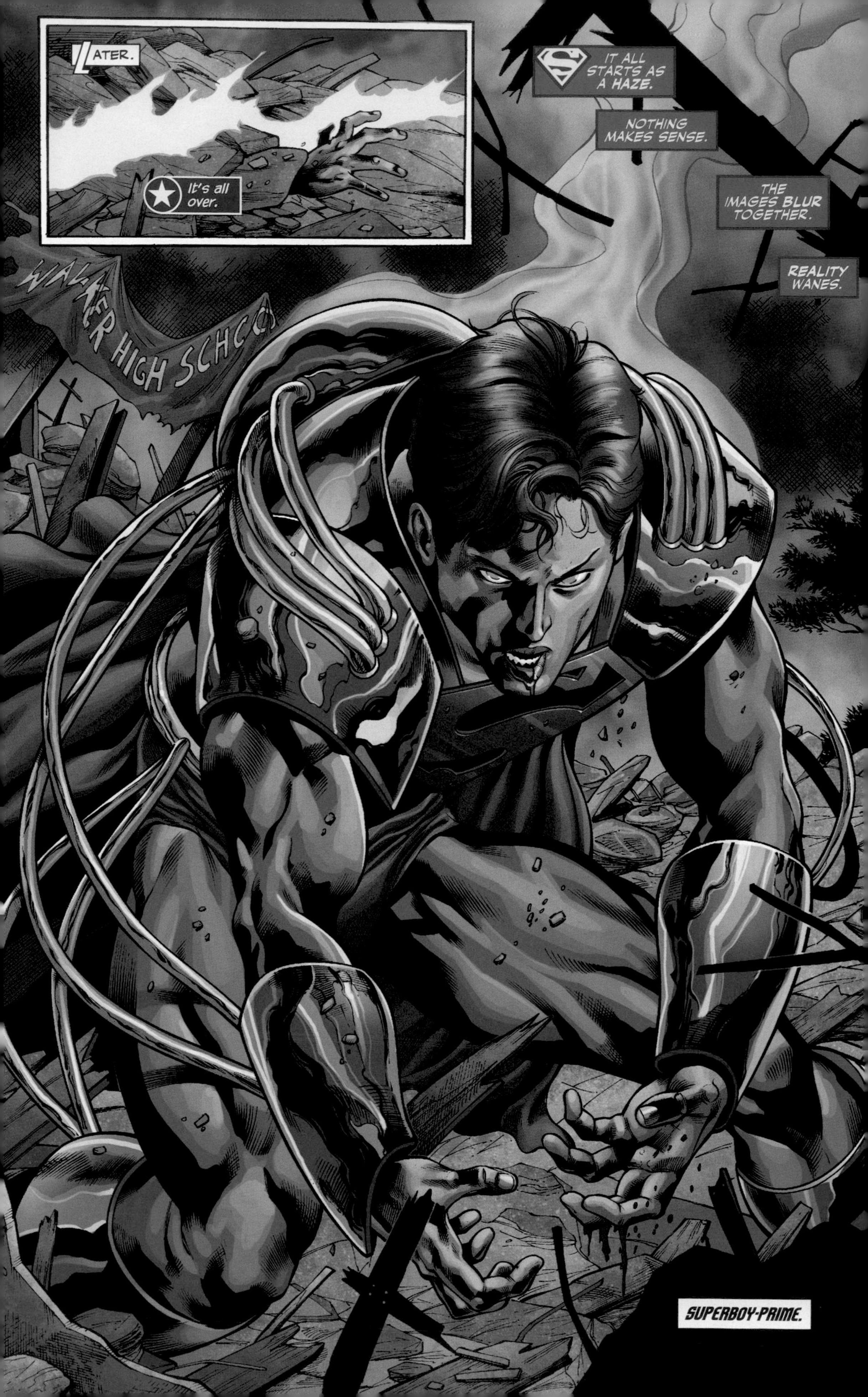
LATER.
It's all over.
IT ALL STARTS AS A HAZE.
NOTHING MAKES SENSE.
THE IMAGES BLUR TOGETHER.
REALITY WANES.
WALKER HIGH SCHOO
SUPERBOY-PRIME.

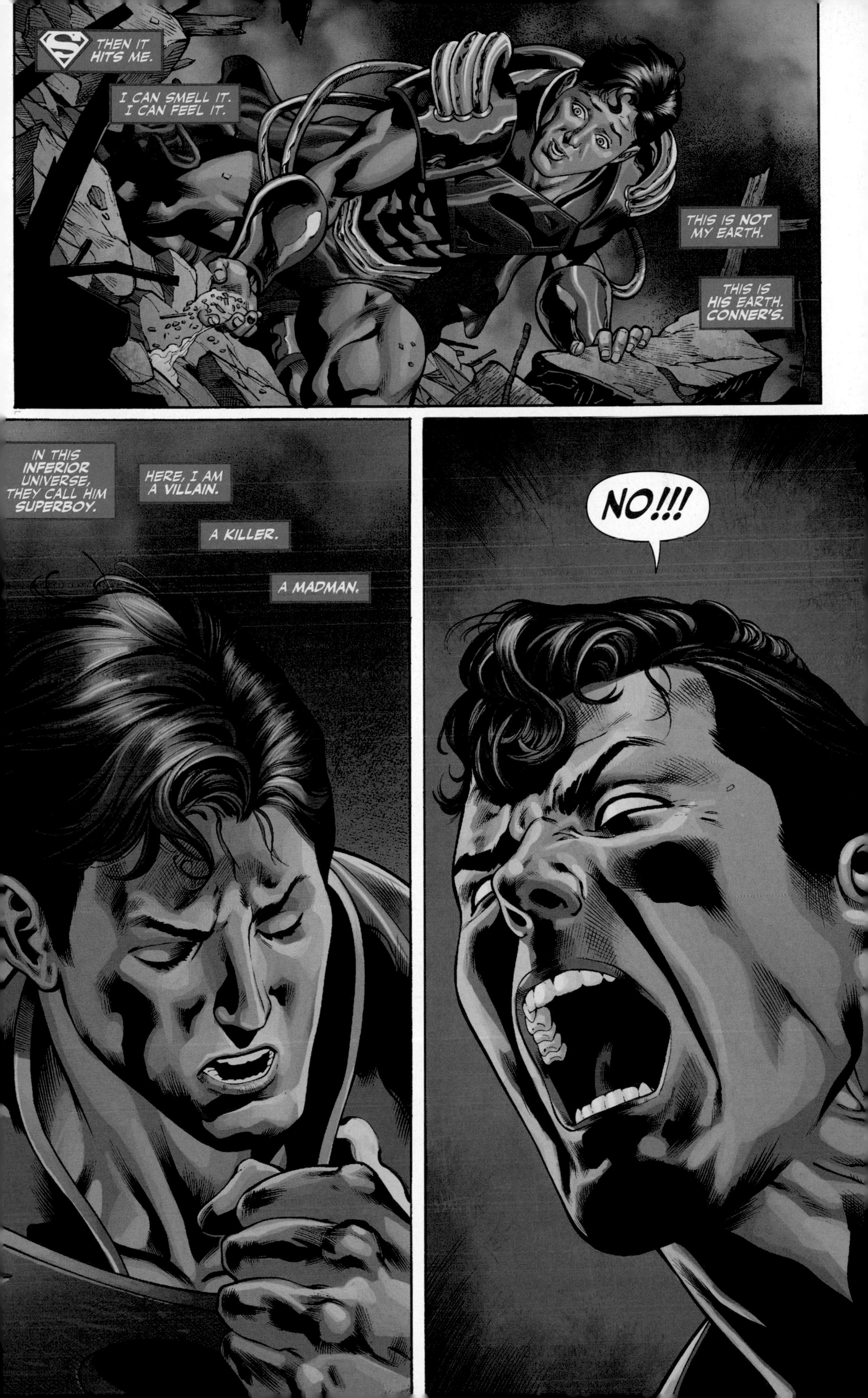
THEN IT HITS ME.
I CAN SMELL IT. I CAN FEEL IT.
THIS IS NOT MY EARTH.
THIS IS HIS EARTH. CONNER'S.
IN THIS INFERIOR UNIVERSE, THEY CALL HIM SUPERBOY.
HERE, I AM A VILLAIN.
A KILLER.
A MADMAN.
NO!!!

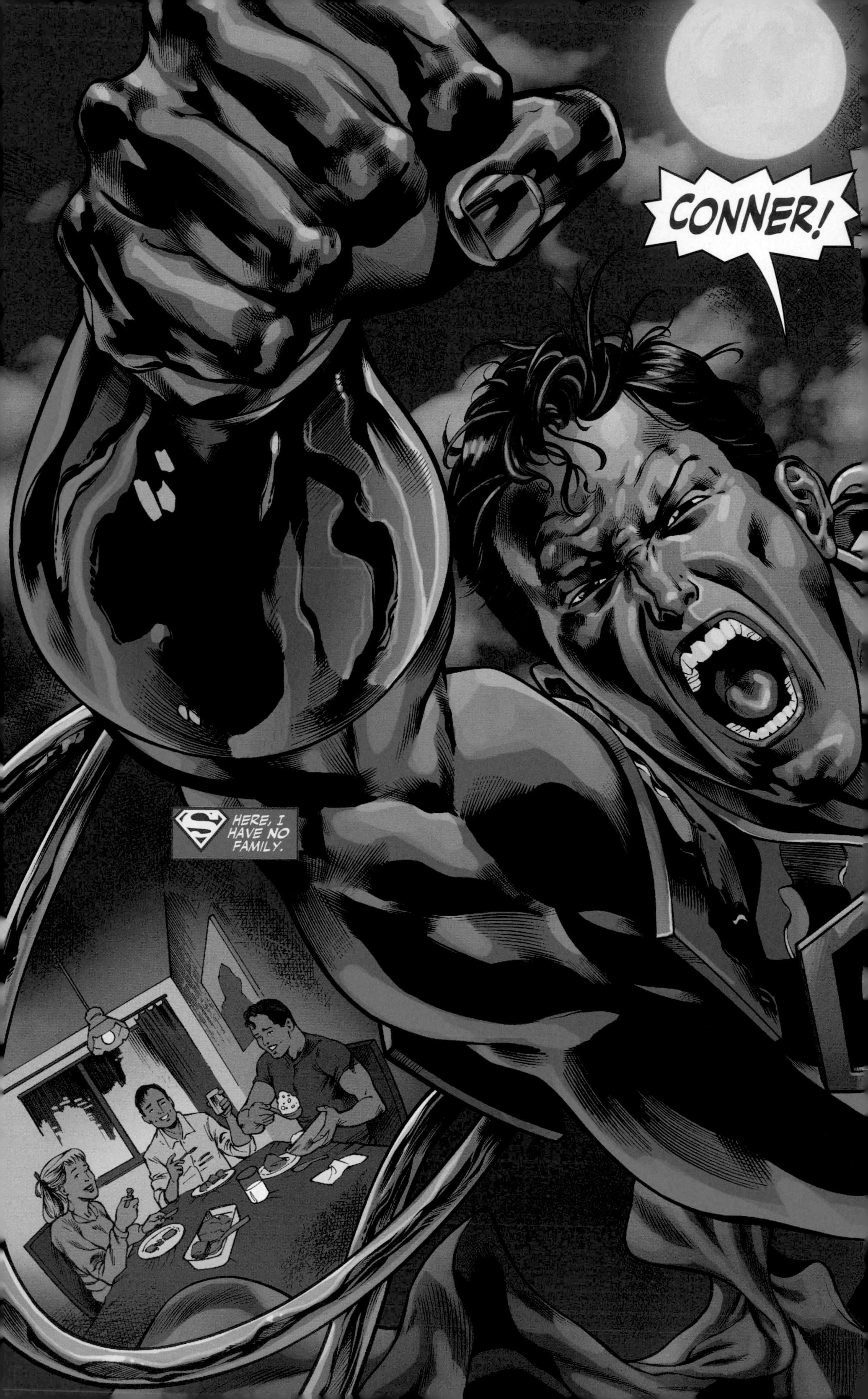
CONNER!
HERE, I HAVE NO FAMILY.

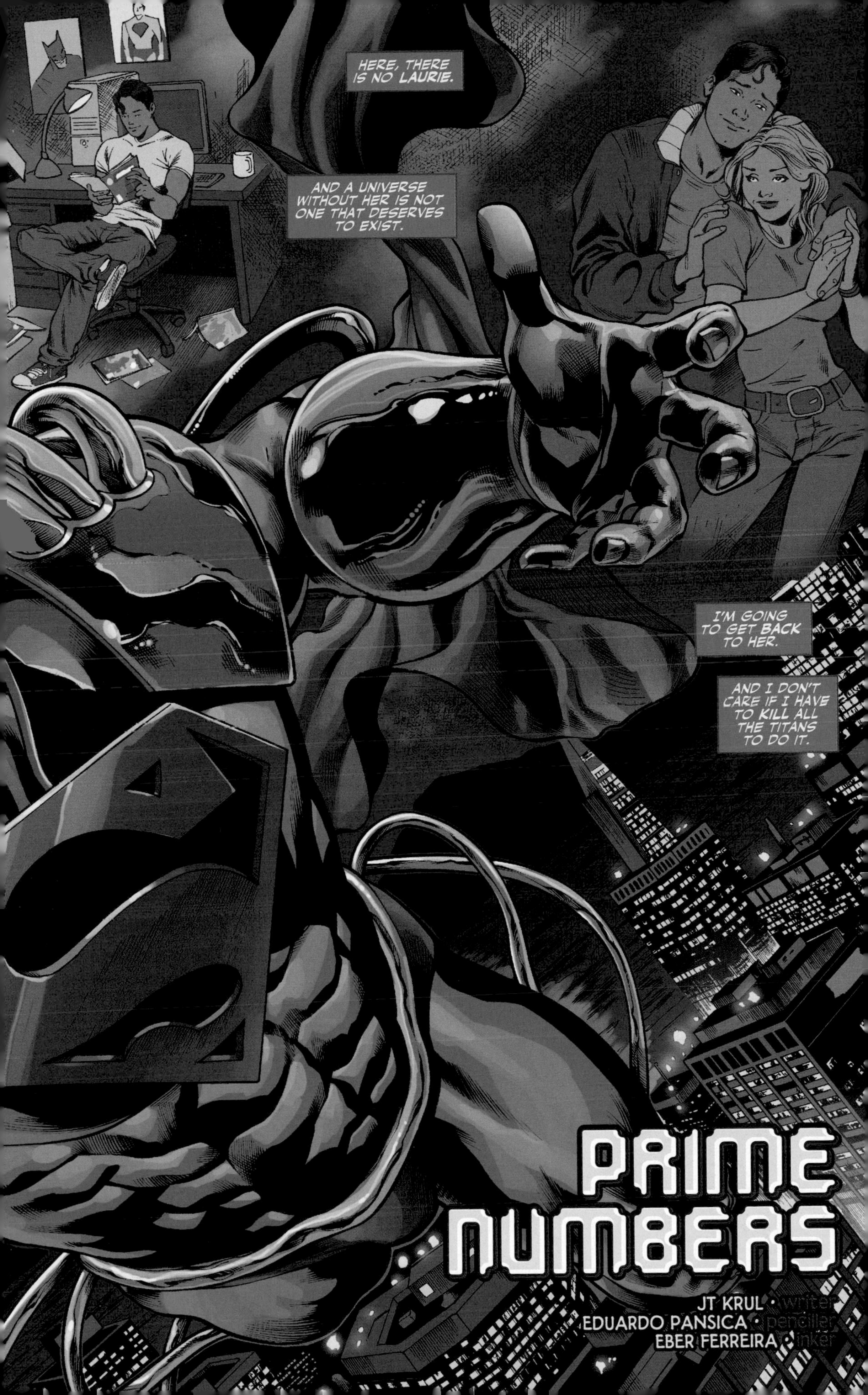
HERE, THERE IS NO LAURIE.
AND A UNIVERSE WITHOUT HER IS NOT ONE THAT DESERVES TO EXIST.
I'M GOING TO GET BACK TO HER.
AND I DON'T CARE IF I HAVE TO KILL ALL THE TITANS TO DO IT.
PRIME NUMBERS
JT KRUL • writer
EDUARDO PANSICA • penciller
EBER FERREIRA • inker

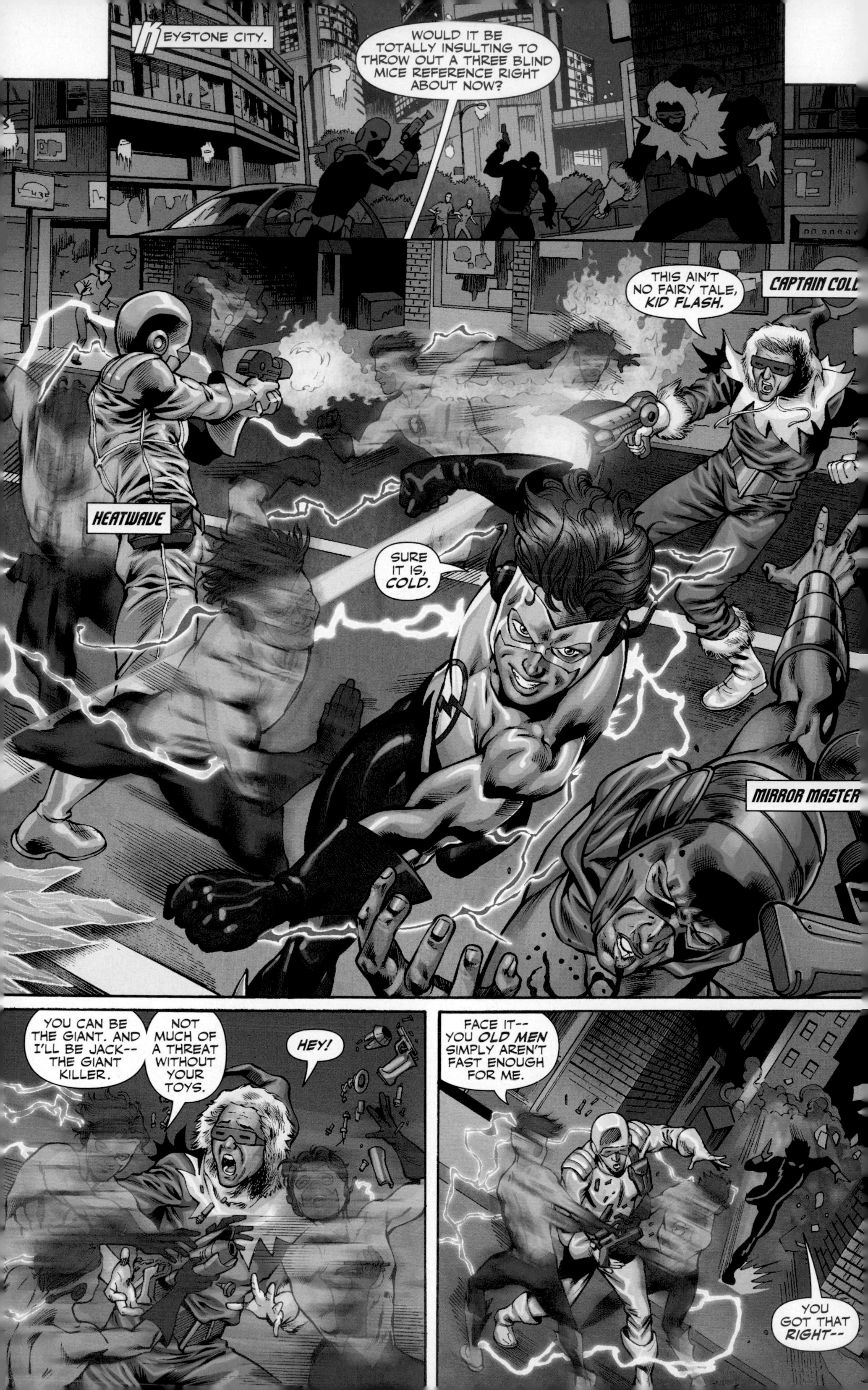
KEYSTONE CITY.
WOULD IT BE TOTALLY INSULTING TO THROW OUT A THREE BLIND MICE REFERENCE RIGHT ABOUT NOW?
THIS AIN'T NO FAIRY TALE, KID FLASH.
CAPTAIN COLD
HEATWAVE
SURE IT IS, COLD.
MIRROR MASTER
YOU CAN BE THE GIANT. AND I'LL BE JACK-- THE GIANT KILLER.
NOT MUCH OF A THREAT WITHOUT YOUR TOYS.
HEY!
FACE IT-- YOU OLD MEN SIMPLY AREN'T FAST ENOUGH FOR ME.
YOU GOT THAT RIGHT--

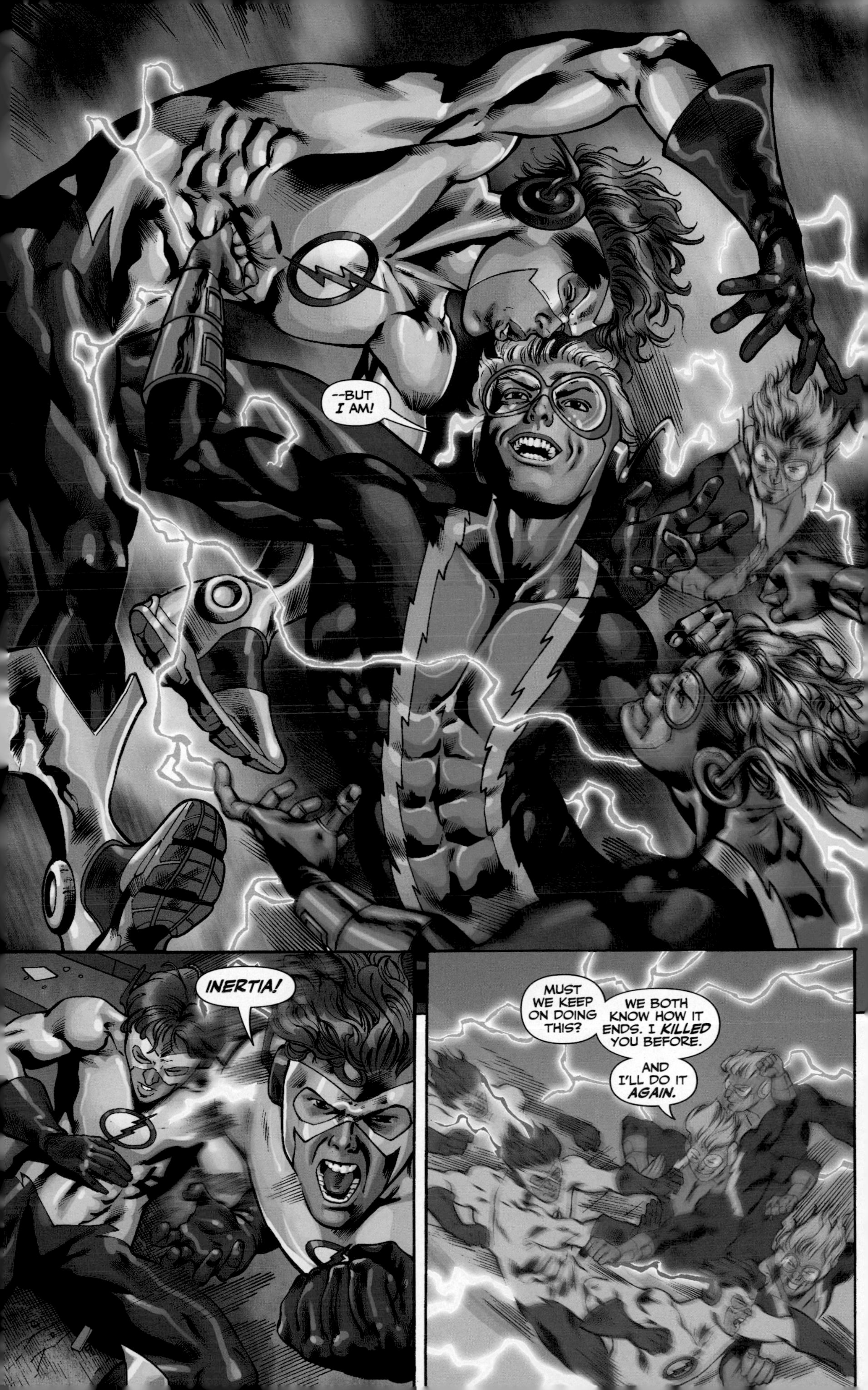
--BUT I AM!
INERTIA!
MUST WE KEEP ON DOING THIS?
WE BOTH KNOW HOW IT ENDS. I KILLED YOU BEFORE.
AND I'LL DO IT AGAIN.

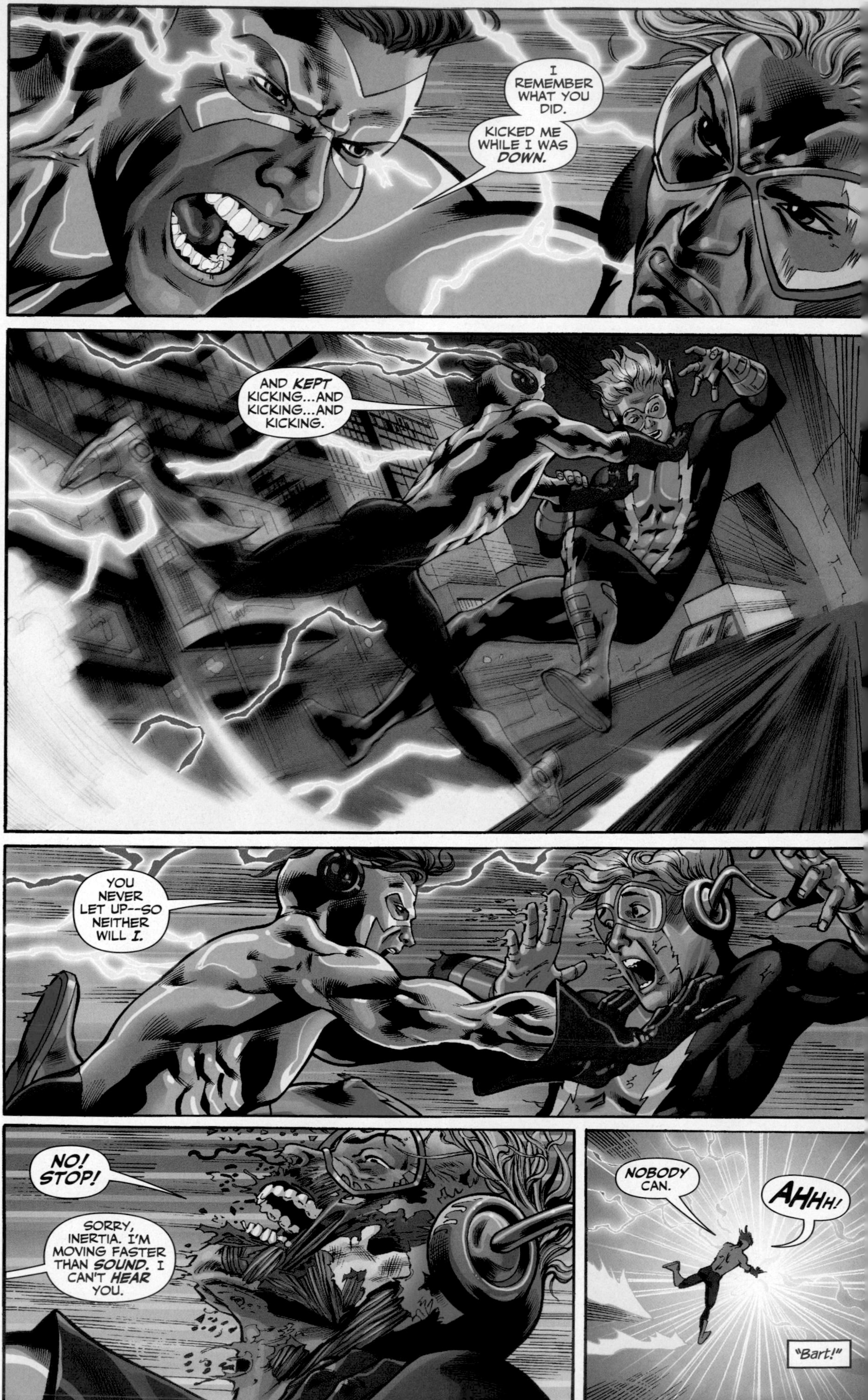
I REMEMBER WHAT YOU DID.
KICKED ME WHILE I WAS DOWN.
AND KEPT KICKING...AND KICKING...AND KICKING.
YOU NEVER LET UP--SO NEITHER WILL I.
NO! STOP!
SORRY, INERTIA. I'M MOVING FASTER THAN SOUND. I CAN'T HEAR YOU.
NOBODY CAN.
AHHH!
"Bart!"

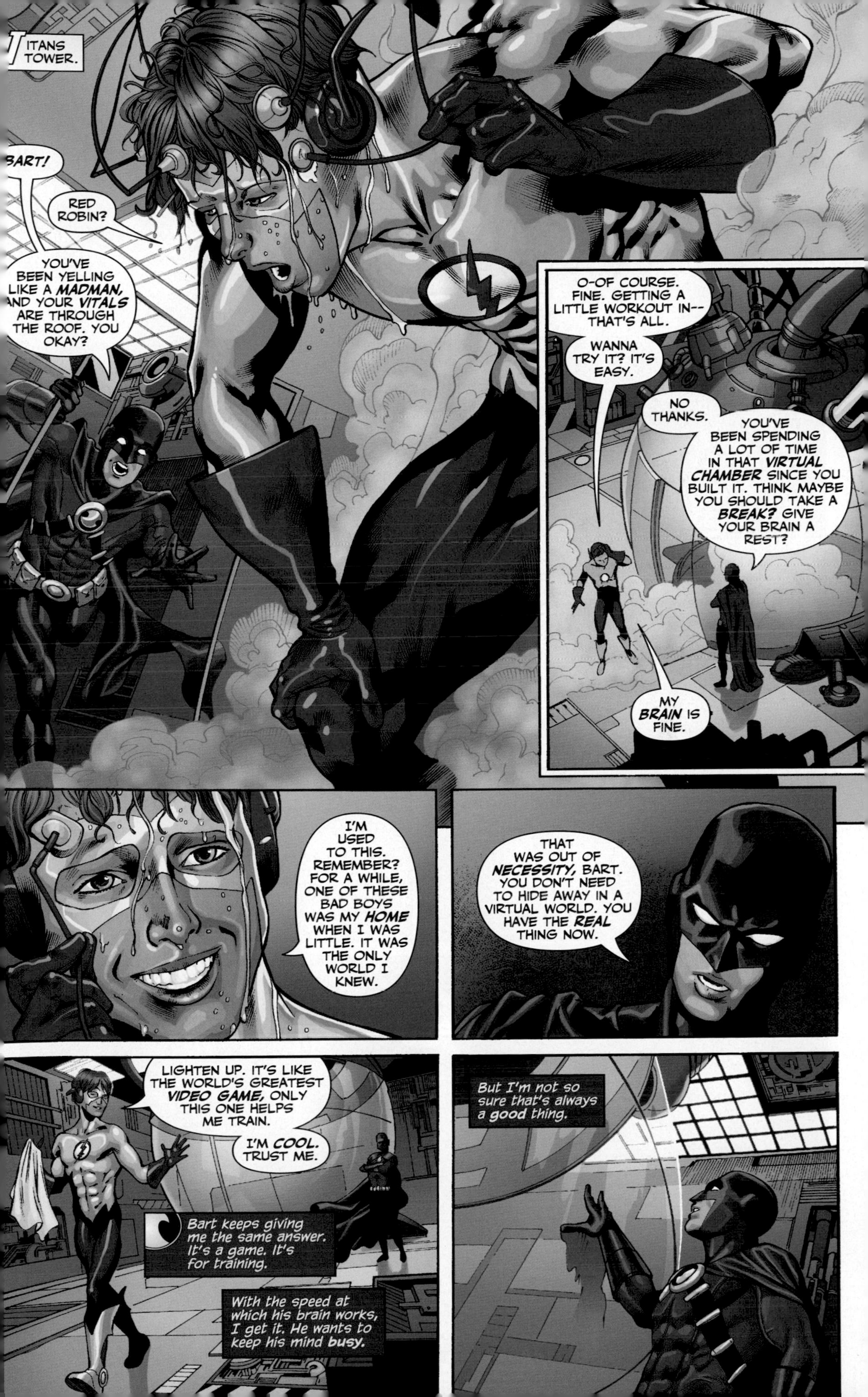

TITANS TOWER.
BART!
RED ROBIN?
YOU'VE BEEN YELLING LIKE A MADMAN, AND YOUR VITALS ARE THROUGH THE ROOF. YOU OKAY?
O-OF COURSE. FINE. GETTING A LITTLE WORKOUT IN-- THAT'S ALL.
WANNA TRY IT? IT'S EASY.
NO THANKS.
YOU'VE BEEN SPENDING A LOT OF TIME IN THAT VIRTUAL CHAMBER SINCE YOU BUILT IT. THINK MAYBE YOU SHOULD TAKE A BREAK? GIVE YOUR BRAIN A REST?
MY BRAIN IS FINE.
I'M USED TO THIS. REMEMBER? FOR A WHILE, ONE OF THESE BAD BOYS WAS MY HOME WHEN I WAS LITTLE. IT WAS THE ONLY WORLD I KNEW.
THAT WAS OUT OF NECESSITY, BART. YOU DON'T NEED TO HIDE AWAY IN A VIRTUAL WORLD. YOU HAVE THE REAL THING NOW.
LIGHTEN UP. IT'S LIKE THE WORLD'S GREATEST VIDEO GAME, ONLY THIS ONE HELPS ME TRAIN.
I'M COOL. TRUST ME.
Bart keeps giving me the same answer. It's a game. It's for training.
With the speed at which his brain works, I get it. He wants to keep his mind busy.
But I'm not so sure that's always a good thing.

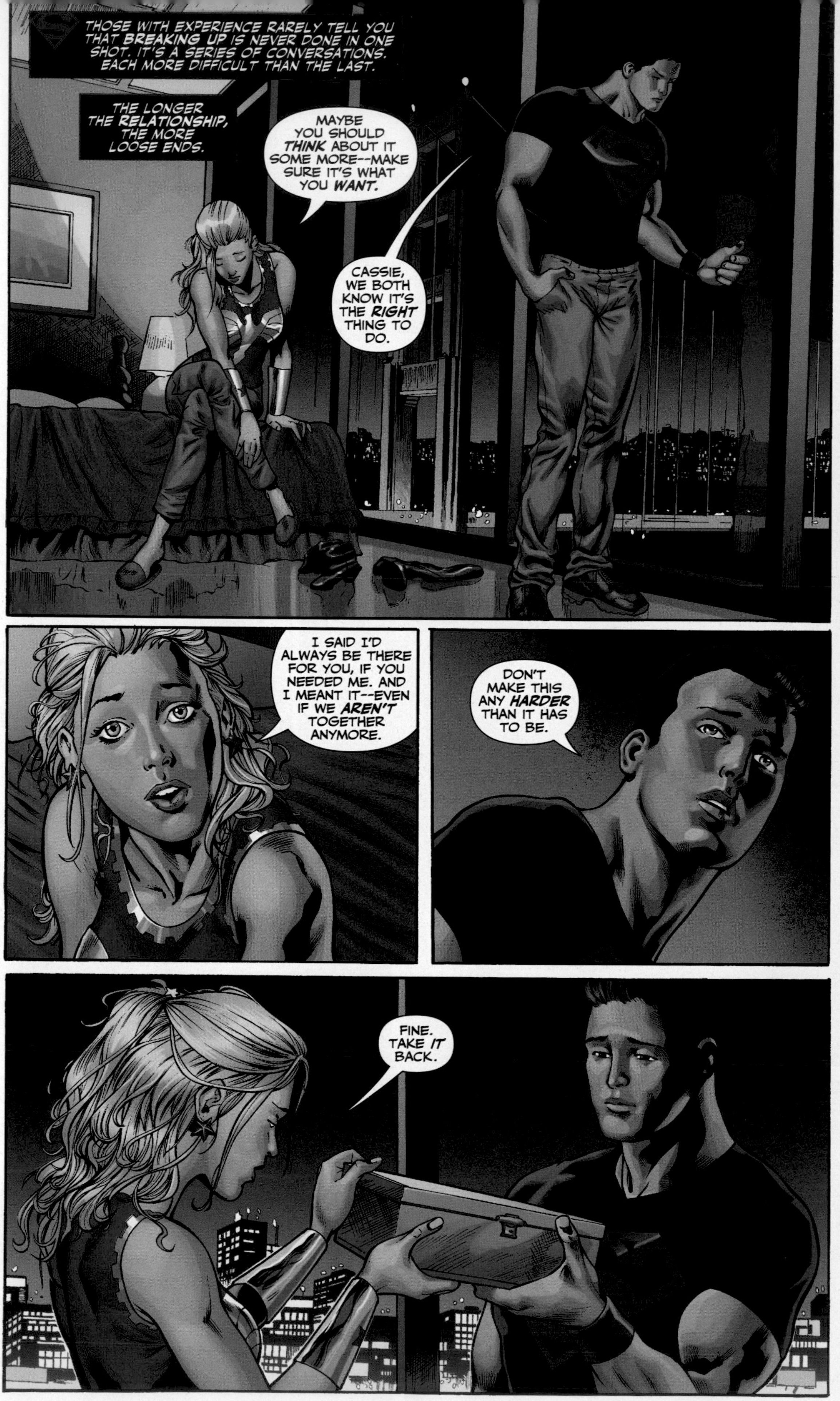
THOSE WITH EXPERIENCE RARELY TELL YOU THAT BREAKING UP IS NEVER DONE IN ONE SHOT. IT'S A SERIES OF CONVERSATIONS. EACH MORE DIFFICULT THAN THE LAST.
THE LONGER THE RELATIONSHIP, THE MORE LOOSE ENDS.
MAYBE YOU SHOULD THINK ABOUT IT SOME MORE--MAKE SURE IT'S WHAT YOU WANT.
CASSIE, WE BOTH KNOW IT'S THE RIGHT THING TO DO.
I SAID I'D ALWAYS BE THERE FOR YOU, IF YOU NEEDED ME. AND I MEANT IT--EVEN IF WE AREN'T TOGETHER ANYMORE.
DON'T MAKE THIS ANY HARDER THAN IT HAS TO BE.
FINE. TAKE IT BACK.

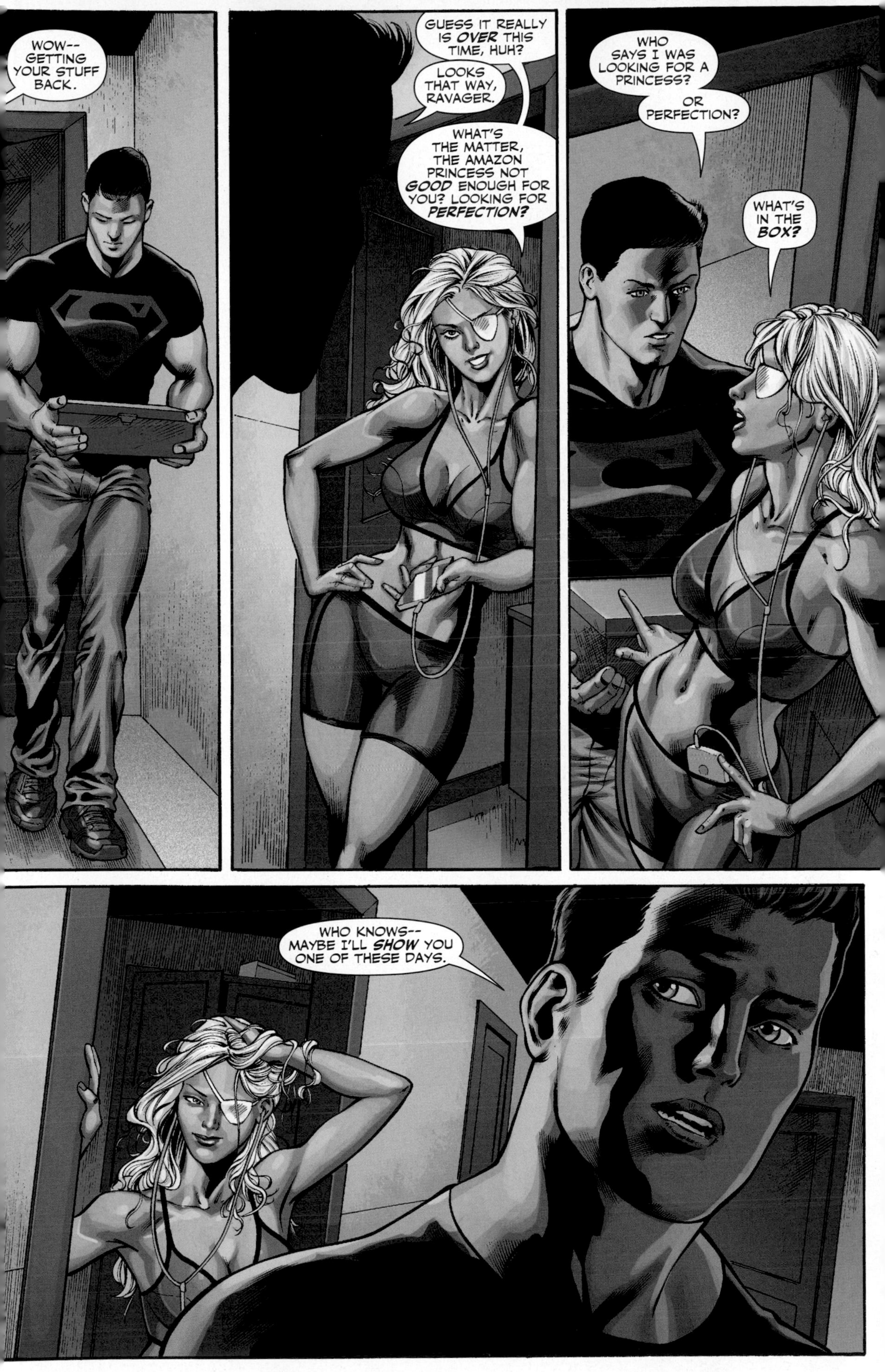
WOW--
GETTING YOUR STUFF BACK.
GUESS IT REALLY IS *OVER* THIS TIME, HUH?
LOOKS THAT WAY, RAVAGER.
WHAT'S THE MATTER, THE AMAZON PRINCESS NOT *GOOD* ENOUGH FOR YOU? LOOKING FOR *PERFECTION?*
WHO SAYS I WAS LOOKING FOR A PRINCESS?
OR PERFECTION?
WHAT'S IN THE *BOX?*
WHO KNOWS--
MAYBE I'LL *SHOW* YOU ONE OF THESE DAYS.

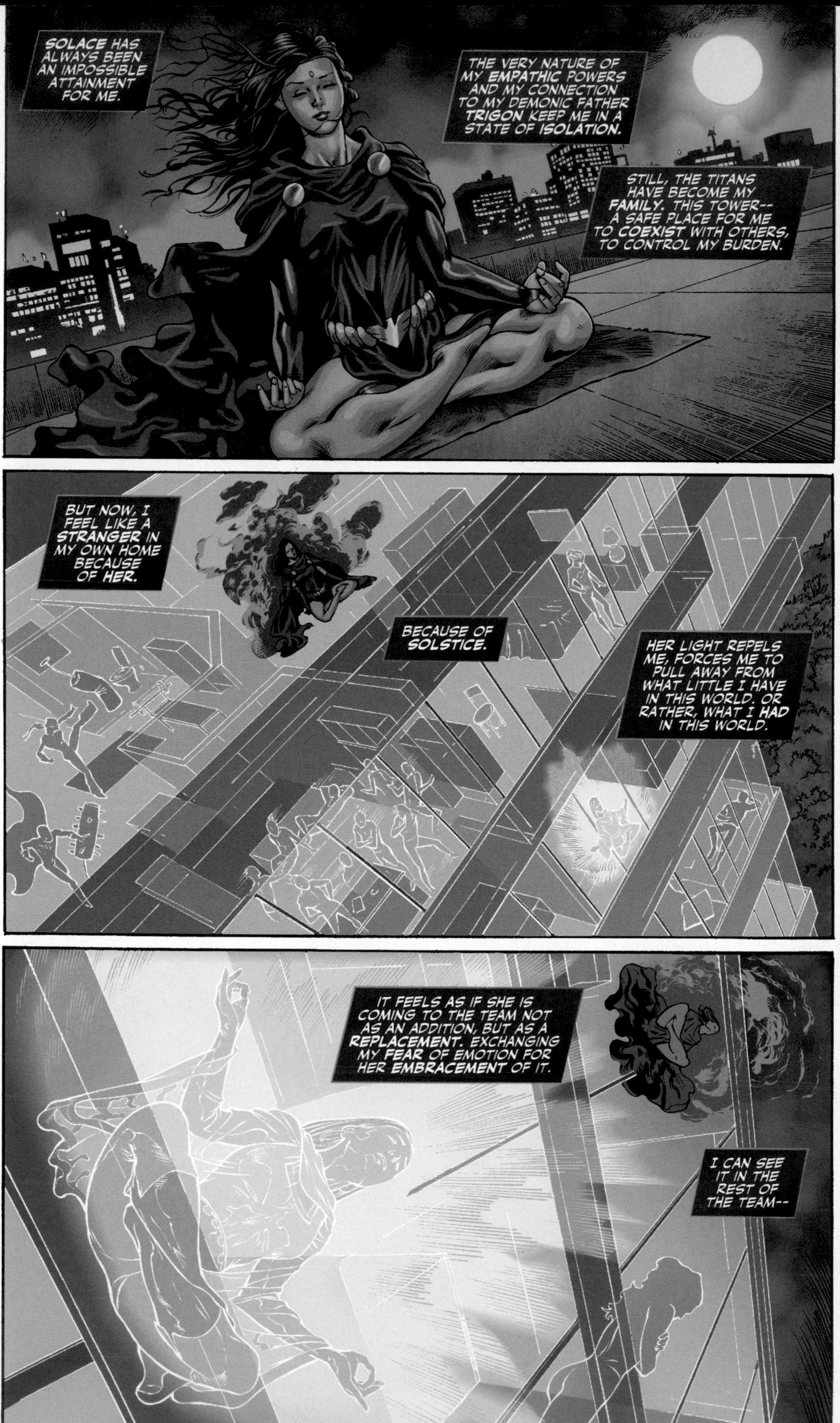
SOLACE HAS ALWAYS BEEN AN IMPOSSIBLE ATTAINMENT FOR ME.
THE VERY NATURE OF MY EMPATHIC POWERS AND MY CONNECTION TO MY DEMONIC FATHER TRIGON KEEP ME IN A STATE OF ISOLATION.
STILL, THE TITANS HAVE BECOME MY FAMILY. THIS TOWER-- A SAFE PLACE FOR ME TO COEXIST WITH OTHERS, TO CONTROL MY BURDEN.
BUT NOW, I FEEL LIKE A STRANGER IN MY OWN HOME BECAUSE OF HER.
BECAUSE OF SOLSTICE.
HER LIGHT REPELS ME, FORCES ME TO PULL AWAY FROM WHAT LITTLE I HAVE IN THIS WORLD. OR RATHER, WHAT I HAD IN THIS WORLD.
IT FEELS AS IF SHE IS COMING TO THE TEAM NOT AS AN ADDITION, BUT AS A REPLACEMENT. EXCHANGING MY FEAR OF EMOTION FOR HER EMBRACEMENT OF IT.
I CAN SEE IT IN THE REST OF THE TEAM--

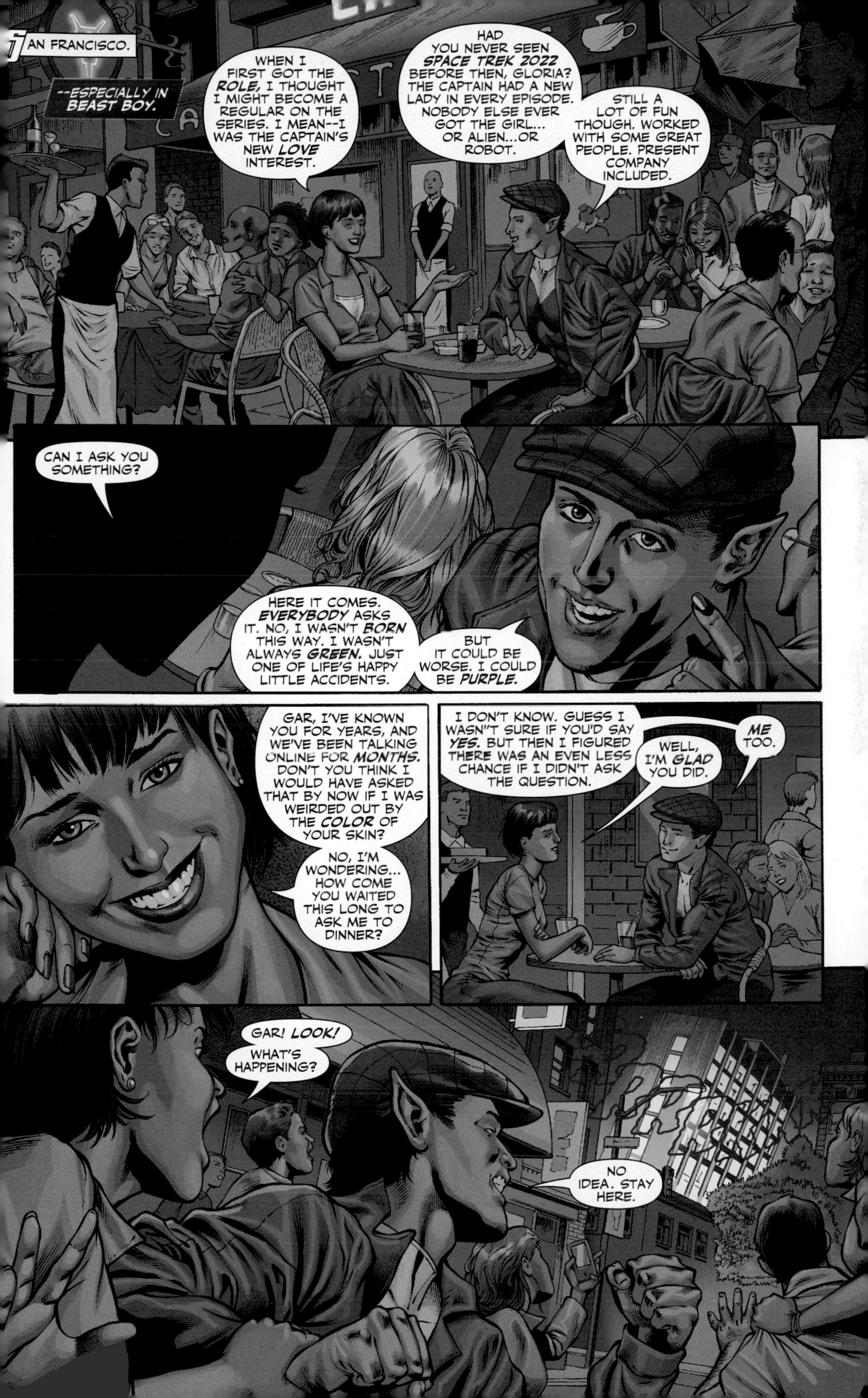
SAN FRANCISCO.
--ESPECIALLY IN BEAST BOY.
WHEN I FIRST GOT THE ROLE, I THOUGHT I MIGHT BECOME A REGULAR ON THE SERIES. I MEAN--I WAS THE CAPTAIN'S NEW LOVE INTEREST.
HAD YOU NEVER SEEN SPACE TREK 2022 BEFORE THEN, GLORIA? THE CAPTAIN HAD A NEW LADY IN EVERY EPISODE. NOBODY ELSE EVER GOT THE GIRL... OR ALIEN...OR ROBOT.
STILL A LOT OF FUN THOUGH. WORKED WITH SOME GREAT PEOPLE. PRESENT COMPANY INCLUDED.
CAN I ASK YOU SOMETHING?
HERE IT COMES. EVERYBODY ASKS IT. NO, I WASN'T BORN THIS WAY. I WASN'T ALWAYS GREEN. JUST ONE OF LIFE'S HAPPY LITTLE ACCIDENTS.
BUT IT COULD BE WORSE. I COULD BE PURPLE.
GAR, I'VE KNOWN YOU FOR YEARS, AND WE'VE BEEN TALKING ONLINE FOR MONTHS. DON'T YOU THINK I WOULD HAVE ASKED THAT BY NOW IF I WAS WEIRDED OUT BY THE COLOR OF YOUR SKIN?
NO, I'M WONDERING... HOW COME YOU WAITED THIS LONG TO ASK ME TO DINNER?
I DON'T KNOW. GUESS I WASN"T SURE IF YOU'D SAY YES. BUT THEN I FIGURED THERE WAS AN EVEN LESS CHANCE IF I DIDN'T ASK THE QUESTION.
WELL, I'M GLAD YOU DID.
ME TOO.
GAR! LOOK!
WHAT'S HAPPENING?
NO IDEA. STAY HERE.

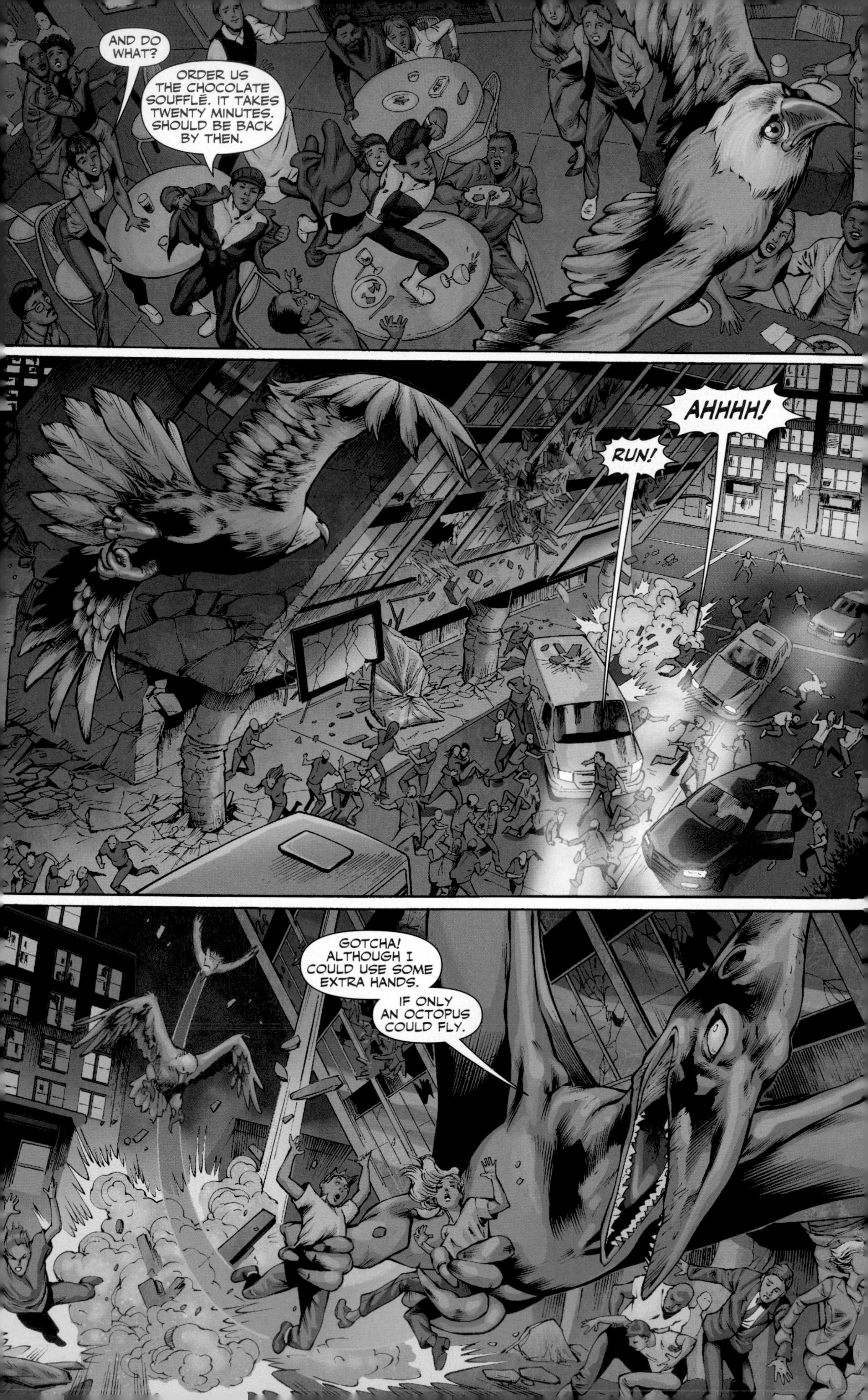
AND DO WHAT?
ORDER US THE CHOCOLATE SOUFFLÉ. IT TAKES TWENTY MINUTES. SHOULD BE BACK BY THEN.
AHHHH!
RUN!
GOTCHA! ALTHOUGH I COULD USE SOME EXTRA HANDS.
IF ONLY AN OCTOPUS COULD FLY.

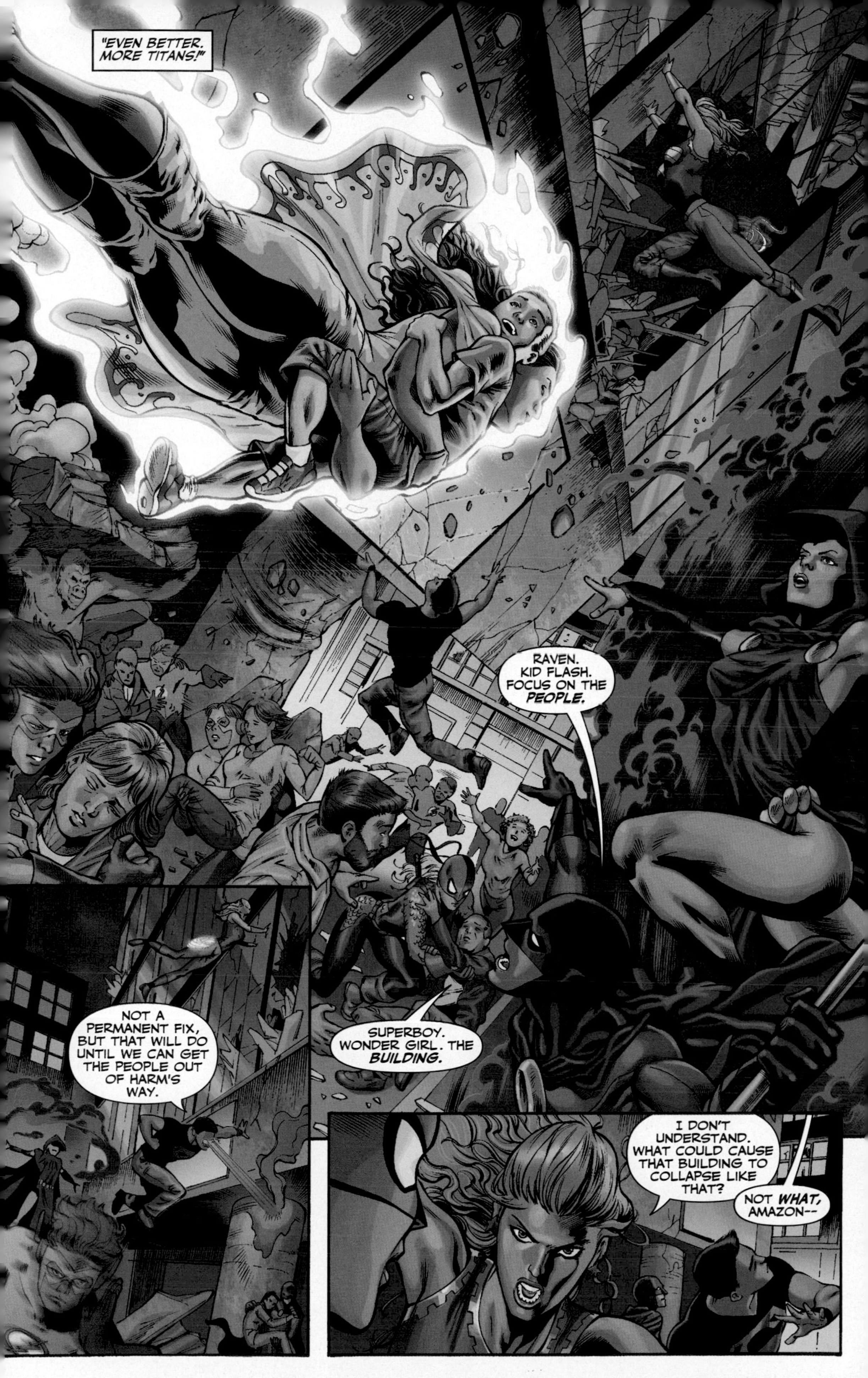
"EVEN BETTER. MORE TITANS!"
RAVEN. KID FLASH. FOCUS ON THE PEOPLE.
SUPERBOY. WONDER GIRL. THE BUILDING.
NOT A PERMANENT FIX, BUT THAT WILL DO UNTIL WE CAN GET THE PEOPLE OUT OF HARM'S WAY.
I DON'T UNDERSTAND. WHAT COULD CAUSE THAT BUILDING TO COLLAPSE LIKE THAT?
NOT WHAT, AMAZON--

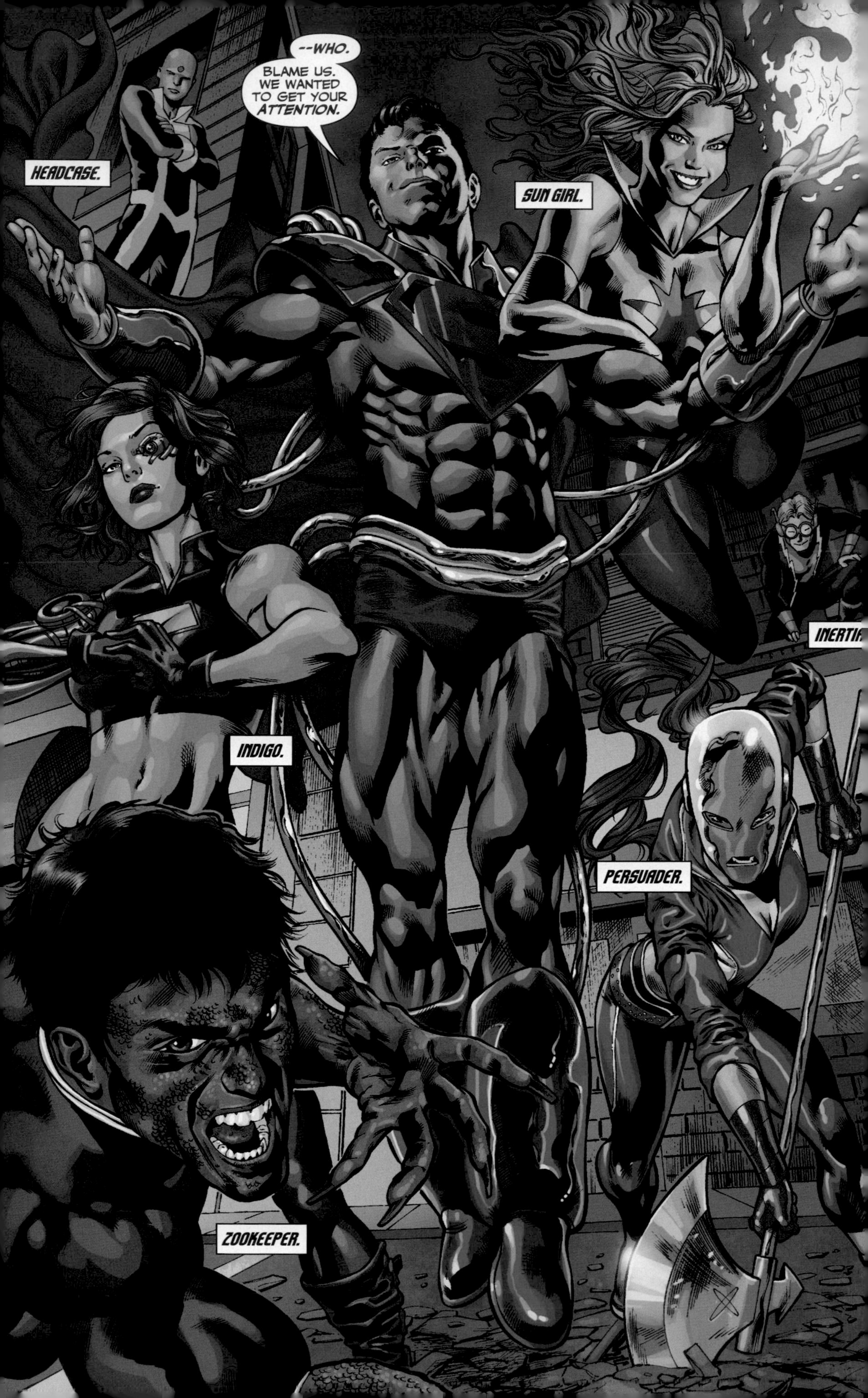
--WHO.
BLAME US. WE WANTED TO GET YOUR ATTENTION.
HEADCASE.
SUN GIRL.
INERTIA
INDIGO.
PERSUADER.
ZOOKEEPER.

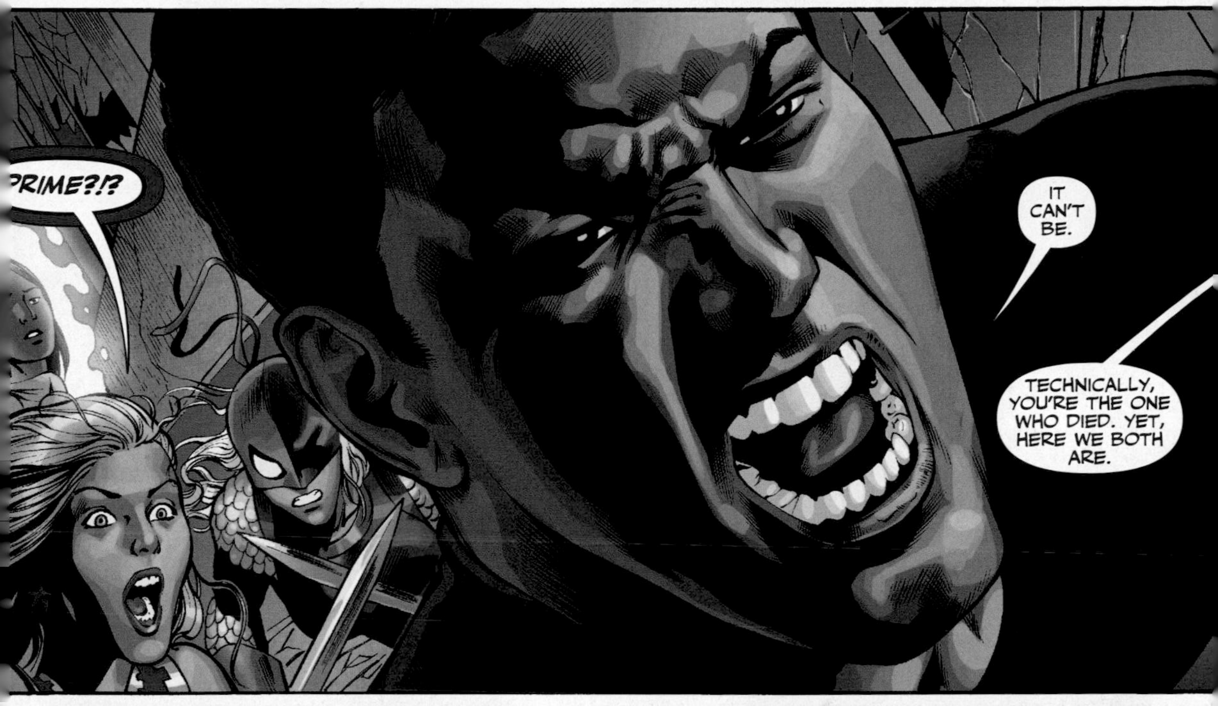
PRIME?!?
IT CAN'T BE.
TECHNICALLY, YOU'RE THE ONE WHO DIED. YET, HERE WE BOTH ARE.
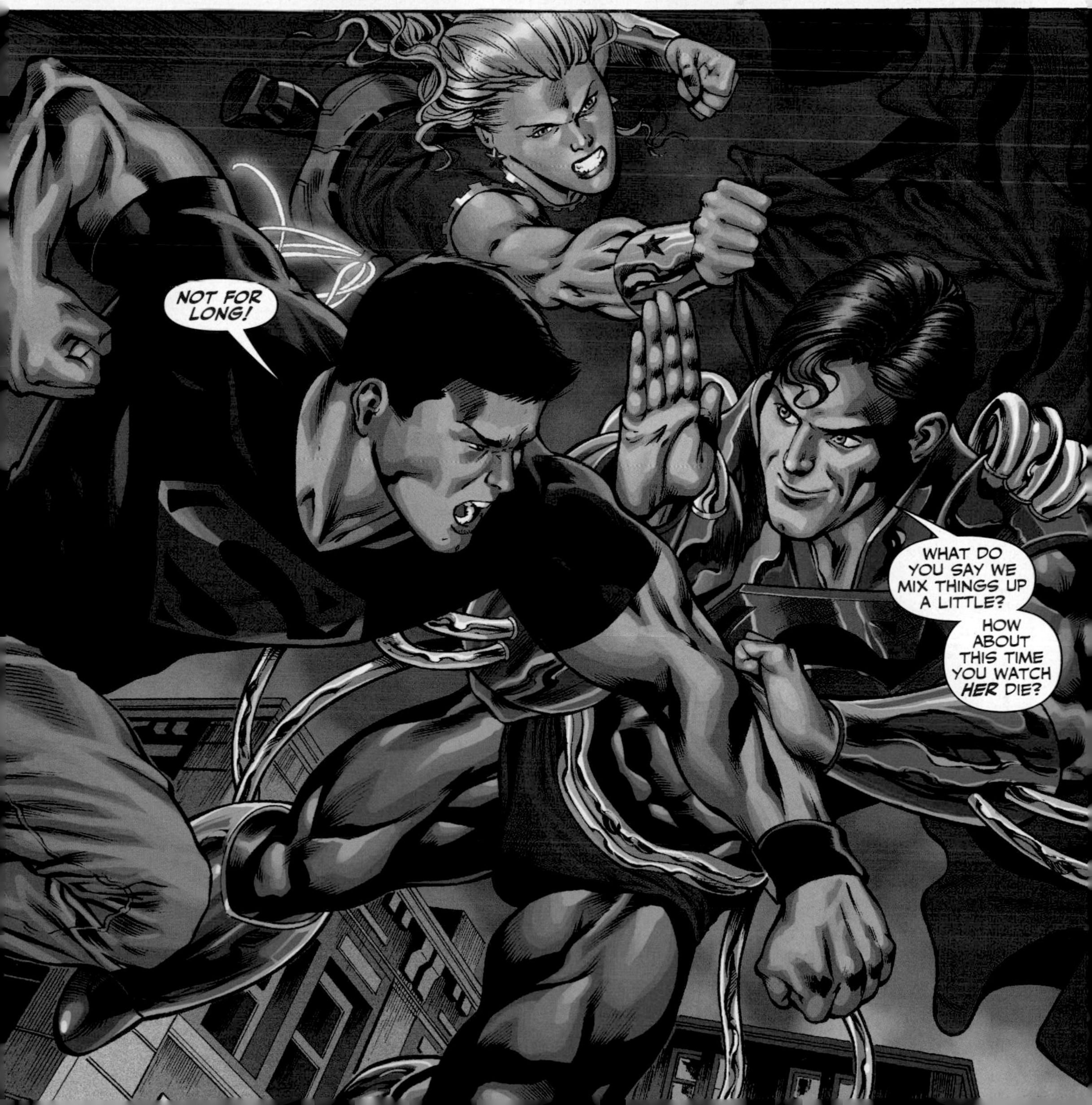
NOT FOR LONG!
WHAT DO YOU SAY WE MIX THINGS UP A LITTLE?
HOW ABOUT THIS TIME YOU WATCH *HER* DIE?

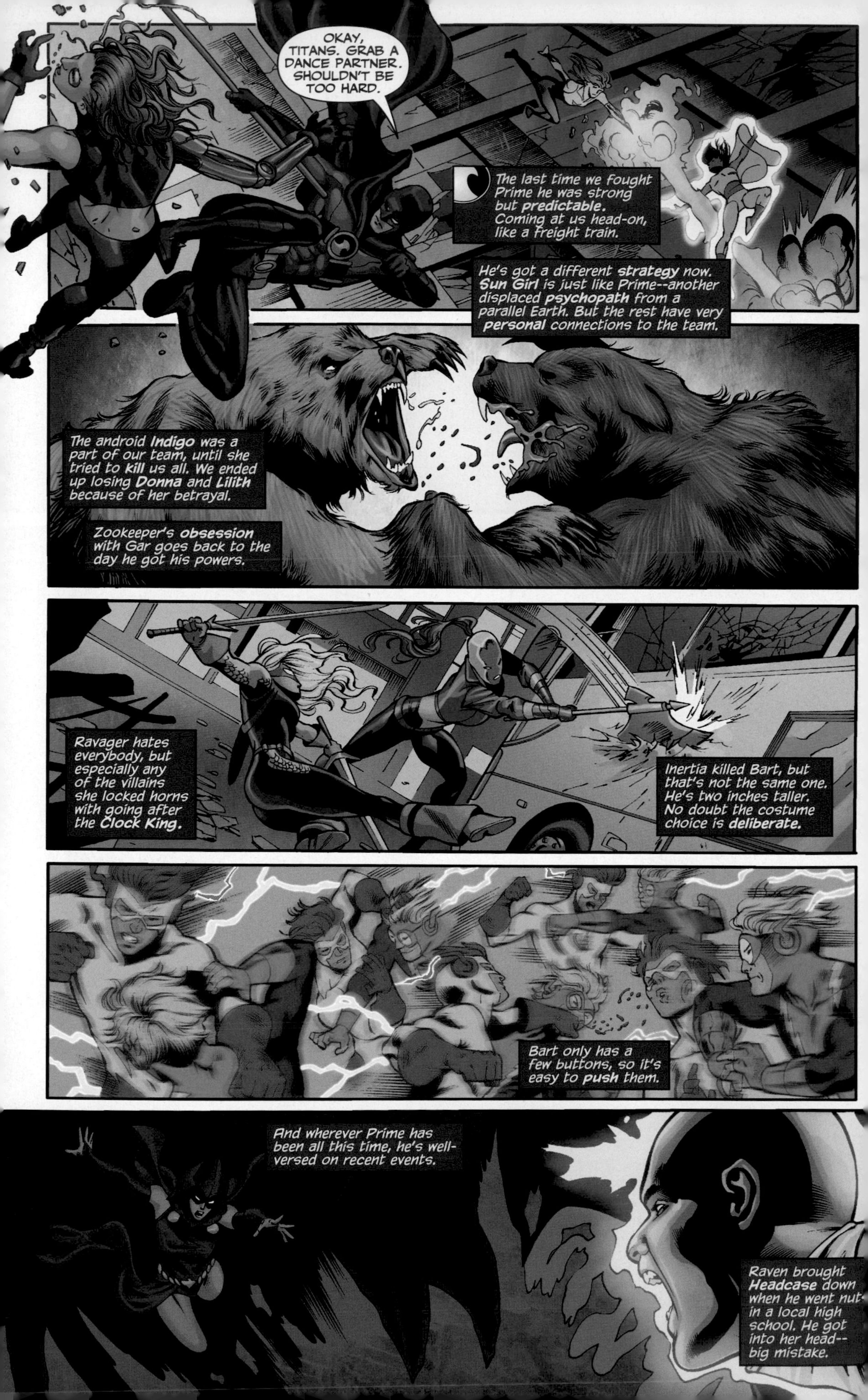
OKAY, TITANS. GRAB A DANCE PARTNER. SHOULDN'T BE TOO HARD.
The last time we fought Prime he was strong but predictable. Coming at us head-on, like a freight train.
He's got a different strategy now. Sun Girl is just like Prime--another displaced psychopath from a parallel Earth. But the rest have very personal connections to the team.
The android Indigo was a part of our team, until she tried to kill us all. We ended up losing Donna and Lilith because of her betrayal.
Zookeeper's obsession with Gar goes back to the day he got his powers.
Ravager hates everybody, but especially any of the villains she locked horns with going after the Clock King.
Inertia killed Bart, but that's not the same one. He's two inches taller. No doubt the costume choice is deliberate.
Bart only has a few buttons, so it's easy to push them.
And wherever Prime has been all this time, he's well-versed on recent events.
Raven brought Headcase down when he went nut in a local high school. He got into her head--big mistake.

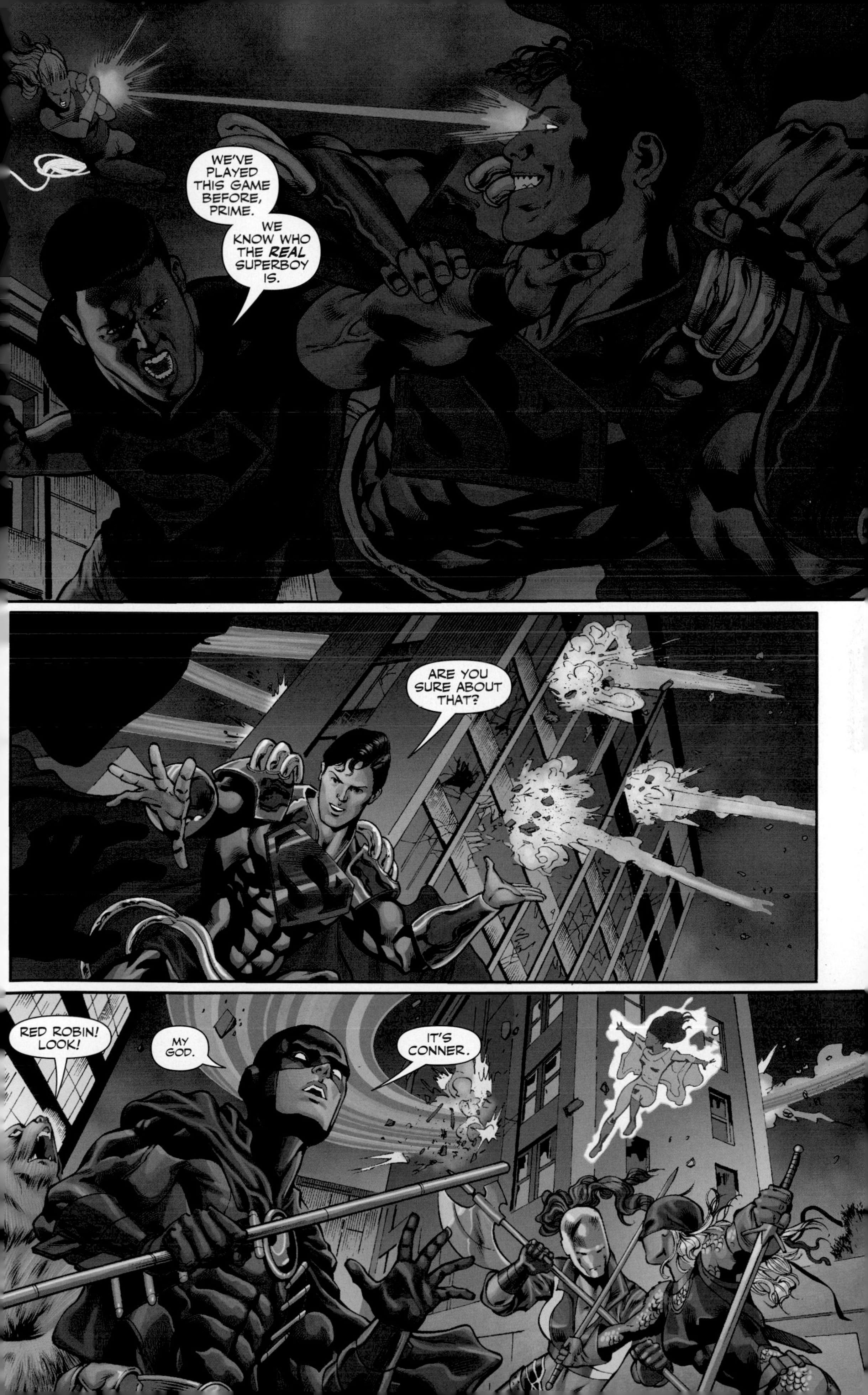
WE'VE PLAYED THIS GAME BEFORE, PRIME.
WE KNOW WHO THE *REAL* SUPERBOY IS.
ARE YOU SURE ABOUT THAT?
RED ROBIN! LOOK!
MY GOD.
IT'S CONNER.

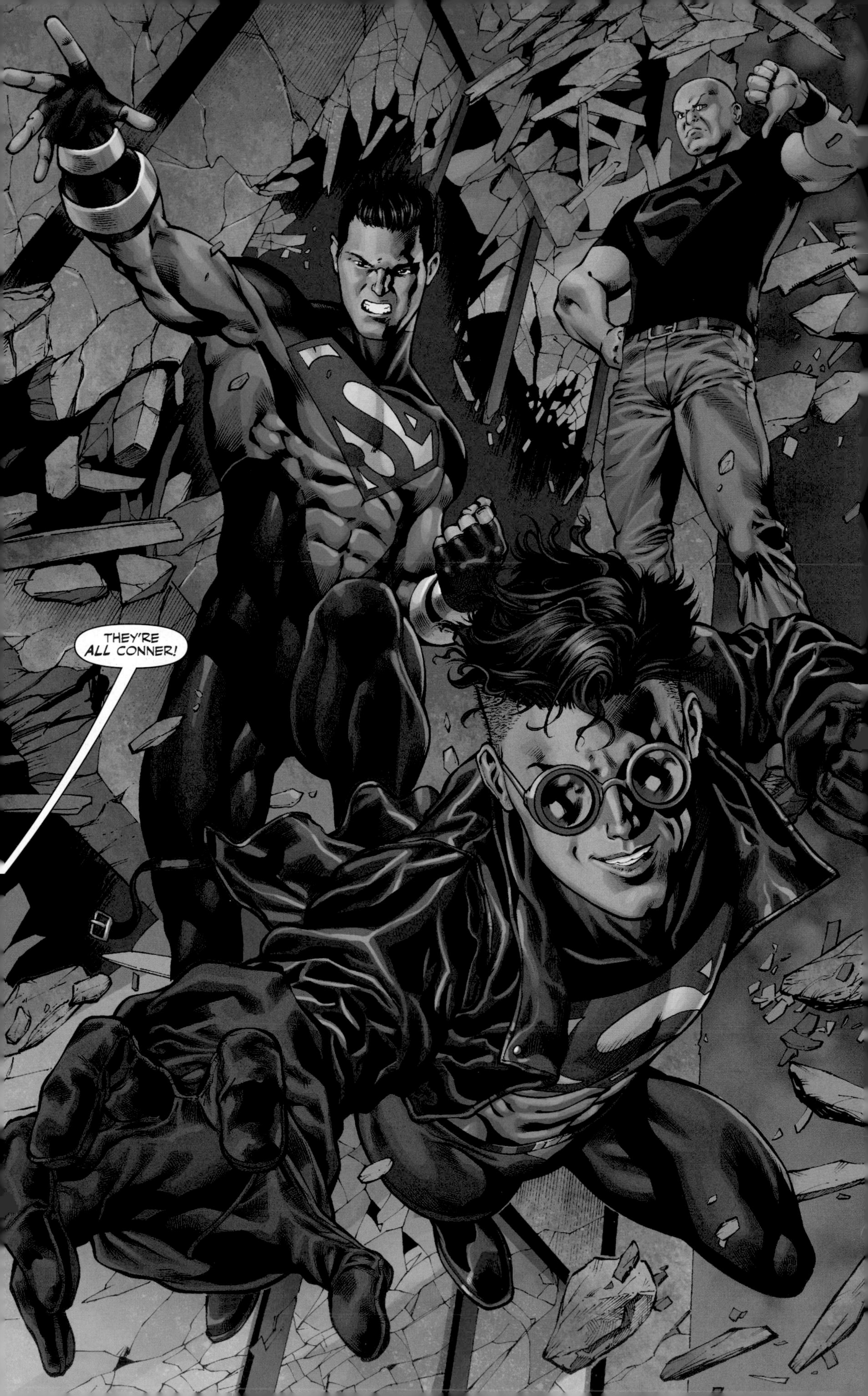
THEY'RE ALL CONNER!

I NEVER WAS ONE FOR ELABORATE SCHEMES.

I USUALLY HAVE NO DESIRE FOR SUCH DRAMATIC MACHINATIONS.

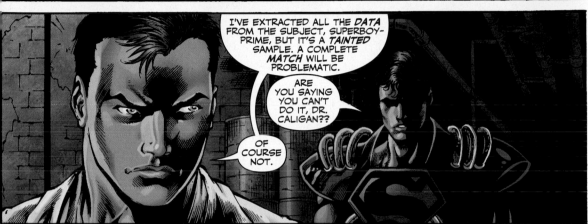

I'VE EXTRACTED ALL THE *DATA* FROM THE SUBJECT, SUPERBOY-PRIME, BUT IT'S A *TAINTED* SAMPLE. A COMPLETE *MATCH* WILL BE PROBLEMATIC.

ARE YOU SAYING YOU CAN'T DO IT, DR. CALIGAN??

OF COURSE NOT.

BUT SOMETIMES, AN IDEA IS TOO *GOOD* TO PASS UP.

I AM MERELY POINTING OUT THAT *CLONING* IS NOT MY FIELD OF INTEREST.

MATCH. Defective Superboy clone.

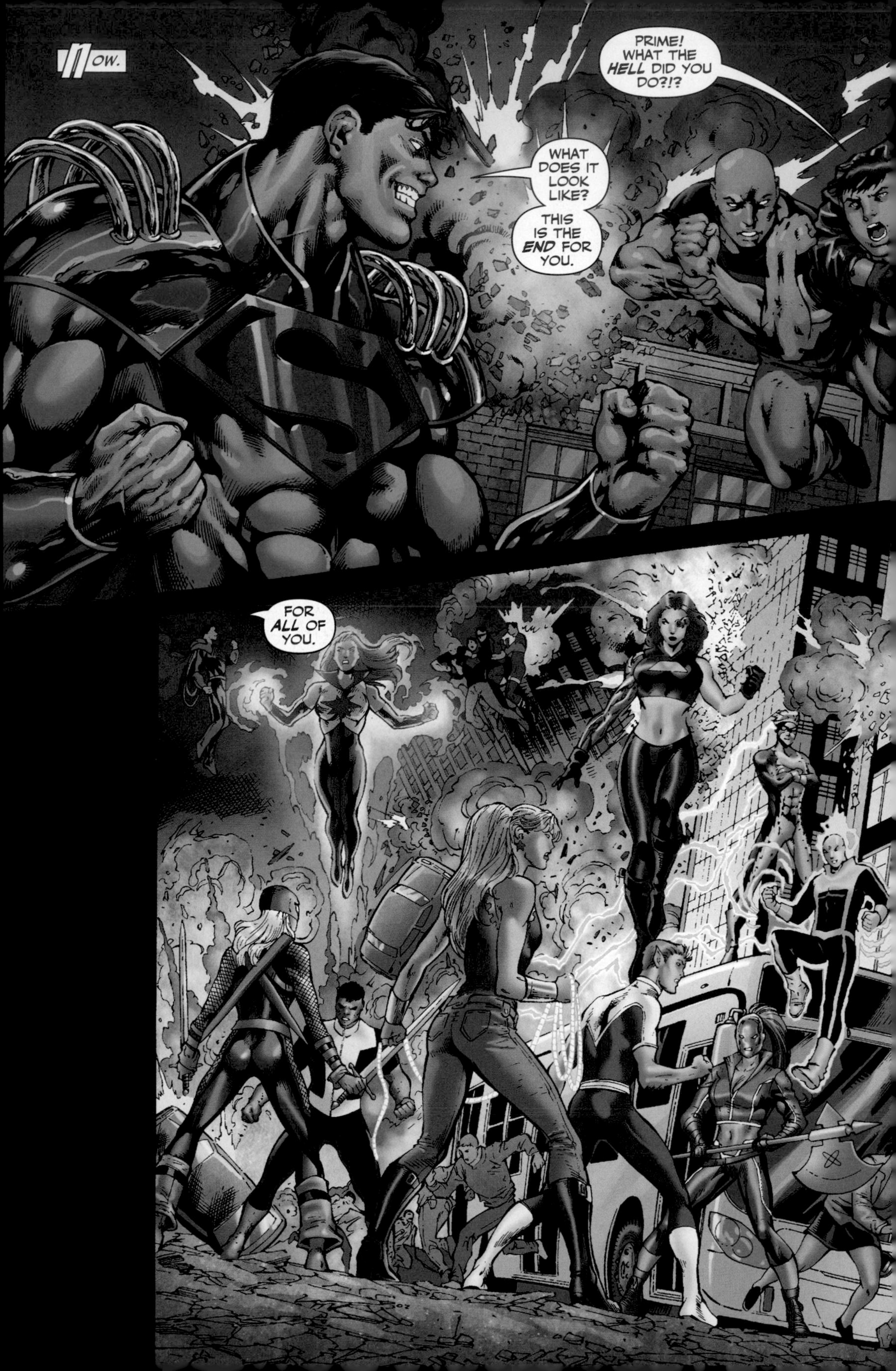
NOW.
PRIME! WHAT THE HELL DID YOU DO?!?
WHAT DOES IT LOOK LIKE?
THIS IS THE END FOR YOU.
FOR ALL OF YOU.

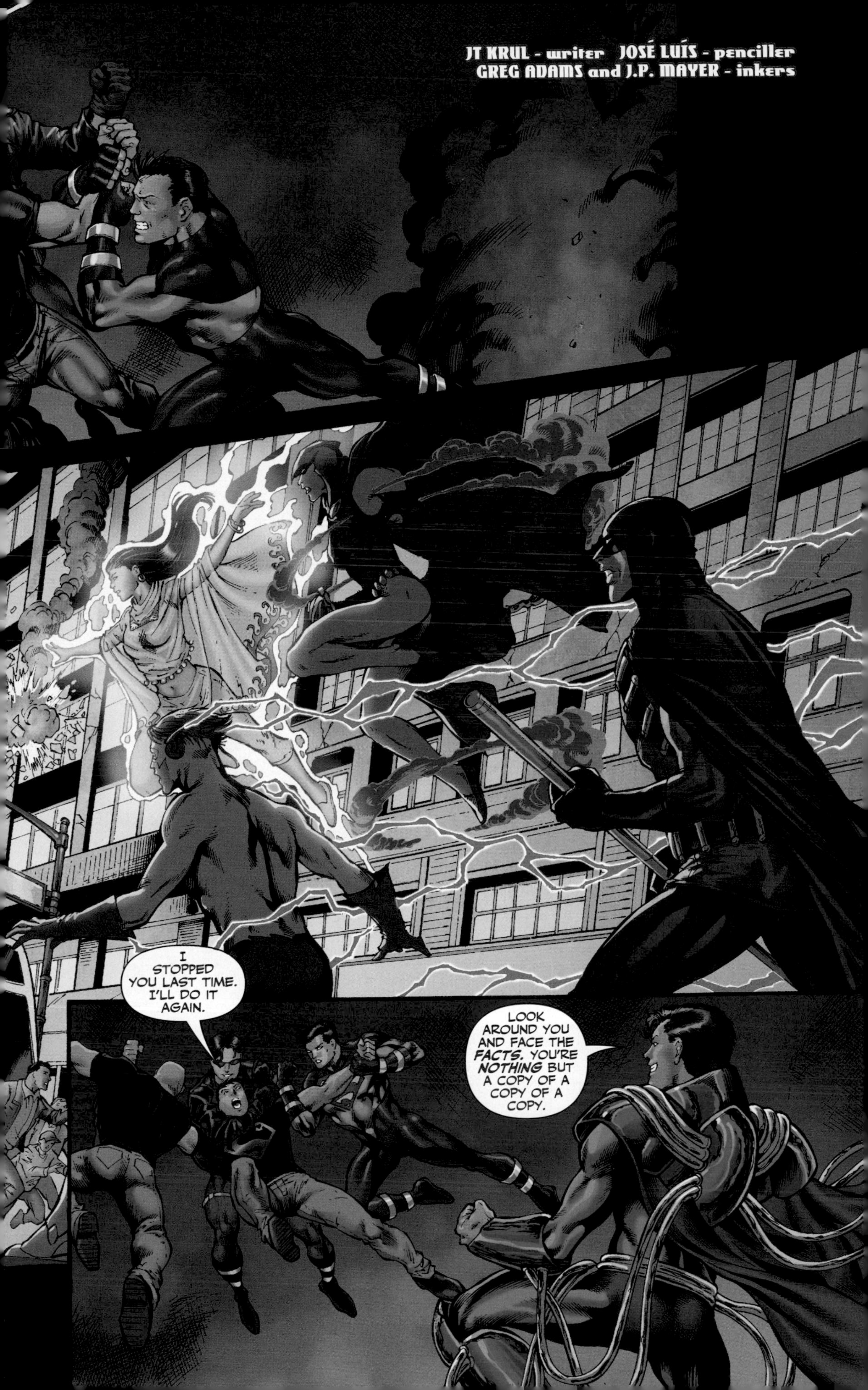
JT KRUL - writer JOSÉ LUÍS - penciller
GREG ADAMS and J.P. MAYER - inkers
I STOPPED YOU LAST TIME. I'LL DO IT AGAIN.
LOOK AROUND YOU AND FACE THE FACTS. YOU'RE NOTHING BUT A COPY OF A COPY OF A COPY.

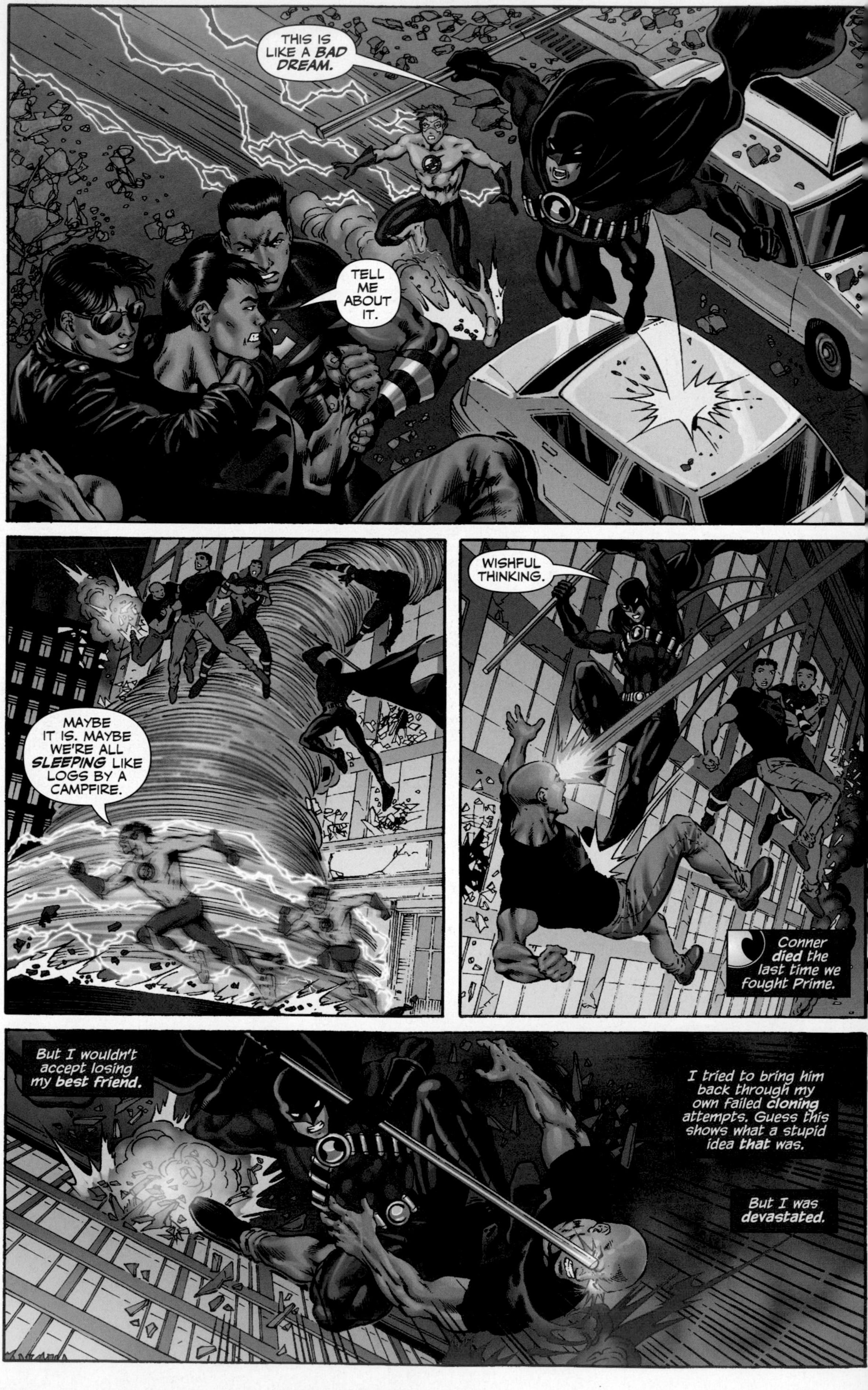
THIS IS LIKE A BAD DREAM.
TELL ME ABOUT IT.
MAYBE IT IS. MAYBE WE'RE ALL SLEEPING LIKE LOGS BY A CAMPFIRE.
WISHFUL THINKING.
Conner died the last time we fought Prime.
But I wouldn't accept losing my best friend.
I tried to bring him back through my own failed cloning attempts. Guess this shows what a stupid idea that was.
But I was devastated.

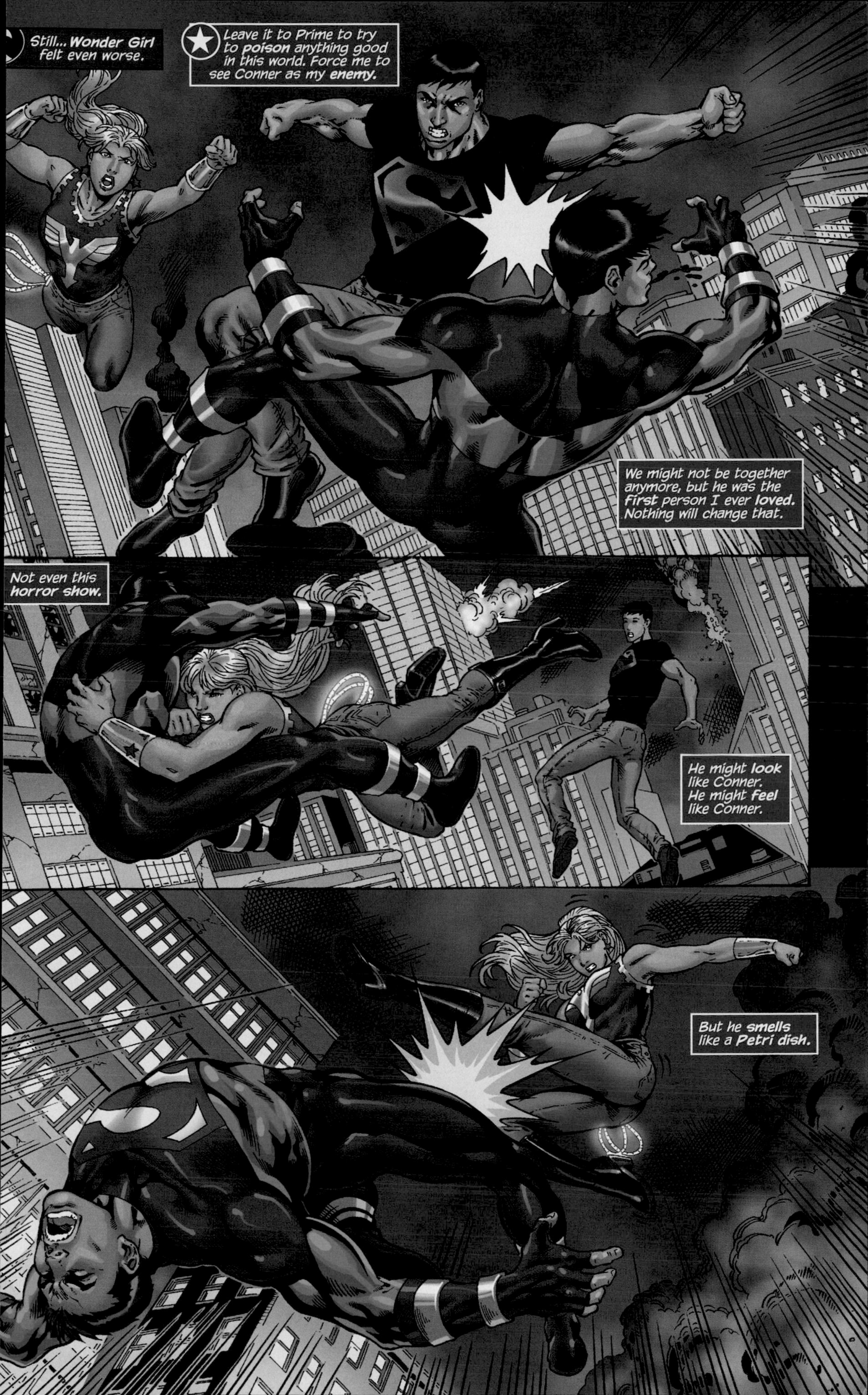
Still... Wonder Girl felt even worse.
Leave it to Prime to try to poison anything good in this world. Force me to see Conner as my enemy.
We might not be together anymore, but he was the first person I ever loved. Nothing will change that.
Not even this horror show.
He might look like Conner. He might feel like Conner.
But he smells like a Petri dish.

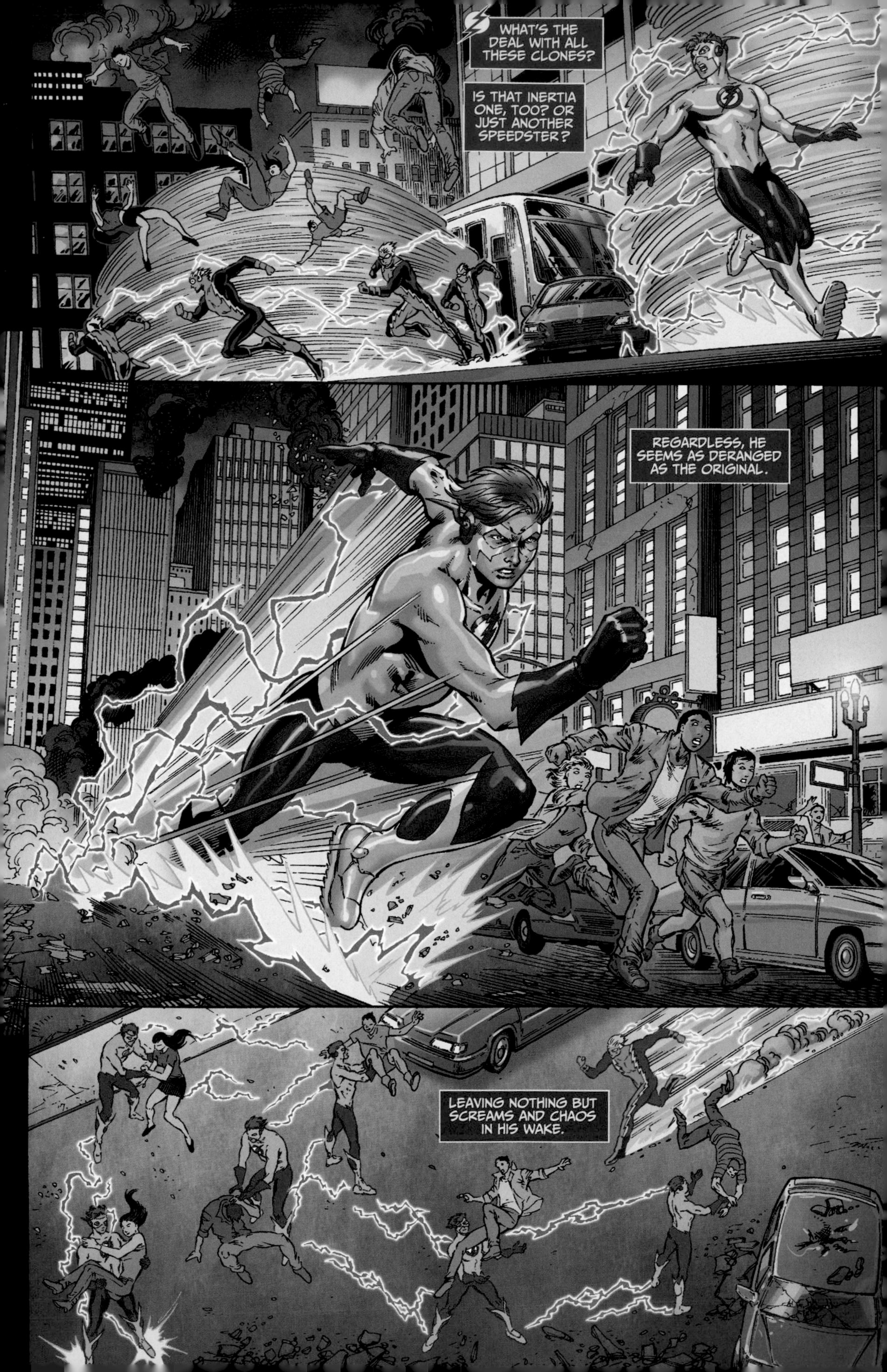
WHAT'S THE DEAL WITH ALL THESE CLONES?
IS THAT INERTIA ONE, TOO? OR JUST ANOTHER SPEEDSTER?
REGARDLESS, HE SEEMS AS DERANGED AS THE ORIGINAL.
LEAVING NOTHING BUT SCREAMS AND CHAOS IN HIS WAKE.

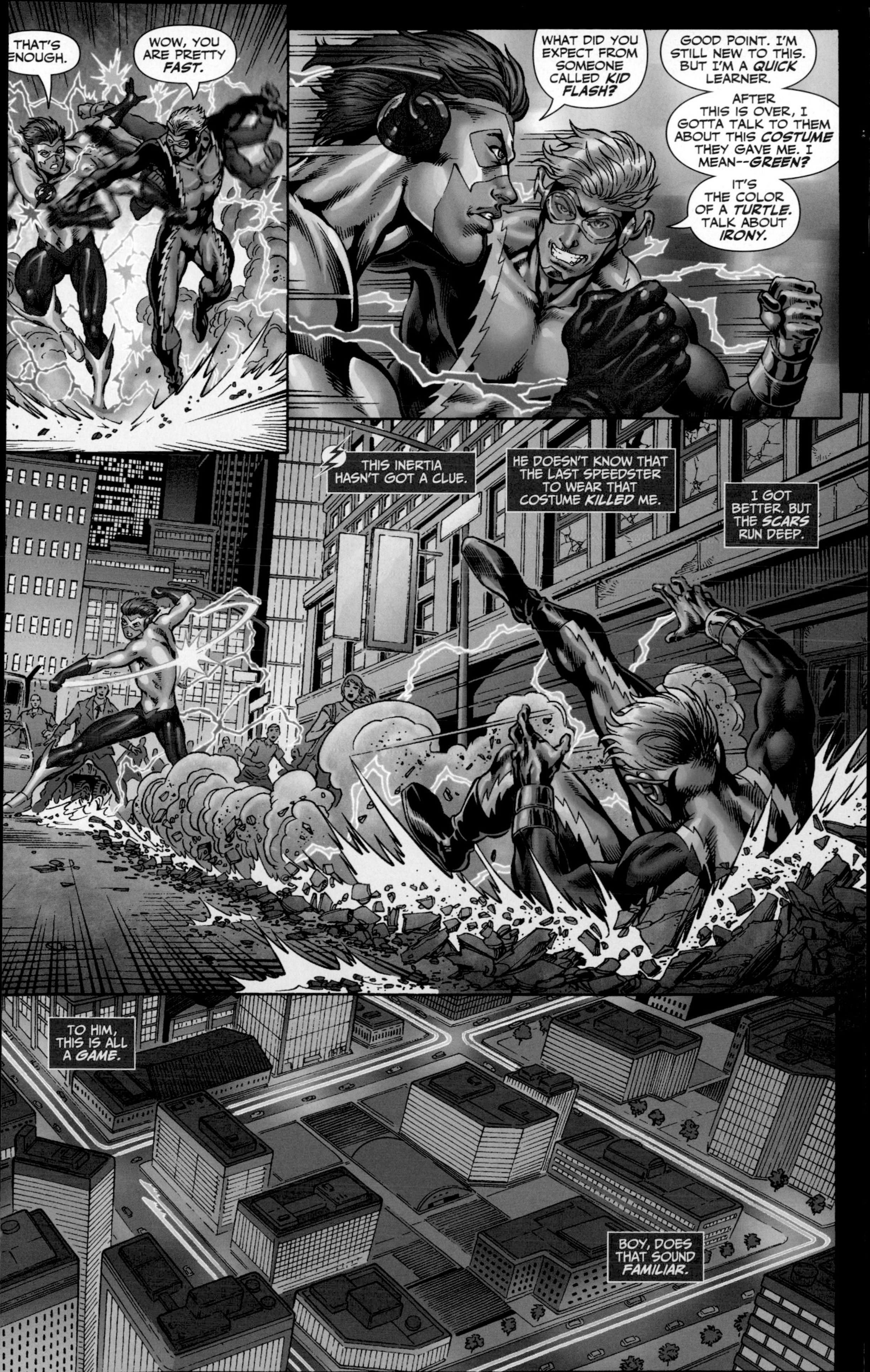
THAT'S ENOUGH.
WOW, YOU ARE PRETTY *FAST.*
WHAT DID YOU EXPECT FROM SOMEONE CALLED *KID FLASH?*
GOOD POINT. I'M STILL NEW TO THIS. BUT I'M A *QUICK* LEARNER.
AFTER THIS IS OVER, I GOTTA TALK TO THEM ABOUT THIS *COSTUME* THEY GAVE ME. I MEAN--*GREEN?*
IT'S THE COLOR OF A *TURTLE.* TALK ABOUT *IRONY.*
THIS INERTIA HASN'T GOT A CLUE.
HE DOESN'T KNOW THAT THE LAST SPEEDSTER TO WEAR THAT COSTUME *KILLED* ME.
I GOT BETTER. BUT THE *SCARS* RUN DEEP.
TO HIM, THIS IS ALL A *GAME.*
BOY, DOES THAT SOUND *FAMILIAR.*

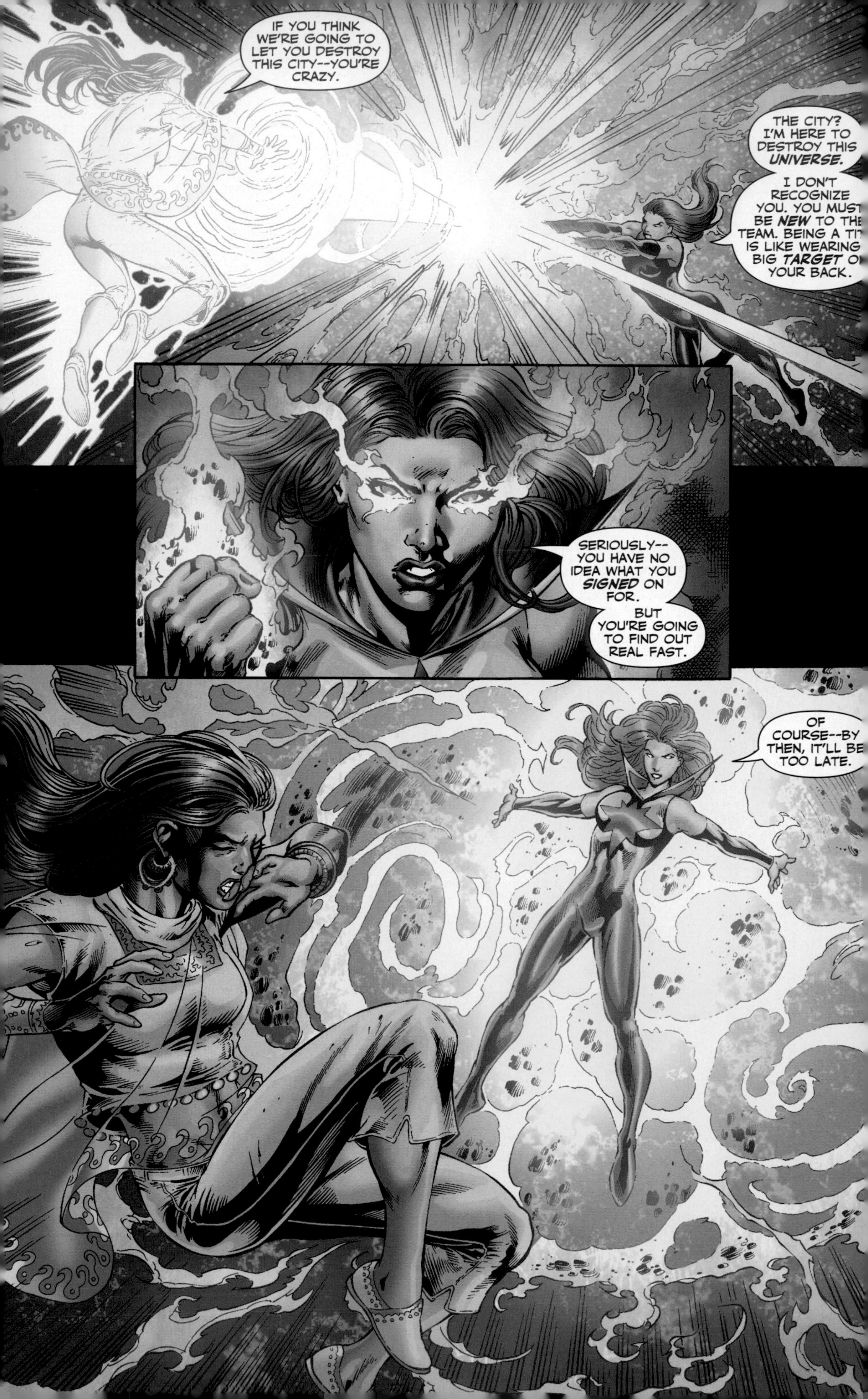

IF YOU THINK WE'RE GOING TO LET YOU DESTROY THIS CITY--YOU'RE CRAZY.
THE CITY? I'M HERE TO DESTROY THIS UNIVERSE.
I DON'T RECOGNIZE YOU. YOU MUST BE NEW TO THE TEAM. BEING A TIT IS LIKE WEARING BIG TARGET O YOUR BACK.
SERIOUSLY-- YOU HAVE NO IDEA WHAT YOU SIGNED ON FOR.
BUT YOU'RE GOING TO FIND OUT REAL FAST.
OF COURSE--BY THEN, IT'LL BE TOO LATE.

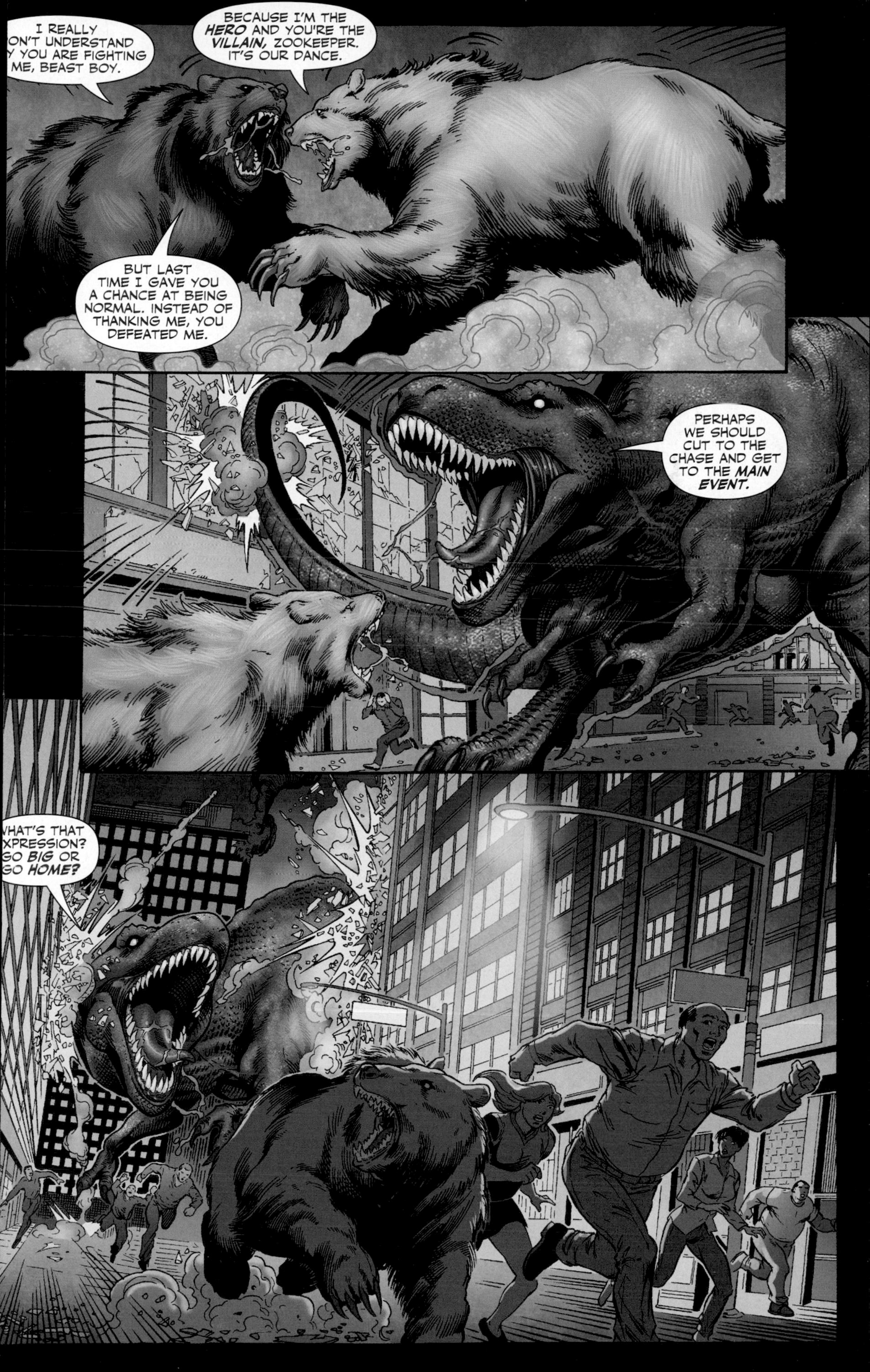
I REALLY ON'T UNDERSTAND Y YOU ARE FIGHTING ME, BEAST BOY.
BECAUSE I'M THE *HERO* AND YOU'RE THE *VILLAIN,* ZOOKEEPER. IT'S OUR DANCE.
BUT LAST TIME I GAVE YOU A CHANCE AT BEING NORMAL. INSTEAD OF THANKING ME, YOU DEFEATED ME.
PERHAPS WE SHOULD CUT TO THE CHASE AND GET TO THE *MAIN EVENT.*
HAT'S THAT XPRESSION? GO *BIG* OR GO *HOME?*

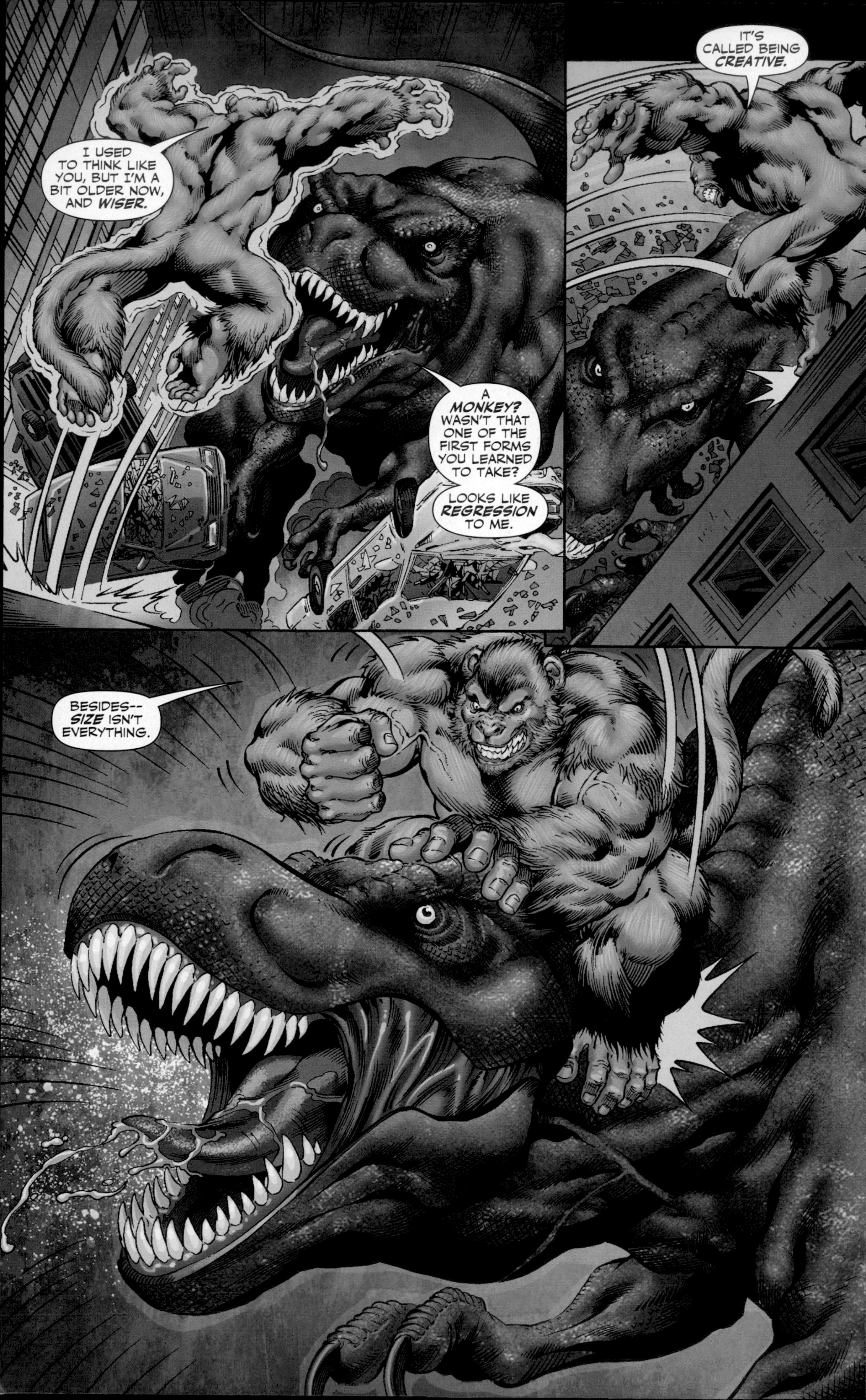
I USED TO THINK LIKE YOU, BUT I'M A BIT OLDER NOW, AND WISER.
A MONKEY? WASN'T THAT ONE OF THE FIRST FORMS YOU LEARNED TO TAKE?
LOOKS LIKE REGRESSION TO ME.
IT'S CALLED BEING CREATIVE.
BESIDES-- SIZE ISN'T EVERYTHING.

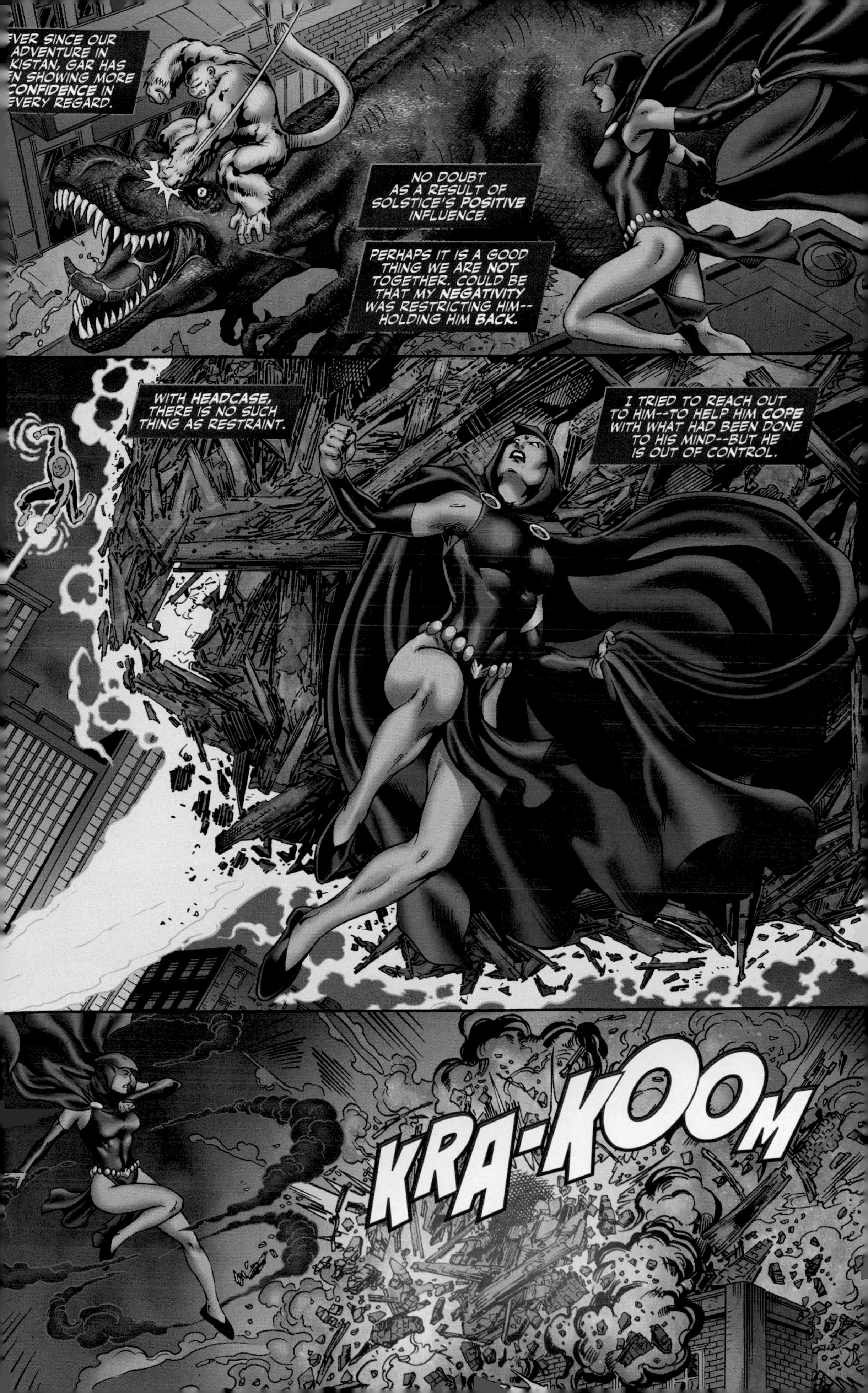
EVER SINCE OUR ADVENTURE IN KISTAN, GAR HAS EN SHOWING MORE CONFIDENCE IN EVERY REGARD.
NO DOUBT AS A RESULT OF SOLSTICE'S POSITIVE INFLUENCE.
PERHAPS IT IS A GOOD THING WE ARE NOT TOGETHER. COULD BE THAT MY NEGATIVITY WAS RESTRICTING HIM--HOLDING HIM BACK.
WITH HEADCASE, THERE IS NO SUCH THING AS RESTRAINT.
I TRIED TO REACH OUT TO HIM--TO HELP HIM COPE WITH WHAT HAD BEEN DONE TO HIS MIND--BUT HE IS OUT OF CONTROL.
KRA-KOOM

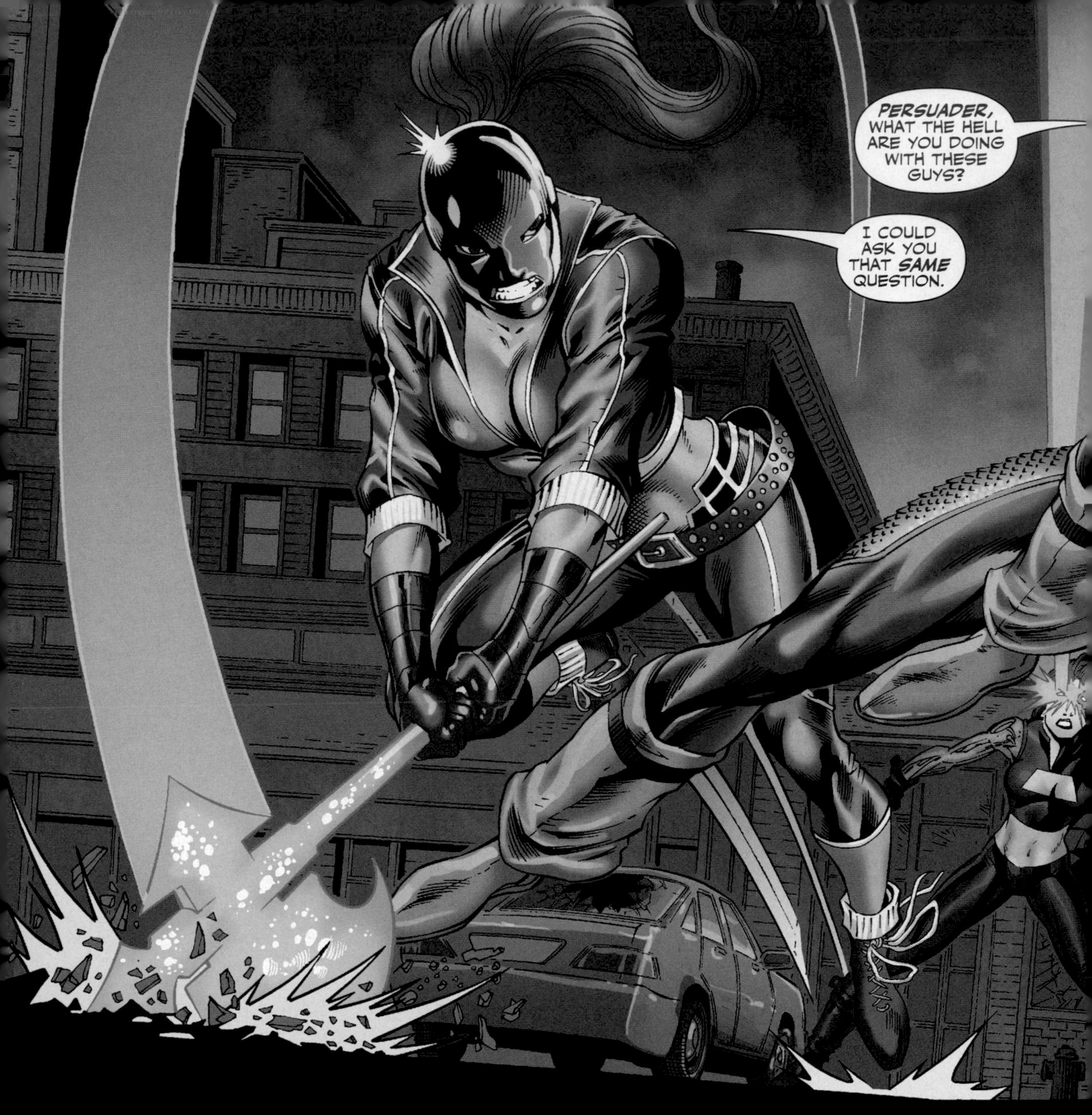
PERSUADER, WHAT THE HELL ARE YOU DOING WITH THESE GUYS?
I COULD ASK YOU THAT SAME QUESTION.

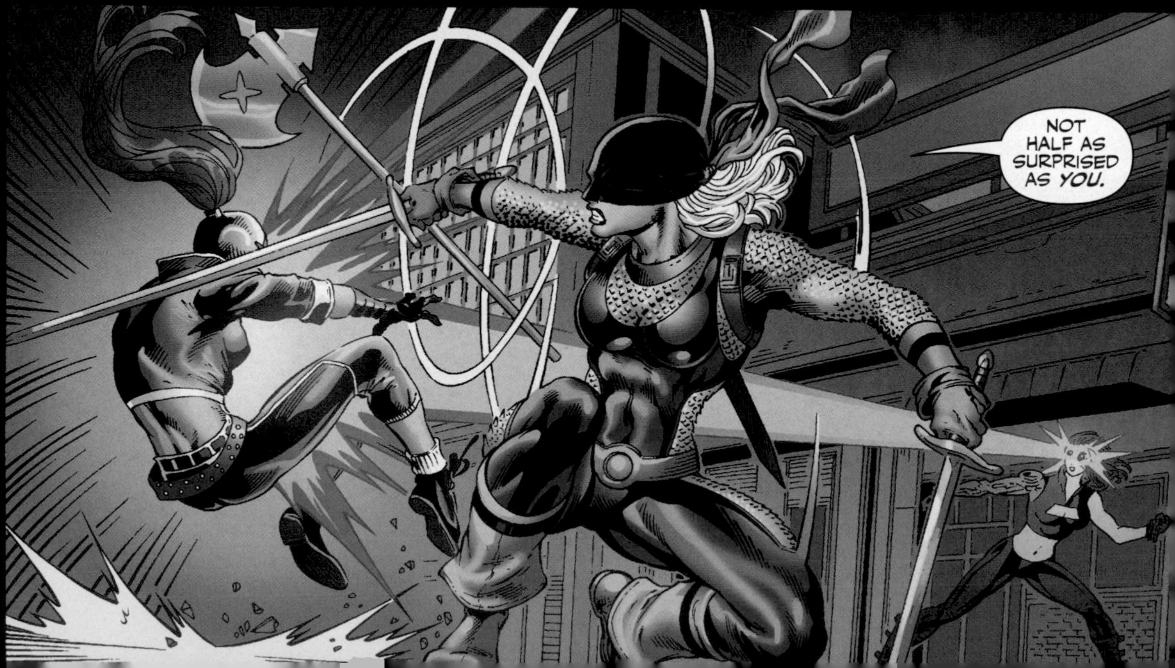
NOT HALF AS SURPRISED AS YOU.

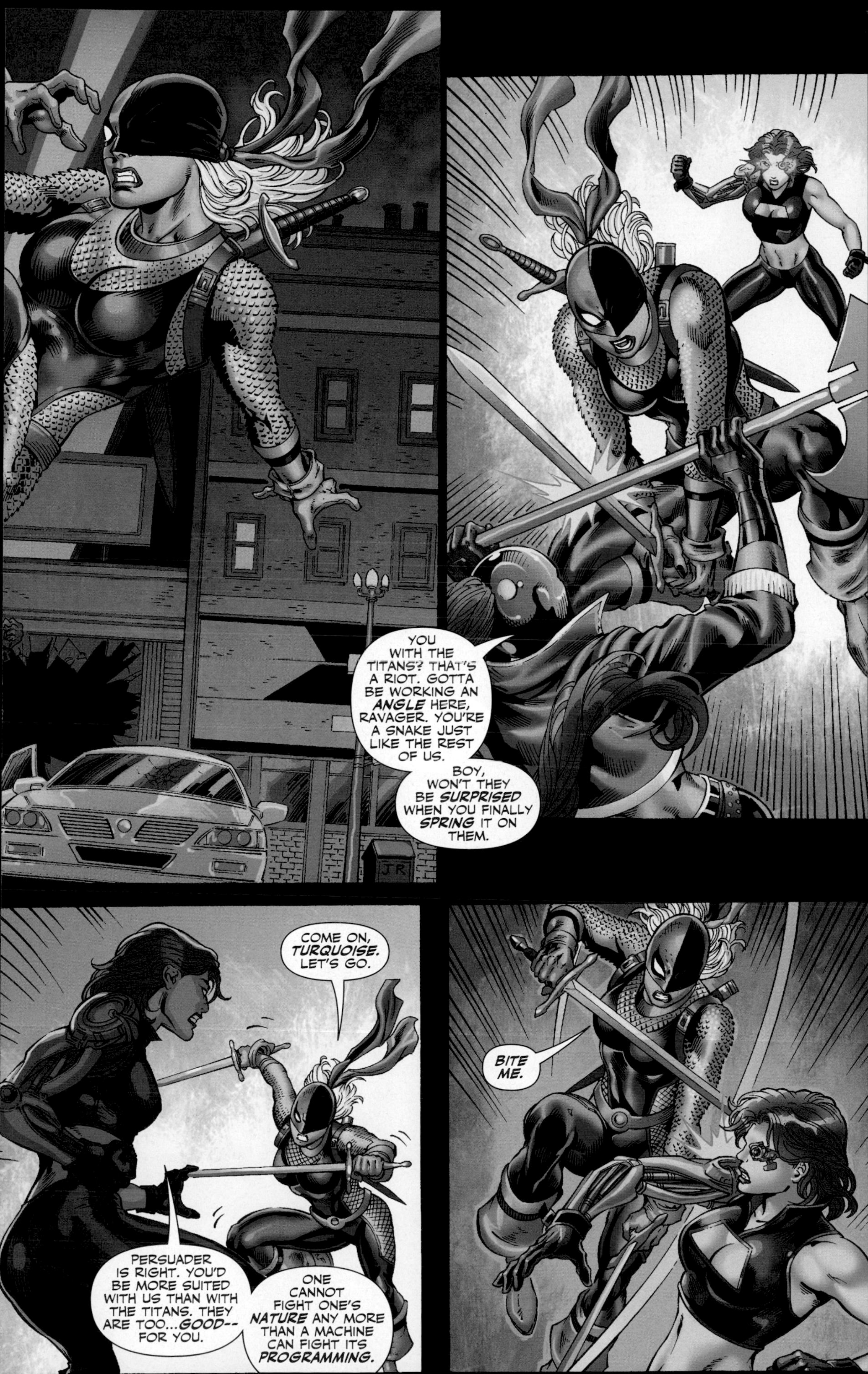
YOU WITH THE TITANS? THAT'S A RIOT. GOTTA BE WORKING AN ANGLE HERE, RAVAGER. YOU'RE A SNAKE JUST LIKE THE REST OF US.
BOY, WON'T THEY BE SURPRISED WHEN YOU FINALLY SPRING IT ON THEM.
JR
COME ON, TURQUOISE. LET'S GO.
PERSUADER IS RIGHT. YOU'D BE MORE SUITED WITH US THAN WITH THE TITANS. THEY ARE TOO...GOOD-- FOR YOU.
ONE CANNOT FIGHT ONE'S NATURE ANY MORE THAN A MACHINE CAN FIGHT ITS PROGRAMMING.
BITE ME.

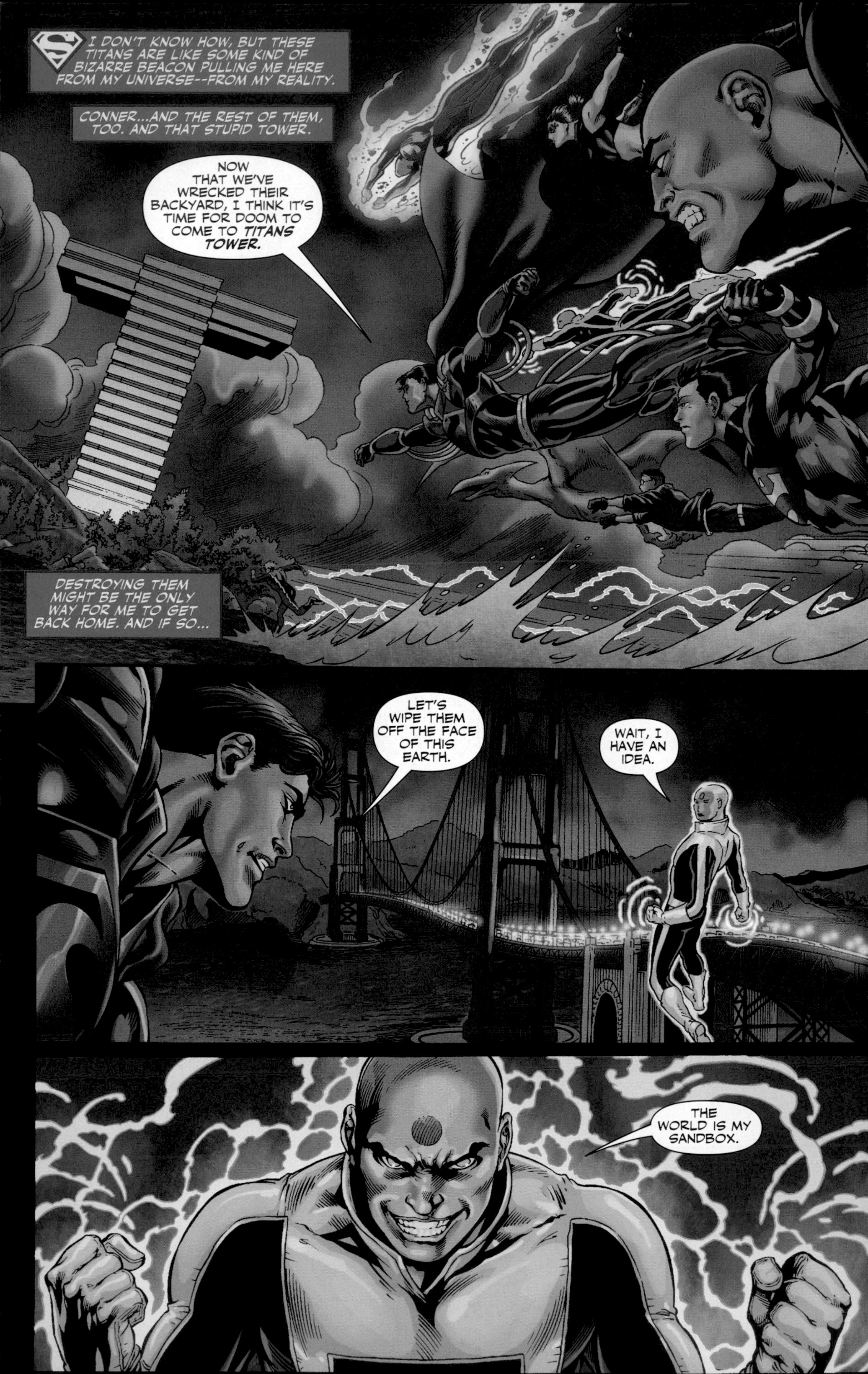
I DON'T KNOW HOW, BUT THESE TITANS ARE LIKE SOME KIND OF BIZARRE BEACON PULLING ME HERE FROM MY UNIVERSE--FROM MY REALITY.
CONNER...AND THE REST OF THEM, TOO. AND THAT STUPID TOWER.
NOW THAT WE'VE WRECKED THEIR BACKYARD, I THINK IT'S TIME FOR DOOM TO COME TO TITANS TOWER.
DESTROYING THEM MIGHT BE THE ONLY WAY FOR ME TO GET BACK HOME. AND IF SO...
LET'S WIPE THEM OFF THE FACE OF THIS EARTH.
WAIT, I HAVE AN IDEA.
THE WORLD IS MY SANDBOX.

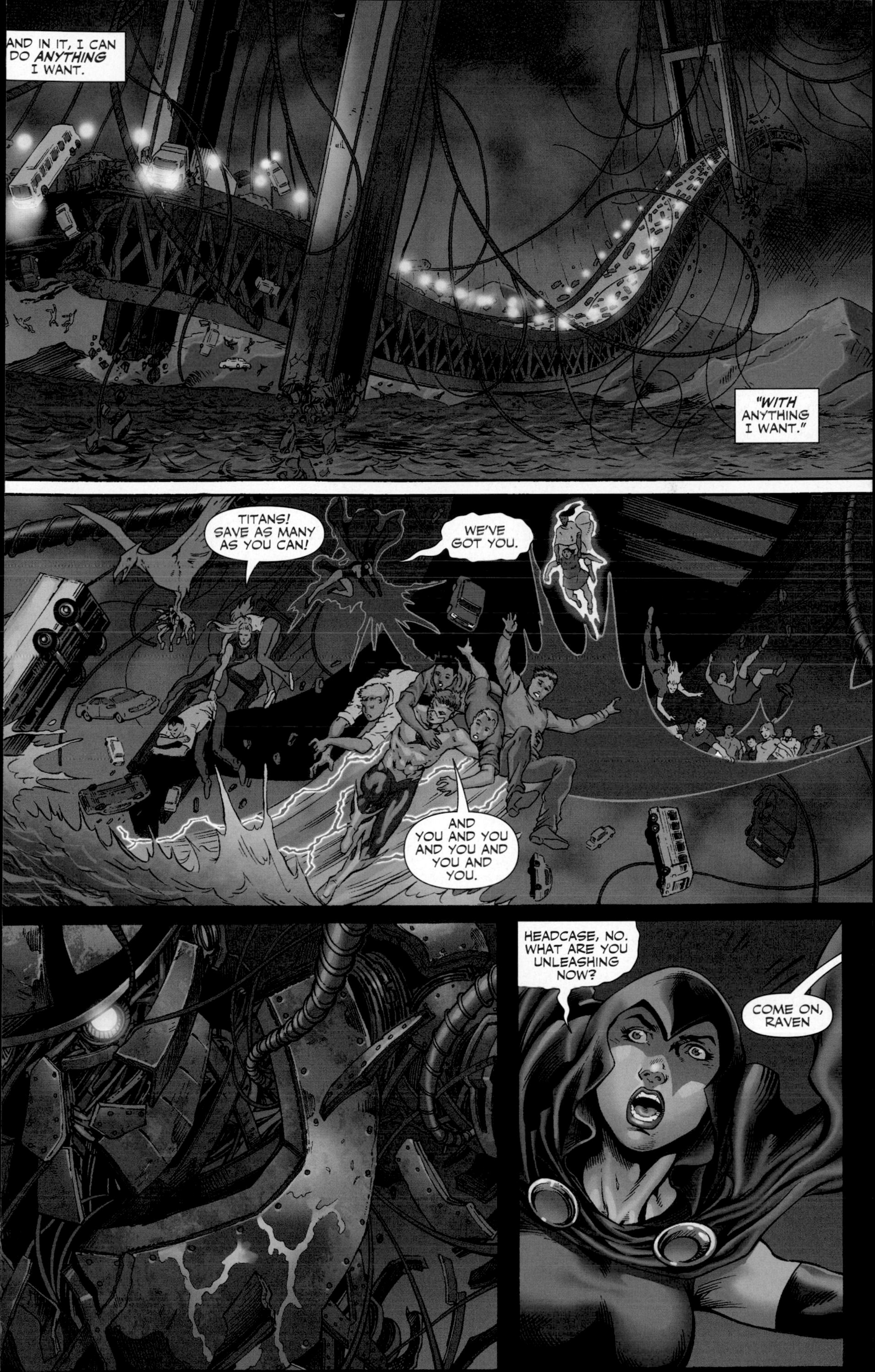
AND IN IT, I CAN DO ANYTHING I WANT.
"WITH ANYTHING I WANT."
TITANS! SAVE AS MANY AS YOU CAN!
WE'VE GOT YOU.
AND YOU AND YOU AND YOU AND YOU AND YOU.
HEADCASE, NO. WHAT ARE YOU UNLEASHING NOW?
COME ON, RAVEN

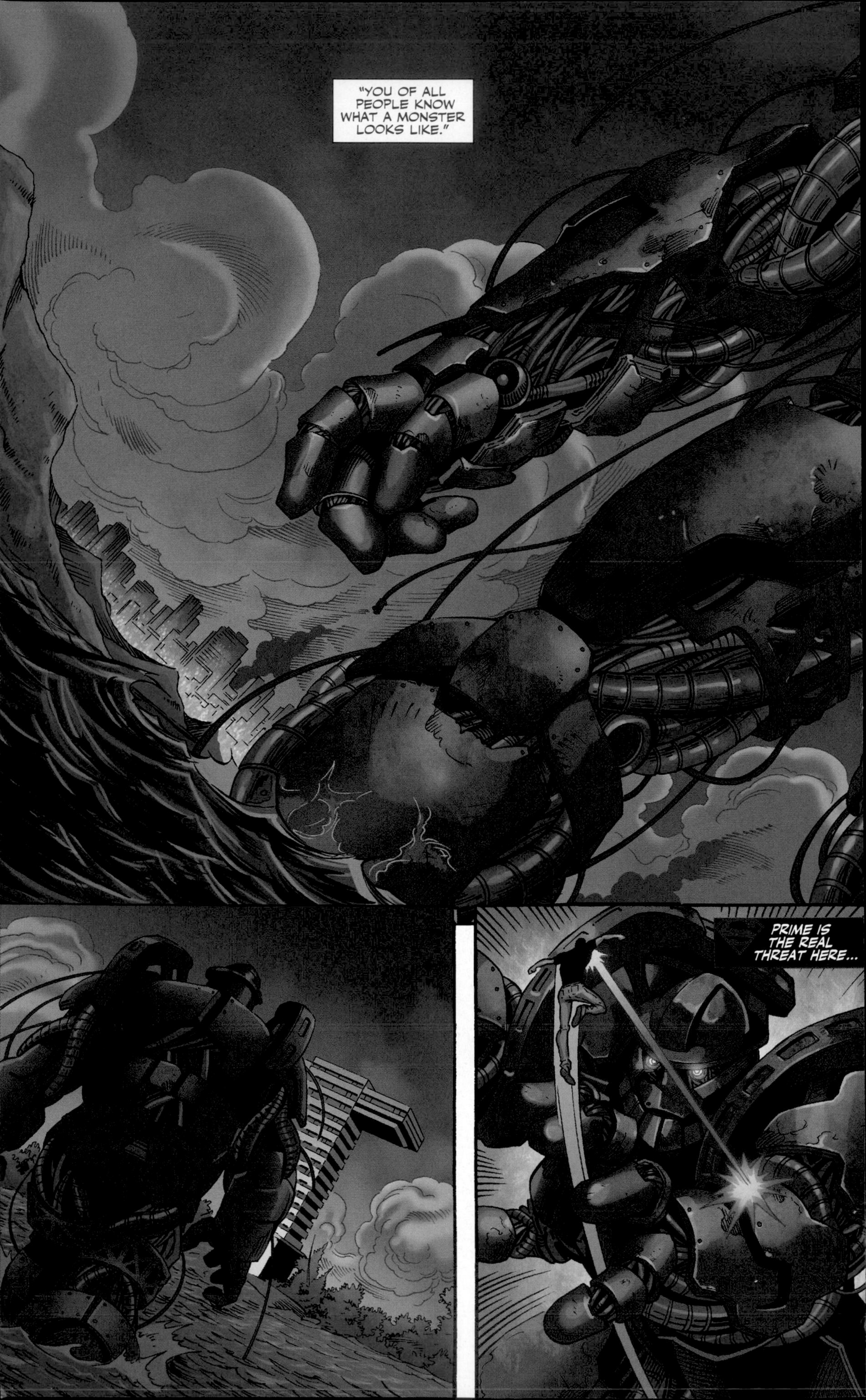
"YOU OF ALL PEOPLE KNOW WHAT A MONSTER LOOKS LIKE."
PRIME IS THE REAL THREAT HERE...

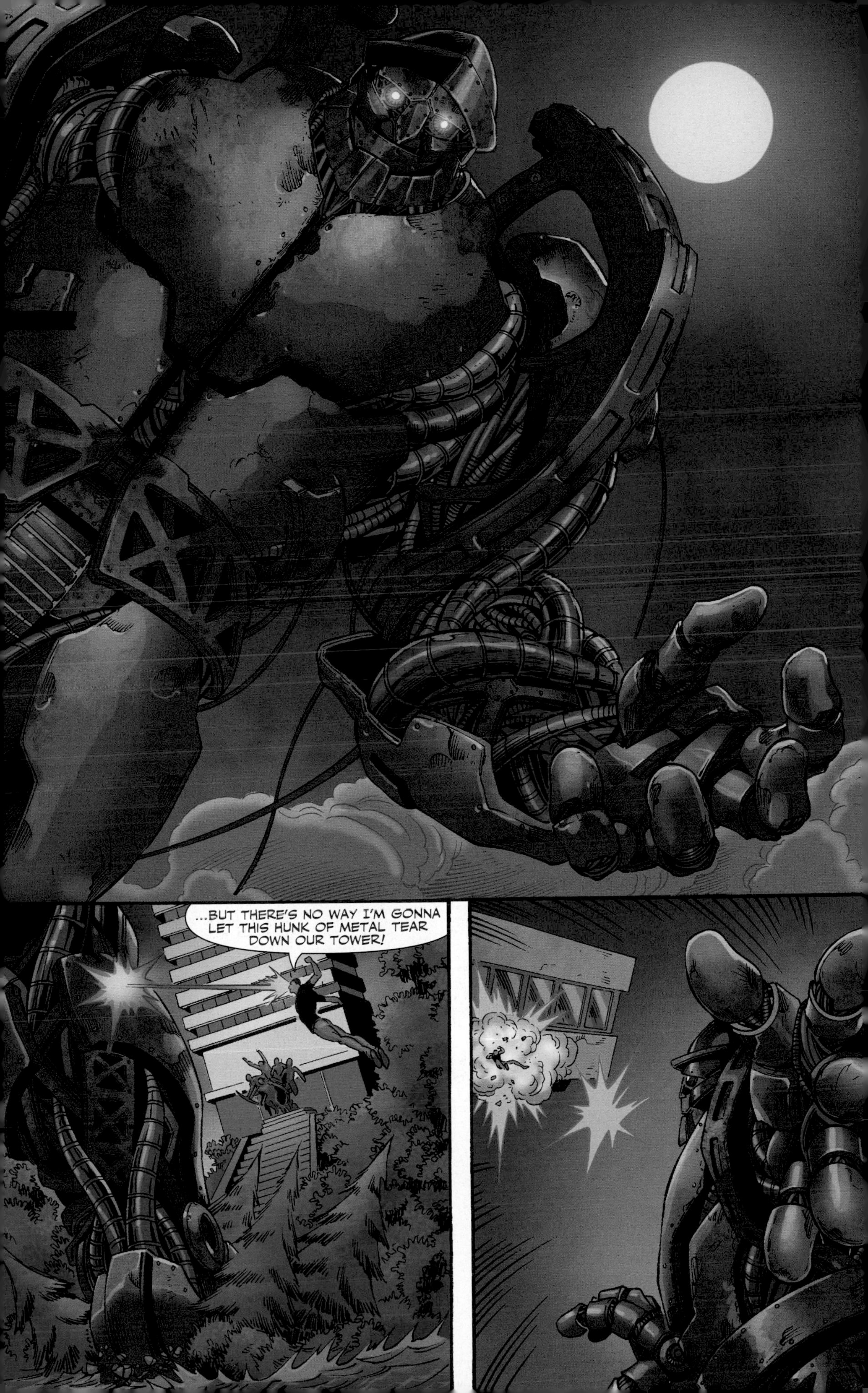
...BUT THERE'S NO WAY I'M GONNA LET THIS HUNK OF METAL TEAR DOWN OUR TOWER!

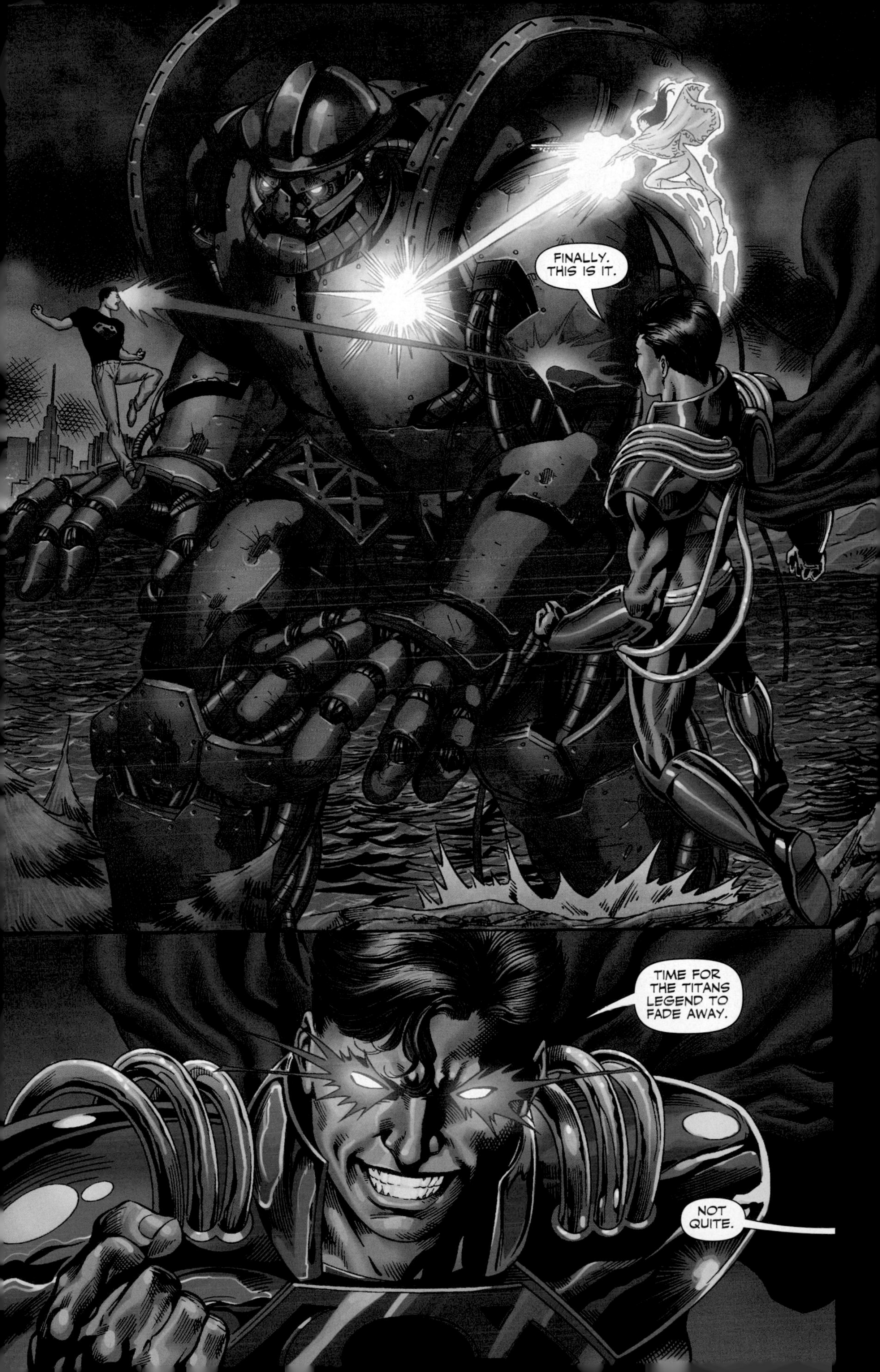
FINALLY. THIS IS IT.
TIME FOR THE TITANS LEGEND TO FADE AWAY.
NOT QUITE.

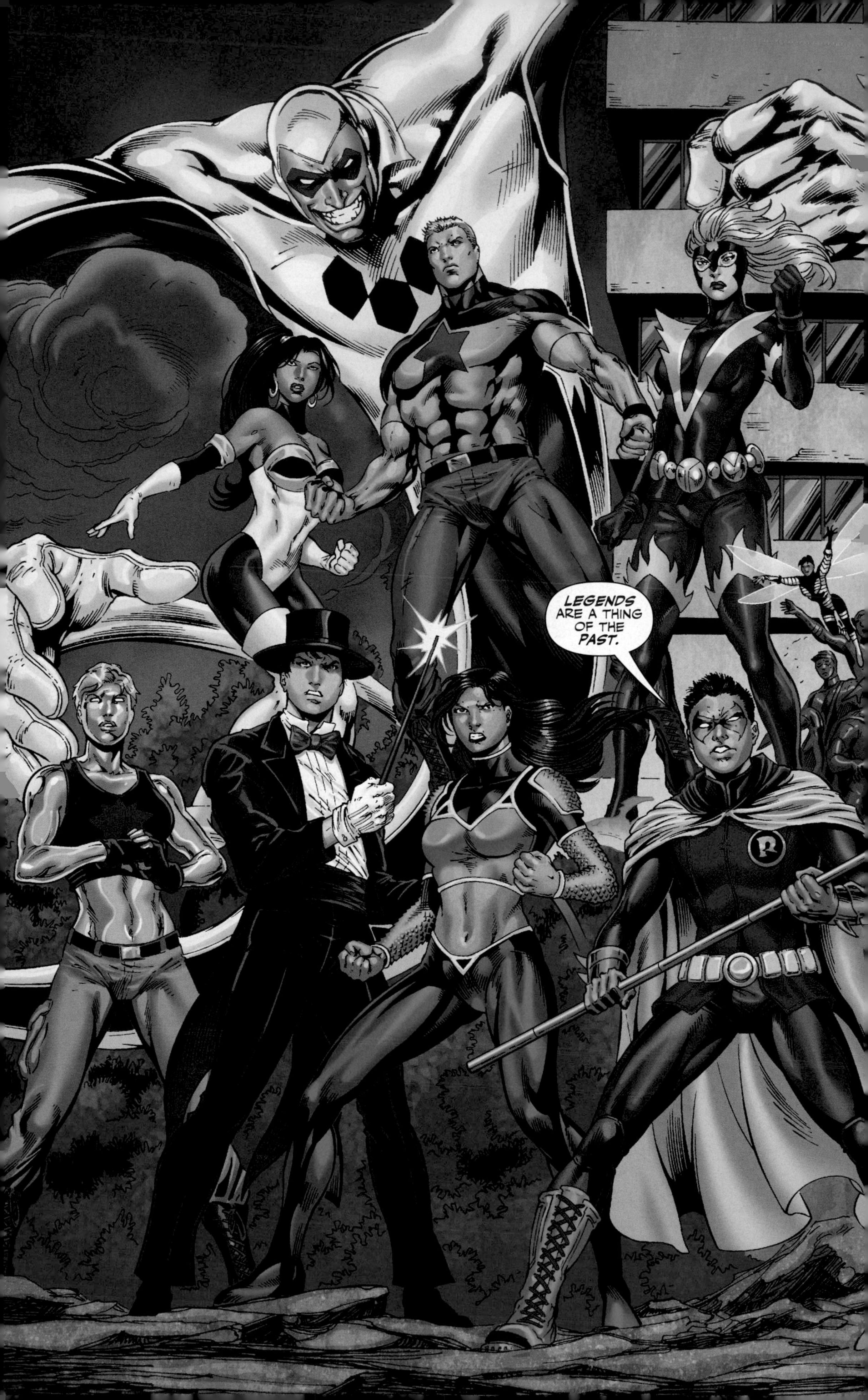
LEGENDS ARE A THING OF THE PAST.

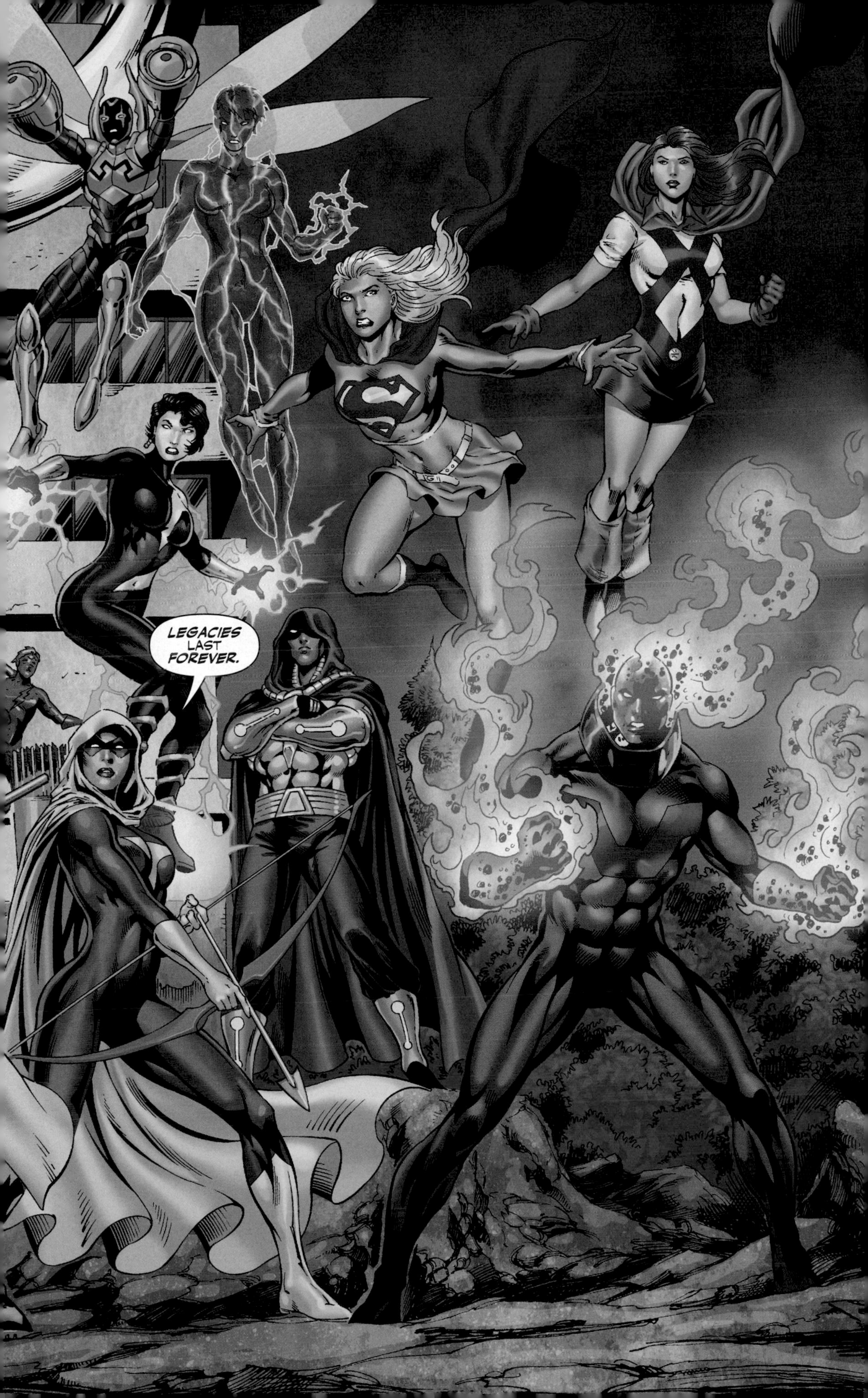
LEGACIES LAST FOREVER.

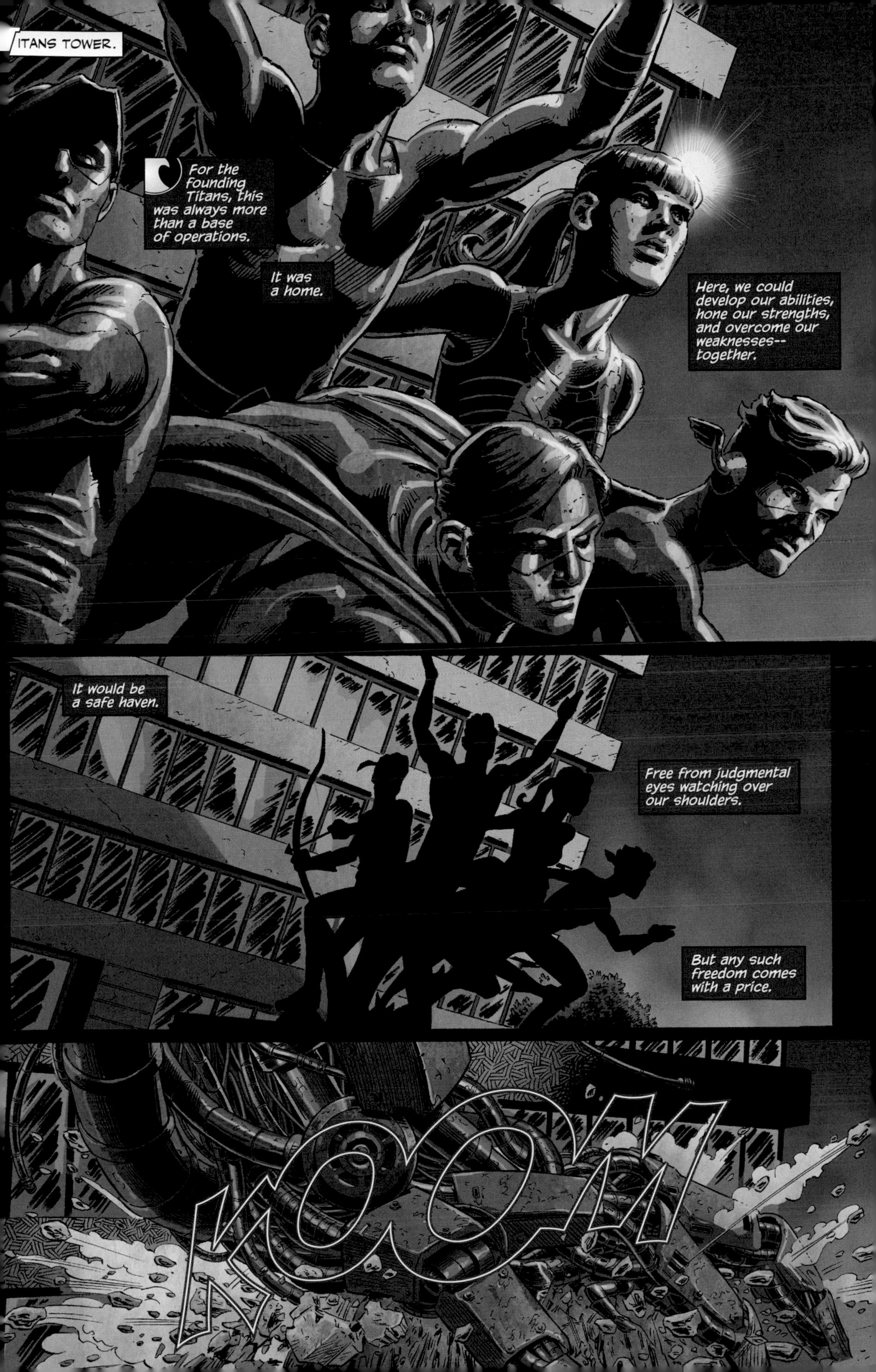
TITANS TOWER.
For the founding Titans, this was always more than a base of operations.
It was a home.
Here, we could develop our abilities, hone our strengths, and overcome our weaknesses-- together.
It would be a safe haven.
Free from judgmental eyes watching over our shoulders.
But any such freedom comes with a price.
KOOM

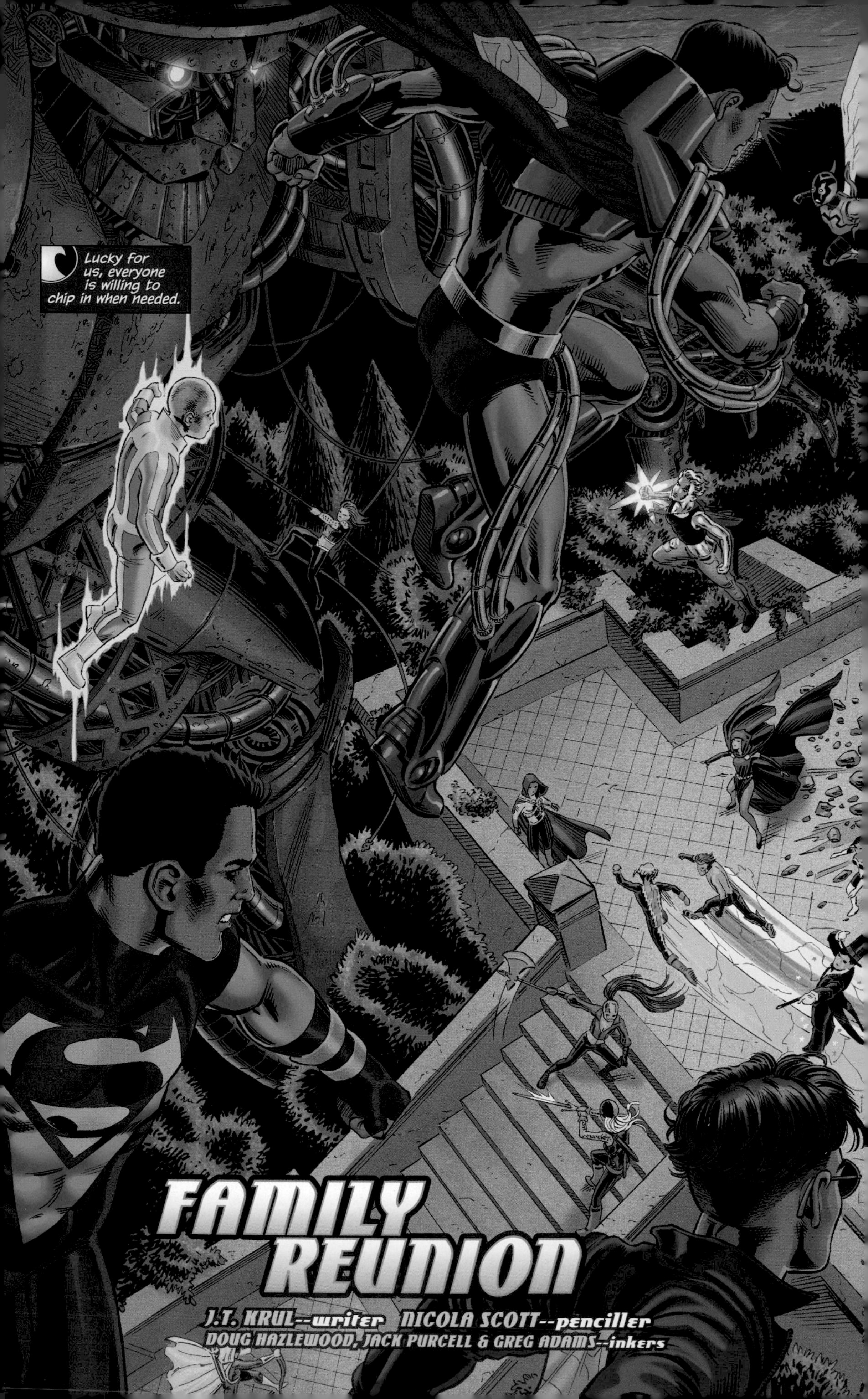
Lucky for us, everyone is willing to chip in when needed.
FAMILY REUNION
J.T. KRUL--writer NICOLA SCOTT--penciller
DOUG HAZLEWOOD, JACK PURCELL & GREG ADAMS--inkers

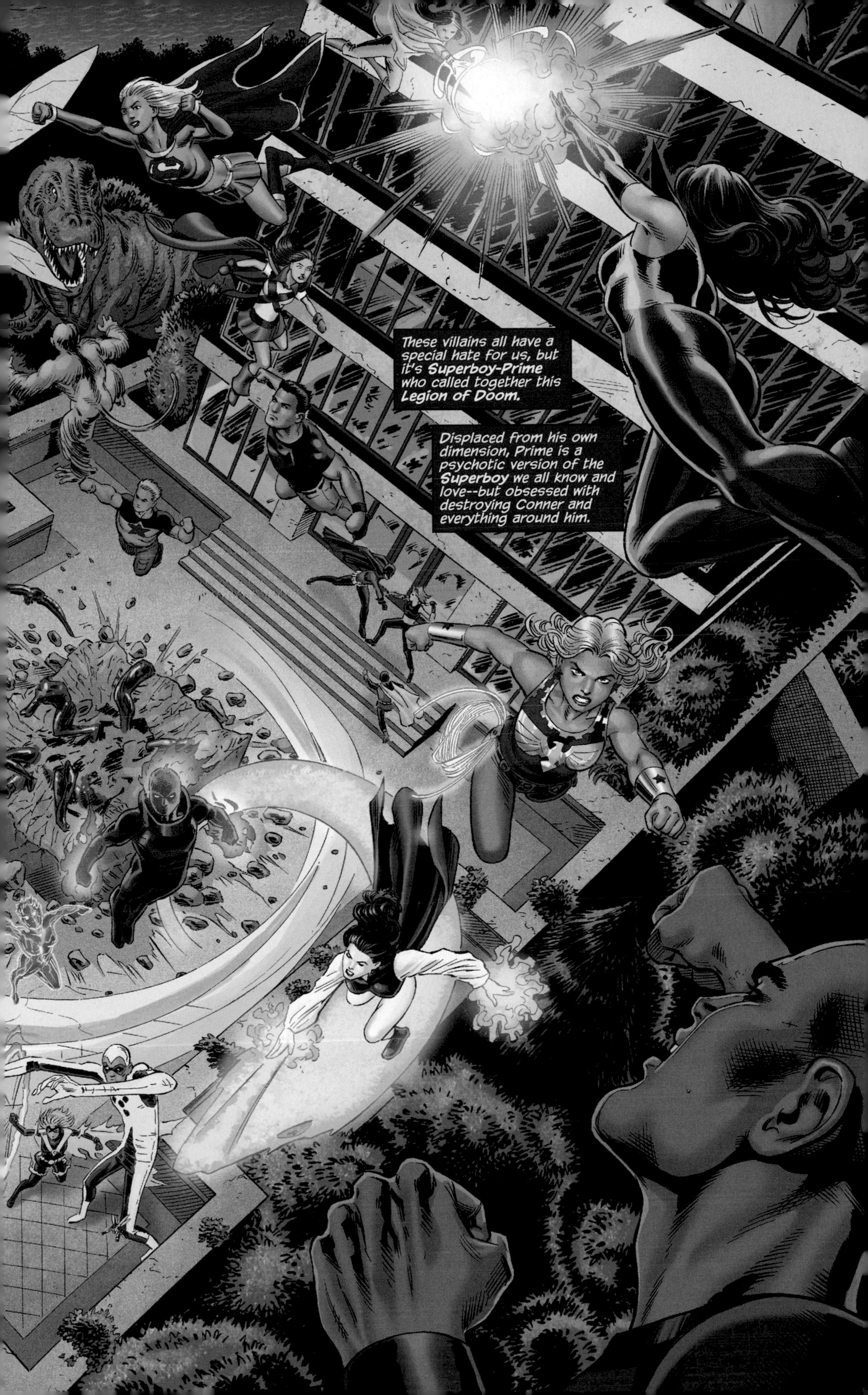
These villains all have a special hate for us, but it's **Superboy-Prime** who called together this **Legion of Doom.**
Displaced from his own dimension, Prime is a psychotic version of the **Superboy** we all know and love--but obsessed with destroying Conner and everything around him.

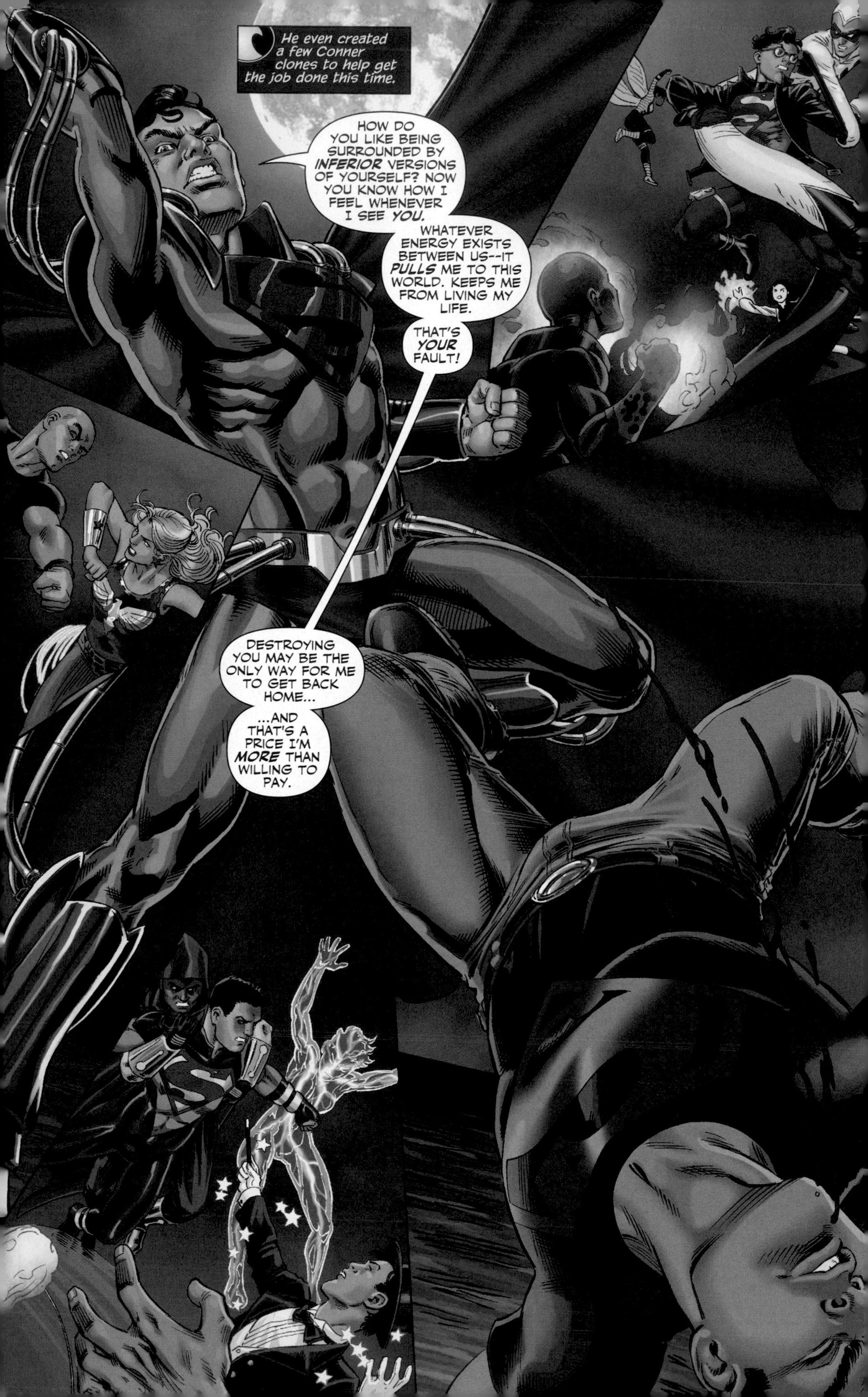
He even created a few Conner clones to help get the job done this time.
HOW DO YOU LIKE BEING SURROUNDED BY INFERIOR VERSIONS OF YOURSELF? NOW YOU KNOW HOW I FEEL WHENEVER I SEE YOU.
WHATEVER ENERGY EXISTS BETWEEN US--IT PULLS ME TO THIS WORLD. KEEPS ME FROM LIVING MY LIFE.
THAT'S YOUR FAULT!
DESTROYING YOU MAY BE THE ONLY WAY FOR ME TO GET BACK HOME...
...AND THAT'S A PRICE I'M MORE THAN WILLING TO PAY.

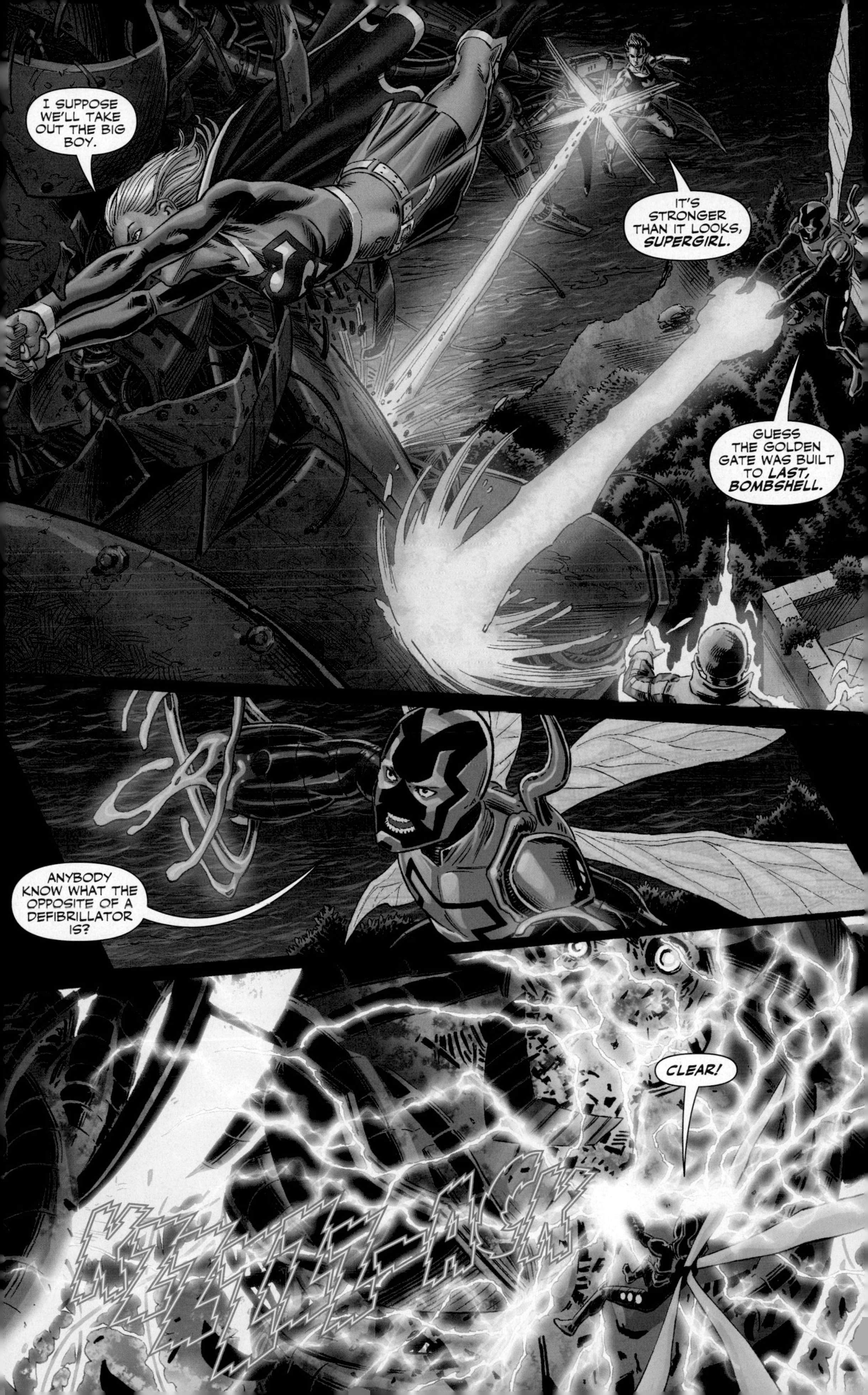
I SUPPOSE WE'LL TAKE OUT THE BIG BOY.
IT'S STRONGER THAN IT LOOKS, *SUPERGIRL.*
GUESS THE GOLDEN GATE WAS BUILT TO *LAST, BOMBSHELL.*
ANYBODY KNOW WHAT THE OPPOSITE OF A DEFIBRILLATOR IS?
CLEAR!

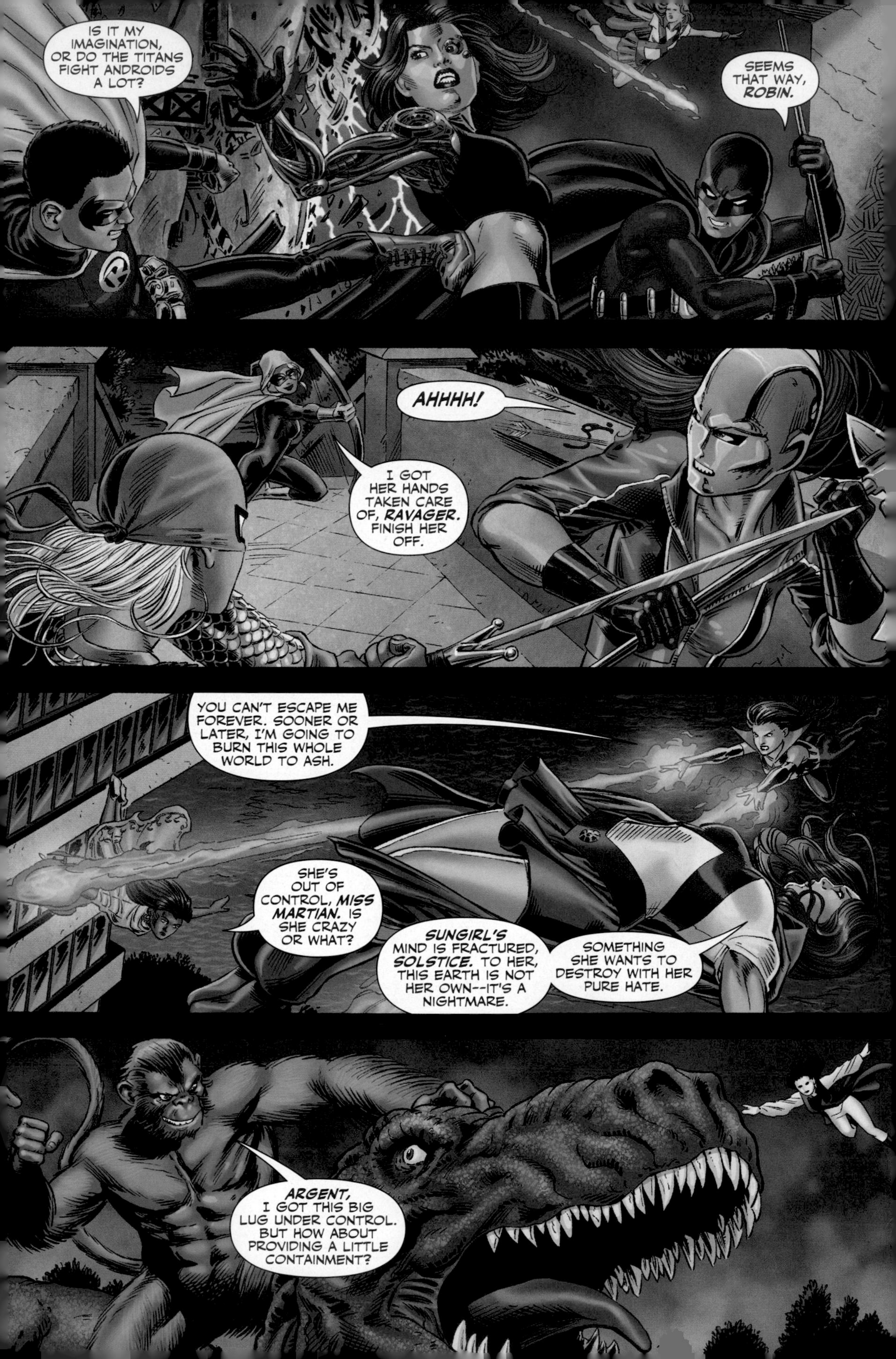
IS IT MY IMAGINATION, OR DO THE TITANS FIGHT ANDROIDS A LOT?
SEEMS THAT WAY, ROBIN.
AHHHH!
I GOT HER HANDS TAKEN CARE OF, RAVAGER. FINISH HER OFF.
YOU CAN'T ESCAPE ME FOREVER. SOONER OR LATER, I'M GOING TO BURN THIS WHOLE WORLD TO ASH.
SHE'S OUT OF CONTROL, MISS MARTIAN. IS SHE CRAZY OR WHAT?
SUNGIRL'S MIND IS FRACTURED, SOLSTICE. TO HER, THIS EARTH IS NOT HER OWN--IT'S A NIGHTMARE.
SOMETHING SHE WANTS TO DESTROY WITH HER PURE HATE.
ARGENT, I GOT THIS BIG LUG UNDER CONTROL. BUT HOW ABOUT PROVIDING A LITTLE CONTAINMENT?

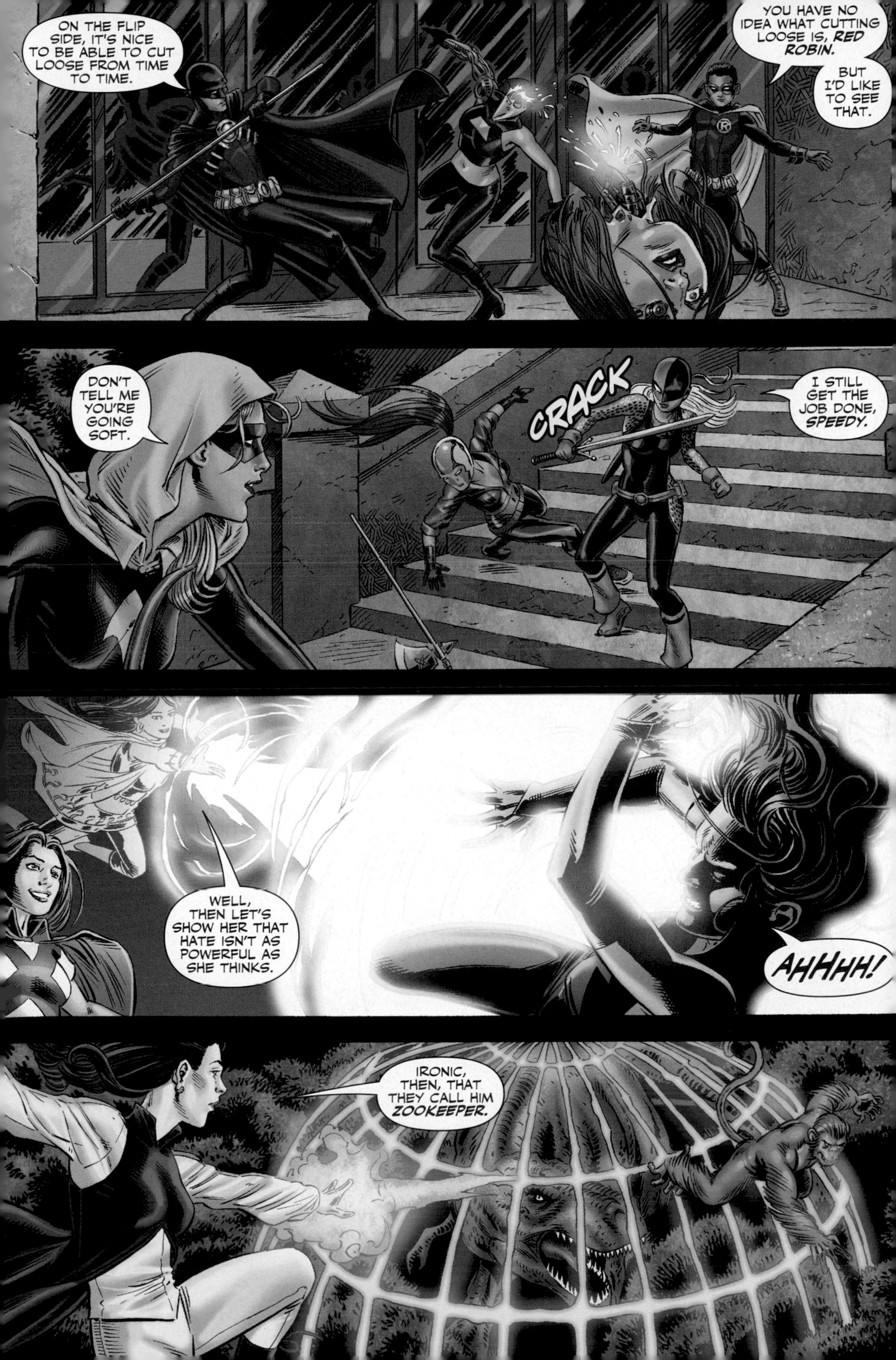
ON THE FLIP SIDE, IT'S NICE TO BE ABLE TO CUT LOOSE FROM TIME TO TIME.
YOU HAVE NO IDEA WHAT CUTTING LOOSE IS, RED ROBIN.
BUT I'D LIKE TO SEE THAT.
DON'T TELL ME YOU'RE GOING SOFT.
CRACK
I STILL GET THE JOB DONE, SPEEDY.
WELL, THEN LET'S SHOW HER THAT HATE ISN'T AS POWERFUL AS SHE THINKS.
AHHHH!
IRONIC, THEN, THAT THEY CALL HIM ZOOKEEPER.

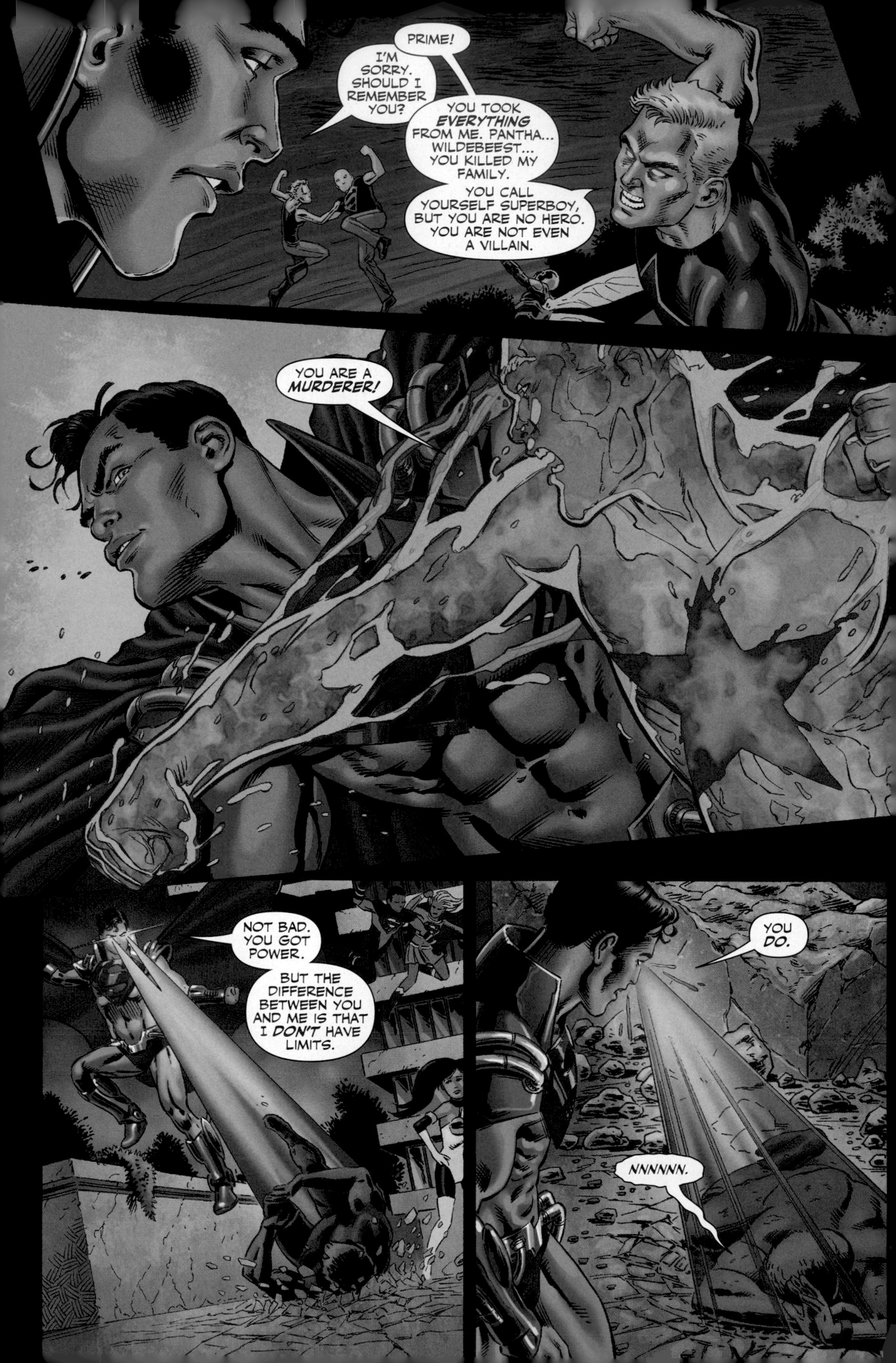
PRIME!
I'M SORRY. SHOULD I REMEMBER YOU?
YOU TOOK EVERYTHING FROM ME. PANTHA... WILDEBEEST... YOU KILLED MY FAMILY.
YOU CALL YOURSELF SUPERBOY, BUT YOU ARE NO HERO. YOU ARE NOT EVEN A VILLAIN.
YOU ARE A MURDERER!
NOT BAD. YOU GOT POWER.
BUT THE DIFFERENCE BETWEEN YOU AND ME IS THAT I DON'T HAVE LIMITS.
YOU DO.
NNNNNN.

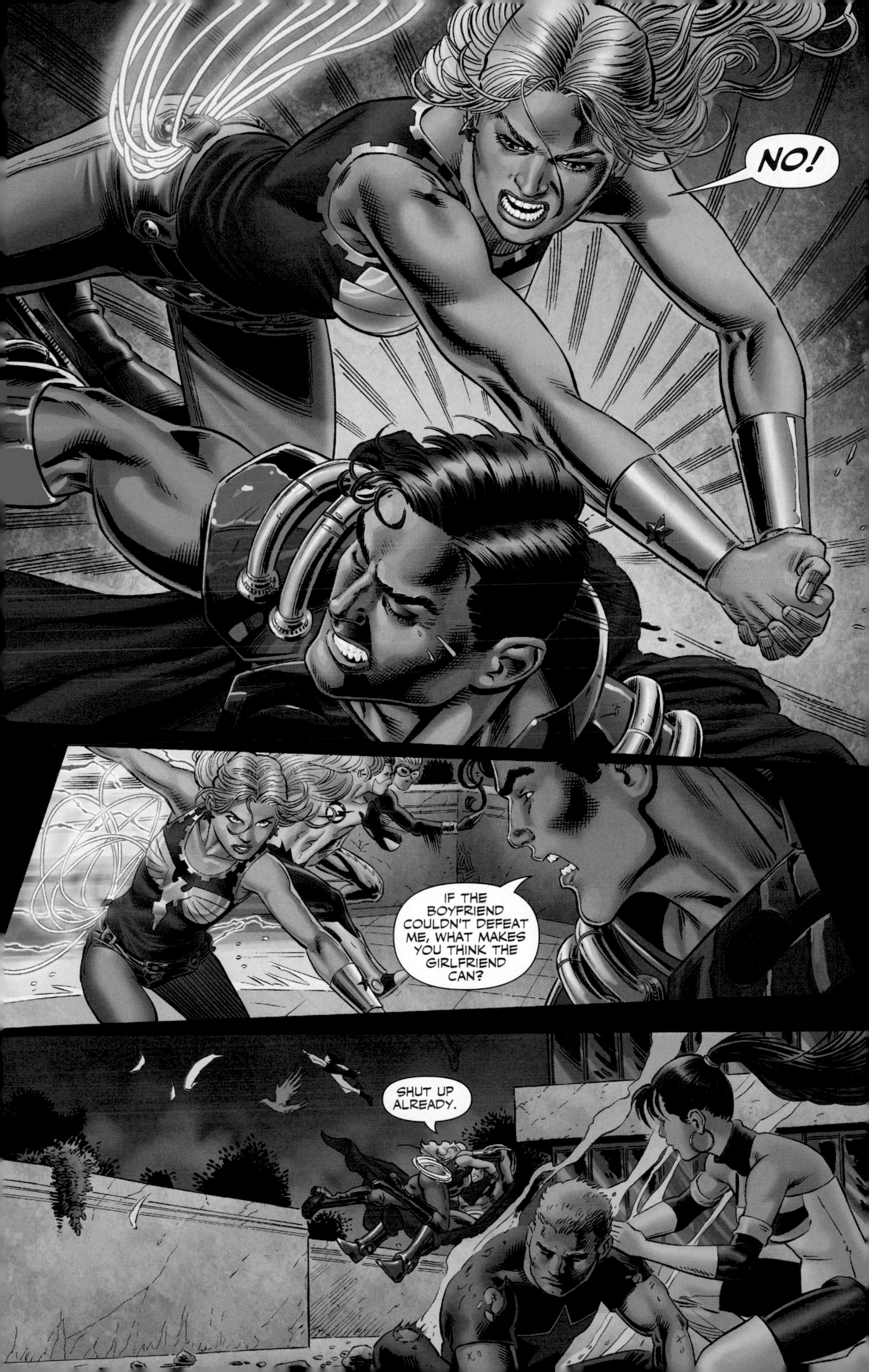
NO!
IF THE BOYFRIEND COULDN'T DEFEAT ME, WHAT MAKES YOU THINK THE GIRLFRIEND CAN?
SHUT UP ALREADY.

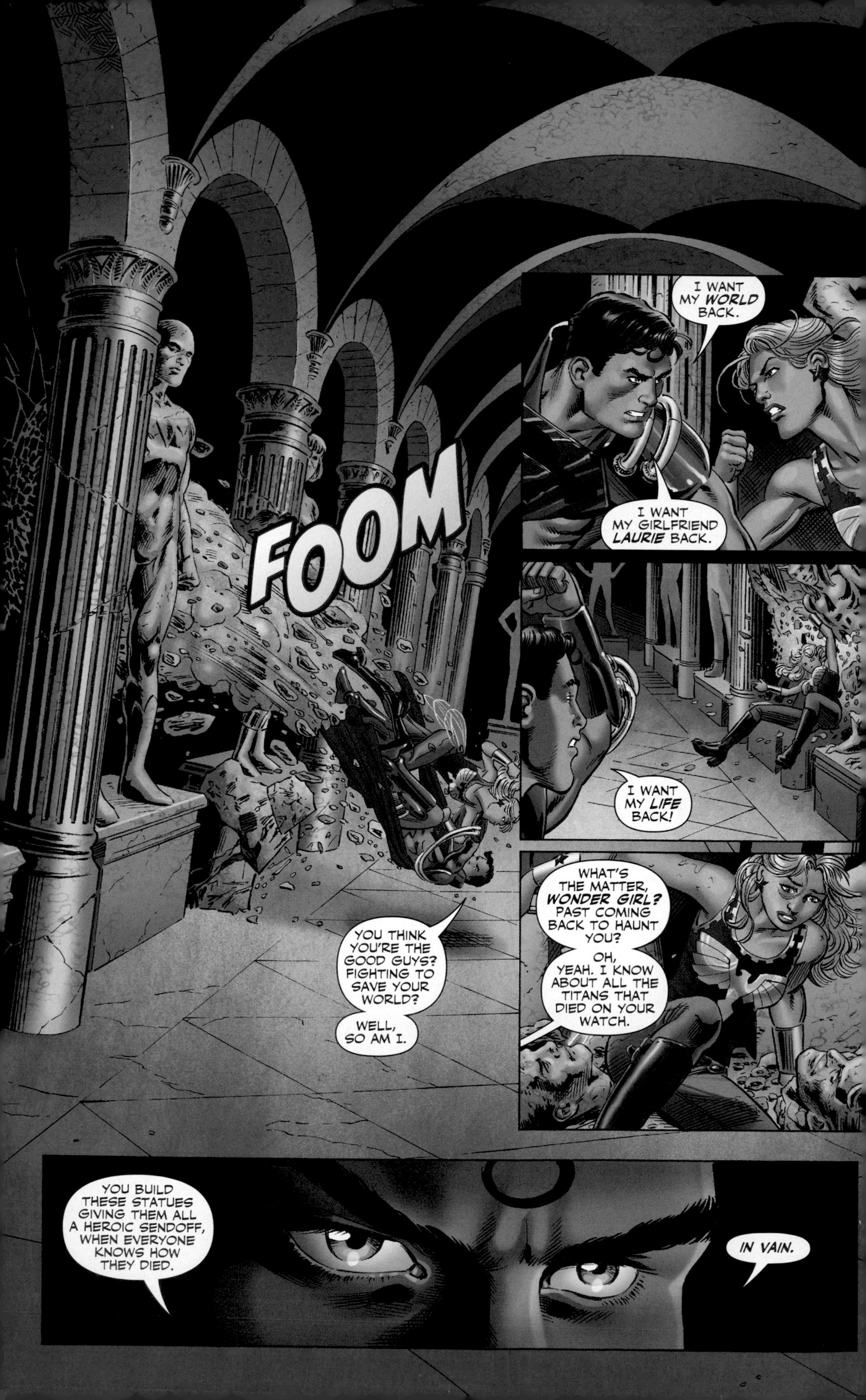
FOOM
I WANT MY WORLD BACK.
I WANT MY GIRLFRIEND LAURIE BACK.
I WANT MY LIFE BACK!
YOU THINK YOU'RE THE GOOD GUYS? FIGHTING TO SAVE YOUR WORLD?
WELL, SO AM I.
WHAT'S THE MATTER, WONDER GIRL? PAST COMING BACK TO HAUNT YOU?
OH, YEAH. I KNOW ABOUT ALL THE TITANS THAT DIED ON YOUR WATCH.
YOU BUILD THESE STATUES GIVING THEM ALL A HEROIC SENDOFF, WHEN EVERYONE KNOWS HOW THEY DIED.
IN VAIN.

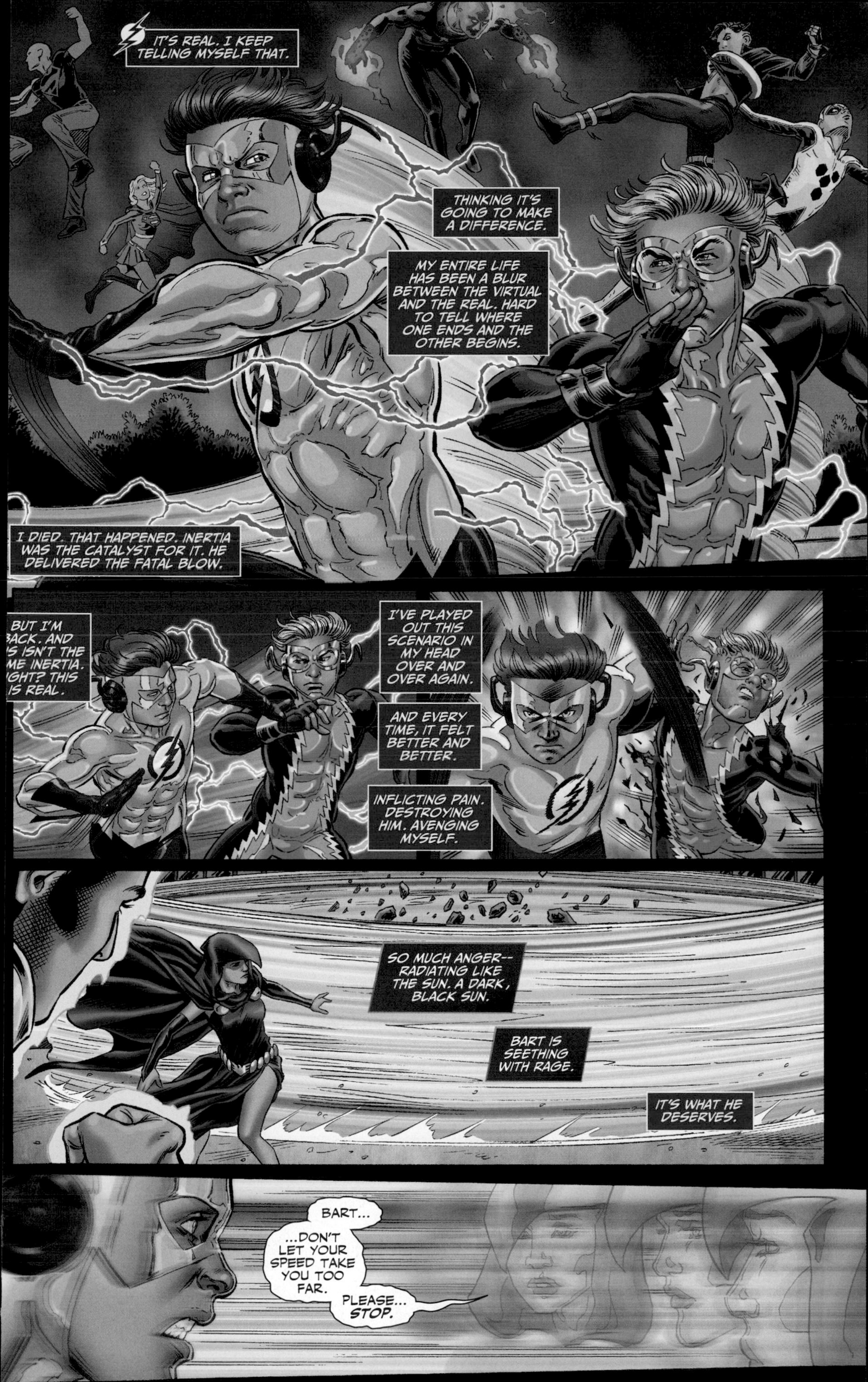
IT'S REAL. I KEEP TELLING MYSELF THAT.
THINKING IT'S GOING TO MAKE A DIFFERENCE.
MY ENTIRE LIFE HAS BEEN A BLUR BETWEEN THE VIRTUAL AND THE REAL. HARD TO TELL WHERE ONE ENDS AND THE OTHER BEGINS.
I DIED. THAT HAPPENED. INERTIA WAS THE CATALYST FOR IT. HE DELIVERED THE FATAL BLOW.
BUT I'M BACK. AND S ISN'T THE ME INERTIA. GHT? THIS IS REAL.
I'VE PLAYED OUT THIS SCENARIO IN MY HEAD OVER AND OVER AGAIN.
AND EVERY TIME, IT FELT BETTER AND BETTER.
INFLICTING PAIN. DESTROYING HIM. AVENGING MYSELF.
SO MUCH ANGER-- RADIATING LIKE THE SUN. A DARK, BLACK SUN.
BART IS SEETHING WITH RAGE.
IT'S WHAT HE DESERVES.
BART...
...DON'T LET YOUR SPEED TAKE YOU TOO FAR.
PLEASE... STOP.

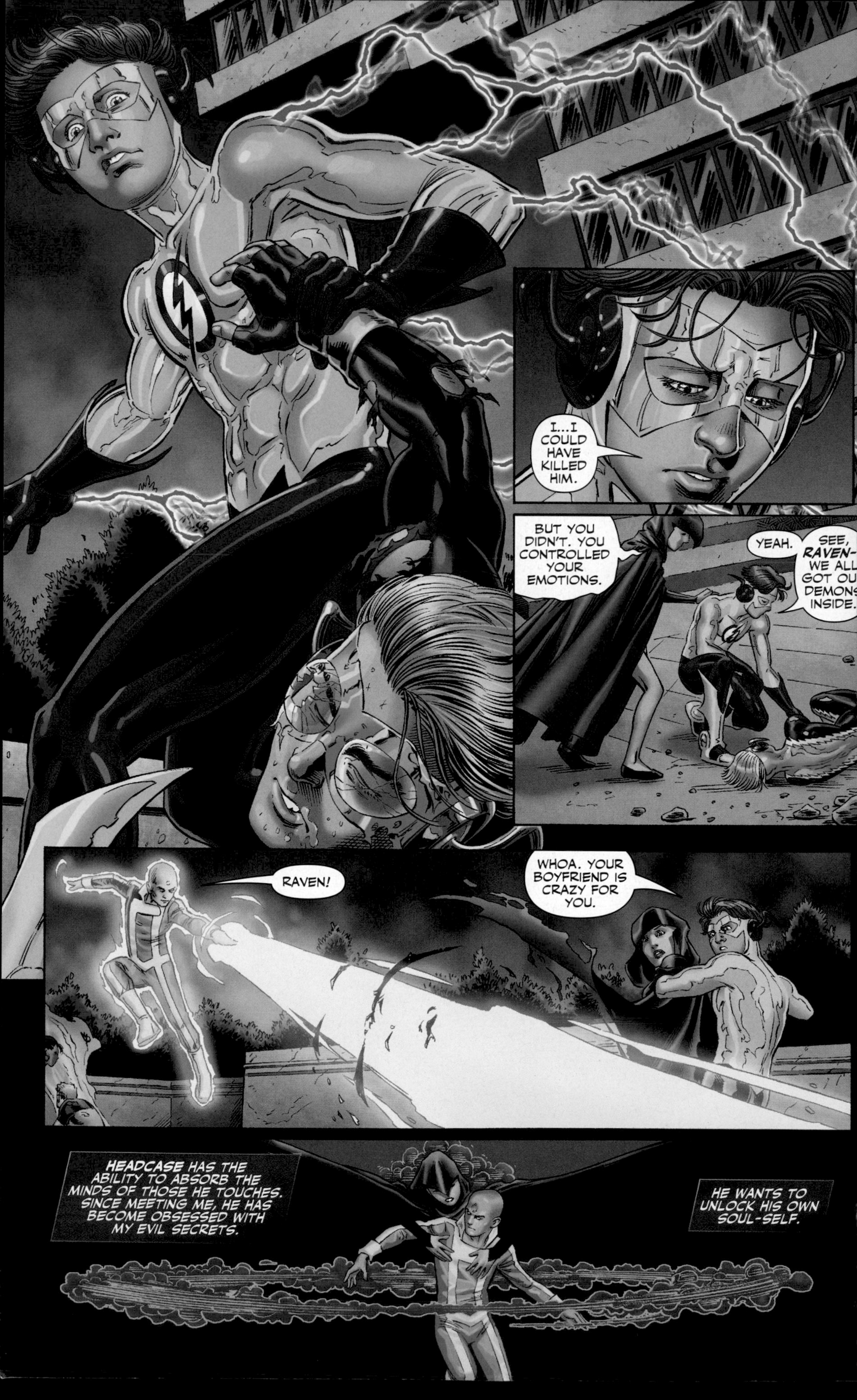

I...I COULD HAVE KILLED HIM.
BUT YOU DIDN'T. YOU CONTROLLED YOUR EMOTIONS.
YEAH.
SEE, RAVEN-- WE ALL GOT OU DEMONS INSIDE.
RAVEN!
WHOA. YOUR BOYFRIEND IS CRAZY FOR YOU.
HEADCASE HAS THE ABILITY TO ABSORB THE MINDS OF THOSE HE TOUCHES. SINCE MEETING ME, HE HAS BECOME OBSESSED WITH MY EVIL SECRETS.
HE WANTS TO UNLOCK HIS OWN SOUL-SELF.

PERHAPS I SHOULD GIVE HIM WHAT HE WANTS.
THIS SUPPOSED TO SCARE ME?
I'M NOT THE SAME KID YOU FOUGHT LAST TIME. I'VE BEEN LEARNING ABOUT THE DARK ARTS-- PREPARING TO ABSORB WHAT YOU KNOW.
MINE IS NOT A REALM OF MAGIC. IT IS ANOTHER DIMENSION-- AN EMPTY VOID.
YOU THINK YOU KNOW WHAT DARKNESS TRULY IS?
OR DESPAIR?
I'LL TELL YOU WHAT YOU SHALL FIND HERE--

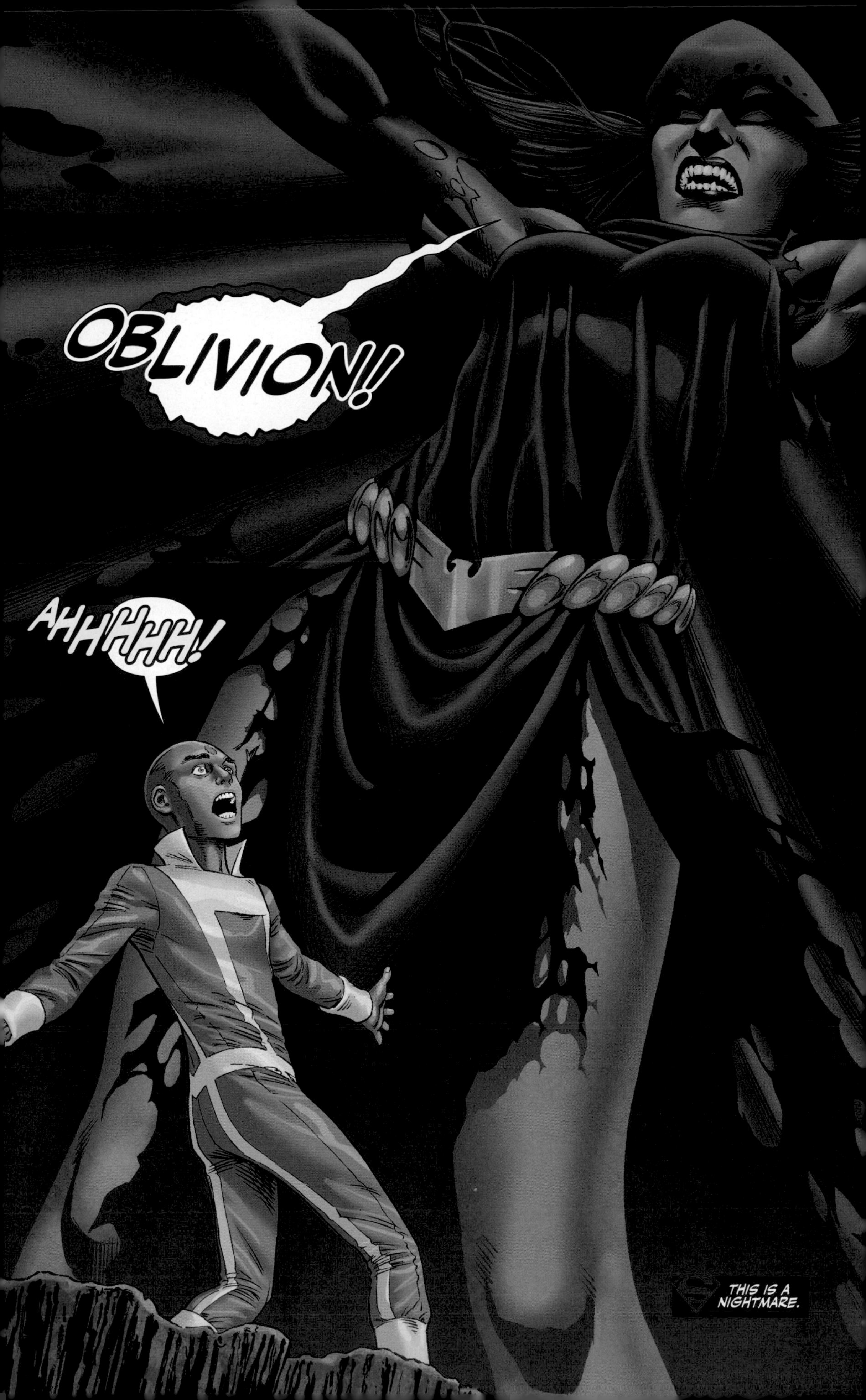
OBLIVION!!
AHHHHHH!
THIS IS A NIGHTMARE.

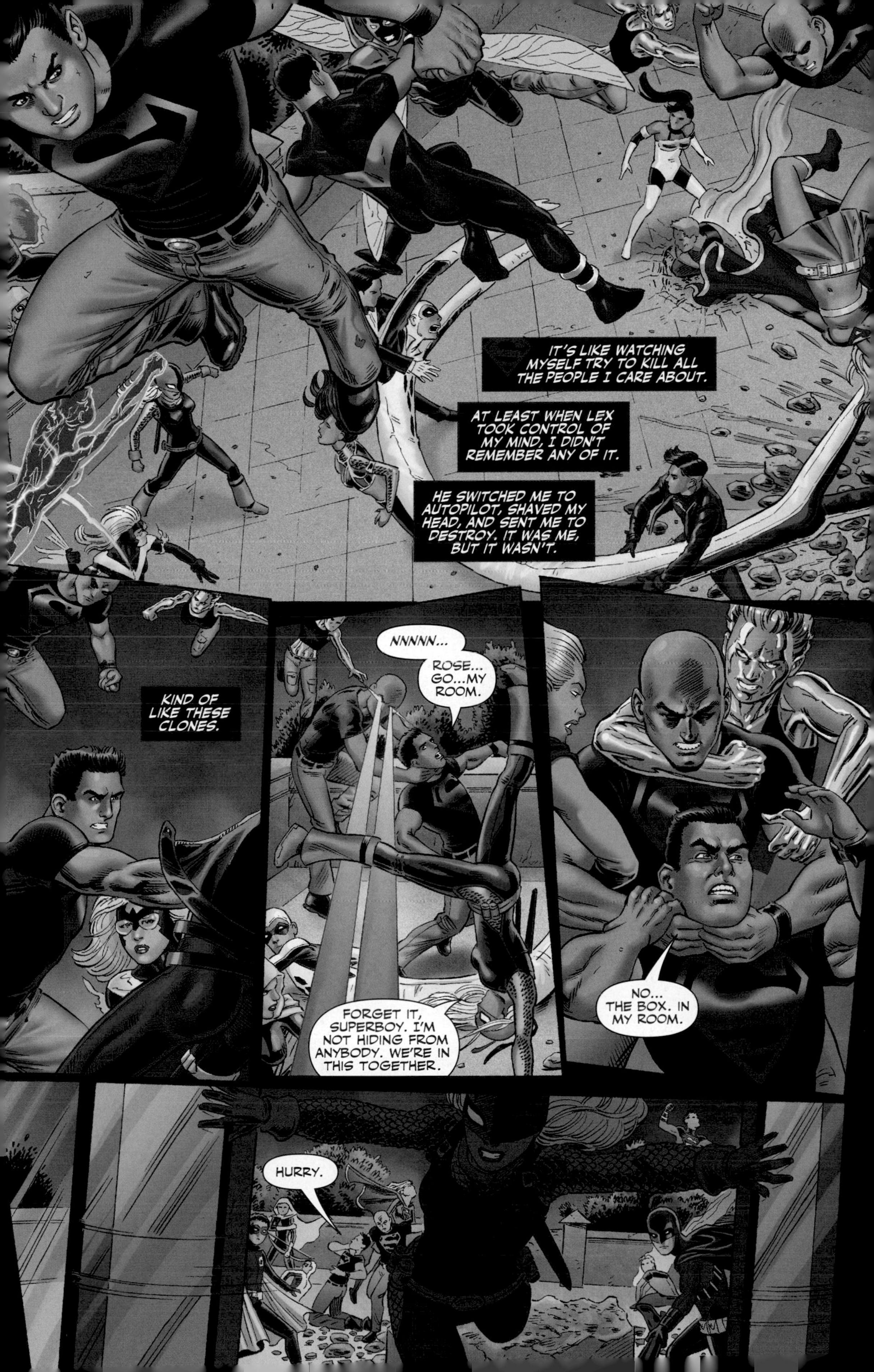
IT'S LIKE WATCHING MYSELF TRY TO KILL ALL THE PEOPLE I CARE ABOUT.
AT LEAST WHEN LEX TOOK CONTROL OF MY MIND, I DIDN'T REMEMBER ANY OF IT.
HE SWITCHED ME TO AUTOPILOT, SHAVED MY HEAD, AND SENT ME TO DESTROY. IT WAS ME, BUT IT WASN'T.
KIND OF LIKE THESE CLONES.
NNNNN...
ROSE... GO...MY ROOM.
FORGET IT, SUPERBOY. I'M NOT HIDING FROM ANYBODY. WE'RE IN THIS TOGETHER.
NO... THE BOX. IN MY ROOM.
HURRY.

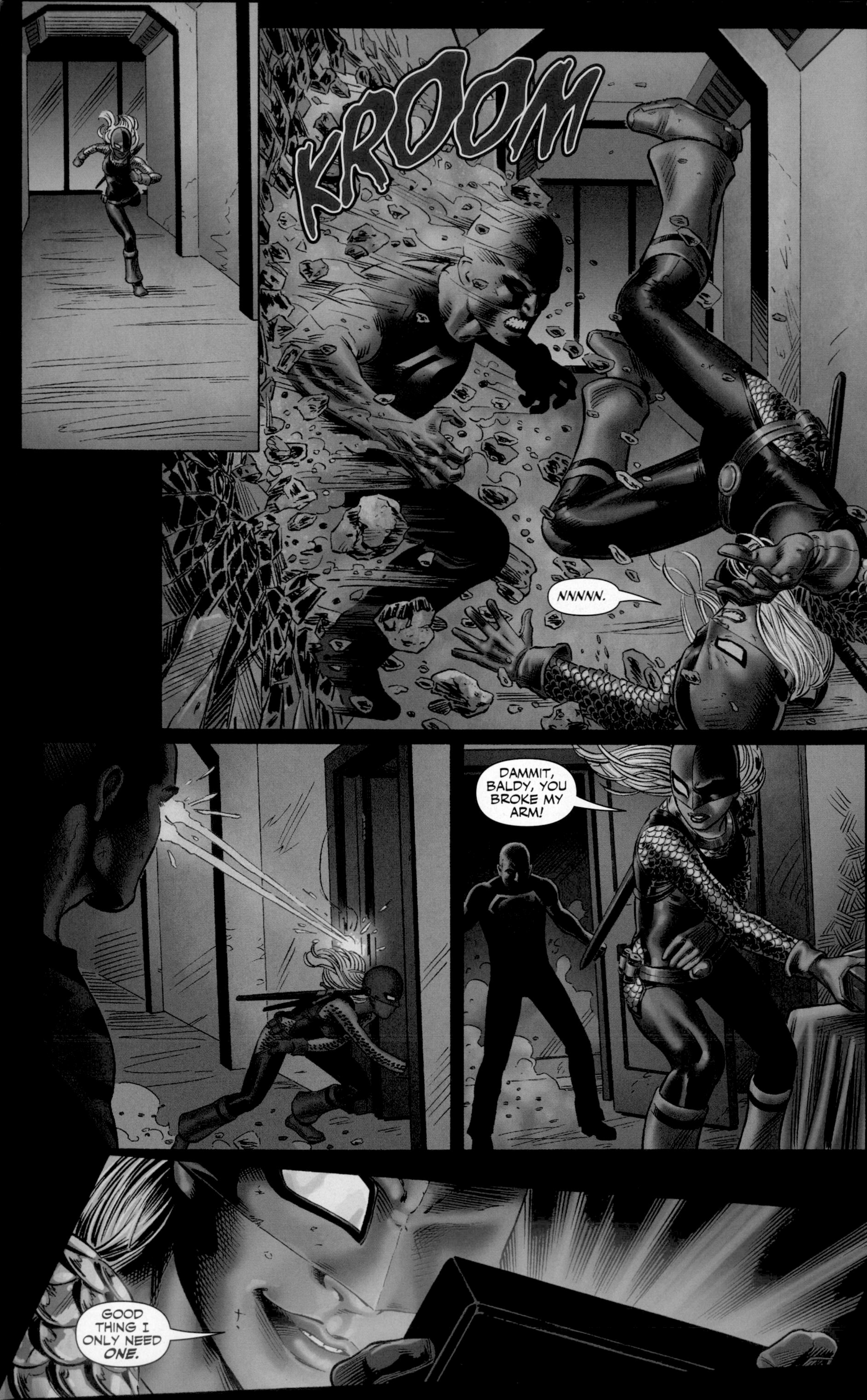
KROOM
NNNNN.
DAMMIT, BALDY, YOU BROKE MY ARM!
GOOD THING I ONLY NEED ONE.

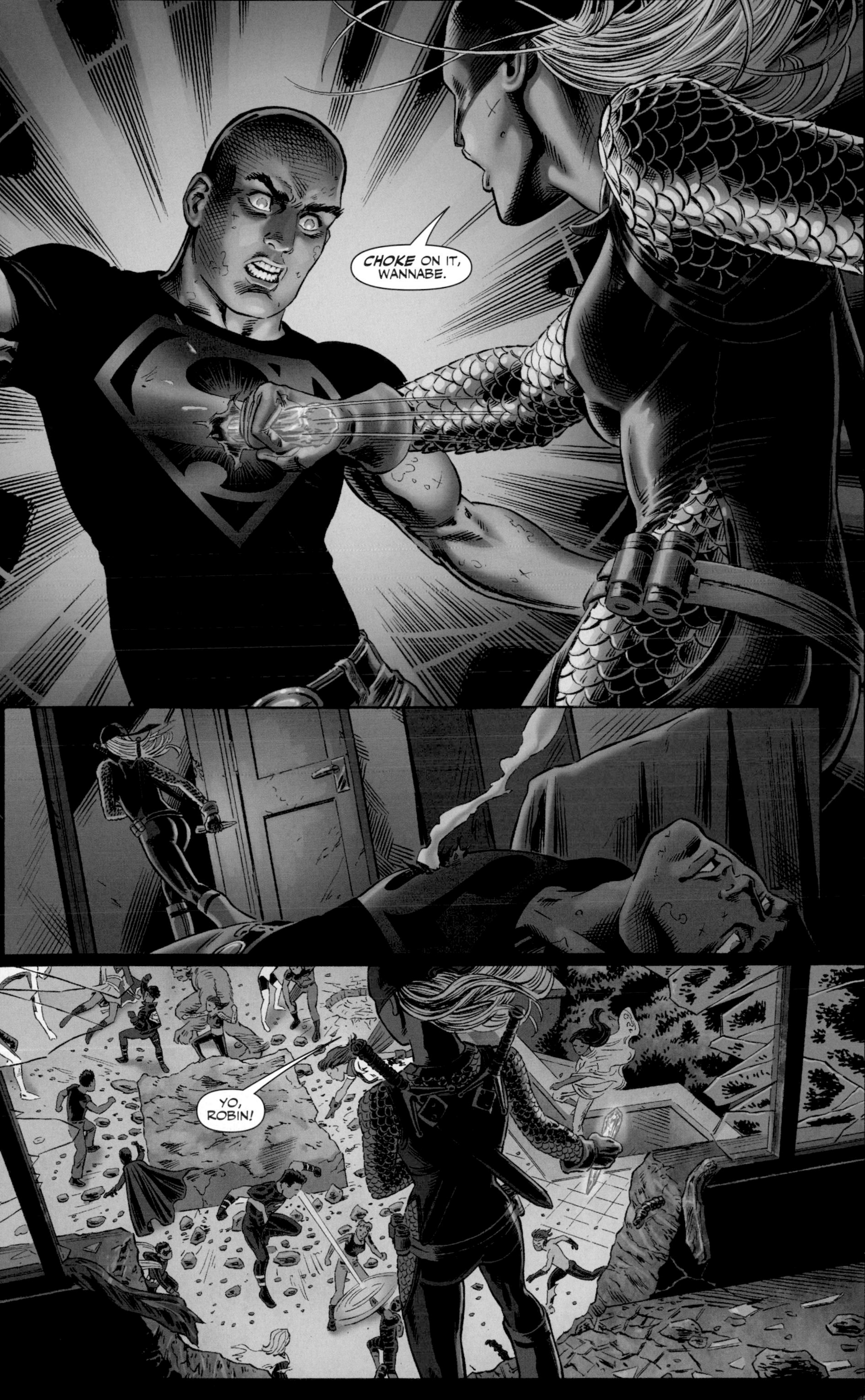
CHOKE ON IT, WANNABE.
YO, ROBIN!

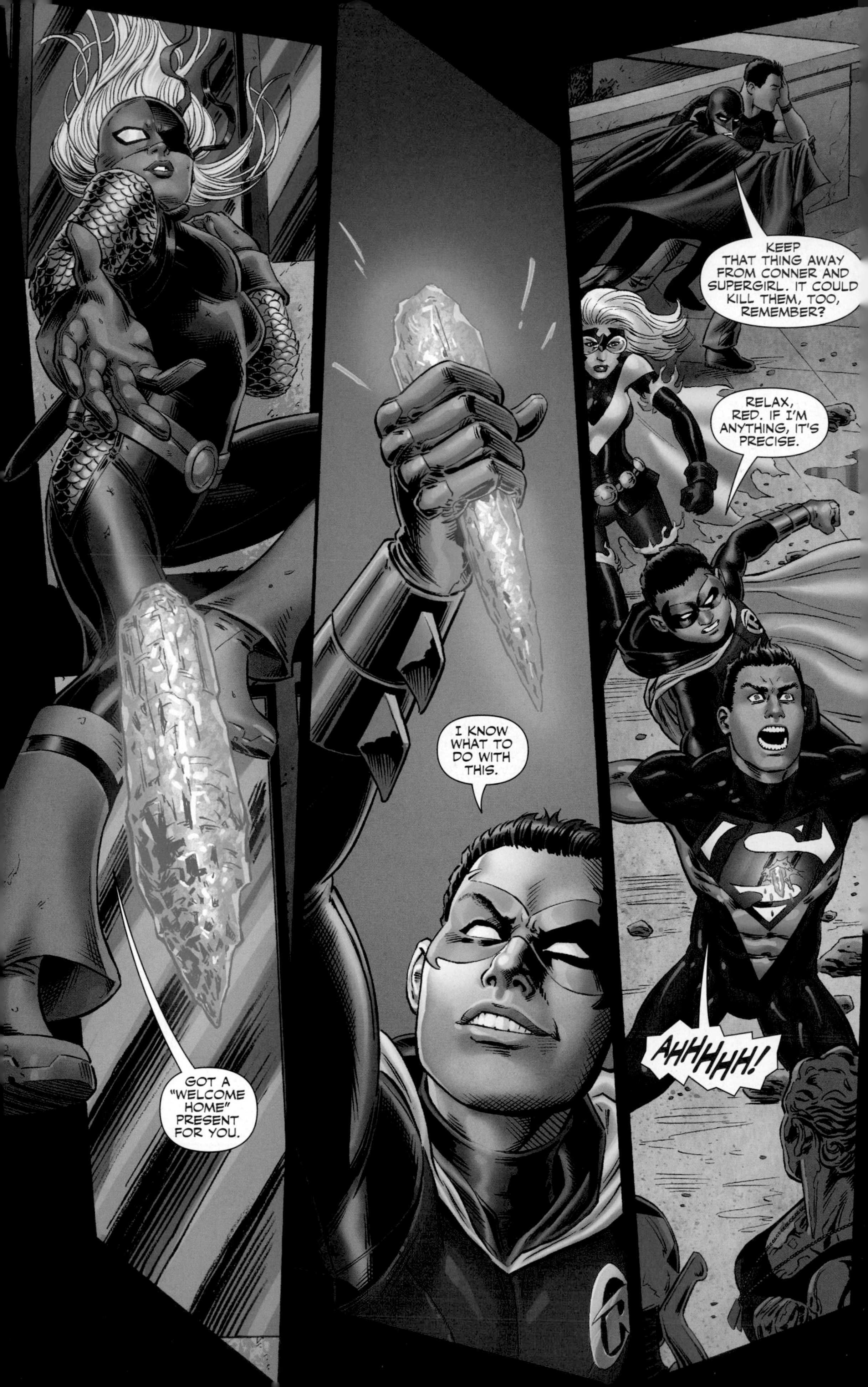
GOT A "WELCOME HOME" PRESENT FOR YOU.
I KNOW WHAT TO DO WITH THIS.
KEEP THAT THING AWAY FROM CONNER AND SUPERGIRL. IT COULD KILL THEM, TOO, REMEMBER?
RELAX, RED. IF I'M ANYTHING, IT'S PRECISE.
AHHHHH!

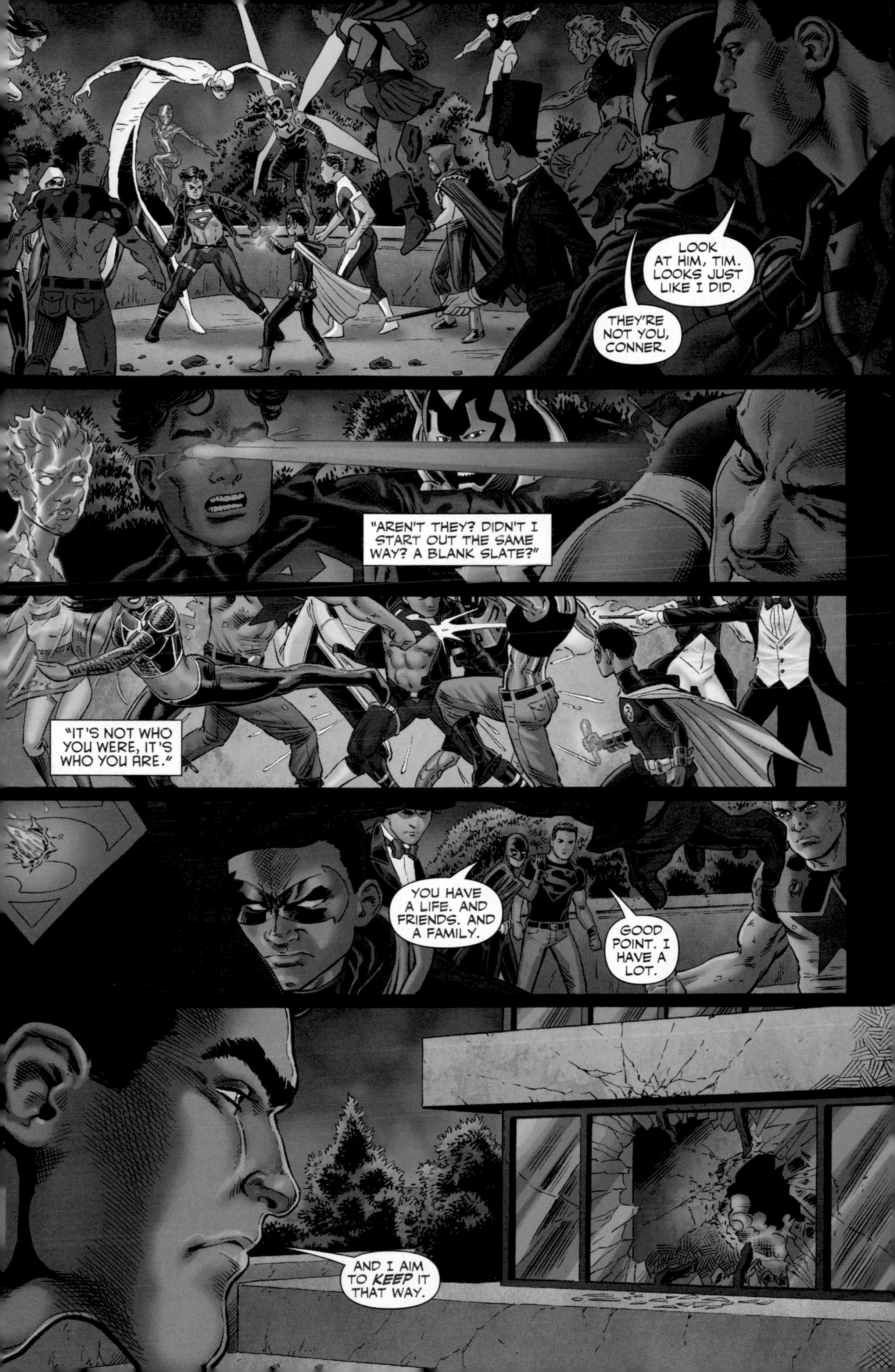
LOOK AT HIM, TIM. LOOKS JUST LIKE I DID.
THEY'RE NOT YOU, CONNER.
"AREN'T THEY? DIDN'T I START OUT THE SAME WAY? A BLANK SLATE?"
"IT'S NOT WHO YOU WERE, IT'S WHO YOU ARE."
YOU HAVE A LIFE. AND FRIENDS. AND A FAMILY.
GOOD POINT. I HAVE A LOT.
AND I AIM TO *KEEP* IT THAT WAY.

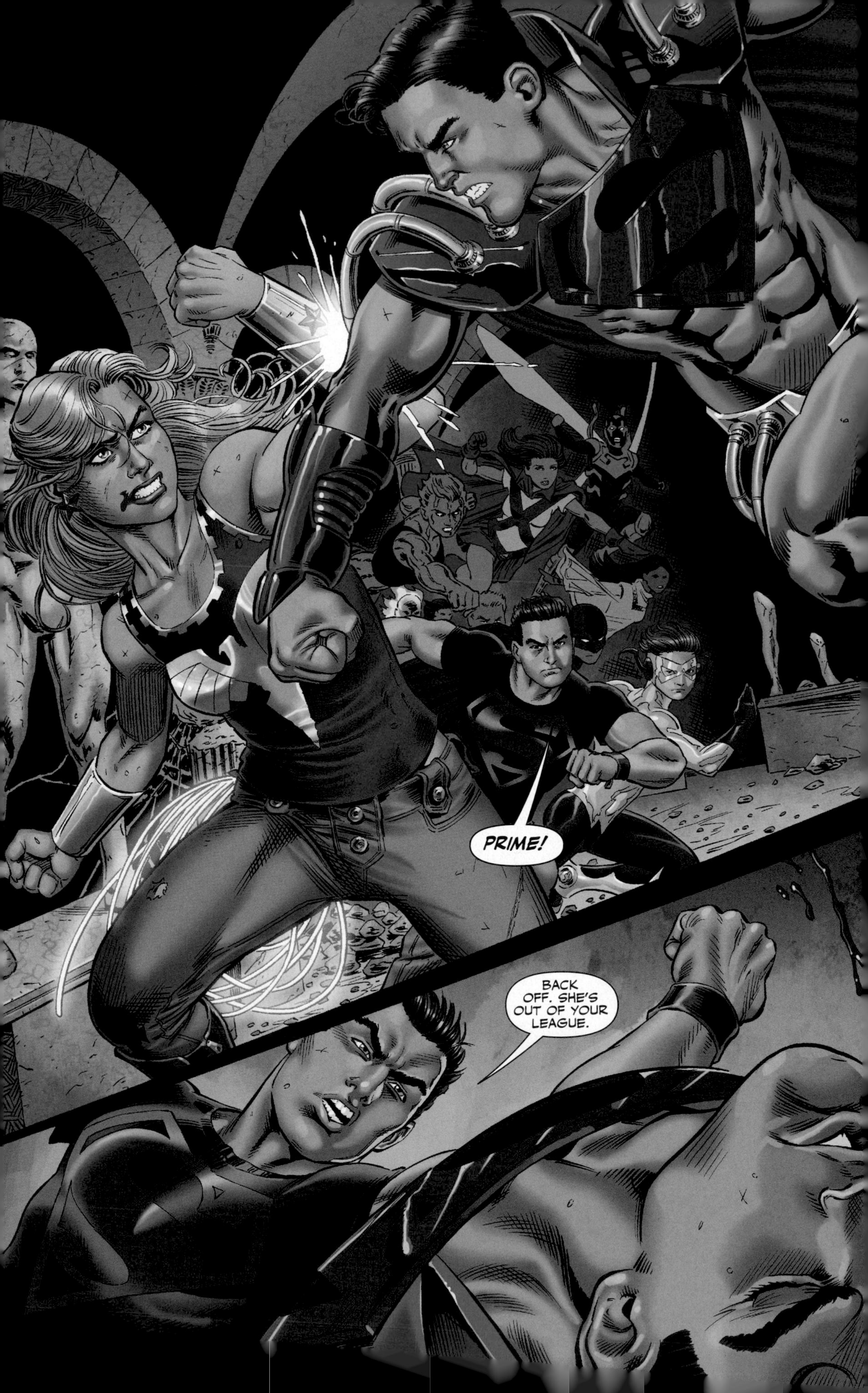
PRIME!
BACK OFF. SHE'S OUT OF YOUR LEAGUE.

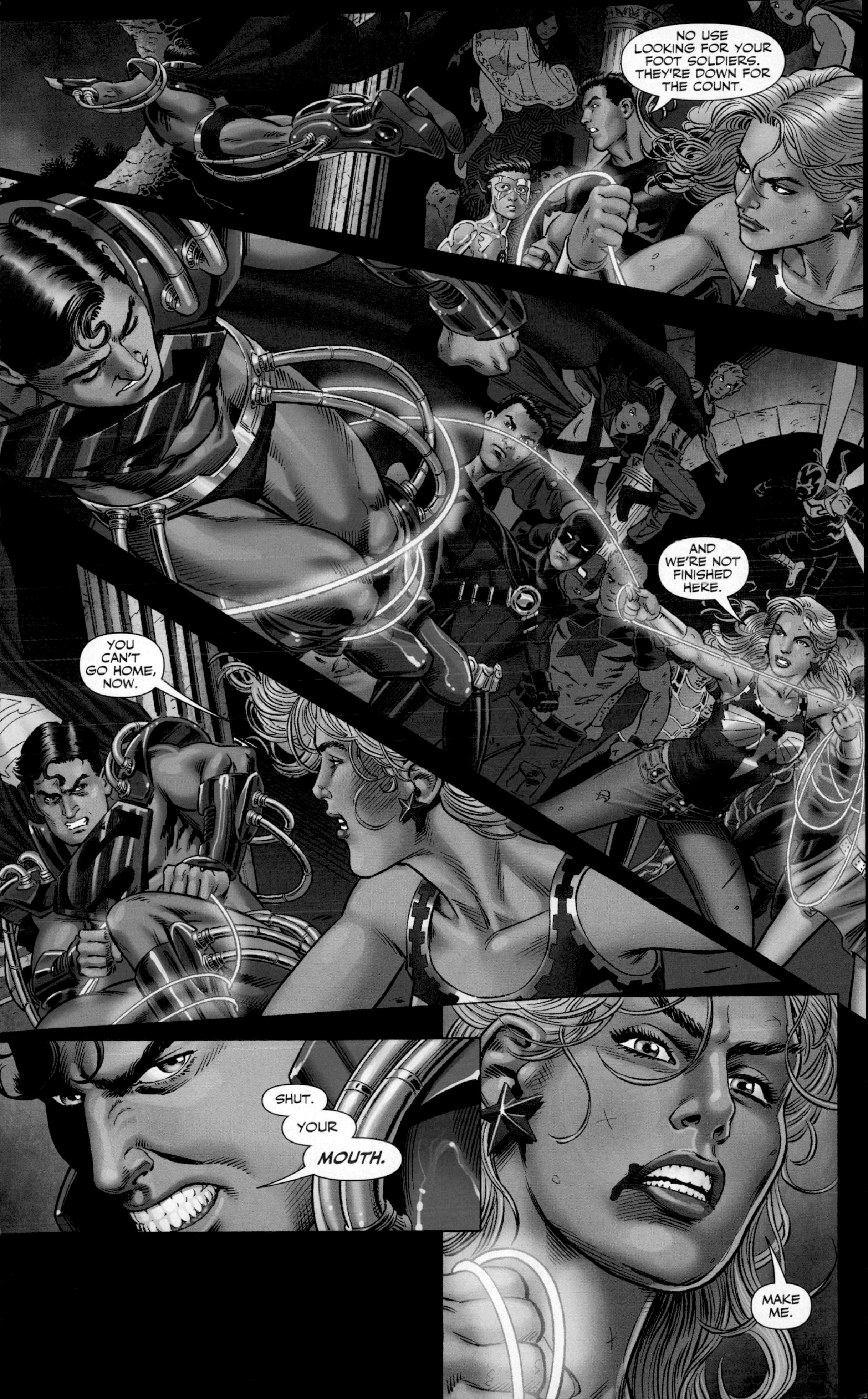
NO USE LOOKING FOR YOUR FOOT SOLDIERS. THEY'RE DOWN FOR THE COUNT.
AND WE'RE NOT FINISHED HERE.
YOU CAN'T GO HOME, NOW.
SHUT. YOUR MOUTH.
MAKE ME.

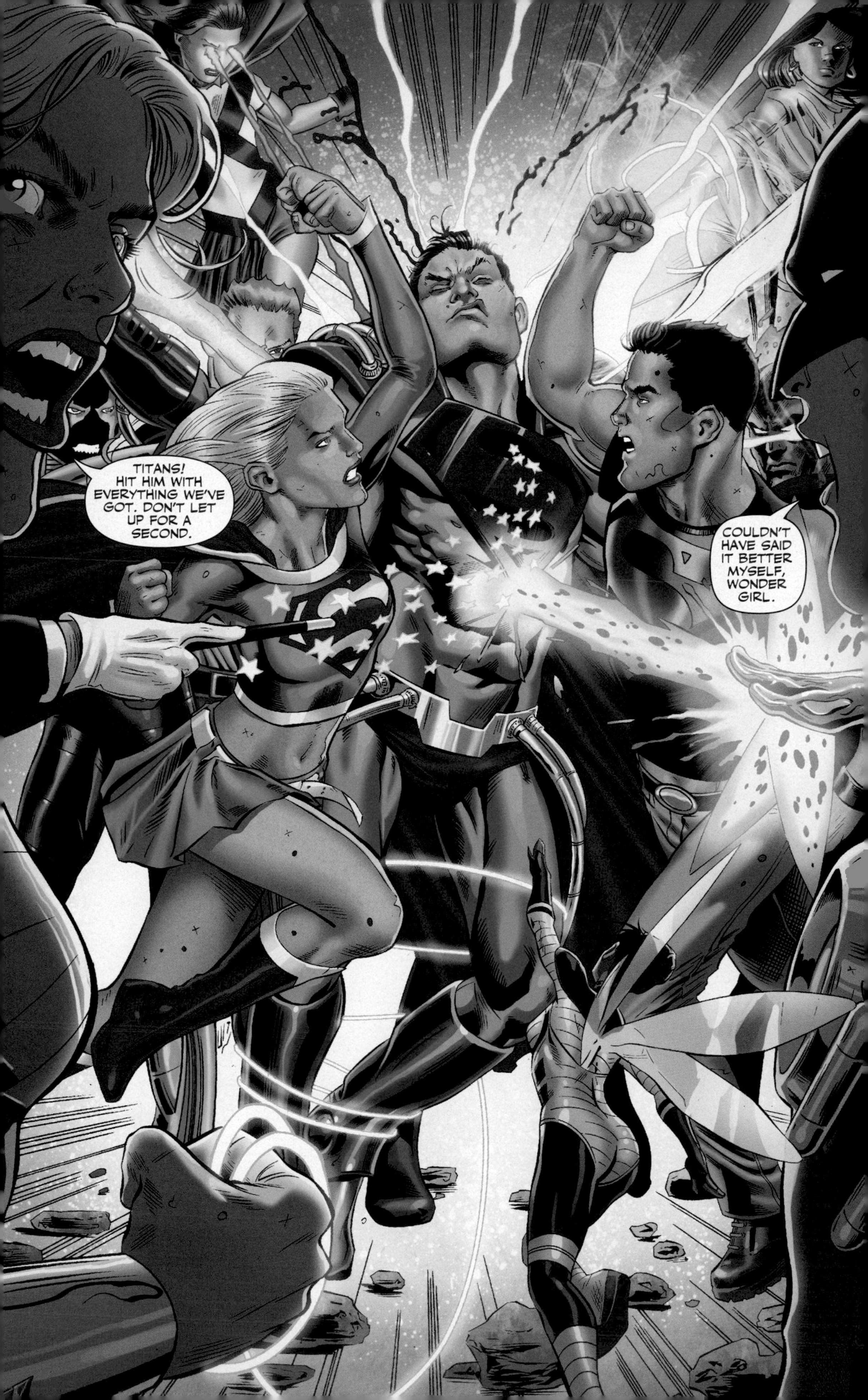
TITANS! HIT HIM WITH EVERYTHING WE'VE GOT. DON'T LET UP FOR A SECOND.
COULDN'T HAVE SAID IT BETTER MYSELF, WONDER GIRL.

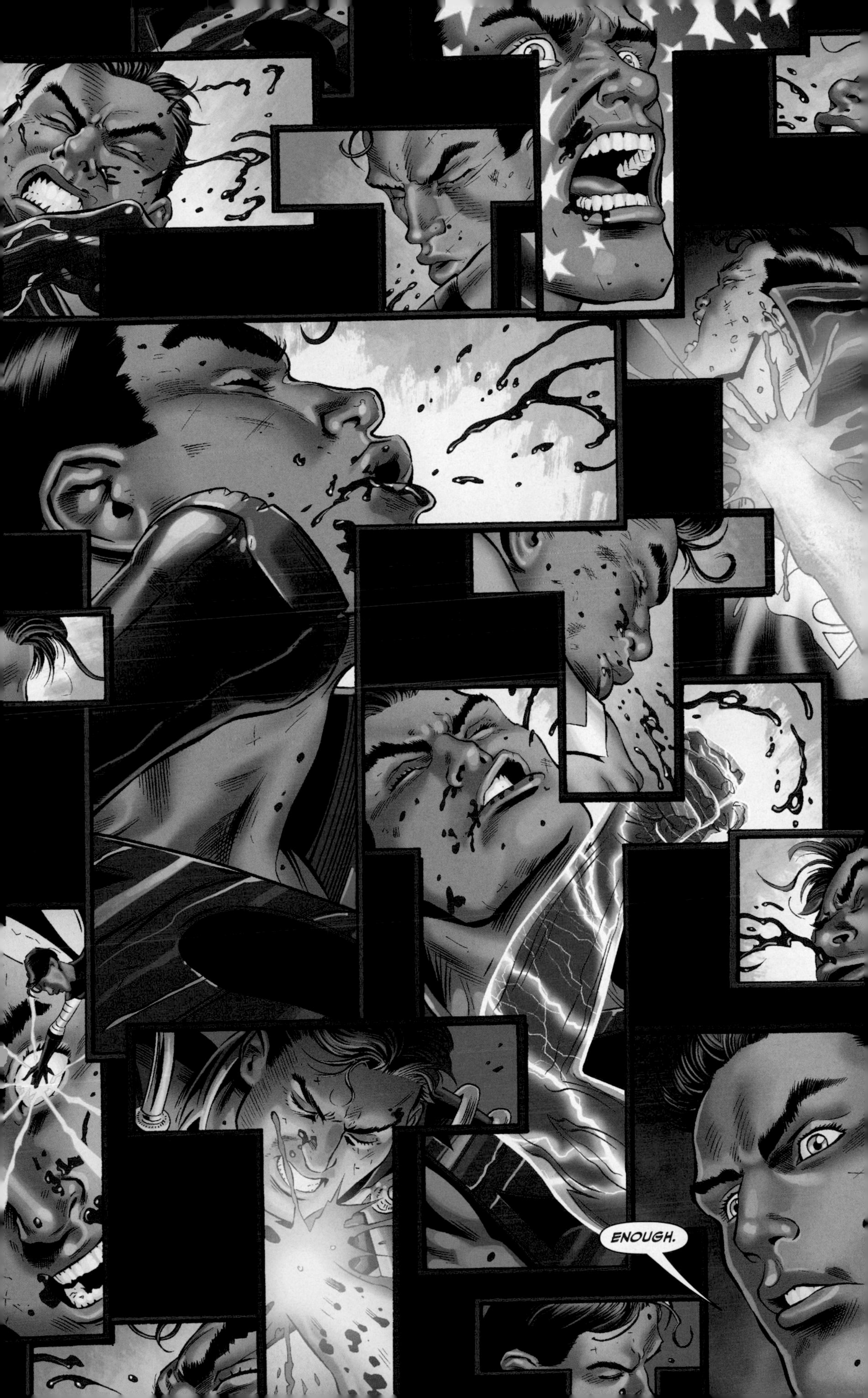
ENOUGH.

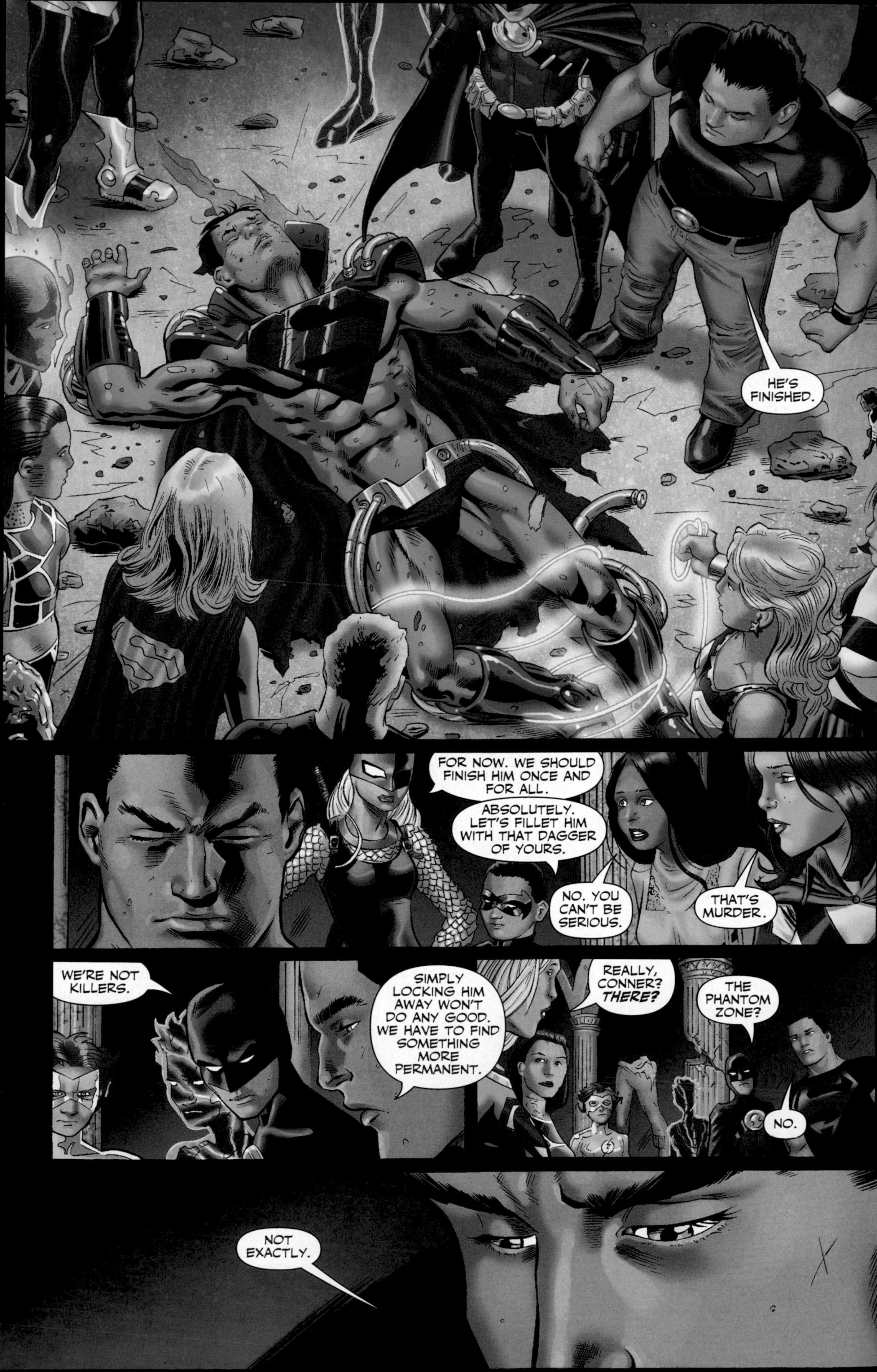
HE'S FINISHED.
FOR NOW. WE SHOULD FINISH HIM ONCE AND FOR ALL.
ABSOLUTELY. LET'S FILLET HIM WITH THAT DAGGER OF YOURS.
NO. YOU CAN'T BE SERIOUS.
THAT'S MURDER.
WE'RE NOT KILLERS.
SIMPLY LOCKING HIM AWAY WON'T DO ANY GOOD. WE HAVE TO FIND SOMETHING MORE PERMANENT.
REALLY, CONNER? THERE?
THE PHANTOM ZONE?
NO.
NOT EXACTLY.

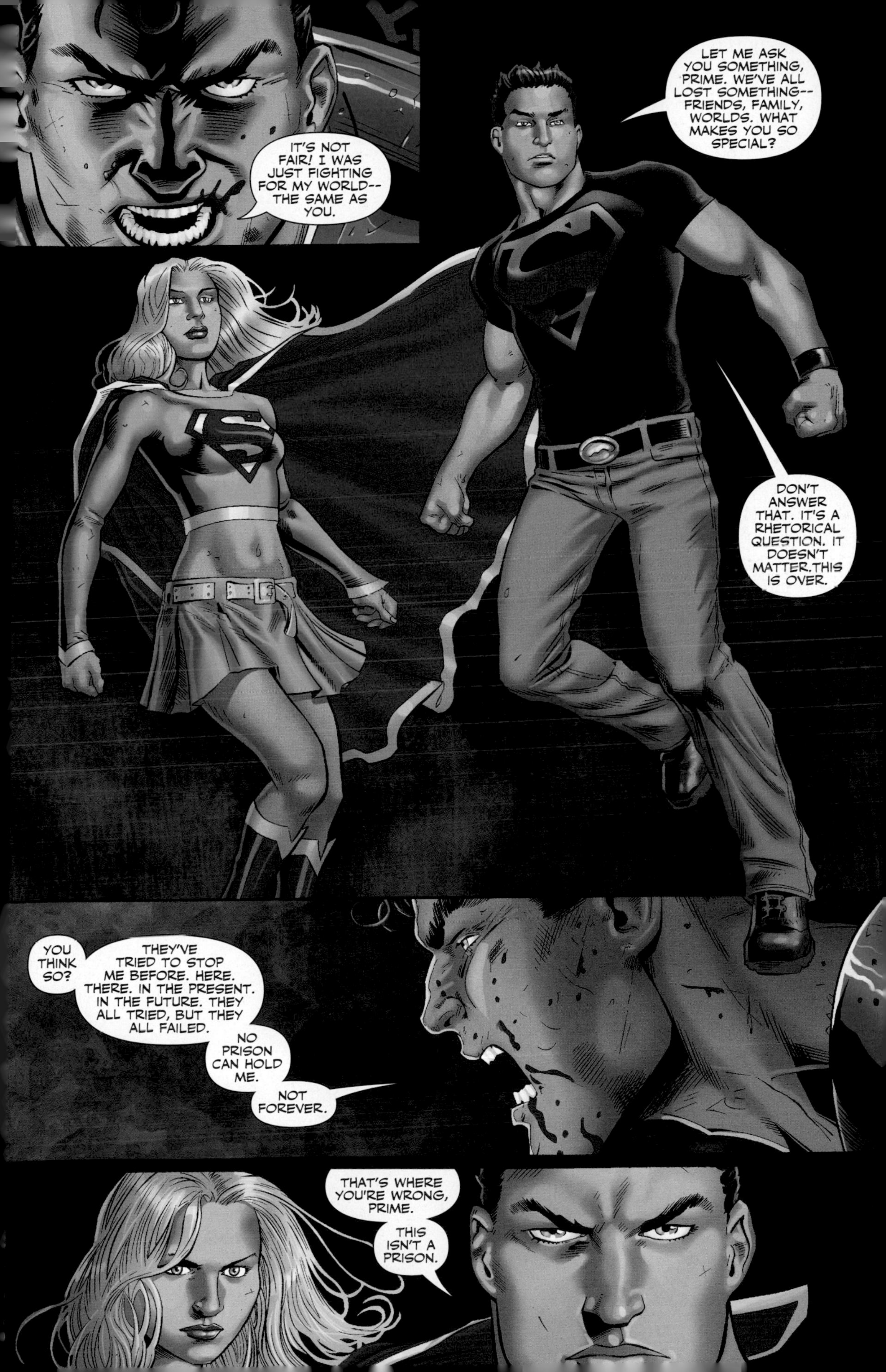
IT'S NOT FAIR! I WAS JUST FIGHTING FOR MY WORLD-- THE SAME AS YOU.
LET ME ASK YOU SOMETHING, PRIME. WE'VE ALL LOST SOMETHING-- FRIENDS, FAMILY, WORLDS. WHAT MAKES YOU SO SPECIAL?
DON'T ANSWER THAT. IT'S A RHETORICAL QUESTION. IT DOESN'T MATTER.THIS IS OVER.
YOU THINK SO?
THEY'VE TRIED TO STOP ME BEFORE. HERE. THERE. IN THE PRESENT. IN THE FUTURE. THEY ALL TRIED, BUT THEY ALL FAILED.
NO PRISON CAN HOLD ME.
NOT FOREVER.
THAT'S WHERE YOU'RE WRONG, PRIME.
THIS ISN'T A PRISON.

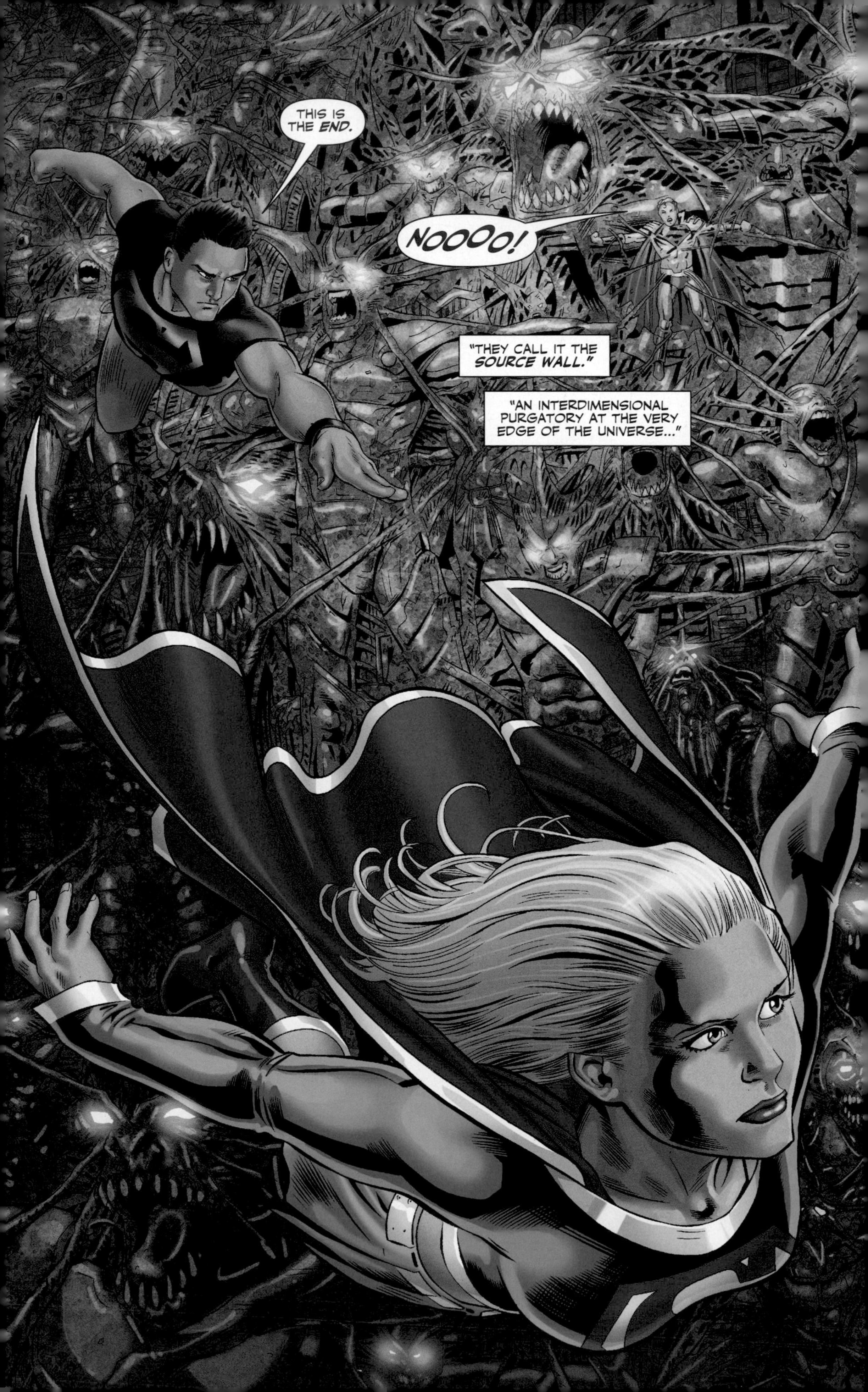
THIS IS THE END.
NOOOO!
"THEY CALL IT THE SOURCE WALL."
"AN INTERDIMENSIONAL PURGATORY AT THE VERY EDGE OF THE UNIVERSE..."

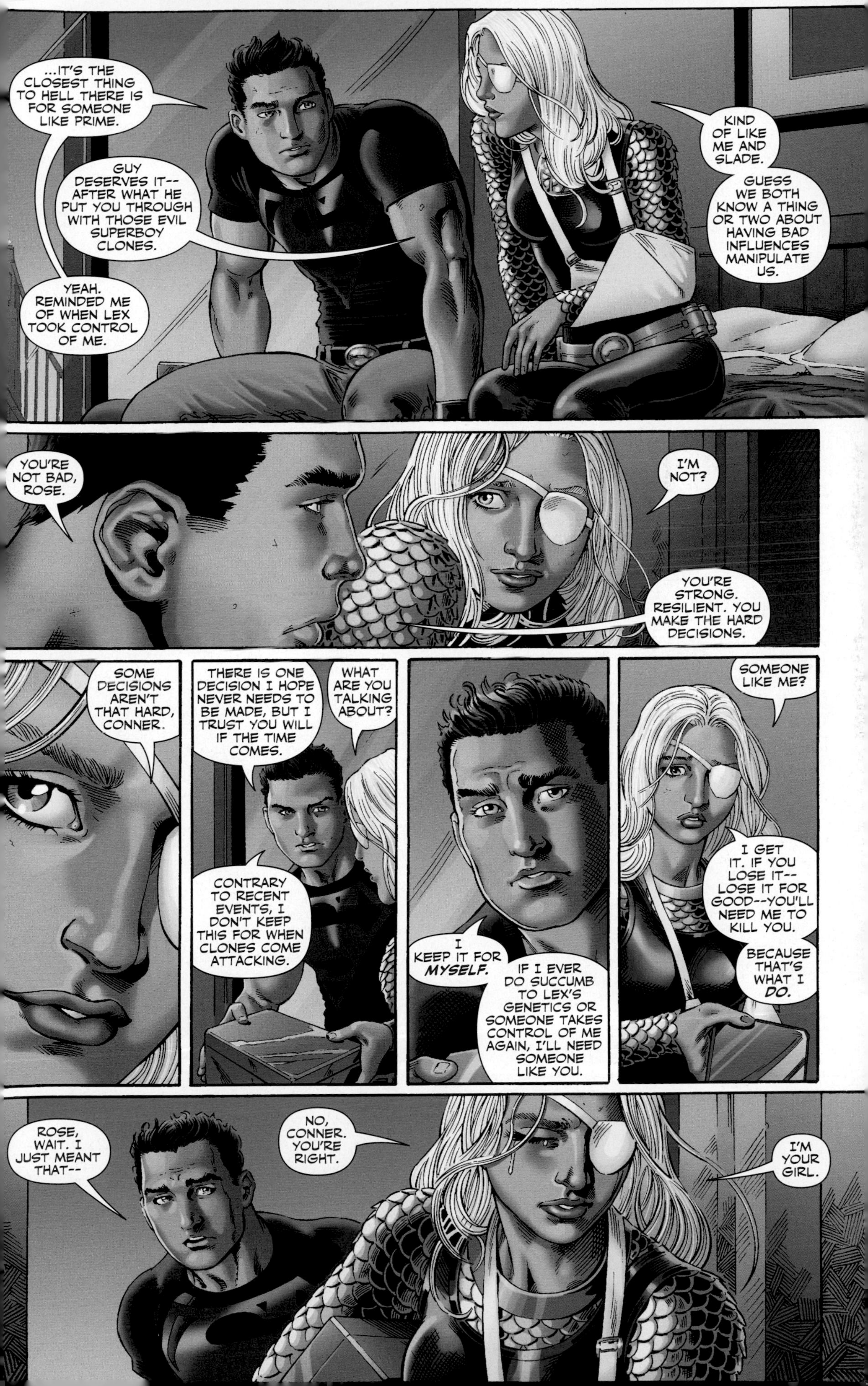
...IT'S THE CLOSEST THING TO HELL THERE IS FOR SOMEONE LIKE PRIME.
GUY DESERVES IT-- AFTER WHAT HE PUT YOU THROUGH WITH THOSE EVIL SUPERBOY CLONES.
YEAH. REMINDED ME OF WHEN LEX TOOK CONTROL OF ME.
KIND OF LIKE ME AND SLADE.
GUESS WE BOTH KNOW A THING OR TWO ABOUT HAVING BAD INFLUENCES MANIPULATE US.
YOU'RE NOT BAD, ROSE.
I'M NOT?
YOU'RE STRONG. RESILIENT. YOU MAKE THE HARD DECISIONS.
SOME DECISIONS AREN'T THAT HARD, CONNER.
THERE IS ONE DECISION I HOPE NEVER NEEDS TO BE MADE, BUT I TRUST YOU WILL IF THE TIME COMES.
WHAT ARE YOU TALKING ABOUT?
CONTRARY TO RECENT EVENTS, I DON'T KEEP THIS FOR WHEN CLONES COME ATTACKING.
I KEEP IT FOR *MYSELF.*
IF I EVER DO SUCCUMB TO LEX'S GENETICS OR SOMEONE TAKES CONTROL OF ME AGAIN, I'LL NEED SOMEONE LIKE YOU.
SOMEONE LIKE ME?
I GET IT. IF YOU LOSE IT-- LOSE IT FOR GOOD--YOU'LL NEED ME TO KILL YOU.
BECAUSE THAT'S WHAT I *DO.*
ROSE, WAIT. I JUST MEANT THAT--
NO, CONNER. YOU'RE RIGHT.
I'M YOUR GIRL.

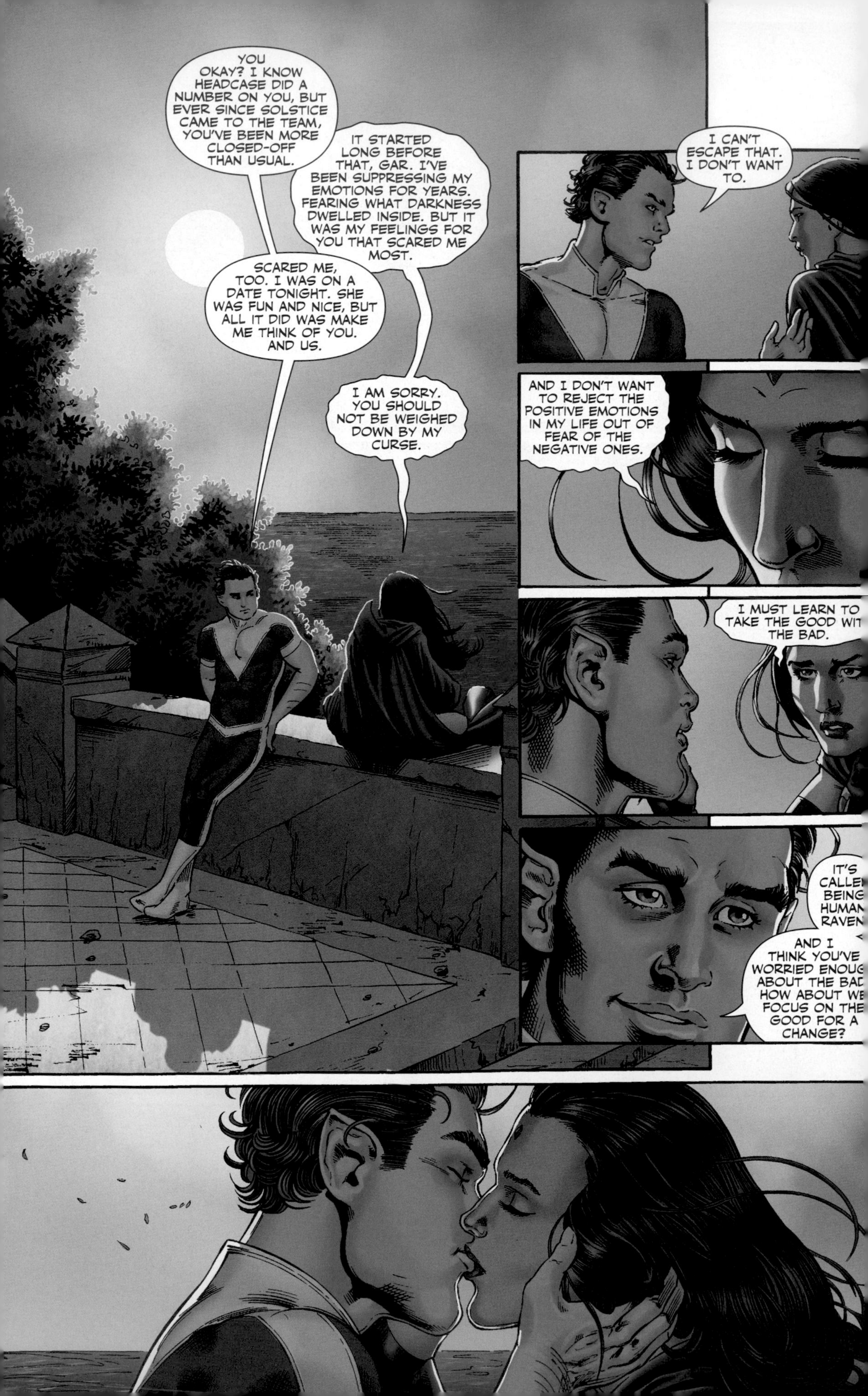
YOU OKAY? I KNOW HEADCASE DID A NUMBER ON YOU, BUT EVER SINCE SOLSTICE CAME TO THE TEAM, YOU'VE BEEN MORE CLOSED-OFF THAN USUAL.
IT STARTED LONG BEFORE THAT, GAR. I'VE BEEN SUPPRESSING MY EMOTIONS FOR YEARS. FEARING WHAT DARKNESS DWELLED INSIDE. BUT IT WAS MY FEELINGS FOR YOU THAT SCARED ME MOST.
SCARED ME, TOO. I WAS ON A DATE TONIGHT. SHE WAS FUN AND NICE, BUT ALL IT DID WAS MAKE ME THINK OF YOU. AND US.
I AM SORRY. YOU SHOULD NOT BE WEIGHED DOWN BY MY CURSE.
I CAN'T ESCAPE THAT. I DON'T WANT TO.
AND I DON'T WANT TO REJECT THE POSITIVE EMOTIONS IN MY LIFE OUT OF FEAR OF THE NEGATIVE ONES.
I MUST LEARN TO TAKE THE GOOD WIT THE BAD.
IT'S CALLE BEING HUMAN RAVEN
AND I THINK YOU'VE WORRIED ENOUG ABOUT THE BAD HOW ABOUT WE FOCUS ON THE GOOD FOR A CHANGE?

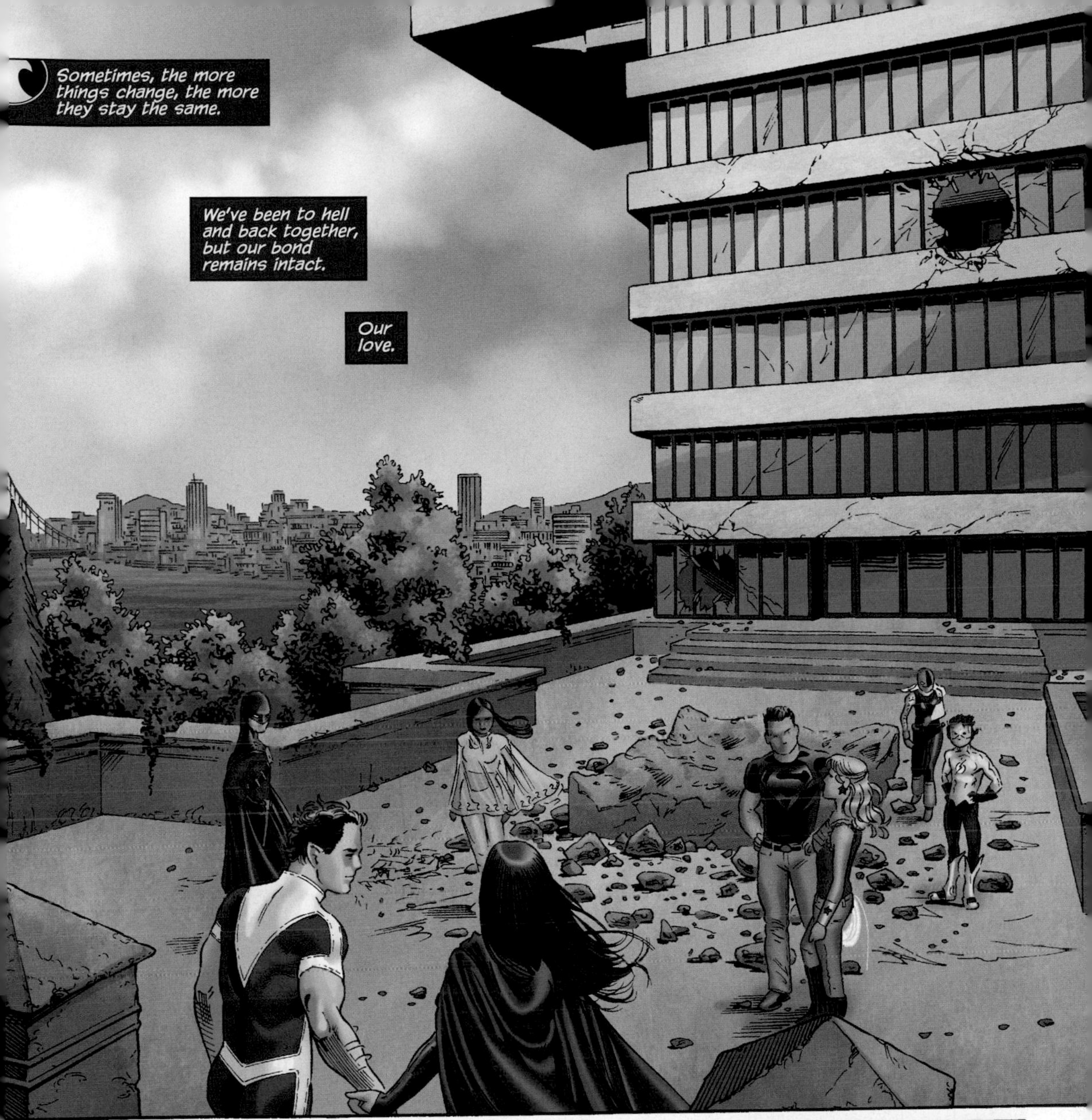
Sometimes, the more things change, the more they stay the same.
We've been to hell and back together, but our bond remains intact.
Our love.

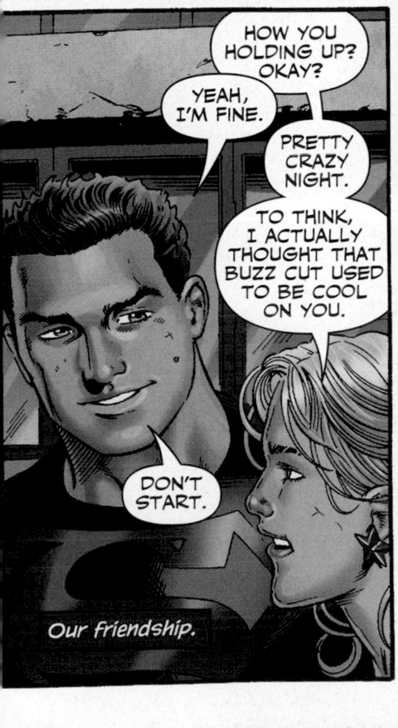
HOW YOU HOLDING UP? OKAY?
YEAH, I'M FINE.
PRETTY CRAZY NIGHT.
TO THINK, I ACTUALLY THOUGHT THAT BUZZ CUT USED TO BE COOL ON YOU.
DON'T START.
Our friendship.

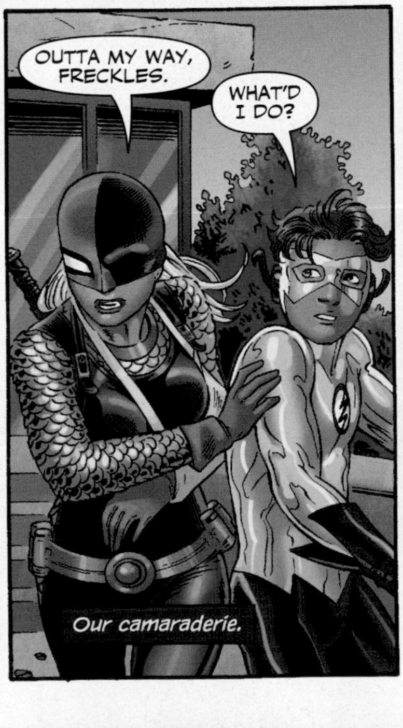
OUTTA MY WAY, FRECKLES.
WHAT'D I DO?
Our camaraderie.

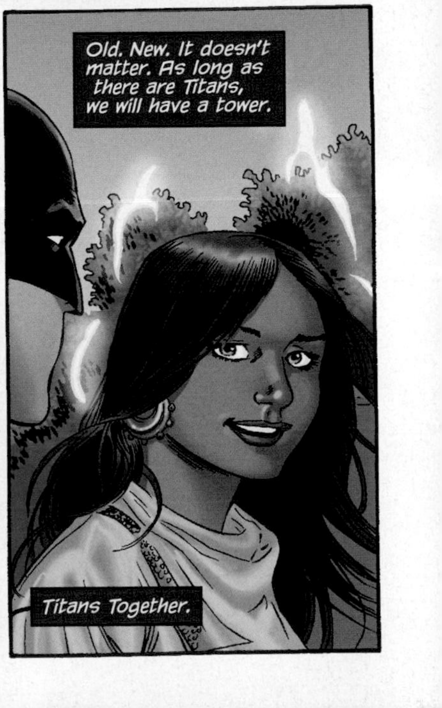
Old. New. It doesn't matter. As long as there are Titans, we will have a tower.
Titans Together.

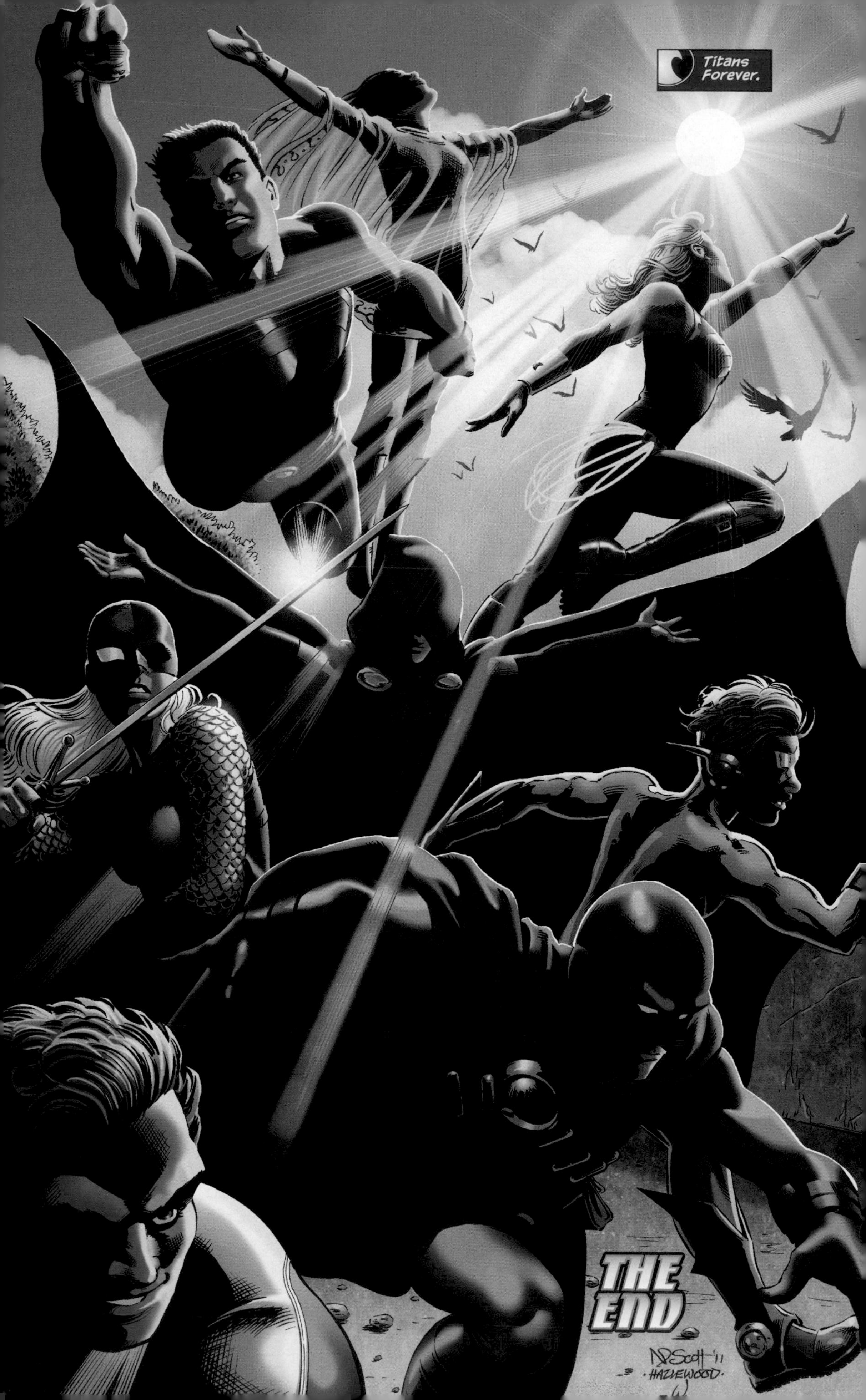
Titans Forever.
THE END
DPScott '11
HAZLEWOOD

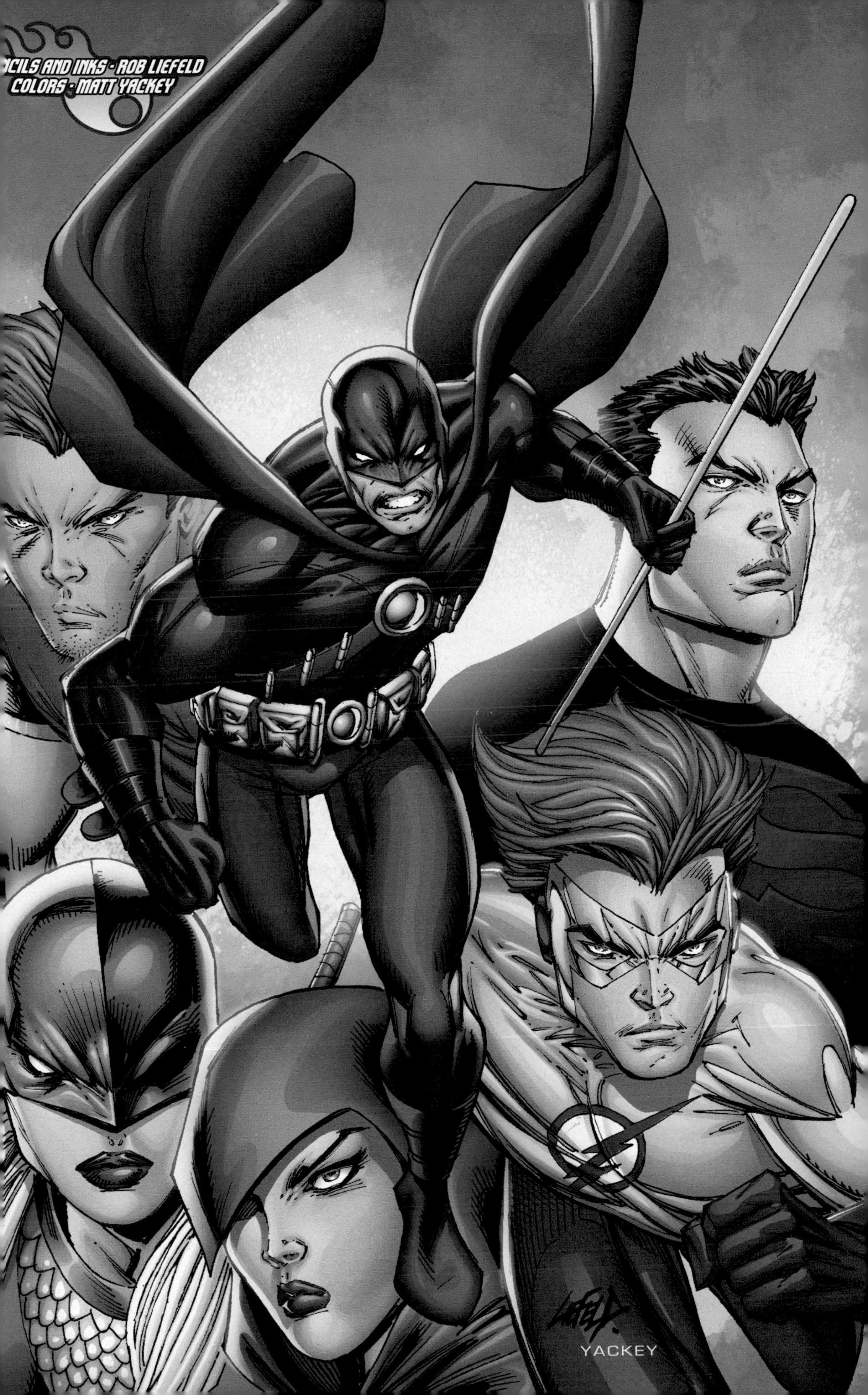
CILS AND INKS - ROB LIEFELD
COLORS - MATT YACKEY
YACKEY

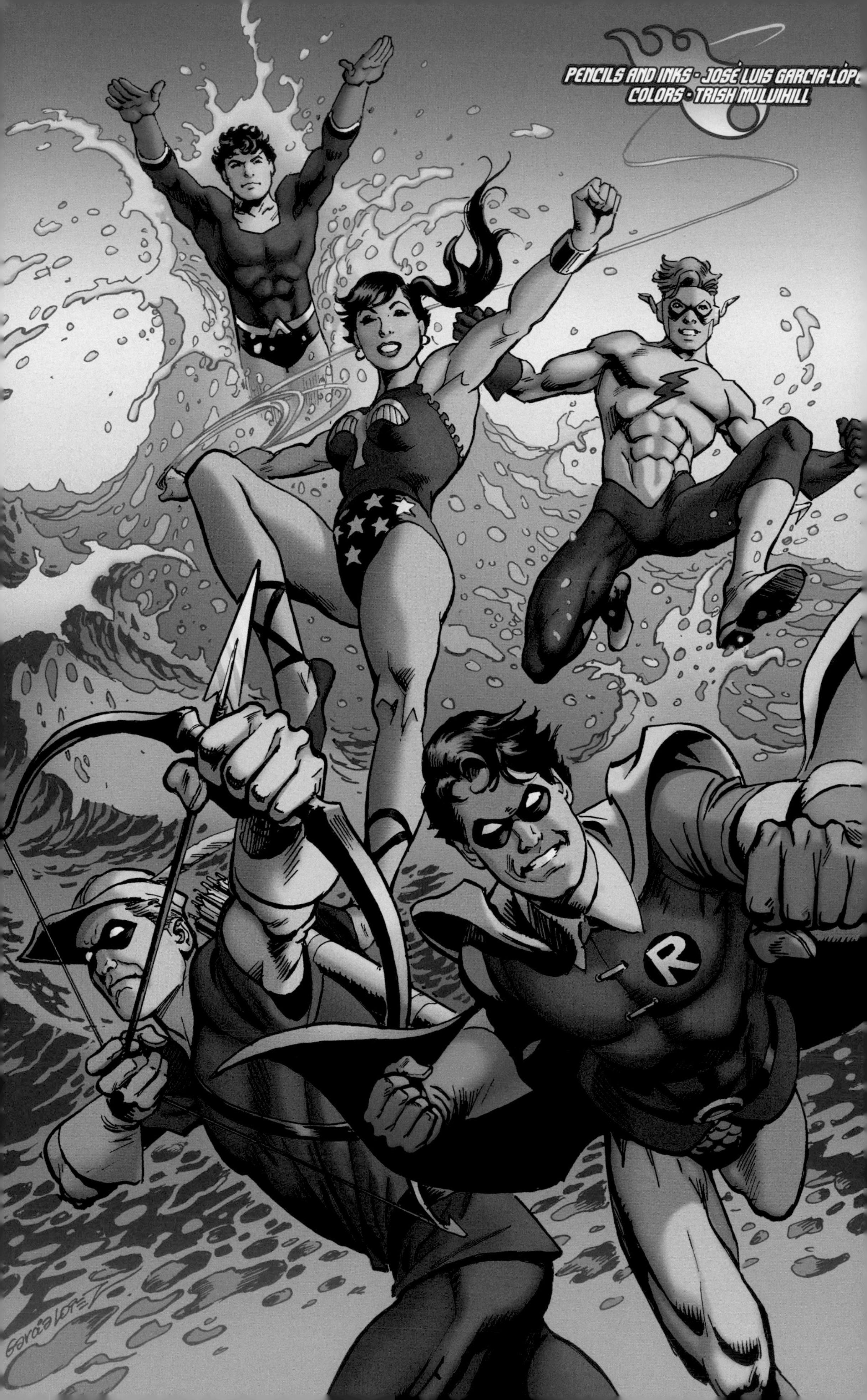
PENCILS AND INKS - JOSÉ LUIS GARCIA-LÓPE
COLORS - TRISH MULVIHILL
Garcia Lopez

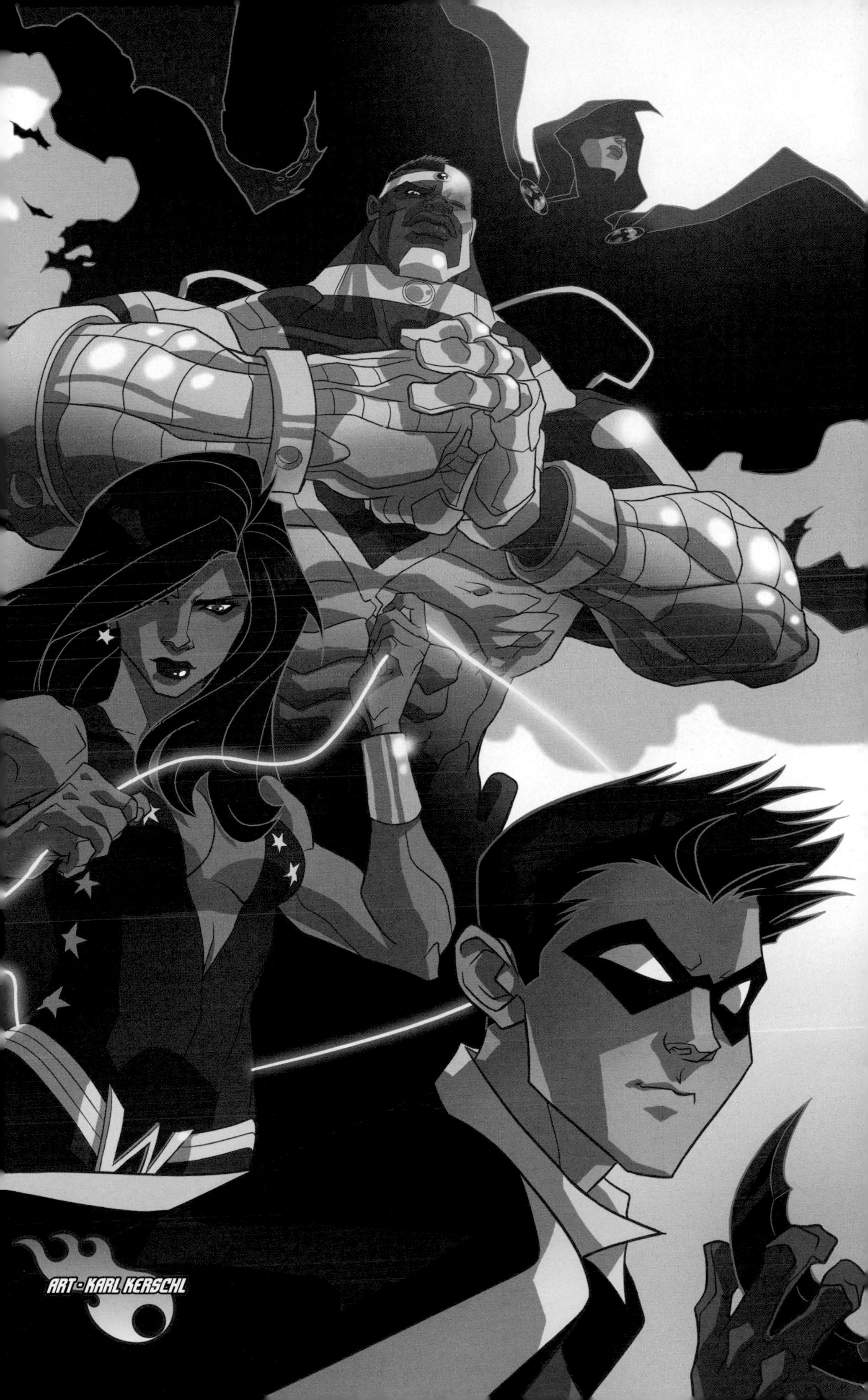
ART • KARL KERSCHL

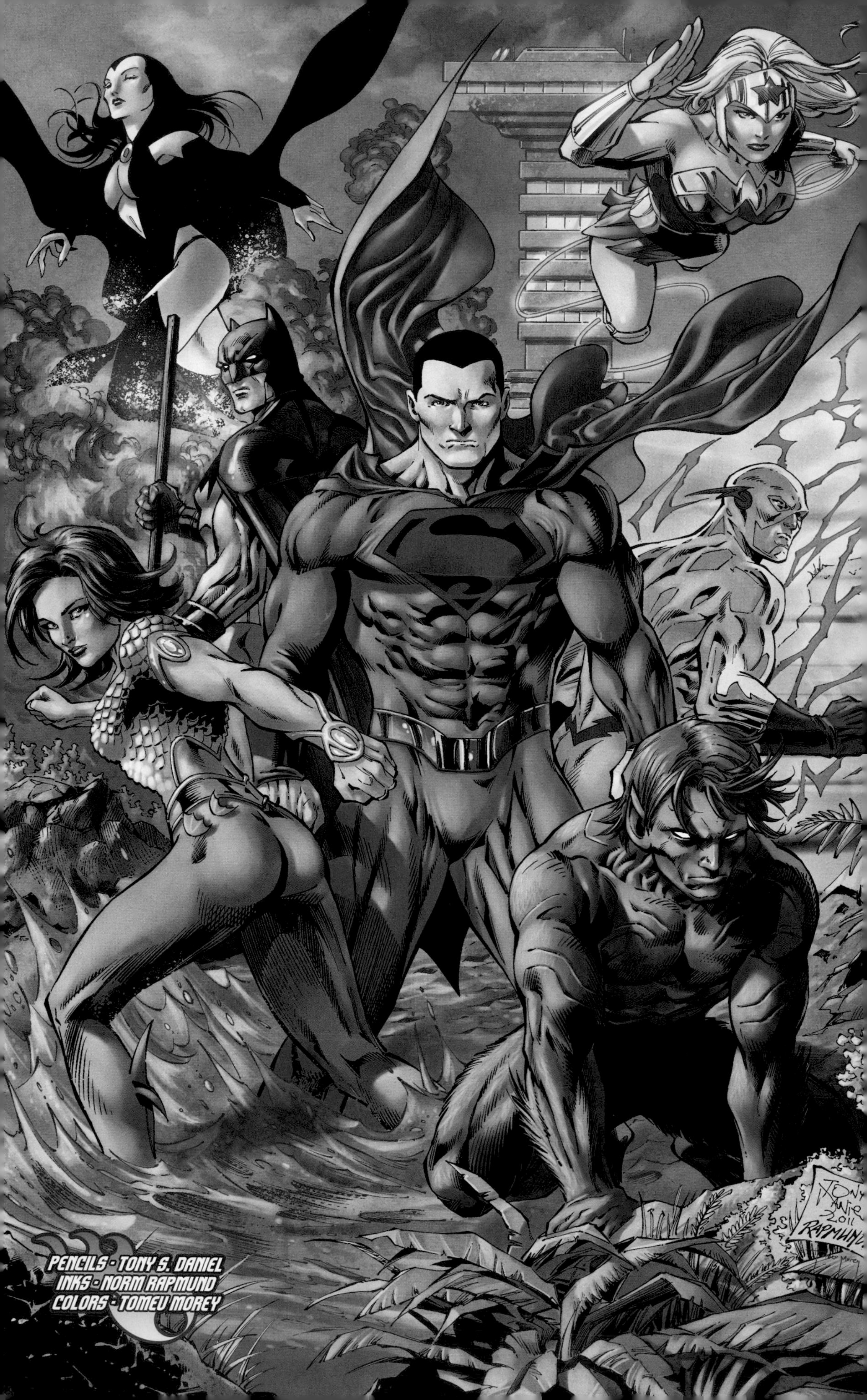
PENCILS - TONY S. DANIEL
INKS - NORM RAPMUND
COLORS - TOMEU MOREY

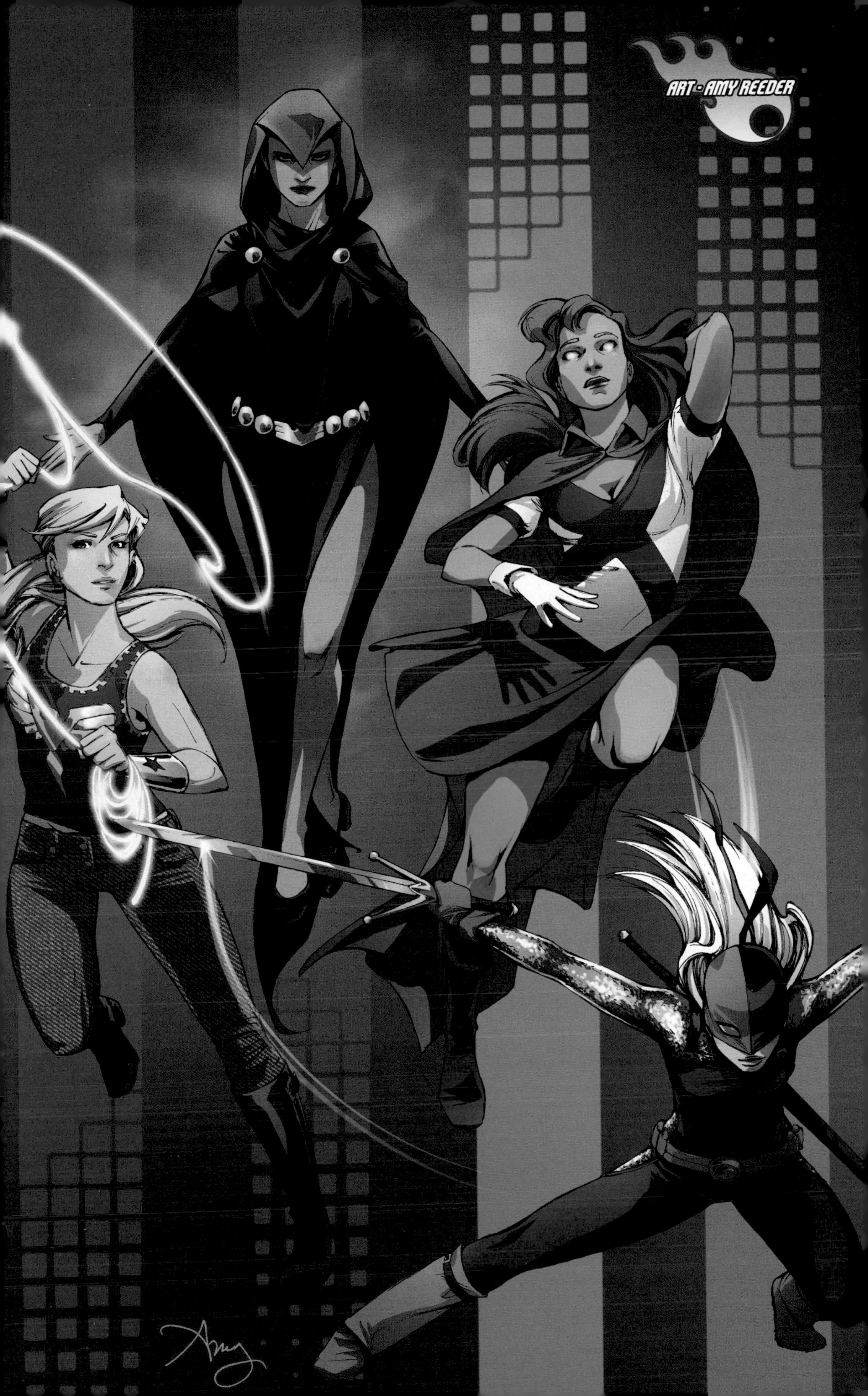
ART - AMY REEDER
Amy

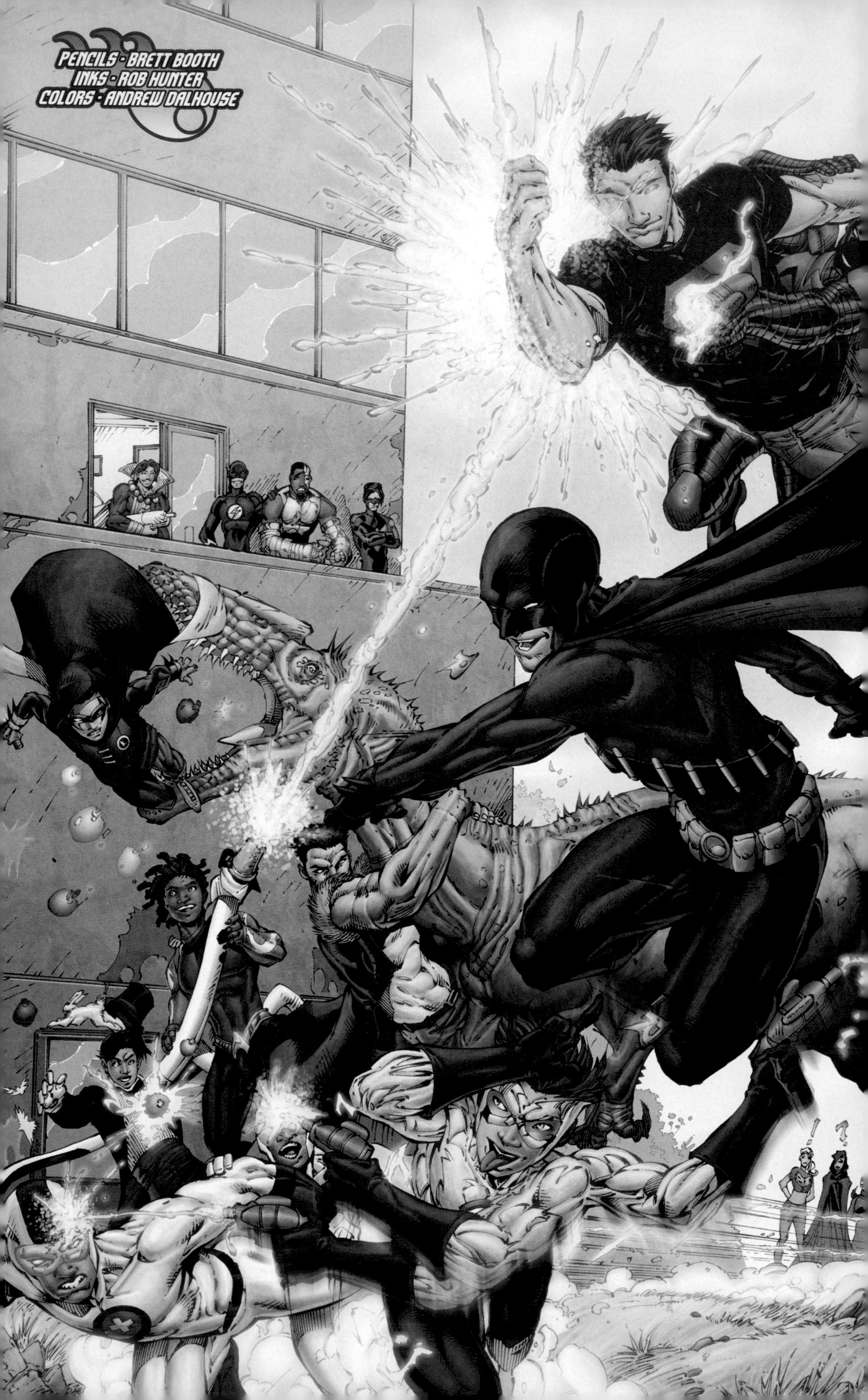
PENCILS - BRETT BOOTH
INKS - ROB HUNTER
COLORS - ANDREW DALHOUSE

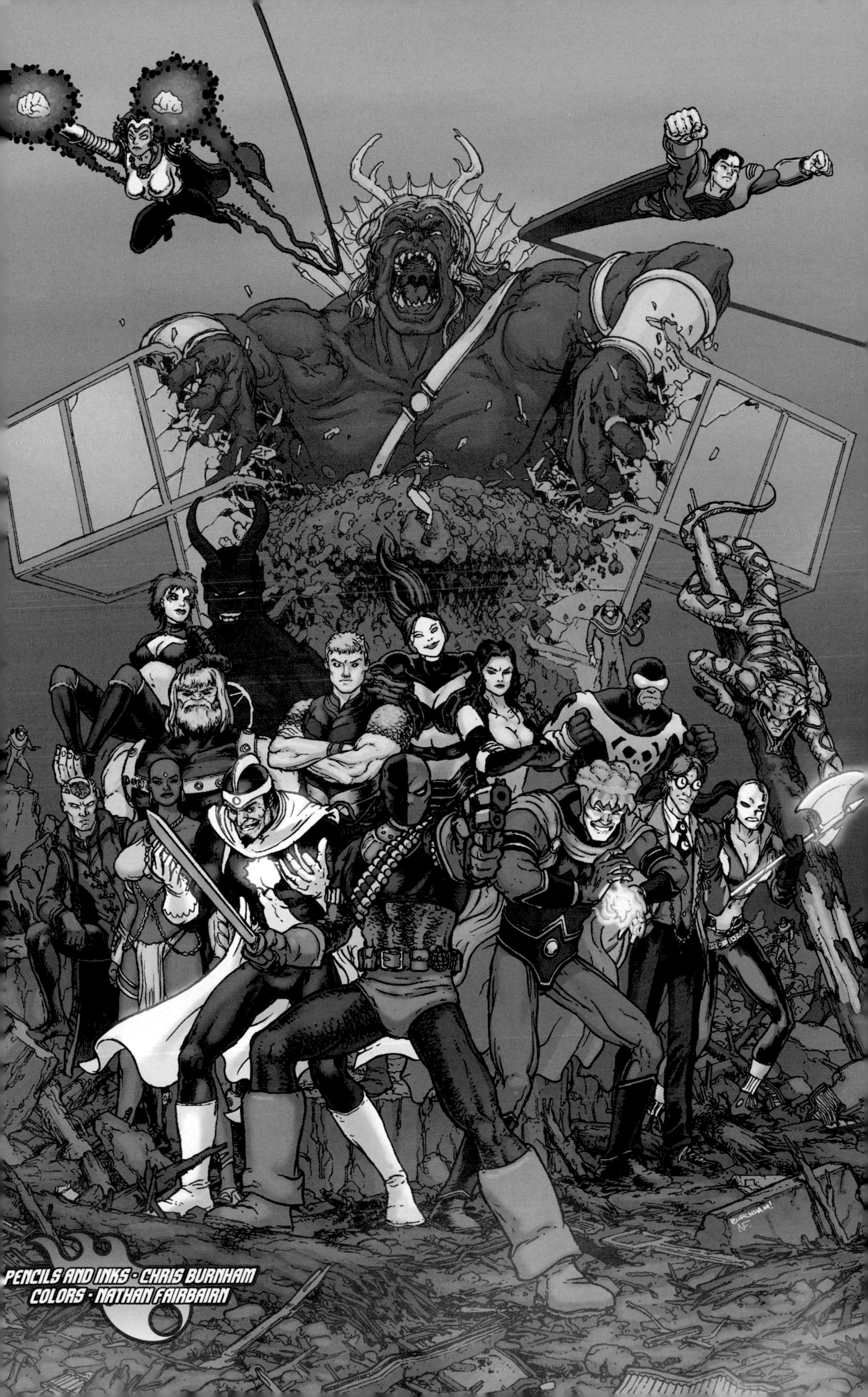
PENCILS AND INKS - CHRIS BURNHAM
COLORS - NATHAN FAIRBAIRN

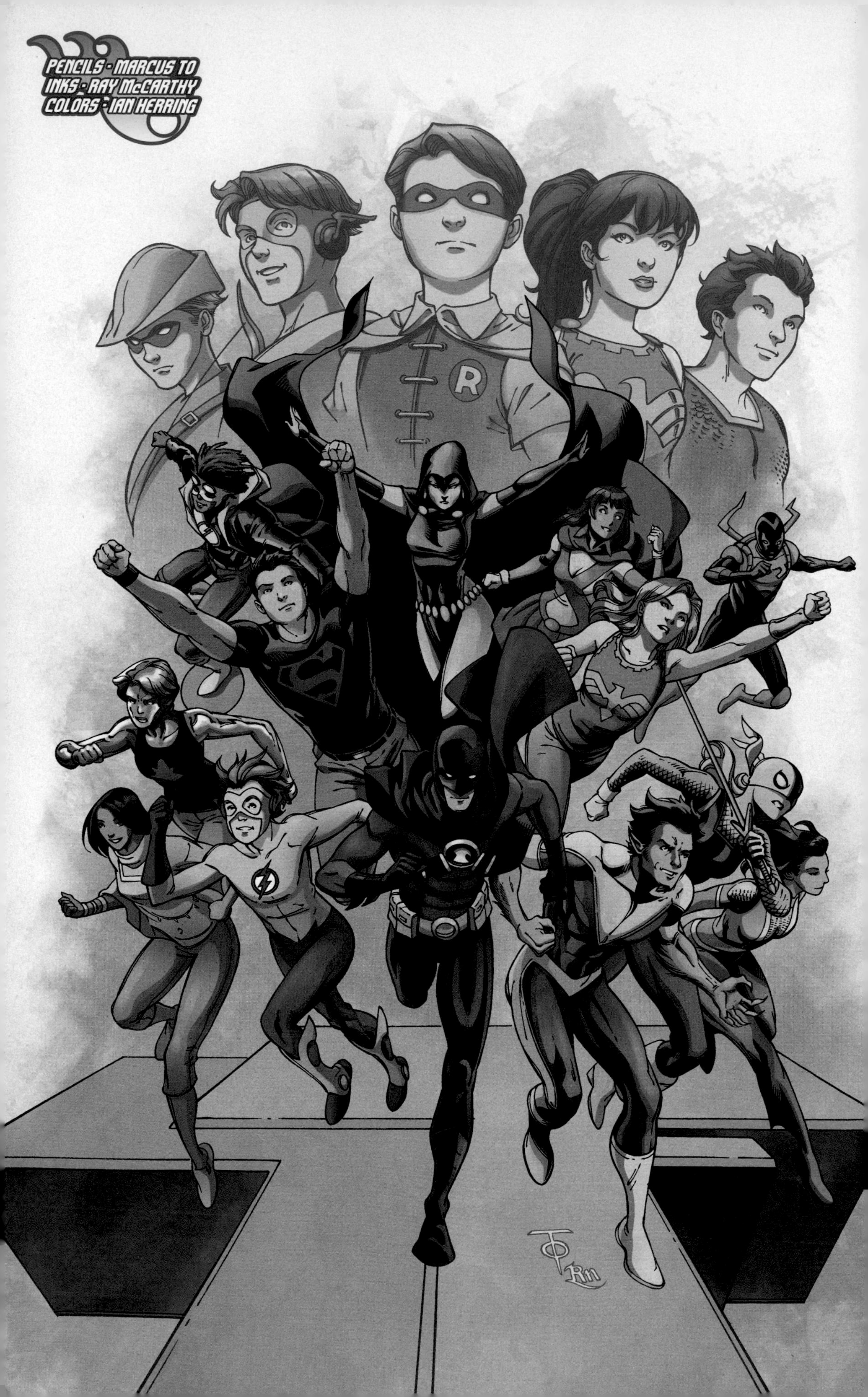
PENCILS - MARCUS TO
INKS - RAY McCARTHY
COLORS - IAN HERRING

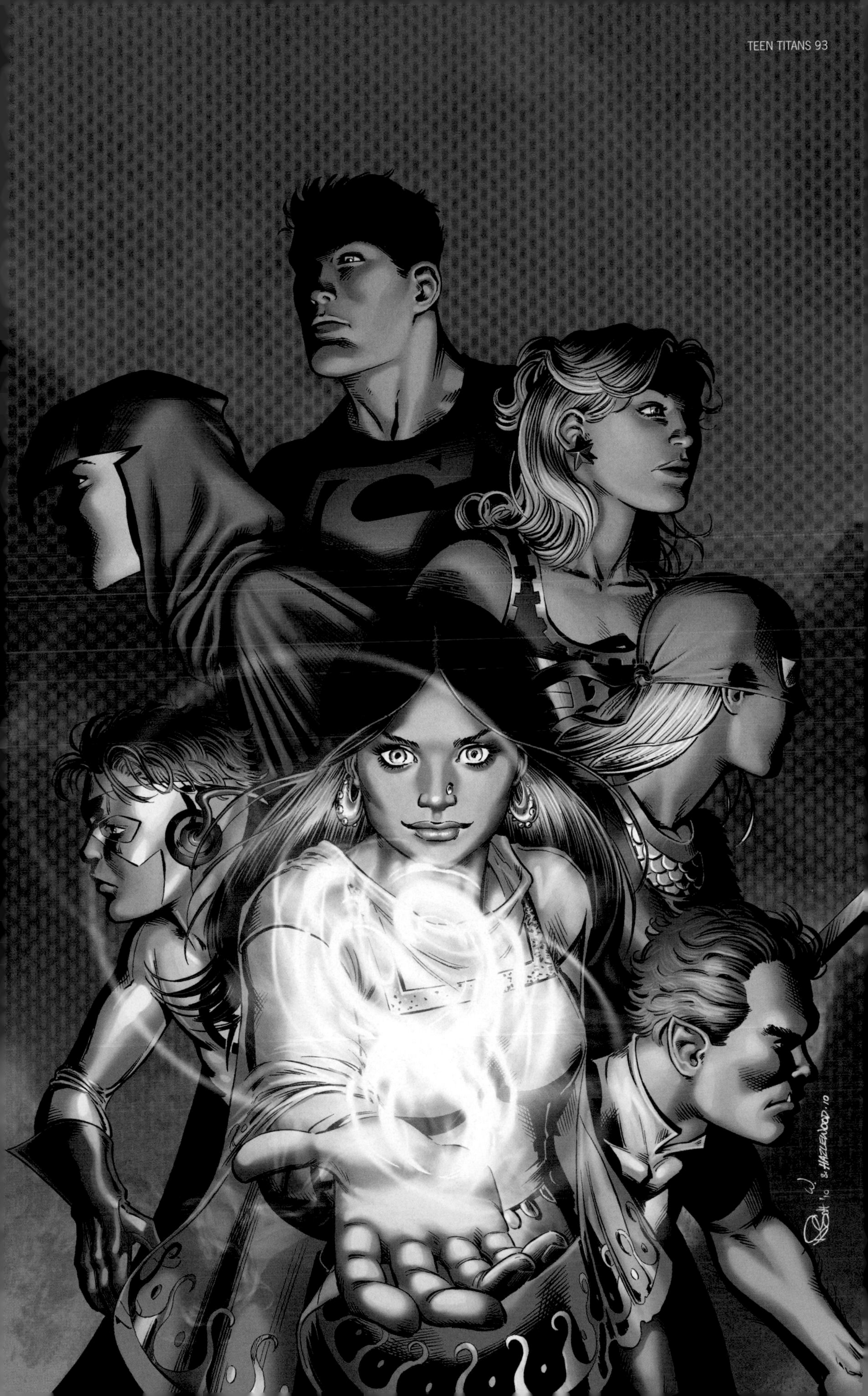

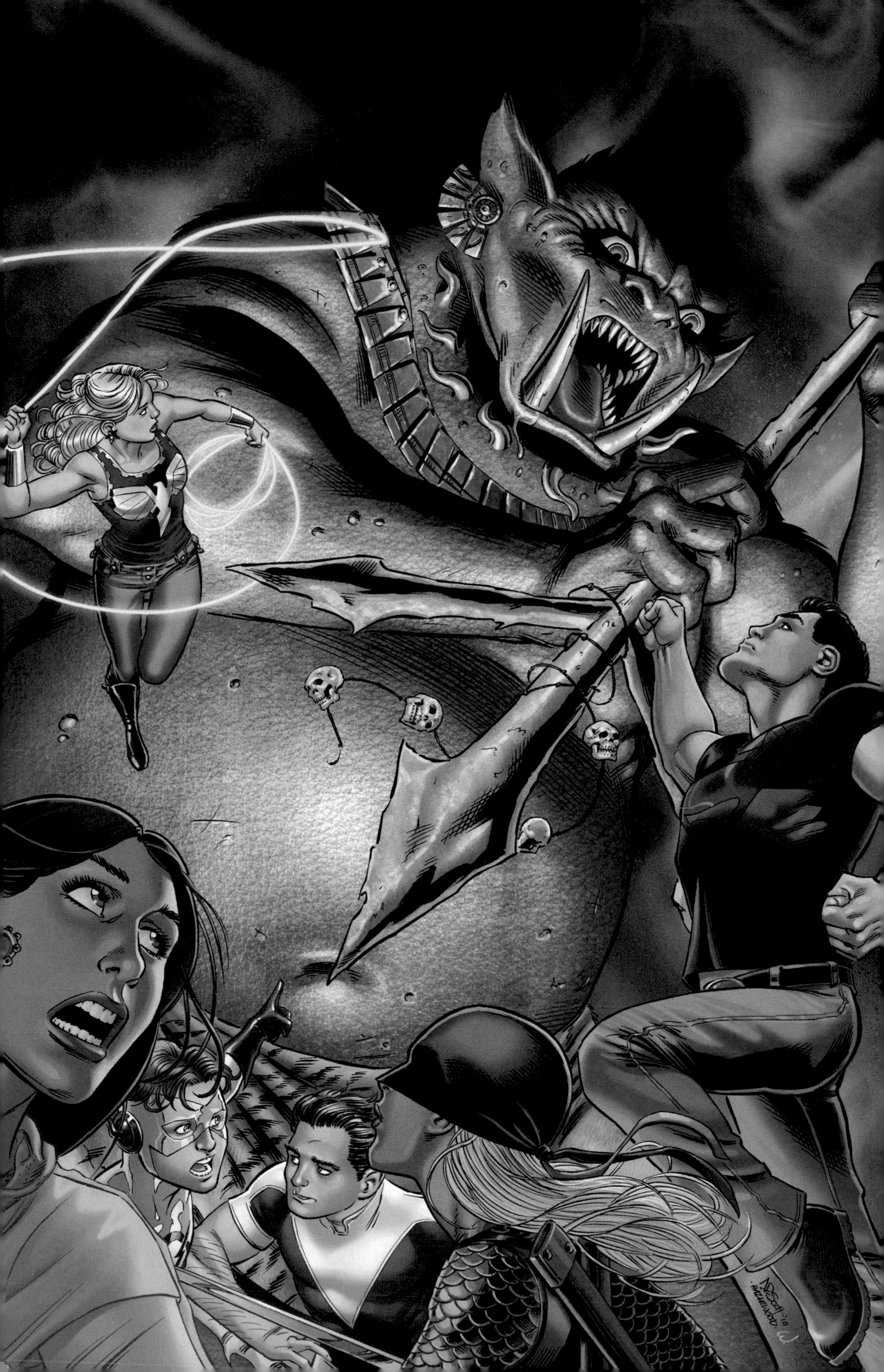

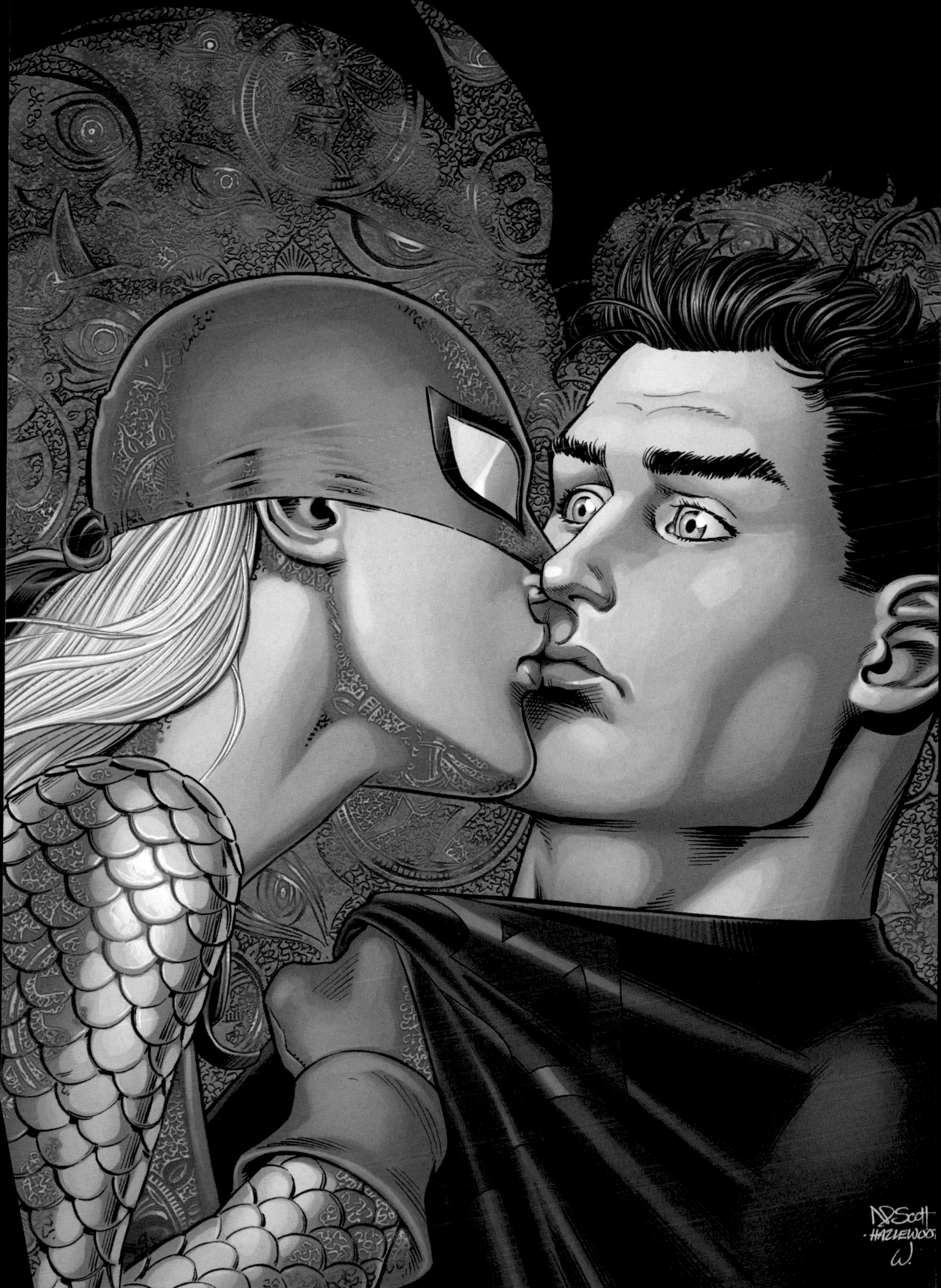

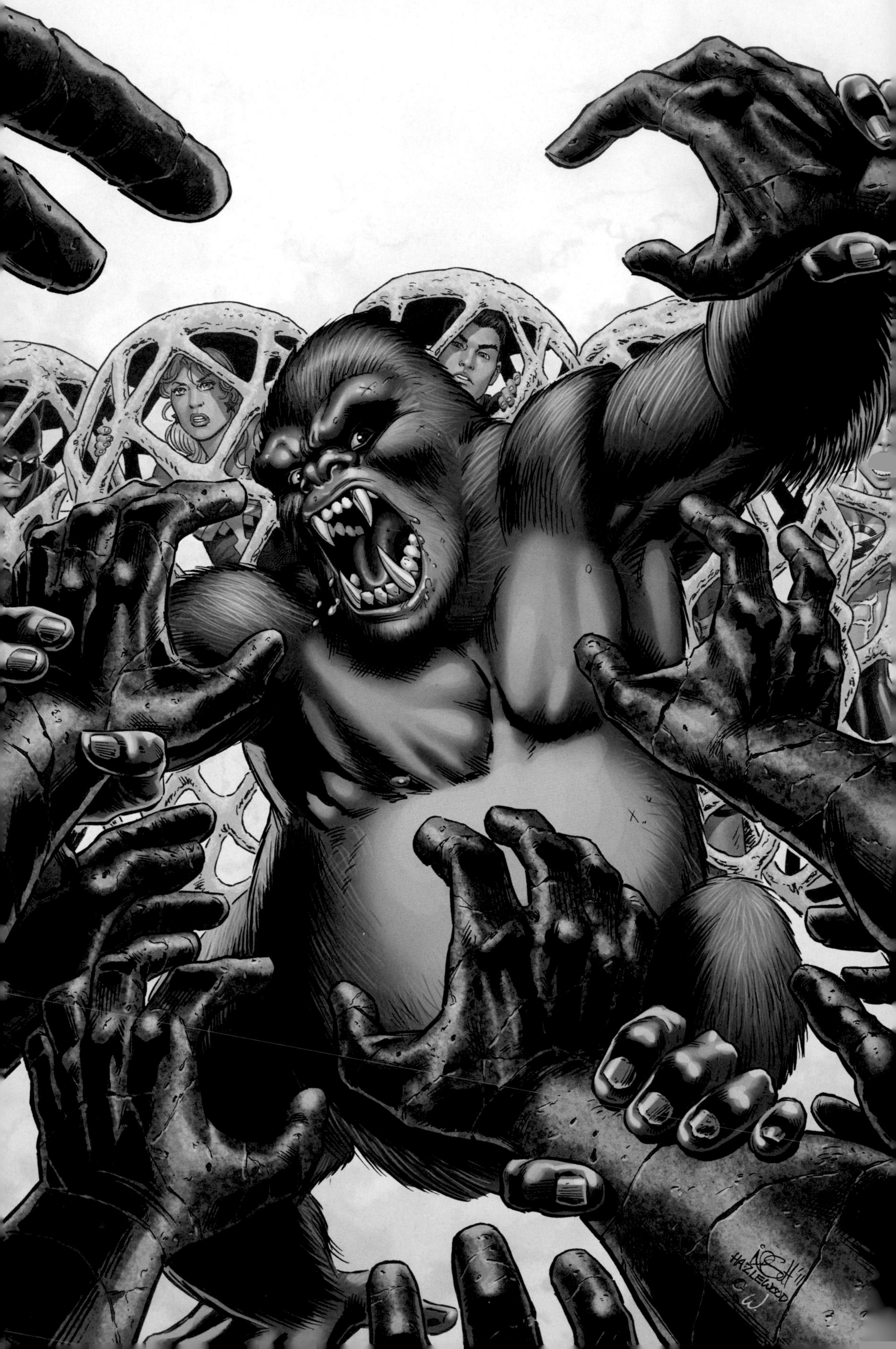
HAZLEWOOD

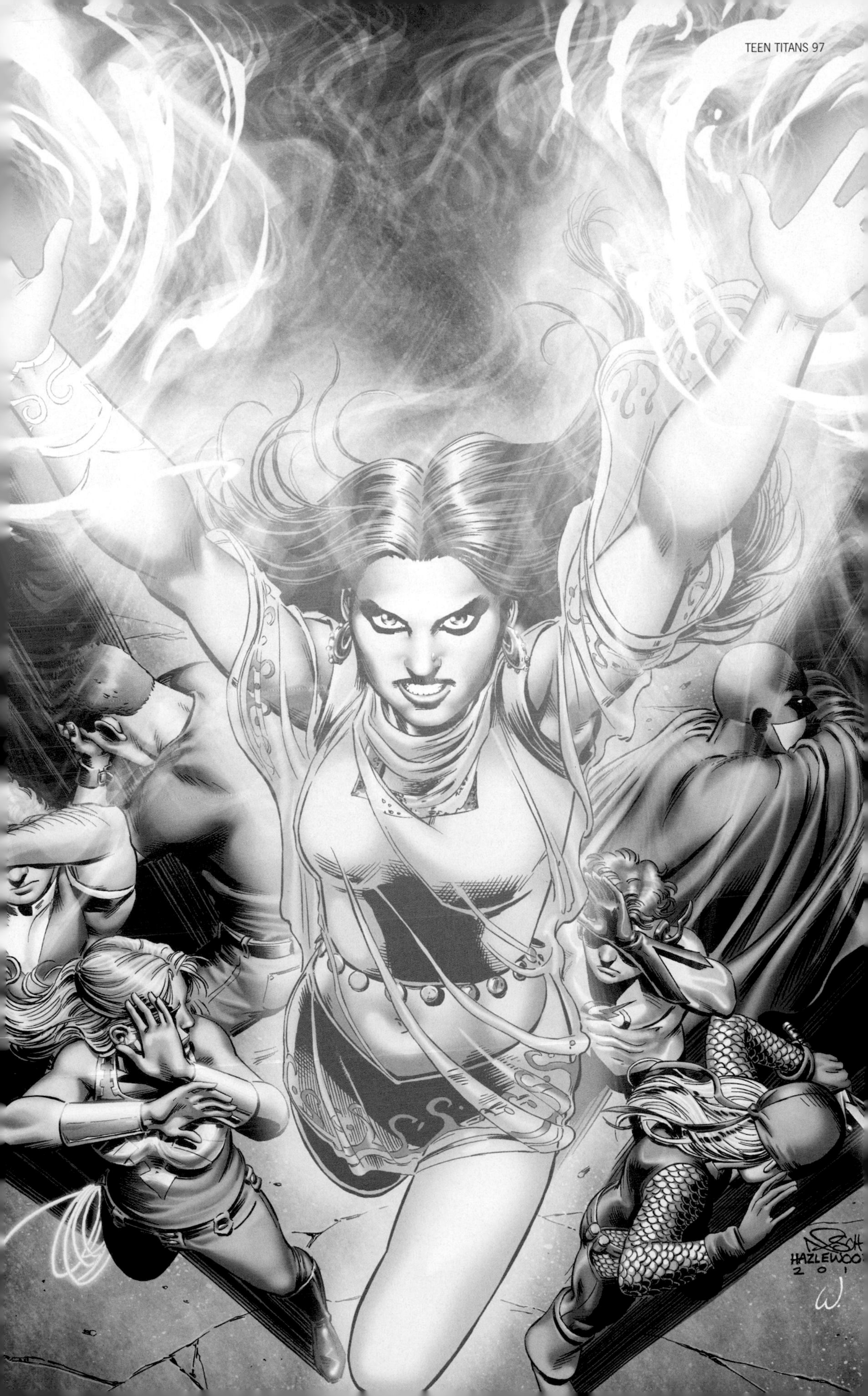

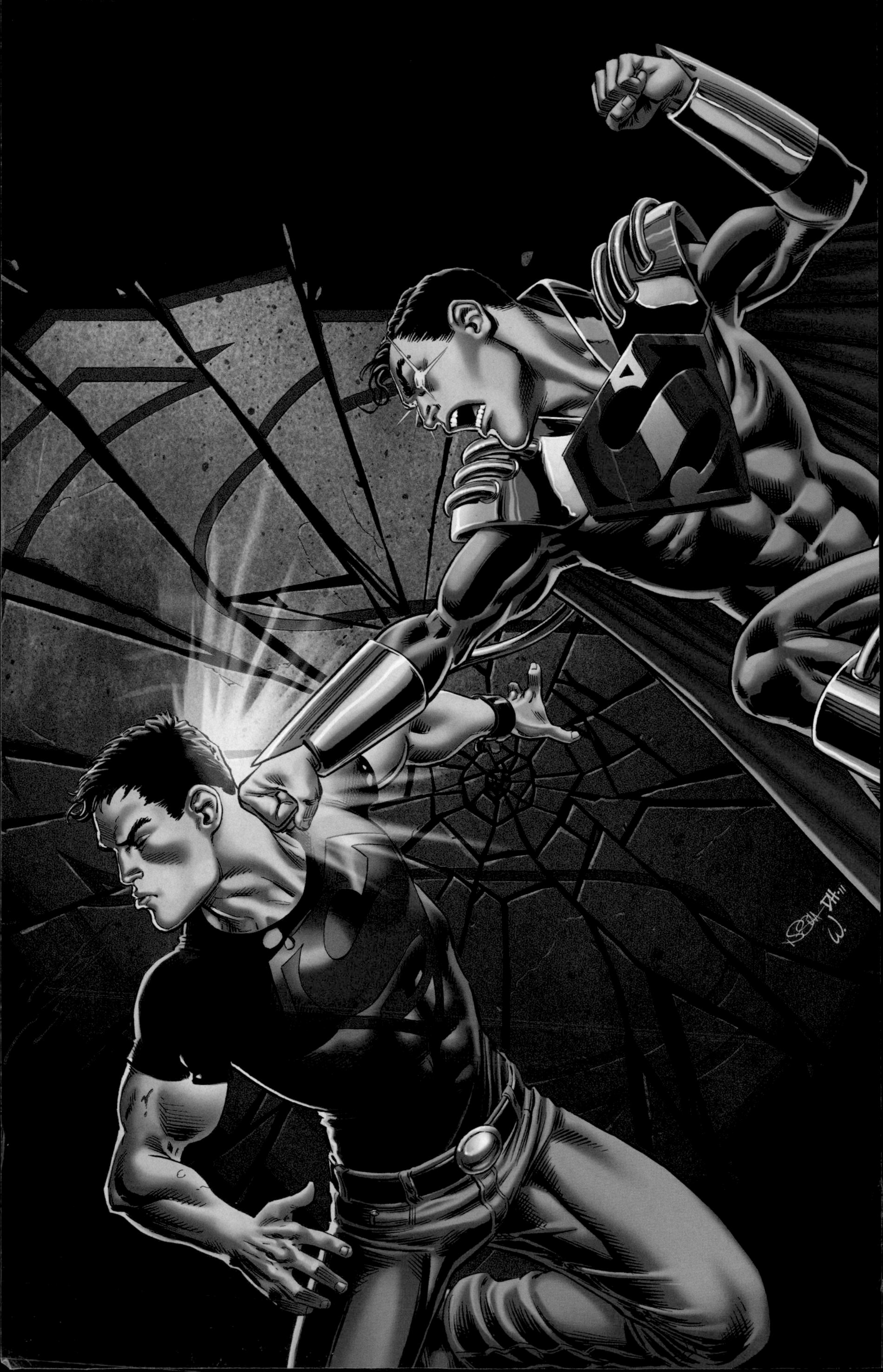

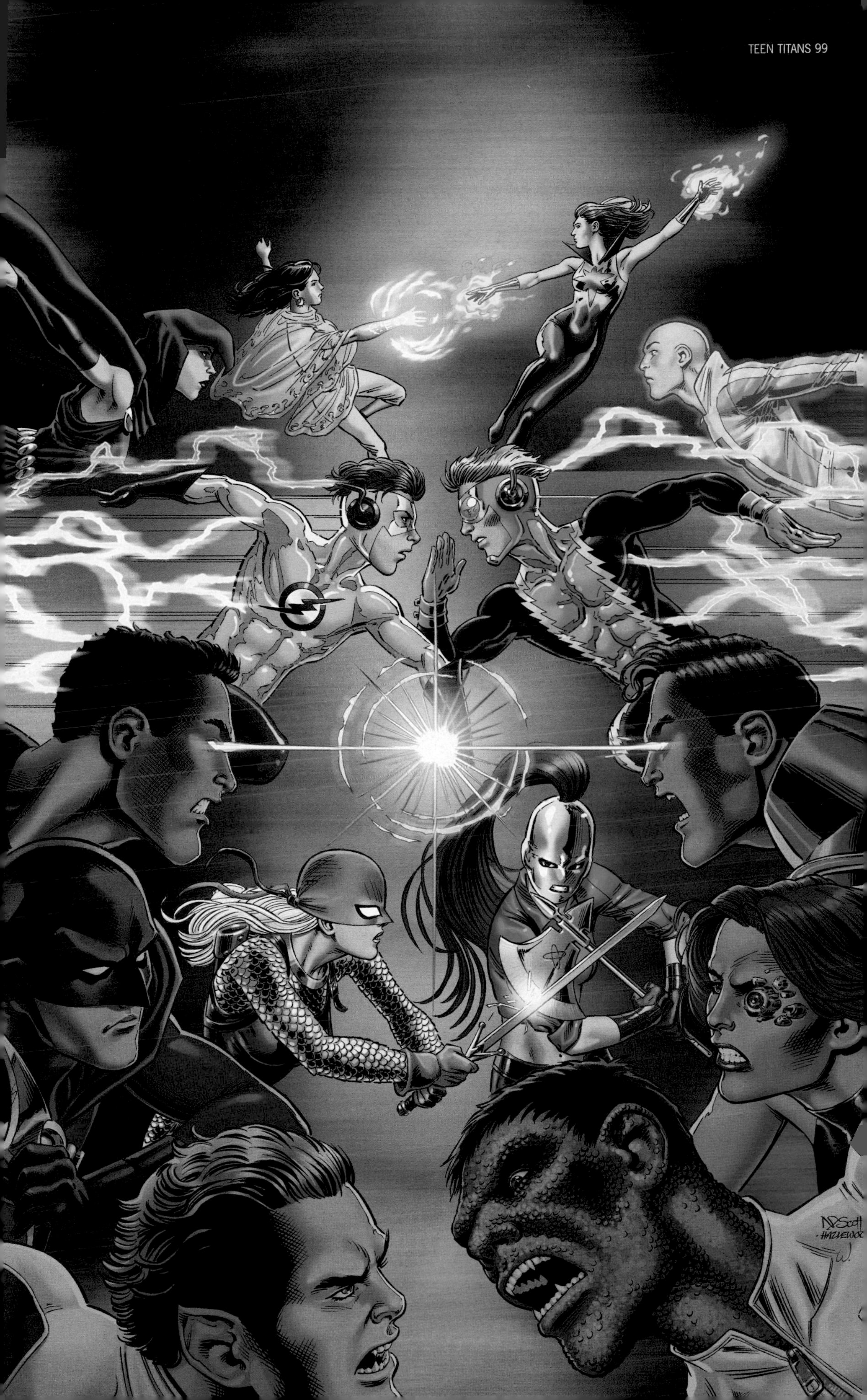

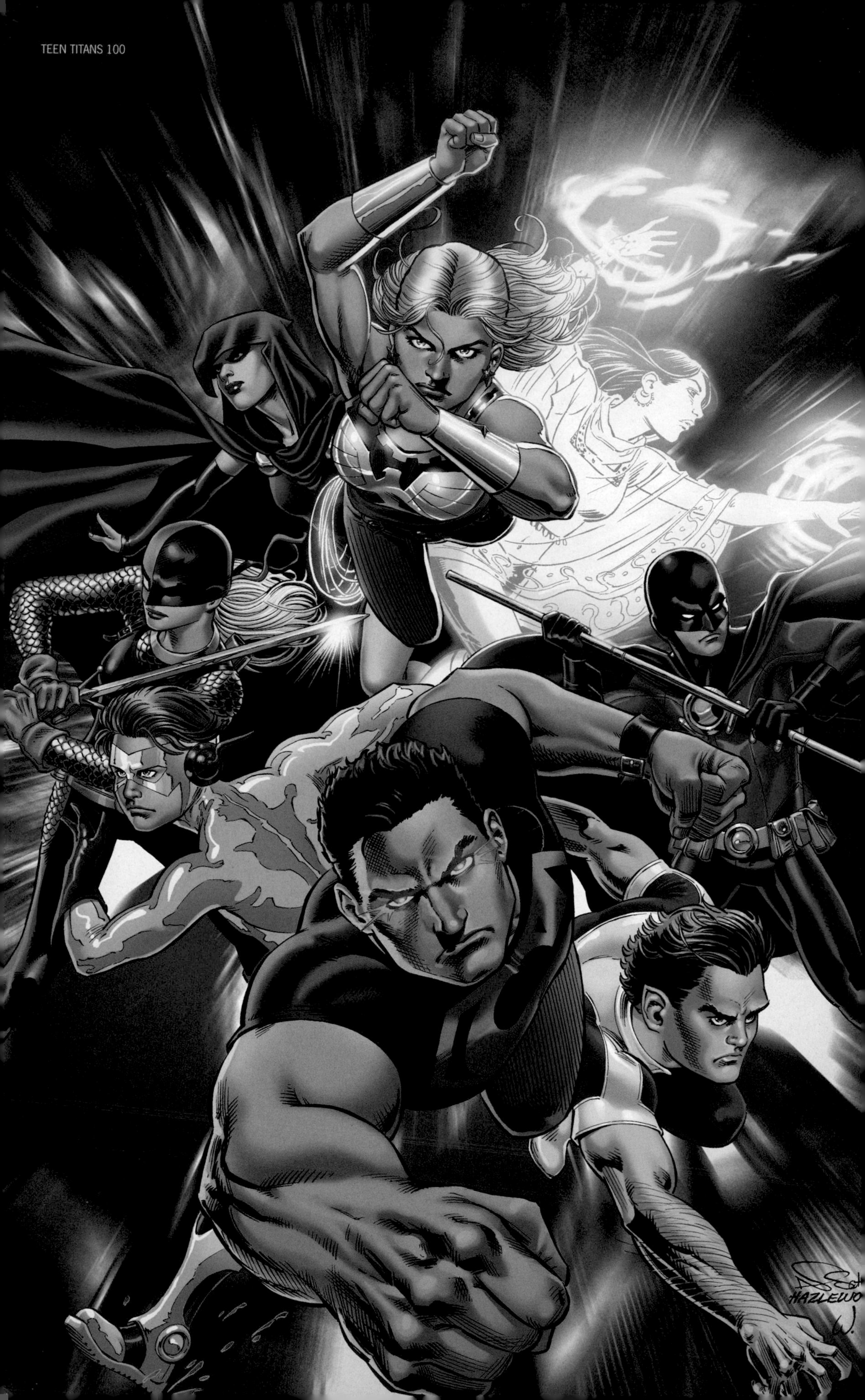

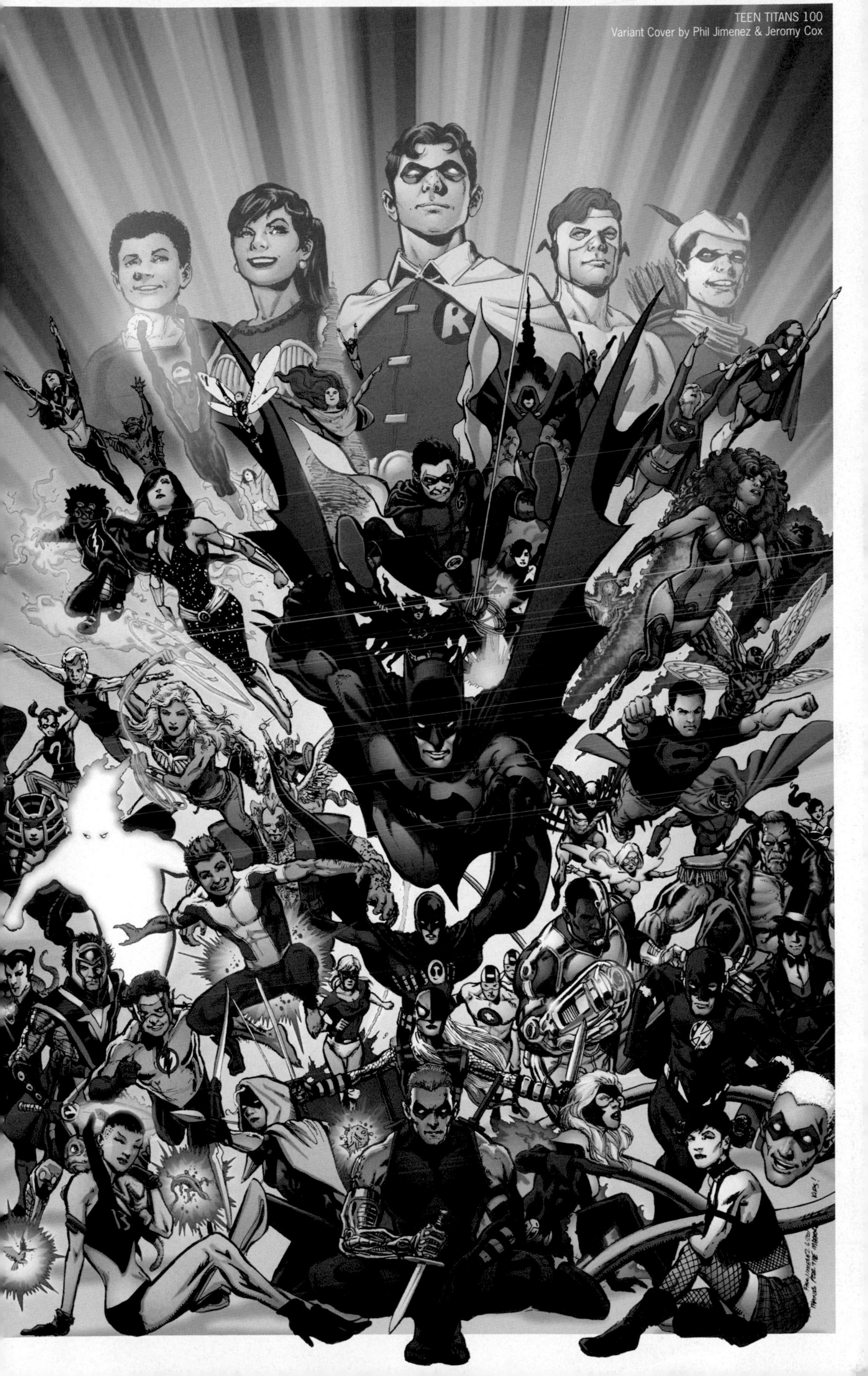

TEEN TITANS 100
Variant Cover by Phil Jimenez & Jeromy Cox